Microsoft
Visual
J++™ 6.0
Programmer's
Guide

Microsoft Press

PUBLISHED BY
Microsoft Press
A Division of Microsoft Corporation
One Microsoft Way
Redmond, Washington 98052-6399

Library of Congress Cataloging-in-Publication Data
Microsoft Visual J++ 6.0 Programmer's Guide / Microsoft Corporation.
      p. cm.
   Includes index.
   ISBN 1-57231-869-4
   1. Java (Computer program language)   2. Microsoft Visual J++.
 I. Microsoft Corporation.
QA76.73.J38M534   1998
005.2'762--dc21   98-30056
                                             CIP

Printed and bound in the United States of America.

1 2 3 4 5 6 7 8 9 WCWC 3 2 1 0 9 8

Distributed in Canada by ITP Nelson, a division of Thomson Canada Limited.

A CIP catalogue record for this book is available from the British Library.

Microsoft Press books are available through booksellers and distributors worldwide. For further information about international editions, contact your local Microsoft Corporation office or contact Microsoft Press International directly at fax (425) 936-7329. Visit our Web site at mspress.microsoft.com.

Acquisitions Editor: Eric Stroo
Project Editors: Anne Taussig, John Pierce

Contents

Chapter 16   Building and Importing ActiveX Controls. **303**

Chapter 17   Building and Importing COM Objects **311**

Appendix B   Conditional Compilation **485**

Appendix C   Reserved Words (Keywords) **493**

Getting Started with Visual J++ 6.0

Microsoft Visual J++ is an integrated Windows-hosted development tool for Java programming. Visual J++ allows you to create, modify, build, run, debug, and package an application, all within a single environment.

Visual J++ 6.0 introduces the Windows Foundation Classes for Java (WFC). This new application framework accesses the Microsoft Windows API, enabling you to write full-featured Windows applications with the Java programming language. WFC also wraps the Dynamic HTML object model implemented in Internet Explorer 4.0, which allows you to dynamically manipulate HTML on both the client and the server.

Creating a WFC Application

When you create a Windows application with WFC, your project contains a *form* that is the main window of the application. You can then add WFC controls to the form to design the graphical user interface.

For a step-by-step example that shows how to create, build, and run a simple WFC application, see "Creating a Windows Application with WFC," in Chapter 1, "Creating Projects."

For information about other types of Visual J++ projects, see Chapter 1, "Creating Projects." For information about importing a project from Visual J++ 1.1, see "Importing a Visual J++ 1.1 Project," in Chapter 1, "Creating Projects."

Modifying Your Application

Once you have created an application, you can:

- Use the Forms Designer to modify your form. The RAD features of the Forms Designer allow you to quickly drop controls onto your form, configure their properties, and add event handlers.

- Use Class Outline and the Text editor to modify your code. Class Outline provides a dynamic view of the contents and structure of your Java classes, and can assist you in adding methods and member variables. The Text editor supports IntelliSense features, such as Statement Completion, to help you write code.

- Use the WFC data controls and components to access data from your form. WFC uses ADO to retrieve data and perform simple data binding.

Building and Running Your Application

When you build your application, any compilation errors appear in the Task List. After you correct these errors, you can run your application from within the development environment.

Debugging Your Application

Although your application may compile without errors, it may not run as expected. The process of finding and fixing logic and run-time errors is known as *debugging*. Using the integrated debugger, you can set breakpoints to step through your code, one statement at a time, and view the values of variables and properties.

Other features of the integrated debugger include multiprocess debugging, remote debugging, and integration between Java and script.

Packaging Your Application

When you have finished modifying and debugging your application, you can package it into an .exe or .cab file and deploy it to the Web.

PART 1

Getting Started with Visual J++ 6.0

CHAPTER 1

Creating Projects

A project is a collection of files that make up an application. In Visual J++, projects are directory-based, which means the project is defined by the files in the project directory structure on the hard disk.

Visual J++ provides several code templates to help you create a project. A template consists of a skeleton Java class that provides the basic code framework. Using these templates, you can create the following types of projects:

- **Windows application**   You can write full-featured Windows applications using the Windows Foundation Classes for Java (WFC). Your Java class extends com.ms.wfc.ui.Form, and you can use the RAD features of the Forms Designer to modify your form. Visual J++ also provides the Application Wizard to create Windows applications.

- **Dynamic HTML application**   You can use the WFC classes to program in Dynamic HTML. Your Java class extends com.ms.wfc.html.DhDocument.

- **COM DLL**   You can create a Java class, package it into a COM DLL, and use it in any application that supports COM.

- **Control**   You can create your own control using WFC. Your Java class extends com.ms.wfc.ui.UserControl and can be modified in the Forms Designer.

- **Java console application**   A console application has no graphical user interface. You can use the nongraphical classes in either WFC or the Java API to develop your application.

- **Java applet**   An applet is launched from an HTML page. Your Java class extends java.applet.Applet, and typically uses the classes defined in the java.awt package.

You can also create an empty project without using any of the code templates.

A Visual J++ project is associated with a .vjp file, which tracks certain project settings. Each project is then contained within a *solution*. A solution can contain a single project or multiple projects, and is identified by an .sln file. For information about adding multiple projects to a solution, see "Creating a Multiproject Solution," later in this chapter.

In addition to creating a new project, you can:

- Manage your project with Project Explorer

- Set project options

- Import a project from Visual J++ 1.1

Directory-Based Projects

In Visual J++, projects are directory-based, which means the project is defined by the files in the project directory structure on the hard disk. For example:

- Adding a file or folder to the project adds the item to the project directory structure on the hard disk.

- Adding a file to the project directory structure through the file system adds the file to the project, provided the file type is specified in the *project filter*. Visual J++ uses a filter to determine which types of files typically belong to a Java project. For more information, see "The Project Filter," later in this chapter.

- Adding a folder to the project directory structure through the file system adds the folder to the project. All files in the folder, whose types are specified in the project filter, are added to the project as well.

- Moving or copying a file or folder within the project moves or copies the item on the hard disk, and vice versa.

- Renaming a file or folder in the project renames the item on the hard disk, and vice versa.

    Note   When removing a file or folder from the project, you can choose to leave the item on the hard disk or completely delete it.

For more information about directory-based projects, see "Different Project Models in Source Code Control," in the Visual Studio online documentation.

In addition to the relationship between the project structure and the file system, the hierarchy of Java packages in the project directly maps to a hierarchy of folders in the project (or file system). In Project Explorer, you can choose to display your project in one of two views:

- Directory view (the default view) displays a hierarchical list of all project subfolders, according to the project directory structure on the hard disk. Each Java package in the project is displayed as a subfolder.

- Package view displays project subfolders as Java packages, in a flat list. Note that package view displays only .java files and the folders that contain .java files. Each folder that is displayed is listed by its fully-qualified package name. The project node itself is considered the default package.

For more information about setting the view in Project Explorer, see "Choosing the Project View," later in this chapter.

Creating a Windows Application with WFC

Using WFC, you can create Windows applications with the Java programming language. You can also use the RAD features of the Forms Designer to quickly drop controls onto your form, configure their properties, and add event handlers.

Note   Before you use the following procedure to create a Windows application, close any projects that you may already have open. (On the **File** menu, click **Close All**.)

To create a Windows application with WFC

1. On the **File** menu, click **New Project**.

2. On the **New** tab, expand the **Visual J++ Projects** folder and click **Applications**. Then select the **Windows Application** icon.

3. In the **Name** box, enter a name for your project.

4. In the **Location** box, enter the path where you want to save your project, or click **Browse** to navigate to the folder.

5. Click **Open**. A collapsed view of your project appears in Project Explorer.

6. In Project Explorer, expand the project node. A file with the default name of **Form1.java** has been added to your project.

   Note   Renaming this file in Project Explorer does not rename the associated class in the source code, and vice versa. You must manually change all instances of the old name. (Note that you can create an empty project and then add a form with the Form template. This two-step process allows you to name the form before it is created.)

When you use the Windows Application template, your Java class extends com.ms.wfc.ui.Form. To view the source code in the Text editor, right-click **Form1.java** in Project Explorer and click **View Code** on the shortcut menu. Program execution begins with the `main` method. The code in the `initForm` method represents the modifications you make in the Forms Designer.

Modifying the Form in the Forms Designer

The following procedures show how to add controls to your form in the Forms Designer. This example populates a list box whenever a button is clicked.

To add controls to the form

1. To open your form in the Forms Designer, double-click **Form1.java** in Project Explorer.

2. In the Toolbox, select the **WFC Controls** tab. (If the Toolbox is not displayed, click **Toolbox** on the **View** menu.)

3. To add a list box to your form, click the **ListBox** control in the Toolbox and then click the form.

4. To add a button to your form, click the **Button** control in the Toolbox and then click the form.

To set the property of a control

1. Select the Button control on the form to show its properties in the Properties window. (If the Properties window is not displayed, click **Properties Window** on the **View** menu.)

2. Find the button's **text** property and change the value to **Add Item**.

To add an event handler

1. You can also use the Properties window to add handlers to the events of controls. Click the **Events** toolbar button in the Properties window to display the events for the Button control.

2. Find the **click** event and enter **addItemClick** for the name of the method that will handle the event. When you press ENTER, the Text editor opens to an empty event handler named `addItemClick`.

3. Inside the definition of the `addItemClick` event handler, add the following line of code:

   ```
   listBox1.addItem("New string.");
   ```

For more information about modifying your code in the development environment, see Chapter 3, "Editing Code."

Building and Running the Application

When you use the Windows Application template, an .exe file named *ProjectName*.exe is automatically created when you build your project.

To build and run your application

1. On the **Build** menu, click **Build**. Any compilation errors or messages appear in the Task List. (Double-clicking an error in the Task List moves the insertion point in the Text editor to the error.) Correct the errors and rebuild your application.

2. To run the application from the development environment, click **Start** on the **Debug** menu. To run the application from the command line, simply run the .exe file.

3. Click the **Add Item** button. A line of text appears in the list box.

4. To close the application, click the Windows Close button located in the upper-right corner of the form.

For more information about using the Forms Designer and creating WFC applications, see Chapter 2, "Designing Forms," and Chapter 11, "Introduction to WFC Programming."

Creating a Windows Application with the Application Wizard

The Application Wizard automatically generates a Windows application using WFC and provides the option of binding your form to the fields in a database. You can also specify the packaging options for your project.

Note   Before you run the Application Wizard, close any projects that you may already have open. (On the **File** menu, click **Close All**.)

To create a Windows application with the Application Wizard

1. On the **File** menu, click **New Project**.

2. On the **New** tab, expand the **Visual J++ Projects** folder and click **Applications**. Then select the **Application Wizard** icon.

3. In the **Name** box, enter a name for your project.

4. In the **Location** box, enter the path where you want to save your project, or click **Browse** to navigate to the folder.

5. Click **Open**.

6. In the **Welcome** step, you can choose a *profile* from the drop-down list. (If the profile you want to use is not listed, click the ellipsis button (**...**) to locate and open that profile.) For more information about profiles, see Chapter 5, "Introducing Wizards and Builders."

7. Click **Next** to specify the application type:

   • Select **Form Based Application** to generate a Windows form-based application.

   • Select **Form Based Application with Data** to generate a Windows application containing a data-bound form. This option launches the Data Form Wizard to walk you through the process of specifying a database and the fields you want to bind.

8. Click **Next** to specify the features that you want to add to your form:

   • **Menu**   The wizard adds a predefined menu bar.

   • **Edit**   The wizard adds an Edit control that fills the entire client area of the window; the Edit control is used to create a simple "Notepad" application.

   • **Toolbar**   The wizard adds a toolbar with predefined buttons.

   • **Status Bar**   The wizard adds a status bar.

9. Click **Next** to specify the type of source code comments:

   • **Javadoc Comment**   The wizard adds Javadoc comments to all classes and their members. These comments provide useful information about the code that has been generated.

   • **TODO Comment**   The wizard adds TODO comments in sections of the code that can be modified or where code should be added to enhance the application. You can also view TODO comments in the Task List window.

   • **Sample Functionality Comment**   The wizard adds comments for the code it inserts. These comments provide information about what the code is intended to do, and indicate which code was automatically generated by the wizard.

10. Click **Next** to specify the packaging options:

- **Class files**   The wizard will not put the project into a package file of any type. Select this option if you want to use a method other than packaging for distributing your application.

- **EXE file**   When your project is built, an .exe file is created. Select this option if you want to create a single file that can be used to run your application. (This is the default option.)

- **Cabinet (CAB) file**   When your project is built, a .cab file is created. A .cab file is a compressed file that contains all of the important information for your project. Select this option if you plan to distribute your project through the Internet.

- **Deploy to (URL)**   You can define a URL to deploy your application to. Specify the URL in the edit box.

11. Click **Next** to view the summary for your application:

- To review your settings, click **View Report**. To save the report, click **Save** in the **View Report** dialog box.

- To save your settings to an existing profile, select the profile from the drop-down list. To save your settings to a new profile, click the ellipsis button (**...**) to specify a file name. (For more information about profiles, see Chapter 5, "Introducing Wizards and Builders.")

12. Click **Finish** to create the project. Your application is opened in the Forms Designer.

Building and Running the Application

After you build your application, you can run it from the development environment.

To build and run your application

1. On the **Build** menu, click **Build**. Any compilation errors or messages appear in the Task List. (Double-clicking an error in the Task List moves the insertion point in the Text editor to the error.) Correct the errors and rebuild your application.

2. To run the application from the development environment, click **Start** on the **Debug** menu.

3. To close the application, click the Windows Close button located in the upper-right corner of the form.

For more information about creating Windows applications, and for a simple example that shows how to modify a form in the Forms Designer, see "Creating a Windows Application with WFC," earlier in this chapter.

Creating a Dynamic HTML Application

WFC wraps the Dynamic HTML (DHTML) object model that is implemented in Internet Explorer 4.0. When you use the Code-Behind HTML template to create a DHTML application, your Java class extends com.ms.wfc.html.DhDocument and is hosted on an HTML page as a COM object. Using the other classes in the com.ms.wfc.html package, you can manipulate elements on the HTML page.

Note Before you use the following procedure to create a DHTML application, close any projects that you may already have open. (On the **File** menu, click **Close All**.)

To create a DHTML application

1. On the **File** menu, click **New Project**.

2. On the **New** tab, expand the **Visual J++ Projects** folder and click **Web Pages**. Then select the **Code-Behind HTML** icon.

3. In the **Name** box, enter a name for your project.

4. In the **Location** box, enter the path where you want to save your project, or click **Browse** to navigate to the folder.

5. Click **Open**. A collapsed view of your project appears in Project Explorer.

6. In Project Explorer, expand the project node. A Java source file with the default name of **Class1.java** has been added to your project, as well as an HTML page named **Page1.htm**.

   Note Renaming the Class1.java file does not rename the associated class in the source code, and vice versa. You must manually change all instances of the old name. (Note that you can create an empty project and then add a class with the Class template. This two-step process allows you to name the class before it is created; however, the Class template does not provide the basic code framework for a DHTML class.)

Viewing Code in the Text Editor

The Code-Behind HTML template already provides some sample functionality. You can view this sample code in the Text editor.

To view the sample code in your DHTML class

- To view the source code, double-click **Class1.java** in Project Explorer.

  The `initForm` method is used for initializing your code, including binding elements in your class to existing elements on the HTML page, and creating new elements. The sample implementation binds a DhText object called `boundText` to an existing element on Page1.htm (`<SPAN id=bindText>Bound Text</SPAN>`). This is accomplished by first calling `boundText.setID("bindText")` and then calling `setBoundElements`. The sample implementation also adds a new DhText object to the document using the `setNewElements` method.

For information about modifying your code in the development environment, see Chapter 3, "Editing Code."

Building and Running the DHTML Application

Because Class1 is to be hosted as a COM object on an HTML page, your project must be packaged into a .cab file. By using the **Code-Behind HTML** template, a .cab file named *ProjectName*.cab is automatically created when you build your project.

Once you have built your project, you can launch the associated HTML page from the development environment or simply open the HTML page in your browser.

To build and run your DHTML application

1. On the **Build** menu, click **Build**. Any compilation errors or messages appear in the Task List. (Double-clicking an error in the Task List moves the insertion point in the Text editor to the error.) Correct the errors and rebuild your application.

2. To run the applet from the development environment, click **Start** on the **Debug** menu. Internet Explorer is launched and Page1.htm displays the elements from your DHTML class.

For more information about using DHTML, see Chapter 14, "Programming Dynamic HTML in Java."

Creating a COM DLL

When a Java class is packaged into a COM DLL, it can be used by any application that supports COM. All public methods defined in your class are exposed through a COM interface.

Note   Before you use the following procedure to create a COM DLL, close any projects that you may already have open. (On the **File** menu, click **Close All**.)

To create a COM DLL

1. On the **File** menu, click **New Project**.

2. On the **New** tab, expand the **Visual J++ Projects** folder and click **Components**. Then select the **COM DLL** icon.

3. In the **Name** box, enter a name for your project.

4. In the **Location** box, enter the path where you want to save your project, or click **Browse** to navigate to the folder.

5. Click **Open**. A collapsed view of your project appears in Project Explorer.

6. In Project Explorer, expand the project node. A file with the default name of **Class1.java** has been added to your project.

    Note   Renaming this file does not rename the associated class in the source code, and vice versa. You must manually change all instances of the old name. (Note that you can create an empty project and then add a class with the Class template. This two-step process allows you to name the class before it is created; however, the Class template does not provide the basic code framework for a COM DLL.)

Adding Code in the Text Editor

To view the source code that was generated, double-click **Class1.java** in Project Explorer. The `@com.register` directive specifies a GUID for your class. You can also add the `onCOMRegister` method to your class, which is automatically invoked when the DLL is registered; you can use this method to perform additional registration, such as creating any custom registry keys needed by the DLL.

The following procedure shows how to add a constructor and create a method that displays a message box.

To add code to your class

- Inside the class declaration, add the following code:

```
public Class1()
{
}

public void showDialog()
{
    com.ms.wfc.ui.MessageBox.show("Hello, World!", "COM");
}
```

For more information about modifying your code in the development environment, see Chapter 3, "Editing Code."

Building the DLL

When you build your project, a DLL and type library (named *ProjectName*.dll and *ProjectName*.tlb, respectively) are automatically created and registered on your computer.

To build the DLL

- On the **Build** menu, click **Build**. Any compilation errors or messages appear in the Task List. (Double-clicking an error in the Task List moves the insertion point in the Text editor to the error.) Correct the errors and rebuild your project.

Importing the DLL

Once your DLL is registered, it can be used by any application that supports COM. The following procedures show how to import your DLL into another Visual J++ project. This example creates a WFC form that invokes the showDialog method whenever the form is clicked.

To create a WFC application

1. Close your DLL project by clicking **Close All** on the **File** menu.

2. To create a new project, click **New Project** on the **File** menu. On the **New** tab, expand the **Visual J++ Projects** folder, and click **Applications**. Then select the **Windows Application** icon.

3. In the **Name** box, enter a name for your project. In the **Location** box, enter the path where you want to save your project, or click **Browse** to navigate to the folder.

4. Click **Open**. In Project Explorer, expand the project node. A file with the default name of **Form1.java** has been added to your project.

To import the DLL

1. In Project Explorer, right-click the name of the new project. Point to **Add** on the shortcut menu and then click **Add COM Wrapper**.

2. The **COM Wrappers** dialog box lists the type libraries that are registered on your computer. Select the name of the DLL project that you had previously created.

3. Click **OK**.

The DLL is imported into your new project as a subfolder containing two .java files: Class1.java and Class1_Dispatch.java. Class1 implements the Class1_Dispatch interface, which exposes the public methods of the Class1 object in the DLL. To access these methods, use a Class1_Dispatch object to instantiate Class1. This is demonstrated in the following procedure.

To modify the WFC form

1. In Project Explorer, expand the project node. Double-click **Form1.java** in Project Explorer to open it in the Forms Designer.

2. Click the **Events** toolbar button in the Properties window to display the events for the form. (If the Properties window is not displayed, click **Properties Window** on the **View** menu.)

3. Find the **click** event and enter **formClick** for the name of the method that will handle the event. When you press ENTER, the Text editor opens to an empty event handler named formClick.

4. Go to the beginning of the file and add the following import statement:

   ```
   import DLLProjectName.*;
   ```

   where *DLLProjectName* is the name of the DLL project that you imported.

5. Inside the Form1 class definition, before the constructor, declare a Class1_Dispatch interface object:

   ```
   Class1_Dispatch c;
   ```

6. In the Form1 constructor after the //TODO comment, instantiate Class1 through the Class1_Dispatch object:

   ```
   c = new Class1();
   ```

7. Inside the defintion of the formClick method, invoke the showDialog method of Class1 through the Class1_Dispatch object:

   ```
   c.showDialog();
   ```

To build and run the WFC application

1. On the **Build** menu, click **Build**. (If you receive any compilation errors or messages, correct the errors and rebuild your application.)

2. To run the application, click **Start** on the **Debug** menu.

3. Click the form. A message box appears that displays "Hello, World!"

4. To close the application, click the Windows Close button located in the upper-right corner of the form.

For more information about creating COM objects, see Chapter 17, "Building and Importing COM Objects." For more information about WFC applications, see "Creating a Windows application with WFC," earlier in this chapter.

Creating a Control

Using WFC, you can create your own controls. A control created with WFC extends com.ms.wfc.ui.UserControl, which in turn extends com.ms.wfc.ui.Form; this allows you to use the Forms Designer to create the control's user interface.

Note   Before you use the following procedure to create a control, close any projects that you may already have open. (On the **File** menu, click **Close All**.)

To create a control

1. On the **File** menu, click **New Project**.

2. On the **New** tab, expand the **Visual J++ Projects** folder and click **Components**. Then select the **Control** icon.

3. In the **Name** box, enter a name for your project.

4. In the **Location** box, enter the path where you want to save your project, or click **Browse** to navigate to the folder.

5. Click **Open**. A collapsed view of your project appears in Project Explorer.

6. In Project Explorer, expand the project node. A file with the default name of **Control1.java** has been added to your project.

Note   Renaming this file does not rename the associated class in the source code, and vice versa. You must manually change all instances of the old name. (Note that you can create an empty project and then add a control class with the Control template. This two-step process allows you to name the control before it is created.)

Viewing Code in the Text Editor

To view the source code that was generated, right-click **Control1.java** in Project Explorer and click **View Code** on the shortcut menu. The code in the `initForm` method represents the modifications you make in the Forms Designer. The nested class `ClassInfo` specifies the properties and events of your control. (To modify the `ClassInfo`, you can use the WFC Component Builder.)

Note that the Javadoc comments for the Control1 class provide information about how to expose your class as an ActiveX control. For more information, see "Setting COM Classes," later in this chapter.

Modifying the Control in the Forms Designer

The following procedures show how to use the existing WFC controls to design your control. This example adds an edit box and a horizontal scroll bar to your control; whenever the scroll bar is scrolled, the edit box displays the scroll bar's current position.

To add existing controls to your control

1. To open your control in the Forms Designer, double-click **Control1.java** in Project Explorer.

2. In the Toolbox, select the **WFC Controls** tab. (If the Toolbox is not displayed, click **Toolbox** on the **View** menu.)

3. To add an edit box to your control, click the **Edit** control in the Toolbox and then click your control's design surface.

4. To add a horizontal scroll bar to your control, click the **HScrollBar** control in the Toolbox and then click your control's design surface.

5. Position the edit box in the upper-left corner of your control's design surface, and move the scroll bar below the edit box. (To reposition an item, select and drag it with the mouse.)

6. Resize your control's design surface around the edit box and scroll bar to eliminate extra space. (To resize the design surface, select it and drag the resize handles.)

To add an event handler

1. Click the **Events** toolbar button in the Properties window. (If the Properties window is not displayed, click **Properties Window** on the **View** menu.)

2. To display the events of the scroll bar, either select the scroll bar on your control's design surface or select the name of the scroll bar object from the drop-down list in the Properties window.

3. Find the **scroll** event and enter **displayPosition** for the name of the method that will handle the event. When you press ENTER, the Text editor opens to an empty event handler named `displayPosition`.

4. Inside the definition of the `displayPosition` event handler, add the following line of code:

```
edit1.setText("Position = " + HScrollBar1.getValue());
```

For more information about modifying your code in the development environment, see Chapter 3, "Editing Code."

Building the Control

When you build your project, your control is automatically made available to the Toolbox.

To build the control

- On the **Build** menu, click **Build**. Any compilation errors or messages appear in the Task List. (Double-clicking an error in the Task List moves the insertion point in the Text editor to the error.) Correct the errors and rebuild your control.

To add the control to the Toolbox

1. Right-click the Toolbox and click **Customize Toolbox** on the shortcut menu.

2. Click the **WFC Controls** tab and select the name of your control.

3. Click **OK**.

Adding the Control to a Form

To use your control, you can add it to a WFC form.

To add a form to your project

1. In Project Explorer, right-click the name of your project. Point to **Add** on the shortcut menu and then·click **Add Form**.

2. Select the **Form** icon.

3. In the **Name** box, enter a name for the Java class.

4. Click **Open**. A file with the default name of **Form1.java** has been added to your project and is opened in the Forms Designer.

To add your control to the form

1. Find your control in the Toolbox. To scroll through the list of controls, you can click the up and down arrows on the Toolbox tabs.

2. Click your control in the Toolbox and then click the form to add the control.

To build and run the form

1. On the **Build** menu, click **Build**. (If you receive any compilation errors or messages, correct the errors and rebuild your project.)

2. To run the form, click **Start** on the **Debug** menu.

   Note   Because you are running your project for the first time, and because your project contains two .java files, the **Project Properties** dialog box is displayed. On the **Launch** tab, select the **Default** option and specify that Form1 should load when the project runs. Click **OK**. (For more information about project properties, see "Setting Project Options," later in this chapter.)

3. Click the ends of the scroll bar in your control. The edit box displays the current scroll position.

4. To close the form, click the Windows Close button located in the upper-right corner of the form.

For more information about creating WFC controls and applications, see Chapter 13, "WFC Control Development," and Chapter 11, "Introduction to WFC Programming."

Creating a Console Application

A console application has no graphical user interface. You can use the nongraphical classes in either WFC or the Java API to develop your application.

Note   Before you use the following procedure to create a console application, close any projects that you may already have open. (On the **File** menu, click **Close All**.)

To create a console application

1. On the **File** menu, click **New Project**.

2. On the **New** tab, expand the **Visual J++ Projects** folder and click **Applications**. Then select the **Console Application** icon.

3. In the **Name** box, enter a name for your project.

4. In the **Location** box, enter the path where you want to save your project, or click **Browse** to navigate to the folder.

5. Click **Open**. A collapsed view of your project appears in Project Explorer.

6. In Project Explorer, expand the project node. A file with the default name of **Class1.java** has been added to your project.

   Note   Renaming this file does not rename the associated class in the source code, and vice versa. You must manually change all instances of the old name. (Note that you can create an empty project and then add a class with the ClassMain template. This two-step process allows you to name the class before it is created.)

Adding Code in the Text Editor

To view the source code that was generated, double-click **Class1.java** in Project Explorer. Program execution begins with the main method.

To add code to the application

- In the Text Editor, add the following code after the //TODO comment inside the main method:

```
String str = "The quick brown fox jumped over the lazy yellow dog.";

System.out.println("The string is: " + str);
System.out.println("The length of the string is: " + str.length());
System.out.println("The substring from positions 10 to 20 is: " +
                   str.substring(10,20));
System.out.println("The uppercase string is: " +
                   str.toUpperCase());
```

For more information about modifying your code in the development environment, see Chapter 3, "Editing Code."

Building and Running the Application

After you build your application, you can run it from either the development environment or from the command line.

To build and run your application

1. On the **Build** menu, click **Build**. Any compilation errors or messages appear in the Task List. (Double-clicking an error in the Task List moves the insertion point in the Text editor to the error.) Correct the errors and rebuild your applet.

2. To run the application from the development environment, click **Start** on the **Debug** menu.

3. To run the application from the command line, use JVIEW. At the command prompt, type jview Class1 from the directory location of your project.

Creating an Applet

An applet runs from within an HTML page, and is created with the classes in the Java API. Your applet must extend java.applet.Applet, and typically uses the classes in the java.awt package to provide a graphical user interface.

Note   Before you use the following procedure to create an applet, close any projects that you may already have open. (On the **File** menu, click **Close All**.)

To create an applet

1. On the **File** menu, click **New Project**.

2. On the **New** tab, expand the **Visual J++ Projects** folder and click **Web Pages**. Then select the **Applet on HTML** icon.

3. In the **Name** box, enter a name for your project.

4. In the **Location** box, enter the path where you want to save your project, or click **Browse** to navigate to the folder.

5. Click **Open**. A collapsed view of your project appears in Project Explorer.

6. In Project Explorer, expand the project node. A Java source file with the default name of **Applet1.java** has been added to your project, as well as an HTML page named **Page1.htm**.

   Note Renaming the Applet1.java file does not rename the associated class in the source code, and vice versa. You must manually change all instances of the old name. (Note that you can create an empty project and then add a class with the Class template. This two-step process allows you to name the class before it is created; however, the Class template does not provide the basic code framework for an applet.)

Viewing Code in the Text Editor

The Applet template already provides some sample functionality. You can view this sample code in the Text editor.

To view the sample code in the applet

1. To view the source code, double-click **Applet1.java** in Project Explorer. Program execution begins with the `init` method.

2. The `init` method simply calls `initForm` and `usePageParams`. Use Class Outline to locate the `initForm` method:

   - If Class Outline is not displayed, point to **Other Windows** on the **View** menu and click **Document Outline**.

   - Expand your class in Class Outline and double-click `initForm`. The insertion point immediately moves to the `initForm` method.

3. The `initForm` method initializes the background and foreground colors, and adds a java.awt.Label control to the applet.

4. In Class Outline, double-click `usePageParams`. This method retrieves the value of the <PARAM> tags from the associated HTML page, and sets the background color, foreground color, and label text to these values. If `usePageParams` is unable to retrieve the <PARAM> values, then default values are used.

For information about modifying your code in the development environment, see Chapter 3, "Editing Code."

Building and Running the Applet

After you build your applet, you can launch the associated HTML page from the development environment or simply open the HTML page in your browser.

To build and run your applet

1. On the **Build** menu, click **Build**. Any compilation errors or messages appear in the Task List. (Double-clicking an error in the Task List moves the insertion point in the Text editor to the error.) Correct the errors and rebuild your application.

2. To run the applet from the development environment, click **Start** on the **Debug** menu. Internet Explorer is launched and Page1.htm displays the applet.

   Note   To run the applet without an HTML page, you can use JVIEW from the command line. At the command prompt, type `jview /a Applet1` from the directory location of your project. When the `/a` option is specified, the Applet Viewer is launched to display your applet.

Creating an Empty Project

When you create a project in Visual J++, you can use one of the code templates, run the Application Wizard, or create an empty project. When you use the code templates or the wizard, your Java source files use the default names, such as Form1.java or Class1.java. Renaming the file does not automatically rename the associated Java class in the code, and vice versa; you must manually change all instances of the old name. However, creating an empty project provides the flexibility of initially naming your Java source files when you add them.

   Note   Before you use the following procedure to create an empty project, close any projects that you may already have open. (On the **File** menu, click **Close All**.)

To create an empty project

1. On the **File** menu, click **New Project**.

2. On the **New** tab, click the **Visual J++ Projects** folder. Then select the **Empty Project** icon.

3. In the **Name** box, enter a name for your project.

4. In the **Location** box, enter the path where you want to save your project, or click **Browse** to navigate to the folder.

5. Click **Open**. Your project appears in Project Explorer and contains no files.

To add a form or control to the project

1. In Project Explorer, right-click the name of your project. Point to **Add** on the shortcut menu and then click **Add Form**.

2. To add a WFC form, select the **Form** icon. Your Java class extends com.ms.wfc.ui.Form. (You can also select the Data Form Wizard icon to automatically generate a data-bound form.)

3. To add a control, select the **Control** icon. Your Java class extends com.ms.wfc.ui.UserControl.

4. In the **Name** box, enter a name for the Java class.

5. Click **Open**.

For more information about WFC forms, and for a simple example that shows how to modify a form, see "Creating a Windows Application with WFC," earlier in this chapter.

To add a Java class to the project

1. In Project Explorer, right-click the name of your project. Point to **Add** on the shortcut menu and then click **Add Class**.

2. To add an empty Java class, select the **Class** icon. (You can later modify this class to create a COM DLL, a Dynamic HTML application, or an applet.)

3. To add a Java class that contains a **main** method (such as to create a console application), select the **ClassMain** icon.

4. In the **Name** box, enter a name for the Java class.

5. Click **Open**.

To add an HTML page to the project

1. In Project Explorer, right-click the name of your project. Point to **Add** on the shortcut menu and then click **Add Web Page**.

2. Select the **Page** icon to add an HTML page.

3. In the **Name** box, enter a name for the page.

4. Click **Open**.

To import a COM DLL into the project

1. In Project Explorer, right-click the name of your project. Point to **Add** on the shortcut menu and then click **Add COM Wrapper**.

2. In the **COM Wrappers** dialog box, select the type library that you want to import.

3. Click **OK**.

    Note By default, when you create a project with the Empty Project icon, your project will not be packaged when you build it. However, if you are creating a Windows application with WFC, you may want to package your project into an .exe file that can be run from the command line; if you are creating a COM DLL, you need to package your project into the DLL format. For more information, see Chapter 7, "Packaging and Deploying Projects."

Creating a Multiproject Solution

Each project you create is contained within a solution, and a solution can contain multiple projects.

Note Before you use the following procedure to create a multiproject solution, close any projects that you may already have open. (On the **File** menu, click **Close All**.)

To create the first project in the solution

1. On the **File** menu, click **New Project**.

2. On the **New** tab, expand the **Visual J++ Projects** folder, and click **Applications**. Then select the **Windows Application** icon.

3. In the **Name** box, enter a name for your project.

4. In the **Location** box, enter the path where you want to save your project, or click **Browse** to navigate to the folder.

5. Click **Open**. A collapsed view of the project appears in Project Explorer.

    Note Because no project (or solution) was open when you created the Windows application project, the new project is created in a new solution.

To add another project to the solution

1. With the first project open, click **New Project** on the **File** menu.

2. On the **New** tab, expand the **Visual J++ Projects** folder and click **Web Pages**. Then select the **Code-Behind HTML** icon.

3. In the **Name** box, enter a name for your project.

4. In the **Location** box, enter the path where you want to save your project, or click **Browse** to navigate to the folder.

5. Because there is a solution that is currently open, you have two options:

   - **Close current solution**   Closes the current solution and creates the project in a new solution.

   - **Add to current solution**   Keeps the current solution open and simply adds the new project to it.

6. Select the **Add to current solution** option and click **Open**. A collapsed view of the project appears in Project Explorer.

Building a Multiproject Solution

When you create a multiproject solution, you can build either a single project within the solution or all projects in the solution.

To build a single project in the solution

1. In Project Explorer, select the name of the project you want to build.

2. On the **Build** menu, click **Build** *ProjectName*.

To build all projects in the solution

   - On the **Build** menu, click **Build Solution**.

When you build the entire solution, typically each project is built in the order that it was added to the solution. However, if one project depends on another project to be built first, you can explicitly change the build order.

To change the build order of the projects in the solution

1. In Project Explorer, right-click the name of the solution, and click **Property Pages** on the shortcut menu.

2. The **Build Order** tab in the **Property Pages** dialog box displays the current build order. To change the order of a project, select the project name, and click one of the **Move** buttons.

3. Click **OK** when you have finished changing the build order of the projects.

Setting the Startup Project

When you create a multiproject solution, the first project that was added is set as the *startup project* and appears in bold font in Project Explorer. The startup project is the project that runs when you click Start on the Debug menu.

To change the startup project

1. In Project Explorer, right-click the project that you want to set as the startup project.

2. On the shortcut menu, click **Set as Startup Project**.

Managing Projects with Project Explorer

The Project Explorer window displays the items that belong to the open project(s). In Visual J++, projects are directory-based. Each file and folder in the project corresponds to a file and folder on the hard disk. Adding a file to the project adds the file to the project directory structure on the hard disk, and vice versa. Note, however, that you can remove a file from the project without removing it from the hard disk.

By default, Project Explorer is automatically opened when you create or open a project. To manually open Project Explorer, click **Project Explorer** on the **View** menu.

Choosing the Project View

A Java package is essentially a folder in your Java project. The hierarchy of Java packages in a project maps to a hierarchy of folders in the file system. Because of this relationship, Project Explorer provides two ways to view your Java project: directory view and package view.

Directory view, the default view, displays a hierarchical list of all project subfolders, according to the project directory structure on the hard disk. Each Java package in the project is displayed as a subfolder. Package view displays project subfolders as Java packages, in a flat list. Note that package view displays only .java files and the folders that contain .java files. Each folder that is displayed is listed by its fully qualified package name. The project node itself is considered the default package.

The following diagram shows the same project in both directory view and package view:

Directory View

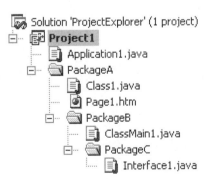

Package View

For more information about the relationship between Java packages and the file system, see "Storing Packages in a File System" in the *Java Language Specification*.

To view the project in package view

- On the **Project** menu, click **Package View**, or click the **Package View** button in Project Explorer. Only the project's .java files, and the folders (packages) that contain them, are displayed. (If a non-Java source file is currently open, then it remains displayed in Project Explorer.)

  Note The structure of files and folders displayed in package view is based on the location of the .java files, not the location of the built .class files. Therefore, if the package statements in the .java files do not match their location on the hard disk, package view will not accurately display the packages in your project.

To view the project in directory view

- On the **Project** menu, click **Directory View**, or click the **Directory View** button in Project Explorer. All files and folders in the project are displayed.

By default, Project Explorer does not display any nonproject files and folders that reside in the project directory structure on the hard disk. However, if the project view is set to directory view, you can display these items by clicking the **Show All Files** button in Project Explorer. Note that in package view, this button is disabled. For more information about nonproject items that reside in the project directory structure, see "Displaying All Files in the Project Directory Structure," later in this chapter.

Opening a File

You can use Project Explorer to open the files in your Java project. Each file is associated with a source editor. If the file supports graphical editing, then it is also associated with a graphical editor.

To open a file in its source editor

- In Project Explorer, right-click the name of the file, and click **View Code** on the shortcut menu. You can also click the **View Code** button in Project Explorer.

To open a file in its graphical editor

- If the file supports graphical editing, right-click the name of the file in Project Explorer, and click **View Designer** on the shortcut menu. You can also click the **View Designer** button in Project Explorer. (If the file does not support graphical editing, neither the button nor the menu command is available.)

  Tip Double-clicking the name of the file opens it in the default editor for that file type. For example, double-clicking a WFC form opens it in the Forms Designer.

For information about adding files to your project, see the next section, "Adding a File."

Miscellaneous Files

To open a file that is not part of the open project, use the **Open File** command on the **File** menu. Project Explorer lists the file under the **Miscellaneous Files** node. Once a nonproject file is listed under **Miscellaneous Files**, you can simply double-click it in Project Explorer to reopen it.

Note that if you remove a file from the project, it still resides in the project directory structure. However, you must still use the **Open File** command to open the file, since the file no longer belongs to the project. For information about removing files, see "Removing a File or Folder," later in this chapter.

Adding a File

When you add a file to your project, it is included in the project's build process. Adding a file to a Java project also adds the file to the project directory structure on the hard disk:

- Creating a new file in the project creates a new file on the disk.

- Adding a file that already exists on the disk copies the file to the appropriate location in the project directory structure.

  Note   Some files may reside in the project directory structure without belonging to the project. For example, removing a file from the project still leaves the file in the project directory structure. This file can be added back to the project in its same location on the disk.

You can add a file to the top-level project or to a specific folder. For information about adding folders to the project, see "Adding a Folder," later in this chapter.

To add a file to the project

1. In Project Explorer, select the project or folder node that will contain the file.

2. On the **Project** menu, click **Add Item**.

3. To create a new file, click the **New** tab in the **Add Item** dialog box.

   - In the left pane of the dialog box, select a file category. In the right pane, select the type of file you want to add, based on the selection in the left pane.

   - In the **Name** box, type a name for the file. For information about valid Java file names, see "Identifiers" in the *Java Language Specification*.

   - Click **Open**. Note that when you add a new .java file, Visual J++ automatically inserts the proper package statement into the file. (If you add a .java file to the project node itself, no package statement is inserted, since the project node is considered the default package.)

4. To add an existing file, click the **Existing** tab in the **Add Item** dialog box.

- Find and select the file you want to add. You can select multiple files from the same folder by using the SHIFT or CTRL keys.

- Click **Open**. Note that when you add an existing .java file, you must manually change its package statement to reference the new package. (Note that the project node itself is considered the default package.) If a file's package statement does not map to the folder it resides in, the output directory structure will not match the source directory structure when you build the project.

When a single file is added to the project through Project Explorer, it is automatically opened in its default editor. When multiple files are added at the same time, no file is opened. For information about opening files, see "Opening a File," later in this chapter.

Note   If a file is added to the project directory structure through the file system, it is automatically added to the project if its file type is specified in the project filter. The file is then displayed in Project Explorer, but not opened. For more information about the project filter, see "Displaying All Files in the Project Directory Structure," later in this chapter.

Adding a File that Resides in the Project Directory Structure

If a file does not belong to the project, but it already exists in the project directory structure, you can simply add it to the project in that same location.

To add a file that already resides in the project directory structure

1. Set the project view to directory view by clicking the **Directory View** button in Project Explorer. Only directory view allows you to see the nonproject files that reside in the project directory structure. For more information about views, see "Choosing the Project View," earlier in this chapter.

2. If the nonproject files are not currently displayed, click the **Show All Files** button in Project Explorer to show all files in the project directory structure.

3. Right-click the name of the file that you want to add to the project. Note that you cannot add a file if its folder is not in the project. For information about adding the folder, see "Adding a Folder that Resides in the Project Directory Structure," later in this chapter.

4. On the shortcut menu, click **Add To Project**. The file is added to the project, but not opened. For information about opening files, see the previous section, "Opening a File."

5. To hide any remaining nonproject files, click the **Show All Files** button again.

For more information about nonproject files that reside in the project directory structure, see "Displaying All Files in the Project Directory Structure," later in this chapter.

Adding a Folder

When you add a new folder to your project, a corresponding folder is created on the hard disk. In a Java project, a folder is essentially a Java package. In Project Explorer's directory view, all packages are displayed as project subfolders. In package view, subfolders are displayed as Java packages. For more information about views, see "Choosing the Project View," earlier in this chapter.

> **Note**   A folder may reside in the project directory structure without belonging to the project. For example, removing a folder from the project still leaves the folder in the project directory structure. This folder can be added back to the project in its same location on the disk.

To add a new folder (package) to the project

1. In Project Explorer, right-click the project or folder node that will contain the new folder.

2. On the shortcut menu, click **New Folder**.

3. In the **Add Package/Folder** dialog box, type the name of the new folder. This name must be a valid Java package name. For information about valid names, see "Identifiers" in the *Java Language Specification*.

4. Click **OK**.

Once you have created a folder, you can add files to it. For information about adding files, see "Adding a File," earlier in this chapter.

> **Note**   If a folder is added to the project directory structure through the file system, it is automatically added to the project and displayed in Project Explorer. All files in the folder, whose types are specified in the project filter, are added to the project as well. For more information about the project filter, see "Displaying All Files in the Project Directory Structure," later in this chapter.

Adding a Folder that Resides in the Project Directory Structure

If a folder does not belong to the project, but it already exists in the project directory structure, you can simply add it to the project in that same location.

To add a folder that already resides in the project directory structure

1. Set the project view to directory view by clicking the **Directory View** button in Project Explorer. Only directory view allows you to see the nonproject items that reside in the project directory structure. For more information about views, see "Choosing the Project View," earlier in this chapter.

2. If the nonproject items are not currently displayed, click the **Show All Files** button in Project Explorer to show all files and folders in the project directory structure.

3. Right-click the name of the folder that you want to add to the project.

4. On the shortcut menu, click **Add To Project**. The folder and all subfolders and files contained within the folder are added to the project. (Only those files whose types are specified in the project filter are added.)

5. To hide any remaining nonproject items, click the **Show All Files** button again.

For more information about the project filter and about nonproject items that reside in the project directory structure, see "Displaying All Files in the Project Directory Structure," later in this chapter.

Moving or Copying a File or Folder

When you move or copy a file or folder in your Java project, the file or folder on the hard disk is also moved or copied. Moving or copying a folder also moves or copies all project files in the folder.

> **Important** When moving or copying a .java file to a different folder, you must manually change its package statement to reference the new package. (Note that the project node itself is considered the default package.) Similarly, if you move a folder within the project, you must manually change the package statement of each .java file in the folder. If a file's package statement does not map to the folder it resides in, the output directory structure will not match the source directory structure when you build the project.

When moving or copying items, Project Explorer follows the rules of the file system. For example, you cannot move a folder into any of its subfolders.

To move or copy a file or folder in the project

1. In Project Explorer, right-click the name of the file or folder to be moved or copied.

2. To move the item, click **Cut** on the shortcut menu; to copy the item, click **Copy**.

3. Right-click the new folder or the project node that will contain the file or folder.

4. On the shortcut menu, click **Paste**.

> **Note** If a file or folder is moved or copied through the file system, it is automatically moved or copied within Project Explorer. However, you must still ensure that the package statements in the .java files are correct.

You can also copy files and folders by dragging them in Project Explorer. Note that drag-and-drop operations in Project Explorer only copy the source items. In directory view, you can drag either a single folder or any set of files. In package view, you can only drag files. For more information about views, see "Choosing the Project View," earlier in this chapter.

Renaming a File or Folder

When you rename a file or folder in your Java project, the file or folder on the hard disk is also renamed.

Important   When renaming an item in your project, you must be careful to manually change all references to the old name. For example, Java requires a public class to have the same name as its source file. Therefore, if you rename a .java file, you must also rename the associated public class, and vice versa.

Note that if you rename a folder, you must change the package statement of each .java file in the folder. If a file's package statement does not map to the folder it resides in, the output directory structure will not match the project directory structure when you build the project.

To rename a file or folder in the project

1. In Project Explorer, right-click the name of the file or folder to be renamed.

2. On the shortcut menu, click **Rename**.

3. Type the new name, and press Enter. This name must be a valid file or package name. For information about valid names, see "Identifiers" in the *Java Language Specification*.

    Note   If a file or folder is renamed through the file system, it is automatically renamed in Project Explorer. However, you must still change all references to the old name.

Removing a File or Folder

When you remove a file from your Java project, the file is no longer built with the project; however, the file still remains in the project directory structure on the hard disk. When you remove a folder, the folder and all of its files are removed from the project, but they are still left on the hard disk.

You can also choose to actually delete the file or folder from both the project and the hard disk.

Note   Removing or deleting a .java file does not automatically remove or delete the associated .class file (if it exists). However, you can display the .class file in Project Explorer and then manually remove or delete it.

To remove a file or folder from the project

1. In Project Explorer, right-click the name of the file or folder to be removed.

2. On the shortcut menu, click **Remove From Project**.

To delete a file or folder from the project and the hard disk

1. In Project Explorer, select the name of the file or folder to be deleted.

2. Press DELETE.

    Note   If an item is deleted through the file system, it is automatically deleted from the project and removed from Project Explorer.

Project Explorer provides the option of displaying the items you have removed from your project. For more information, see the next section, "Displaying All Files in the Project Directory Structure." For information about adding a removed file or folder back to the project, see "Adding a File" and "Adding a Folder," earlier in this chapter.

Displaying All Files in the Project Directory Structure

Files and folders may reside in the project directory structure without belonging to your project:

- Removing a file or folder from a Java project still leaves it on the hard disk.

- Files whose types are not in the project filter may not be added to the project. For more information, see the next section, "The Project Filter."

In Project Explorer's directory view, you have the option of displaying all files and folders that reside in the project directory structure, even if they do not belong to the project. The icon for each item denotes whether it currently belongs to the project.

To toggle the display of nonproject items in the project directory structure

1. Set the project view to directory view by clicking the **Directory View** button in Project Explorer. Only directory view allows you to see the nonproject items that reside in the project directory structure. For more information about views, see "Choosing the Project View," earlier in this chapter.

2. Click the **Show All Files** button in Project Explorer.

For information about adding a nonproject file or folder to the project, see "Adding a File" and "Adding a Folder," earlier in this chapter.

The Project Filter

Visual J++ uses a project filter to determine which types of files typically belong to a Java project. The project filter is an inclusive filter, meaning that the extensions in the filter identify valid project files. The following extensions are included in the project filter:

- .java

- .asp, .htm, .html

- .bmp, .gif, .ico, .jpeg, .jpg

- .avi, .au, .wav

- .doc, .rtf, .txt, .ppt, .wri, .xls

- .bat, .cur, .reg, .snd, .tlb, .url

When a file is added to the project directory structure from outside the Visual J++ environment, the project filter is used to determine whether the file actually belongs to the project.

> **Important**   When you add a file within the Visual J++ environment, the file is always added to the project, regardless of its file type.

Setting Project Options

Visual J++ provides a number of options that allow you to configure your application for debugging, optimize your project's compiled output, expose classes within your project as COM objects, and specify the paths for your class's dependencies. You can find all of these options in the *<Project>* properties dialog box (where *<Project>* is the name of your currently selected project). You can display these options by clicking the Project menu and selecting the *<Project>* Properties menu command.

Setting Launch Options

Before a project can be compiled in Visual J++, you need to define the project file that will be loaded first and used as the entry point of the application. You can select this file by either choosing it from a list of available project files, which uses a default program and command line, or select a custom program and command line. For most applications, the default program and command line arguments are sufficient. Specifying a custom program and command line are usually used when you need to define a custom command line to pass to your application when it is run within Visual J++. You can also use the custom program option when you are developing a WFC control or COM DLL that needs to be tested from a separate program.

To select the build configuration

1. On the **Project** menu, click *<Project>* **Properties** (where *<Project>* is the name of the project that is currently selected in the Project Explorer).

    The *<Project>* **Properties** dialog box appears.

2. Select the **Launch** tab.

3. In the **Configuration** drop-down list, choose the build configuration for which you want the **Launch** tab settings to apply.

To choose the entry point file with default program and command line

1. On the *<Project>* **Properties** dialog box, click **Default** to enable the default options.

2. In the **When project runs, load** drop-down box, select the name of the file you wish to use as the entry point to your application. The following are the types of files that can be displayed in the list:

   - Any Java classes that have a **main** method defined.

   - HTML files.

   - Java classes that extend **java.lang.Applet**.

   The **Program** text box identifies the program that will launch your application, based on the type of file selected from the entry point list. The **Arguments** text box shows command line arguments that are to be passed when the program runs.

3. If the file selected from the entry point list is a Java source file, you can select the **Launch as a console application** check box to run your application with **JView** instead of **WJView**. **JView** displays all output from your application in a console window, while **WJView** displays all output in the Output Window.

To choose the entry point file and define a custom program and command line

1. On the *<Project>* **Properties** dialog box, click **Custom**. By default, the **Program** and **Argument** text boxes contain the same project file, program, and arguments that are defined in the **Default** section.

2. In the **Program** text box, enter a new program name to run or modify the existing program name.

3. In the **Arguments** text box, enter a new list of arguments to use or modify the existing arguments list. The default arguments supplied also include the name of the project file that will be used as the entry point.

   Note   If you want to configure a different entry point file for a debug build versus a release build of your project, you can use the **Configuration** drop-down list to specify the new settings.

Setting Compiler Options

Visual J++ provides a number of compiler options to help optimize compiled output and to assist in the debugging process of an application. The Compile tab of the *<Project>* Properties dialog box provides a way to set these options. Most of the options provided in this dialog box are check boxes that you can set to enable or disable a feature. For information each of the options in the dialog box, click the Help button located in the dialog box.

If you want to specify conditional compilation symbols to be used when compiling your code, you can define them using the options on the Compile tab. Enter conditional compilation symbols into the **Conditional compilation symbols** box and separate each entry with a comma. For more information on setting symbols and conditional compilation, see Appendix B, "Conditional Compilation."

In addition to the compiler options that can be changed in the dialog box, you can also define additional compiler options that are passed to the compiler after the other options have been passed. You can specify additional compiler options by entering them in the **Additional compiler options** text box. Each option should be separated by a space. For more information on available compiler options, see "JVC Command-Line Options" in Chapter 9, "Compiling Applications with JVC."

Another compilation setting that you can specify in the Compile tab is the **Output Directory**. This box allows you to specify a directory in which the project's compiled files are to be placed. If your project has any packages defined within it, Visual J++ creates those packages in the output directory and compiles any source files in those packages. You can use this setting to specify a location for a debug or release build of your project. By default, this box is left empty; thus, all project output is placed in the project directory.

> **Note**   The **Configuration** list allows you to have different settings for release and debug builds of your project. You can use this feature to specify specific compiler settings and the output directory for each configuration of your project. An **All Configurations** setting is also available to make changes global to all configurations of your project.

Creating Custom Build Rules

Depending on the type of project you are working with, you may need to have certain tasks completed prior to and after building your project. The Custom Build tab of the *<Project>* Properties dialog box allows you to specify commands that are to be executed before or after building a project. There are two text boxes on this tab — Pre-build and Post-build. The format of the commands entered into these text boxes should be identical to the commands used in a batch file (such as Autoexec.bat).

To add pre-build or post-build commands

1. On the **Project** menu, click *<Project>* **Properties** (where *<Project>* is the name of the project that is currently selected in the Project Explorer).

   The *<Project>* **Properties** dialog box appears.

2. Select the **Custom Build** tab.

3. In the **Configuration** drop-down list, choose the build configuration for which you want the **Custom Build** tab settings to apply.

4. Select the **Pre-build command(s)** box if you want to specify commands that will occur before your project is built. Select the **Post-build command(s)** box if you want to specify commands that will occur after your project has been built.

5. Enter the commands you wish to specify for the selected build command type. Only one command should be specified on each line of the text box. When entering commands into the text box, you can use standard batch commands to specify conditions under which the commands should execute.

Setting the Classpath

In order to utilize Java packages in your projects, it is important that the packages be available on the Classpath. The Classpath is a path the compiler uses to find packages that you reference in your projects. You can add a package to the Classpath by either adding it to your Autoexec.bat file, if you are running Microsoft Windows; or to the environment settings if you are running under Microsoft Windows NT. The following is an example of a Classpath entry:

```
SET CLASSPATH=%PATH%;C:\MYPACKAGE;
```

You may want to have a path added to the Classpath for your Java project. The Classpath tab of the *<Project>* Properties dialog box allows you to add and remove paths that are related to your project.

To display the Classpath tab

1. On the **Project** menu, click *<Project>* **Properties** (where *<Project>* is the name of the project that is currently selected in the Project Explorer).

    The *<Project>* **Properties** dialog box appears.

2. Select the **Classpath** tab.

3. In the **Configuration** drop-down list, choose the build configuration for which you want the **Classpath** tab settings to apply.

To add a path to the project specific Classpath

1. On the *<Project>* **Properties** dialog box, click the **New** button.

    The **Extended Project-specific Classpath** dialog box appears.

2. Enter the path that you wish to add to your project's Classpath. If the path you define does not exist, Visual J++ will ask you if you want to add the path regardless of the path's existence.

3. Click **OK**.

    The path is added to the list of paths.

Note If you have multiple projects open in Visual J++, you can merge all the project-specific Classpaths into a consolidated "solution-specific" Classpath. To do this, click the **Merge all Project-specific Classpaths in Solution** check box.

To delete a Classpath from the list, select the Classpath in the list and then click **Delete**. You can also use the **Up** or **Down** buttons to change the order of the Classpaths in the list.

Setting COM Classes

Exposing a class as a COM class is a way of creating powerful and reusable applications. By selecting a class as a COM class, the class and its public methods can be accessed from other applications and programming languages. The COM Classes tab of the *<Project>* Properties dialog box allows you to specify which public classes in your project should be exposed as COM classes. Once a class has been defined as a COM class, Visual J++ creates a type library for your project's COM classes so that it can be accessed by other applications and registered as a COM object in the system registry.

The COM Classes tab also allows you to use an existing type library to expose your project's classes or to create class templates for existing type libraries or embedded COM object ActiveX controls. A COM template allows you to use Java source code to implement COM components that are described in type libraries or pre-existing COM components. If you have a type library or COM component that you wish to implement using Java, you can select the type library or COM component from the list and Visual J++ will build the template code in your project. You can then implement each of the methods provided by the templates, and compile to create a COM component.

To make a class in your project a COM class

1. On the **Project** menu, click *<Project>* **Properties** (where *<Project>* is the name of the project that is currently selected in the Project Explorer).

   The *<Project>* **Properties** dialog box appears.

2. Select the **COM Classes** tab.

   Note Any settings made in the **COM Classes** tab of the *<Project>* **Properties** dialog box are not affected by changes in the build configuration settings in the **Configuration** list.

3. In the **COM Classes** tab, click **Automatically generate Type Library**.

4. Place a check mark next to the class you wish to make a COM class.

5. By default, Visual J++ creates a type library file based on the name of the project. To change this and other information related to the type library, such as the library name, description, help file, and help context ID, click **Options**. This displays the Type Library Options dialog box where you can modify the information for the type library.

To use an existing type library

1. On the **COM Classes** tab, click **Use existing Type Library** and then click **Select**.

    The COM Templates dialog box appears.

2. From the list of **Installed COM Components**, locate and place a check mark next to the type library you wish to use. If the type library is not registered in your system registry, you can click **Browse** to select the type library you wish to use.

3. Click **OK**.

    Visual J++ creates a package directory in your project directory and also creates the template classes in the new package directory.

Importing a Visual J++ 1.1 Project

You can open and use Java projects created with Visual J++ 1.1 in the new Visual J++ 6.0 development environment. The following procedure provides the steps for converting these files.

> **Caution**   Before importing your Visual J++ 1.1 project, it is important that you understand the new project structure. The new project structure is directory-based in contrast to the file-based structure of Visual J++ 1.1. This change in project structure means that every file that exists in the root directory of your project and all directories below the project root directory are automatically included as part of your project. You can remove files from a new project with the **Remove From Project** item on Project Explorer's shortcut menu. If you remove an item from a project, you can add it back to the project by using the **Add To Project** item on Project Explorer's shortcut menu. However, when you delete a file from a project, it is physically deleted from the directory and cannot be recovered from the development environment, but may be recoverable from the Recycle Bin.

To import a Visual J++ 1.1 project

1. On the **File** menu, click **Open Project**.

    The **New Project** dialog box appears.

2. Click the **Existing** tab, and locate the root directory of the Visual J++ 1.1 project you want to import.

3. Click the root directory of Visual J++ 1.1 project.

4. In the **New Project** dialog box, click **Import Project Folder**.

    Your imported Visual J++ 1.1 project appears in the Project Explorer.

5. In the Project Explorer, expand your project's folder to view the files in your project.

Your project is now ready for you to modify, build, and run.

CHAPTER 2

Designing Forms

The Forms Designer provides you with a dynamic way to visually create forms for your applications. You can turn a two-dimensional form into source code that is based on the Windows Foundation Classes for Java (WFC). The Forms Designer contains Rapid Application Development (RAD) features, such as code generation and code completion, that provide quick syntax analysis, debugging information, and other tools for:

- Creating a form and specifying the alignment and formatting without having to write Java code.

- Managing the Toolbox containing WFC, ActiveX, and custom controls.

- Adding controls to a form by dragging WFC and ActiveX controls onto it. The Forms Designer generates the appropriate Java source code.

- Adding event handlers to controls.

- Formatting forms to position and size your forms and controls by dragging their handles and objects visually without having to write Java code.

- Setting properties with the Properties window without having to write Java code. Properties include form elements such as color, size, position, and font.

- Creating menus for your form through the addition of a single WFC control.

- Code generation synchronization for visual representation of code changes and form views.

- Writing or modifying Java code for a form and viewing the results in the Forms Designer.

- Authoring WFC controls for your forms.

Creating a Form

You can add a form to your application through the Project menu.

Objects that include components and controls can be dragged from the Toolbox to the form. The form is persisted as a block of source code that defines an instance of the WFC Form class. The default Form class contains:

- A constructor that invokes the initForm method.

- A set of instance variables, one for each item on the form.

- An initForm method that specifies the default properties for the items. You can change these defaults by setting item properties.

The Forms Designer generates this code based on values set in the Properties window for each control and the form itself. Be careful when modifying the initForm method, because the Forms Designer also reads this code when displaying the form. Also, avoid conditionals, such as **if**, **while**, and **switch** statements, and component methods. If you modify the initForm code, restrict changes to properties that begin with **set**, and restrict values to constants. Do not use variables to set values.

For example:

Correct   `setSize(10,100);`

Incorrect   `x=10; y = 100; setSize(x,y);`

To create a form

1. Open an existing project, or create a new project.

2. In Project Explorer, select the name of your project.

3. On the **Project** menu, click **Add Form**.

4. In the **Add Item** dialog box, click either the **New** or **Existing** tab. For this example, click the **New** tab.

5. In the **Add Item** dialog box, click the **Form** icon.

   This template creates a class capable of hosting controls.

6. In the **Name** box, edit the name of the class file. The default name is Form1.java.

7. Click **Open**.

   The form window is displayed, showing the form surface.

The form is automatically opened in design mode if you are creating a new form from a template.

If the Forms Designer is not currently active, use the following procedure to open it.

To view the form in the Forms Designer

- On the **View** menu, click **Designer**.

  – or –

  Double-click the node in the Project Explorer, or right-click the form file name, and then click **View Designer** on the context menu. Your form now appears in the Forms Designer.

By default, controls are aligned to the form grid. Set grid options using the Tools command on the Options menu. Form properties can be directly modified in the property page for the form.

The Toolbox contains WFC Controls and can include other tabs containing ActiveX and custom controls.

Once you have the basic form template, you are ready to add controls to it.

Managing the Toolbox

The Forms Designer includes a Toolbox of default controls. The default control types are divided by tabs. You can add custom tabs to the Toolbox and add custom controls to any of the tabs.

To add objects to the Toolbox

- On the **Tools** menu, click **Customize Toolbox**.

  – or –

  Paste an item that has been copied to the Clipboard into the Toolbox.

  – or –

  Drag selected scraps of code or text from the Text editor into the Toolbox and then drag them into other files or windows where you want to use them.

    Note   Only components that extend com.ms.wfc.core.Component and have the **ShowInToolbox** attribute set (this is set to **true** by default) are displayed.

To organize your tools, you can:

- Copy a Toolbox item from one tab to another tab by pressing CTRL and dragging the selected item to the new tab.

- Move a Toolbox item from one tab to another tab by dragging the selected item to the new tab.

    Note   If you try to move a nonremovable item, dragging it to a new tab will copy it to the new tab instead of moving it.

You can add and customize Toolbox tabs by:

- Clicking **Add Tab** on the context menu when you right-click the Toolbox to create tabs for customized groupings.

- Rearranging items on a tab and rearranging the tabs by dragging them to the location you want.

- Clicking the tab label and typing the new name description text of items or by using **Rename Item** on the context menu.

To view Toolbox objects as a list

- Right-click the Toolbox to display the context menu, and then click **List View**. This displays the contents of the active tab in the Toolbox in a list format. This list contains the icons and descriptive information associated with the active Toolbox tab.

To view Toolbox objects as icons

- Right-click the Toolbox to display the context menu, and then clear the **List View** check box. This displays the contents of the active tab in the Toolbox as icons only.

To delete objects from the Toolbox

- Select the item to be deleted, and press DELETE.

To recover a deleted control

1. Right-click the Toolbox to display the context menu, and then click **Customize Toolbox**.

2. In the **Customize Toolbox** dialog box, click the **WFC Controls** tab.

3. In the **WFC Controls** tab, click the check box for the control you want to add.

Adding Controls to a Form

You can add controls to your form in design mode by selecting them from the Toolbox.

To add a control

- In the Toolbox, click the control you want to add to your form and drag it onto your form. The control appears on your form in its default size.

  – or –

  In the Toolbox, double-click the control to add it to the center of your form. The control appears on your form in its default size. You can then drag it to the desired location.

  > **Note**   When a control is placed onto a form at design time, only the class name for the control is added. Code for the control is not generated until you close the form. If you modify an existing control in the Toolbox, you must close and reopen the form or reload the project so that the form picks up the updated class files for the control.

To resize a control

- Select the control you want to resize, and resize it with the sizing handles.

    Note You can also use SHIFT + arrow keys to size the control.

To add event handler templates to a control

- Double-click a form or control to generate a method for the default event of the form or control. The event handler method is created in the Form class.

    Note You can also add event handlers through the events view in the Properties window.

Adding an Event Handler

You can use the Forms Designer to create *event handlers*. An event handler is a routine in your code that determines which actions to perform when an event occurs, such as the user's clicking a button.

For example, the event handler for the mouseDown event provides a mouseEvent object that allows you to determine which mouse button was pressed, where the mouse was positioned on the form, and which keys on the keyboard were pressed during the click.

You can add an event handler using the events view in the Properties window. A handler for the default event can also be added by double-clicking. Moreover, you can assign an existing handler to the events of other controls if the signatures of the events are the same.

To add an event handler using the events view of the Properties window

1. Click the control (such as a button control) or form you want an event handler created for.

2. In the Properties window, click the events view button (indicated by a thunderbolt symbol).

3. In the list of available events, click an event (for example, **click**).

4. In the box to the right of the event name, type the name of the handler (for example, MyButton_click), and press ENTER.

    A code template is generated in your code similar to the following:

    ```
    private void MyButton_click(Object sender, Event e) {

    }
    ```

    In this example, *sender* is the source of the event and *e* is an Event object that provides information about the event.

To add a handler for the default event

- Double-click a form or control to generate a handler method for the default event of the form or control.

  – or –

  In the events view in the Properties window, double-click the event to create the handler for the default event.

To use to the same handler for events shared by multiple controls

1. In the events view in the Properties window, click an event for the first control.

2. In the box to the right of the event name, type the name of the handler, and press ENTER.

3. On the form, select the second control.

4. In the Properties window, click the same event for the second control.

5. Click the drop-down arrow to view a list of existing handlers for this type of event.

6. Select the name of the event handler. Only the existing handler is used. No new templates are created in the code.

Formatting Forms

You can format objects you have placed on your form using the location properties for the form, the grid options on the Tools menu, and various options on the Format menu.

To change a control's location properties

1. Click the control you want to change.

2. On the **View** menu, click **Properties Window**.

3. In the Properties window, double-click the **location** property to expand the node.

4. Enter the x and y coordinate properties for your control.

   Note   You can also change the location programmatically by setting the x and y location properties.

To set grid options

1. On the **Tools** menu, click **Options**.

2. In the **Options** dialog box tree-view area of your project, double-click **Forms Designers**, and then click **WFC**.

You can use this dialog box to set the defaults for displaying the grid, the grid height and width in pixels, and to toggle alignment to the grid.

To format controls on a form, you can use the options on the **Format** menu to:

- Align controls.

- Make multiple controls the same size.

- Size to grid.

- Adjust horizontal and vertical spacing.

- Adjust the front-to-back order.

- Lock controls in place.

To align two controls on a form

1. Click the first control (this control becomes the reference), and then press the CTRL key and click the second control.

2. On the **Format** menu, point to **Align**, and then click **Lefts**.

   The second control aligns with the left edge of the first control.

   Note Controls can be stacked on top of each other.

Modifying the Form Layout Behavior

With the Forms Designer, you can define the behaviors of controls that are placed on your form. For example, you can anchor a label control at the top of the form using the anchor property, or you can modify the docking behavior of your form.

To anchor the control within the form

1. Place the control on the form.

2. Click the control so that the control's properties appear in the Properties window.

3. In the Properties window, double-click the **anchor** property.

4. In the Anchor editor, click the cross bars to enable and disable anchoring between the control and the form edge.

To modify docking behavior

1. Place the control on the form.

2. Click the control so that the control's properties appear in the Properties window.

3. In the Properties window, double-click the **dock** property.

4. In the Docking editor, click the bars to enable and disable docking for the control. Click **None** to disable docking.

   Note The control is automatically resized to fit the boundaries of the docked edge.

Most controls can be docked to the edges of a form or can be made to fill the entire form.

Setting Properties with the Properties Window

Properties are attributes that define how a control appears and runs at run time. Each form and each control have an associated custom property page. Modifying the properties in the page (the Properties window) affects the code that is generated for the control in the initForm method. Properties include the appearance, behavior, and position for the control. The background color, enable and disable state, show state, font, default size and position, and so forth, can be set in the Properties window for the form.

To edit the properties of a control or form

1. On the form, click the control you want to edit; or to edit the form, click the form itself.

    The property page associated with the selected control is displayed in the Properties window.

2. In the Properties window, select the property for the control that you want to modify. For example, select the **font** property to change the font style for the name on a button control.

    Note   If you select multiple controls, a custom property page appears that displays only the common properties.

Complex properties use common dialog boxes and editors for:

*   Text input — size and strings (in-place string edit changes appear in real-time)
*   Combo box selection — cursors, enumerators and Booleans
*   Font picker — common dialog box for selecting font characteristics
*   Color picker — common dialog box with a palette for color selection
*   List items — window for creating initial list items
*   Anchor and Dock editors — for setting position behavior

Click the node of compound properties to access subproperties.

Creating Menus for Forms

You can create main menus and context menus using the menu controls provided by the Forms Designer.

Adding and Modifying a Menu

If you want your application to provide a set of commands to users, menus offer a convenient and consistent way to group commands and an easy way for users to access them. The menu bar appears immediately below the title bar on the form and contains one or more menu titles. When you click a menu title (such as File), a menu containing a list of menu items appears. Menu items can include commands (such as New and Exit), separator bars, and submenu titles. Each menu item the user sees corresponds to a menu control property you define. Multiple menus can be added to one form.

To add a menu to your form

1. Under **WFC Controls** in the Toolbox, double-click the **MainMenu** control.

   Note   You can also select the **MainMenu** control and drag it onto your form.

   The **MainMenu** control is inserted onto your form, and the default location for the first item on the menu bar is displayed. Two visual markers (**Type Here**) appear directly to the right and below to signify the next available editing location.

   Note   By default, the **MainMenu** property for the form is set to MainMenu1.

2. Type the name of your first menu caption in the default location text box. (For example, type **File** to add the **File** menu.)

   The menu caption is added to your menu, and the default location text box moves to the next menu caption location. Continue typing your menu captions until all your captions are complete.

Forms can have several menu items, such as File/Save and File/SaveAs, that change depending on the state of the application. Menus can be enabled or disabled, checked or unchecked, made visible or hidden using properties for each menu item.

If you want to change the main menu used by a form, you change the **menu** property for the form to a different menu name, for example, mainMenu2.

You can add *access keys* to your menu. Access keys provide a way for the user to access the menu using only the keyboard. An access key corresponds to an underlined letter on the menu.

To add access keys to a menu

1. Click the menu caption in which you want to add an access key.

2. Place the cursor immediately before the letter in the caption box that you want to be your access key letter and type an ampersand (&). For example, on the **File** menu, click **File**, place your cursor before the "F" in **File,** and then type an ampersand. You can also edit the caption title through the **Text** property for the menu item.

Shortcut keys add accessibility to your menus. A shortcut key is a keyboard combination, such as CTRL+C for copy, that invokes a particular command.

To add a shortcut key to a menu item

1. Click to the immediate right of the menu item caption to which you want to add a shortcut key. A drop-down list appears.

2. Select a key combination from the drop-down list.

   – or –

   In the Properties window, click the **shortcut** property and select a key combination.

To remove a shortcut key

1. Select a menu item.

2. Set the **shortcut** property to **none**.

At times, you may want to give users various commands that they can apply to the application. For example, there may be several available toolbars in an application. The user can select which toolbar will be displayed by clicking the toolbar name on the menu, and a check mark appears next to the toolbar name.

To enable check marks on a menu

1. Select a menu item.

2. Click to the immediate left of the menu item name. A check box apears.

   – or –

   In the Properties window, click the **checked** property.

To move a menu

1. Select the desired menu item caption.

2. Drag the menu caption to the new position.

   The menu caption moves and snaps to place. Other menu captions that are affected by this change are moved as appropriate.

   Note   Moving top-level menu captions moves all submenus as well. Submenus are not displayed during the move.

To modify a menu caption

1. Click the menu caption you want to modify.

2. In the text box containing the menu caption, make any necessary changes.

Separator bars are used in menus to add a distinct line between groups of commands.

To create a menu separator bar

1. Click the menu caption that is above the location where you want to add a separator bar.

2. Press the HYPHEN (–) key, and then press ENTER.

A separator bar appears directly below your menu caption.

– or –

Click the right mouse button, and then click **Insert Separator** on the context menu.

Separator bars can be moved and deleted in the same manner as menu captions.

To delete a menu item from your form

*   Right-click the menu item caption you want to delete, and click **Delete** on the context menu.

    Note To delete the entire menu, select each menu caption and press DELETE, or click the MainMenu control you want to delete and press DELETE.

Confirmation on deletion occurs only on menu captions with submenus.

To edit the name associated with a menu item

1. Click the right mouse button over a menu item.

2. Click **Edit Names** to toggle the Edit Names mode for the menu.

3. Click on and edit the name associated with the menu item you wish to modify (for example, menuItem1).

Context Menus

Context menus can be associated with controls on your form. These menus appear when the user right-clicks the control.

To add a context menu to a form

1. Under the **WFC Controls** in the Toolbox, double-click the **ContextMenu** control.

    Note Use any of the methods to add a control to a form. You can also select the **ContextMenu** control in the Toolbox and drag the control onto your form.

2. To enter design mode, double-click the **ContextMenu** control.

To assign a context menu to a control

1. Click the control you want to assign a context menu to.

2. In the Properties window, add the name of the context menu to the **contextMenu** property. By default, the first context menu is named contextMenu1.

Context menu controls can be edited in the same way as MainMenu controls. For more information, see the previous section, "Adding and Modifying a Menu."

Adding ToolTips to Controls on a Form

ToolTips are text strings that appear as you "hover" over a control with the mouse pointer. In Visual J++, a separate WFC control enables ToolTip functionality for controls on the form. The time, delay, and other properties can be set using the property page for each control on the form.

To add ToolTips to controls

1. In the WFC Toolbox, add a ToolTip control to your form.

2. Edit the property for each control to add the desired text.

Code Generation

Visual J++ synchronizes visual representation of code changes and form views (code generation from visual layout) in both directions. Information about which methods (and classes) are being modified is formatted into the source code. Similarly, modifications to the source code are sent to the Forms Designer.

The two-way editing does not simultaneously modify source code and visual layout. The code that is used to create the visual layout is disabled while the Forms Designer is in use. The layout is stored as code when the Forms Designer window is closed or the form is saved. Editing of the entire initForm function is locked until the Forms Designer window is closed.

Edits in the Forms editor are not serialized as code until you click Save on the File menu, or when the Forms editor is closed.

You can use the Forms Designer to edit classes that adhere to the following syntax:

```
class isEditable extends [UserControl, Form, Design Page] {
    Container components = new Container(this);
    private void initForm() {
        [form initialization code goes here]
    }
}
```

The initialization code must adhere to certain parsing rules:

- Initialization code must reside in the initForm function.

- No conditional code will be parsed (no **if, while**, or **switch** statements).

CHAPTER 3

Editing Code

Visual J++ provides several ways to create, modify, and manage your project's code. The topics and procedures in this section give you hands-on experience to help you explore the Text editor, Class Outline, WFC Component Builder, and Object Browser.

Managing Files with the Text Editor

The development environment includes an integrated Text editor to manage, edit, and print source files. Most of the procedures for using the editor will seem familiar if you have used other Windows-based text editors. In addition, Visual J++ has enhanced the Text editor with several new timesaving features such as statement completion, dynamic syntax checking, and two-way interaction between the Text editor and Class Outline — these are just a few of the services IntelliSense provides for Visual J++ developers.

Splitting a Window in the Text Editor

To split the Text editor's window

1. Point to the splitter box at the top of the vertical scroll bar.

2. When the pointer changes to a window-sizing cursor, drag the splitter bar to the position you want.

To return to a single window

- Double-click the splitter bar.

To move or copy text between parts of a long document

1. Split the window into two panes.

2. Display the code you want to move or copy in one pane.

3. Display the destination for the code in the other pane.

4. Select and drag the code across the splitter bar to the destination pane.

Viewing a File in Full-Screen Mode

To begin or end full-screen mode

- On the **View** menu, click **Full Screen**.

Finding and Replacing Text in a Single File

To find text in a single file

1. Move the insertion point to the location in your file where you want to begin your search.

2. On the **Edit** menu, click **Find and Replace**.

   The **Find** tool window appears.

3. In the text box next to the **Find** button, type the search text.

   You can also use the drop-down list to select from a list of your previous search strings.

4. From the **Look In** combo box, select **Current Document**.

5. To begin your search, click **Find**.

   This highlights the first occurrence of your search item.

6. To continue searching, click **Find**.

To replace text in a single file

1. Move the insertion point to the location in your file where you want to begin your search.

2. On the **Edit** menu, click **Find and Replace**.

   The **Find** tool window appears.

3. In the text box next to the **Find** button, type the search text.

   You can also use the drop-down list to select from a list of your previous search strings.

4. From the **Look In** combo box, select **Current Document**.

5. In the text box next to the **Replace** button, type the replacement text.

6. Click **Replace**.

   The first occurrence of your search item is highlighted in the Text editor.

   Note   To replace all occurrences within the file, click **Replace All**.

7. Click **Replace** again.

   This replaces the current selection and highlights the next occurrence of the search item.

Finding Text in Multiple Files

To find text in multiple files

1. On the **Edit** menu, click **Find and Replace**.

   The **Find** tool window appears.

2. In the text box next to the **Find** button, type the search text.

   You can also use the drop-down list to select from a list of your previous search strings.

3. From the **Look In** combo box, choose the types of files in which to search.

4. Click **Browse**, to display the **Look In** dialog box.

5. Highlight the top level folder in which to begin the search.

6. Click **Add**.

   The name of the folder appears in the bottom text box of the **Look In** dialog box.

7. Click **OK** to return to the **Find** dialog box.

8. Click the **Subfolders** check box to include files in subdirectories of the previously selected top-level folder.

9. To begin your search, click **Find**.

   A list of files containing the search text appears in bottom window of the **Find** dialog box.

10. Double-click an entry from the list.

    An editor window containing the file opens with the line containing the search text selected.

Finding Matching Delimiters

Source code is often grouped using delimiters such as (), { }, [], and <>. These groupings are called levels. The editor understands nested levels, and matches the correct delimiter even if the level spans several pages and contains many levels within it. The editor's functionality allows you to jump quickly between the start and end of a level.

To find a matching delimiter

1. Place the insertion point immediately before or after any delimiter.

2. Press the keyboard shortcut, CTRL+].

    The insertion point moves forward or backward to the matching delimiter. Choosing the command again returns the insertion point to its starting place. If a matching delimiter cannot be found, the insertion point does not move.

Navigating with Bookmarks

You can set bookmarks to mark frequently accessed lines in your source file. Once a bookmark is set, you can use menu or keyboard commands to move to it. You can remove a bookmark when you no longer need it.

To set a bookmark

1. Move the insertion point to the line where you want to set a bookmark.

2. On the **Edit** menu, click **Bookmarks** and then choose **Toggle Bookmark** from the cascading menu.

    – or –

    Press the **Toggle Bookmark** keyboard shortcut, CTRL + K, CTRL + K.

    A light blue rectangle appears in the margin next to the line selected if you have enabled your editor to display margins.

To navigate to the next bookmark

*   On the **Edit** menu, click **Bookmarks** and then choose **Next Bookmark** from the cascading menu.

    – or –

    Press the **Next Bookmark** keyboard shortcut, CTRL+K, CTRL+N.

To navigate to the previous bookmark

- On the **Edit** menu, click **Bookmarks** and then choose **Previous Bookmark** from the cascading menu.

  – or –

  Press the **Previous Bookmark** keyboard shortcut, CTRL+K, CTRL+P.

To remove a bookmark

1. Move the insertion point to the line where a bookmark exists.

2. On the **Edit** menu, click **Bookmarks** and then choose **Toggle Bookmark** from the cascading menu.

   – or –

   Press the **Toggle Bookmark** keyboard shortcut, CTRL+K, CTRL+K.

   The light blue rectangle disappears from the margin.

To remove all bookmarks

- On the **Edit** menu, click **Bookmarks** and then choose **Clear All Bookmarks** from the cascading menu.

  – or –

  Press the **Clear All Bookmarks** keyboard shortcut, CTRL+K, CTRL+L.

Selecting a Box of Text

You can select a box of text, also known as a column block of text, to perform cut, copy, delete, indent, and unindent operations.

To enable box selection of text

1. On the **Tools** menu, click **Options** to display the **Options** dialog box.

2. Expand the **Text Editor** node of the tree view in the **Options** dialog box.

3. Expand the **Per Language** node and select **Java**.

4. In the **Settings** group of options, select the **Box Selection** radio button.

To select a box of text

1. Point to the beginning of the text you want to select.

2. Hold down the left mouse button and move the mouse to highlight a box of text.

   When you release the left mouse button, a box of text is selected and is available for cut, copy, delete, and indent operations.

   Note   To cancel the selected box of text, click the left mouse button.

Writing Code with Statement Completion

Visual J++'s Statement Completion saves you time by doing the reference look-up work for you. Statement Completion automatically displays member lists and parameter information that gives you a list of classes, members, and method signatures, that are relevant within the context of the current .java source file.

To introduce you to the Statement Completion features, this scenario will show you how to build statement(s) with the `java.lang.String` and `java.lang.System` classes. After you've built your project and run the application, the program will display a message in the console window provided by JVIEW. This scenario includes the following procedures:

- Enabling/Disabling Statement Completion Options in the Text Editor

- Creating Statements with Word Completion

- Selecting an Overloaded Method

- Selecting Methods from a Member List

- Building an Argument List with Parameter Info

  Note This scenario was created with the Visual J++ Console Application template. You may complete the following procedures with any .java source code file in any Visual J++ project. If you would like to create a console application to complete this scenario, please see "Creating a Console Application" in Chapter 1, "Creating Projects," and follow the steps to create and open a project before proceeding.

Enabling/Disabling Statement Completion Options in the Text Editor

Within the development environment, you can enable or disable Statement Completion's **Auto list members** and **Parameter information** options.

To enable Statement Completion options

1. On the **Tools** menu, click **Options** to display the **Options** dialog box.

2. From the tree view in the leftmost pane of the **Options** dialog box, expand the **Text Editor** and then the **Per Language** nodes by clicking the plus ("+") sign next to these nodes.

3. Select **Java** to display the **Text Editor/Per Language/Java** property page.

4. In the **Statement Completion** group of this property page, click the check boxes for **Auto list members** and **Parameter information** to enable these options.

Visual J++ enables Statement Completion's **Auto list members** and **Parameter information** by default.

> **Note**   Clearing the check box for **Auto list members** or **Parameter information** disables the respective option.

Creating Statements with Word Completion

For the examples in this topic, Word Completion provides visual clues when you're typing the name of String and System classes, and creating a new String object. Word Completion is available for any Visual J++ project.

> **Note**   The code examples in the following scenario were created with a Visual J++ Console Application project. If you would like to create a Console Application project to complete this scenario, see "Creating a Console Application" in Chapter 1, "Creating Projects," and follow the steps to create and open the project before proceeding.

To select an item from a list provided by the Word Completion feature

1. On the **View** menu, click Project Explorer to open Project Explorer.

2. In **Project Explorer** click the plus ("+") sign to the left of your project's name to expand your project.

3. Highlight the .java file containing your project's main() method (Class1.java by default), and select **View Code** from the shortcut menu.

   Visual J++ opens the Text editor and loads your .java file. The file is now ready for editing.

4. To get Word Completion assistance for the String class, type an "S" between the braces of the application's main() method and leave the cursor to the right of this letter.

   > **Tip**   Notice the red squiggly line drawn under the letter. Since an "S" has no significance within the context of this program, IntelliSense gives a visual clue for the syntax error. For more information about visual editing clues, see "Finding Errors with Dynamic Syntax Checking," later in this chapter.

5. On the **Edit** menu, click **Complete Word** to display a list box of classes and other elements recognized by IntelliSense.

   > **Tip**   You can use the keyboard shortcut, CTRL+SPACE, instead of selecting the **Complete Word** option on the **Edit** menu, to display this list box.

6. With the list box still displayed, type a "T" after the "S" of the statement you're building in your .java file.

   Statement Completion now selects **StackOverflowError** in its list — the first element that starts with an "ST" in the context of this program.

7. Now type an "R" after the "ST" in your statement and Statement Completion moves the highlight bar to **String** in the list box.

8. Press the **Tab** bar to insert String into the statement you're building.

   Pressing the **Tab** bar or any other non-alphanumeric key, such as a period or opening parenthesis, places the selected item into a statement at the location of the insertion point.

   > **Tip** Instead of typing the letters until Statement Completion finds the element you need, you can use the up and down arrows to highlight your selection.

To select a class name after the new operator

1. Continue to build the statement by typing the following code after String:

   ```
   [String] myStr = new
   ```

2. Type a space after new and Statement Completion automatically displays a list of class names available within the scope of your program.

3. Type "STR", or enough letters of "String" to select the **String** item from the list.

4. Press **Tab** and String is inserted after new.

   Your statement should look like this:

   ```
   String myStr = new String
   ```

To continue building the statement that displays a line of text, you'll need a constructor for the new String object. See the next section, "Selecting an Overloaded Method," for a procedure that selects a String constructor with Statement Completion's **Parameter Info** option.

If you know how to partially spell the name of the class or item, use the following procedure to speed up the process of typing and selecting the correct spelling and capitalization.

To finish typing a word using the Word Completion feature

1. In your .java file, move the cursor to a new line and type "SY."

2. Press CTRL+SPACE (the Word Completion keyboard shortcut).

   Statement Completion completes the word, System, and inserts it into your code since it is the only item that begins with an "SY." If more than one item starts with these letters, Statement Completion displays a list box.

Selecting an Overloaded Method

This example uses Statement Completion to help you select an overloaded constructor method for the `String` class.

> **Note** If you have completed the steps of "Creating Statements with Word Completion" continue working through the following procedure. If not, take a few minutes and complete the procedure before selecting an overloaded constructor method for the `String` object.

Before proceeding, make sure you have loaded a .java file into the Text editor that contains the following code:

```
String myStr = new String
```

To select an overloaded method for a class

1. With the insertion point immediately after the last "`String`" in the statement, type an opening parenthesis, "(".

    A pop-up window appears displaying the signature of one of the constructor methods for the String class. The spin control on the left side of this window indicates how many overloaded constructor methods (**11**) are available for the String class and which one is being displayed (**1**).

    > **Note** For methods and constructors that are not overloaded, this list box is replaced by the **Parameter Info** text box. See Building an Argument List with Parameter Info for an example that uses the **Parameter Info** feature.

2. Click anywhere on the spin control to display the signatures of the other String constructor methods until you find one that takes a `String` argument.

    In this example, constructor number 11 of 11 meets this criteria.

3. After the opening parenthesis, type `"Hello World!");`.

    Your completed statement should look like this:

```
String myStr = new String("Hello World!");
```

Statement Completion also displays a class's public methods and fields. To display a member list for the `String` object, see the following section, "Selecting Methods from a Member List."

Selecting Methods from a Member List

This example uses Statement Completion's **Member list** feature to help you select a method of the `String` class. You may also use this procedure to select class member variables from the **Member list**.

Note If you have completed the steps of Creating Statements with Word Completion and Selecting an Overloaded Method, continue with the following procedure. If not, take a few minutes and work through those procedures before selecting a method for the `String` class.

Before proceeding, make sure you have loaded a .java file into the Text editor that contains the following code:

```
String myStr = new String("Hello World!");
```

To select a class member from the Members List

1. On a new line, type:

    ```
    if(mystr.
    ```

2. When you type the "." (dot operator) after `myStr`, Statement Completion displays a list of the methods belonging to the `String` class.

    Tip If you do not get a member list after you type the dot operator, select **List Members** from the **Edit** menu or use the keyboard shortcut, CTRL+J. If this continues to happen, make sure you've enabled the Statement Completion feature.

3. Type "equalsI" to highlight the `String` class's `equalsIgnoreCase` method in the **Members List**.

4. Press **Tab** to insert the `equalsIgnoreCase` method after the dot operator for `myStr`.

    Both lines of your code should look like the following:

    ```
    String myStr = new String("Hello World!");
    if(myStr.equalsIgnoreCase
    ```

To continue building the next statement with Statement Completion's **Parameter Info** feature, see Building an Argument List with Parameter Info.

Building an Argument List with Parameter Info

This example uses Statement Completion's **Parameter Info** feature to display information for a method's argument.

Note If you have completed the steps of "Creating Statements with Word Completion," "Selecting an Overloaded Method," and "Selecting Methods from a Member List," continue with the following procedure. If not, take a few minutes and work through those procedures before selecting a method for the String class.

Before proceeding, make sure you have loaded a .java file into the Text editor that contains the following code:

```
String myStr = new String("Hello World!");
if(myStr.equalsIgnoreCase
```

To select build an argument list with Parameter Info

1. Continuing to build the if statement, type an opening parenthesis, "(", immediately after myStr.equalsIgnoreCase.

    Parameter Info displays the method's declaration with the single parameter (**String p1**) in a bold-type font.

    Note In this case, the method has only one parameter (**String p1**). If you select a method that takes more than one argument, IntelliSense displays argument types and positions within the method declaration. When you type the opening parenthesis after the method's name, IntelliSense bolds the first argument. As you add commas between the arguments, IntelliSense bolds the type and position information for the next argument that's needed to complete the method's call.

    Tip If you do not get a pop-up window with parameter information after you type the opening parenthesis, select **Parameter Info** from the **Edit** menu or use the keyboard shortcut, CTRL+SHIFT+I. If this continues to happen, make sure you've enabled the Statement Completion feature.

2. After the opening parenthesis, complete the statement by typing:

    ```
    "hello world!"))
    ```

    The completed if statement should look like the following:

    ```
    if(myStr.equalsIgnoreCase("hello world!"))
    ```

3. Using the Statement Completion's Word Completion, Member List, and **Parameter Info** options, complete this example by adding the following code after the closing parenthesis of the if statement:

```
{
System.out.println("The strings are the same.");
}
else
{
System.out.println("The strings are different.");
}
return;
```

4. Build the program.

5. In the Text editor, place the cursor on "return" (the last statement of this program's code). Click the right mouse button and select **Run To Cursor** from the shortcut menu.

6. View the following results in JVIEW's console window:

```
The strings are the same.
```

Finding Errors with Dynamic Syntax Checking

Visual J++ also provides dynamic syntax checking to assist you when you're writing code within the Text editor. In addition to the information Statement Completion provides, you receive visual clues in the form of red squiggly lines and error tips as you build your program's statements.

As you begin typing within a .java file, red squiggly lines appear under code elements, such as class names, member names, and symbols. When you see a red squiggly line, IntelliSense is telling you your code, as it is currently written, has syntactic errors. As you continue typing, the red squiggly lines may disappear as you finish the statement — depending upon the correctness of the completed statement.

For each syntax error marked with a red squiggly line, a task related to the syntax error will appear in the Task List. This provides a list of items that you'll need to correct before you compile your program.

To get error tips and error help from a red squiggly line

1. Rest the cursor over the red squiggly line.

   IntelliSense displays an Error Tip that best suits the context of your source code. On occasion, the tip will simply be "Syntax Error."

   Tip If you do not see a red squiggly line under obvious syntax errors, make sure you've enabled the options that support dynamic syntax checking.

2. While resting the cursor over a red squiggly line, click the right mouse button to access the shortcut menu.

3. From the shortcut menu, select **Error Help** to get online help for the error identified by the red squiggly line.

   See "Creating Statements with Word Completion," earlier in this chapter, for an example that demonstrates the use of red squiggly lines.

Enabling/Disabling Dynamic Syntax Checking Options in the Text Editor

Within the development environment, you can enable or disable the editor's dynamic syntax checking options.

To enable dynamic syntax checking options

1. On the **Tools** menu, click **Options** to display the **Options** dialog box.Ehh

2. From the tree view in the leftmost pane of the **Options** dialog box, expand the **Text Editor** node by clicking the plus ("**+**") sign next to it.

3. Select Java Tasks to display the property page for **Tasks** and **Error display**.

4. In the **Tasks** group of this property page, click the check box for **Check syntax as you type**.

5. In the **Error Display** group of the property page, click the check box for **Underline syntax errors as you type**.

Visual J++ enables these dynamic syntax checking options by default.

   Note Clearing the check box for **Check syntax as you type** or **Underline syntax errors as you type** disables the respective option.

Updating Class Outline from the Text Editor

Visual J++ uses IntelliSense to dynamically update the Class Outline tree view of your file whenever you add a method, member variable, or class to an existing .java source file from the Text editor. If you wish to add a Javadoc comment to your code, IntelliSense creates a comment block and then displays the comment in Class Outline's Javadoc pane.

Adding Items to Class Outline from the Text Editor

Although Visual J++ provides Class Outline and WFC Component Builder to help you add methods, member variables, properties, events, and classes to a project, you can also add these to your project by typing the code directly into your .java file from the Text editor. When you add the code for new classes and class members to a .java file, IntelliSense immediately displays the appropriate icon for the new class or class member in your project's Class Outline.

The following procedure demonstrates the dynamic updating of Class Outline when a new class and method is added to a source file from the Text editor.

> **Note**   The code examples in this and the following topic, Adding Javadoc Comments to Source Files, were created with a Visual J++ Console Application project. You may use any existing Visual J++ project to reproduce the results of these scenarios. If you want to create a Console Application project for the following procedures, see "Creating a Console Application" and follow the steps to create and open the project before proceeding.

To add a new class to Class Outline from the Text editor

1. In **Project Explorer**, click the plus ("+") sign to the left of your project's name to expand your project.

2. Double-click the filename or icon of the .java file containing your project's main() method (Class1 .java by default).

   Visual J++ opens the Text editor and loads your .java file. The file is now ready for editing.

3. On the **View** menu, click **Other Windows** and select **Document Outline** from the cascading menu.

   Class Outline appears with a collapsed tree view of your file.

4. From within the Text editor, after the closing brace of the class definition for `Class1`, add the following code to your .java source file:

```
class Greeting
{
}
```

5. In **Class Outline**, notice that a new class icon has been added to the tree view of your project's file for the `Greeting` class you've just created.

   Note   When you use the Text editor to move the insertion point in the source file, Class Outline does not indicate which definition has been navigated to. To synchronize Class Outline with the source file, right-click the declaration in the Text editor and click **Sync Class Outline** on the shortcut menu.

To add a new method to Class Outline from the Text editor

1. In **Class Outline**, expand the `Greeting` class to display the icons for **Superclasses** and **Inherited Members**.

2. From within the Text editor, add the following code after the opening brace of the `Greeting` class:

```
public static String hello()
{
    String strGreet = new String("Hello World!");
    return strGreet;
}
```

3. In **Class Outline**, notice a new method icon has been added to your project for the `hello()` method you've just created.

   Note   When you use the Text editor to move the insertion point in the source file, Class Outline does not indicate which definition has been navigated to. To synchronize Class Outline with the source file, right-click the declaration in the Text editor and click **Sync Class Outline** on the shortcut menu.

4. To test the `hello()` method of the `Greeting` class, add the following code to your application's `main()` method:

```
System.out.println(Greeting.hello());
return;
```

5. Build the program.

6. In the Text editor, place the cursor on "`return`" (the last statement of this program's code). Click the right mouse button and select **Run To Cursor** from the shortcut menu.

7. View the following results in JVIEW's console window:

```
Hello World!
```

To add a Javadoc comment to the new `hello()` method, see the next section, "Adding Javadoc Comments to Source Files."

Adding Javadoc Comments to Source Files

Below your file's tree view in Class Outline is a Javadoc pane. If a class, method, or member variable has Javadoc comments , the comments appear in this pane. When you add a Javadoc comment to your code, IntelliSense displays the first sentence of the comment in the Javadoc pane whenever you highlight a class, method, or member variable name in Class Outline.

The following procedure explains how to add a Javadoc comment to a method; however, you follow the same steps to add Javadoc comments to classes and member variables.

> **Note** This procedure uses a Console Application project and adds to the code created in the scenario that updates items in Class Outline. If you have not completed the steps that add a Greeting class and hello() method to a basic Console Application, take a few minutes and follow the steps in the previous section, "Adding Items to Class Outline from the Text Editor," before continuing.

To add a Javadoc comment to a method

1. In **Project Explorer**, click the plus ("+") sign to the left of your project's name to expand your project.

2. Double-click the filename or icon of the .java file containing your project's main() method (Class1 .java by default).

   Visual J++ opens the Text editor and loads your .java file. The file is now ready for editing.

3. On the **View** menu, click **Other Windows** and select **Document Outline** from the cascading menu.

   Class Outline appears with a collapsed tree view of your project.

4. In **Class Outline**, expand the Greeting class to display the icons for **Superclasses**, **Inherited Members**, and the hello() method.

5. From within the Text editor, type the opening characters for a Javadoc comment, /**, above the hello() method declaration in your source file.

   IntelliSense creates a Javadoc comment block by inserting the closing characters for a Javadoc comment, */, into your code.

6. After the opening characters of the Javadoc comment block, type the following:

```
/** The hello() method is a static method that takes
 * no arguments and returns a String object to the
 * calling method. The value returned will always
 * be "Hello World!".
 */
```

7. In **Class Outline**, highlight the `hello()` method.

    Notice that the first sentence of the comment you've just added appears in the Javadoc pane.

When you are creating Javadoc comments for your classes, methods, and member variables, you may want or need to add one or more Javadoc fields to a comment. IntelliSense displays a list of Javadoc fields available in Visual J++. The following procedure adds an author field to the Javadoc comment created above.

To add an Javadoc field to a Javadoc comment

1. In **Project Explorer**, click the plus ("+") sign to the left of your project's name to expand your project.

2. Double-click the filename or icon of the .java file containing your project's `main()` method (Class1 .java by default).

    Visual J++ opens the Text editor and loads your .java file. The file is now ready for editing.

3. In the `hello()` method's Javadoc comment, after the last sentence but before the closing Javadoc characters, */, type an @ sign.

    IntelliSense displays a list box of valid Javadoc comment fields.

4. Double-click "**author**" in the list box.

    The word "author" is inserted into your Javadoc comment after the @ sign.

5. Type your name after `@author`.

    Your finished Javadoc comment should look like this:

```
/** The hello() method is a static method that takes
 * no arguments and returns a String object to the
 * calling method. The value returned will always
 * be "Hello World!".
 * @author Mary Doe
 */
```

Managing Code with Class Outline

The Class Outline window lists all classes, interfaces, and delegates defined in a .java source file. All imported classes, and all classes that are contained within the file's package, are also listed. Whenever you open a .java file in the Text editor, Class Outline automatically displays the information for that file.

Class Outline shows the following details for each class:

- The superclass, as well as all other classes in the inheritance hierarchy
- The members that are inherited from the superclass, as well as from the other classes in the inheritance hierarchy
- Any interfaces that the class implements
- Any initializer blocks defined in the class
- Any nested or member classes contained within the class
- Any nested interfaces contained within the class
- The methods and member variables defined by the class

When an item is selected in Class Outline, any associated Javadoc comments are displayed in the lower pane of Class Outline.

Using Class Outline, you can:

- Navigate to a definition in the source file
- Modify a class declaration in the source file
- Add a new declaration to the source file
- Add declarations for interface methods in the source file
- Delete a definition from the source file
- Move or copy a definition in the source file
- Override a method inherited from the superclass
- Set a breakpoint on a method

Class Outline is available whenever you open a .java file in the Text editor, and by default, it is tab-linked with the Toolbox. If you close Class Outline, you can later reopen it by pointing to **Other Windows** on the **View** menu and clicking **Document Outline**.

Refreshing Class Outline

In most cases, the items displayed by Class Outline are automatically synchronized with the associated declarations in the source file; for example, if you change the name of a method in your class, the method name is immediately updated in Class Outline. However, you must manually refresh Class Outline if you change the declaration of an inherited method. Class Outline does not automatically update the list of inherited members.

To refresh Class Outline, right-click the Class Outline window and click **Refresh** on the shortcut menu.

Navigating to a Definition

You can use Class Outline to quickly move the insertion point to a specific definition in your source file. If the definition resides in another .java file (such as the definition of an inherited method), and if that source file is available on your computer, then the file is opened and the insertion point is moved to the definition. If the source file is not available, then the Object Browser is opened.

To navigate to a definition

1. In Class Outline, right-click the item whose definition you want to navigate to.

2. On the shortcut menu, click **Go to definition**.

    – or –

    Double-click the item in Class Outline.

    Note   When you use the Text editor to move the insertion point in the source file, Class Outline does not indicate which definition has been navigated to. To synchronize Class Outline with the source file, right-click the declaration in the Text editor and click **Sync Class Outline** on the shortcut menu.

Modifying a Class Declaration

Using Class Outline, you can easily modify the general attributes of a class.

To modify a class declaration

1. In Class Outline, right-click the name of the class you want to modify.

2. On the shortcut menu, click **Class Properties**.

3. Select an access modifier from the **Access** drop-down list. Nested (or inner) classes can be declared as public, protected, private, or default (package). Non-nested classes can be declared as public or default. For information about nested classes, see "Inner Classes" in the *Java Language Specification*.

4. Select additional modifiers, such as abstract, final, or static. (Only nested classes can be declared as static.)

5. To insert Javadoc comments for the class, enter the comment text in the **Javadoc comment** box.

6. If you are exposing your class as a WFC component, select **Include WFC Component Support (ClassInfo)** to insert a ClassInfo class. (This option is only available for non-nested classes.) ClassInfo is used to describe the properties and events of the component.

7. To expose your class as a COM object, select **COM Class**. When this option is selected, the @com.register directive is inserted to register your class as a COM class, making it accessible to other applications that support COM. (The **COM Class** option is only available for non-nested classes.)

8. To add Microsoft Transaction Server support to your class, select **Enabled** under **MTS Support**. (This option is only available for non-nested classes.) Note that because transaction support is only valid for COM classes, enabling MTS support also selects the **COM Class** option. You can then select one of the following options from the drop-down list:

   - **Required**   The component requires an MTS transaction for its work.

   - **RequiresNew**   The component requires a new MTS transaction for its work. (A new transaction is created, even if one already exists.)

   - **Supported**   The component works regardless of whether a transaction is provided by MTS.

   - **NotSupported**   The component supports neither MTS transactions nor the MTS API.

   The @com.register and @com.transaction directives are automatically added to your class. For more information about Microsoft Transaction Server, see "Getting Started with Microsoft Transaction Server," in the Visual Studio online documentation, Platform SDK.

9. Click **OK** to apply your changes.

   Note   If you use the Text editor to modify a class declaration, Class Outline is automatically updated to show the changes.

Adding a New Declaration

You can use Class Outline to add a method or member variable to a class, or to add a new class to your .java file.

Note If you use the Text editor to add a declaration, the item is automatically added to Class Outline.

To add a new method

1. In Class Outline, right-click the name of the class that will define the method. On the shortcut menu, click **Add Method**.

2. In the **Add Method** dialog box, enter the name of the method in the **Method Name** box.

3. Select a return type from the **Return Type** drop-down list, or enter your own return type.

4. To add method parameters, click the ellipsis (**...**) button under **Parameters**:

   - In the **Edit Parameter List** dialog box, select a parameter type from the **Type** drop-down list or enter your own type. In the **Name** box, enter the name of the parameter.

   - Click **Add** to add the parameter.

   - Repeat this process for each method parameter. Note that to delete a parameter that you have already added, you can select the parameter from the list and click **Delete**. To insert a parameter between two existing parameters, select the parameter after which the new parameter is to appear. When you click **Add**, the new parameter is inserted before the parameter you selected.

   - Click **OK** when you have finished adding all parameters.

5. Select an access modifier from the **Access** drop-down list. Methods can be declared as public, protected, private, or default (package).

6. Select additional modifiers, such as abstract, final, static, synchronized, or native.

7. To insert Javadoc comments for the method, enter the comment text in the **Javadoc comment** box.

8. Click **Add** to insert the method declaration into your file. Class Outline is automatically updated to display the new method.

To add a new member variable

1. In Class Outline, right-click the name of the class that will define the member variable. On the shortcut menu, click **Add Member Variable**.

2. In the **Add Member Variable** dialog box, enter the name of the member variable in the **Member Variable Name** box.

3. Select a data type from the **Data Type** drop-down list or enter your own data type.

4. Select an access modifier from the **Access** drop-down list. Member variables can be declared as public, protected, private, or default (package).

5. Select additional modifiers, such as static, final, volatile, or transient.

6. To initialize the member variable, enter a value in the **Initial Value** box.

7. To insert Javadoc comments for the member variable, enter the comment text in the **Javadoc comment** box.

8. Click **Add** to insert the member variable into your file. Class Outline is automatically updated to display the new member variable.

To add a new class

1. To add a nested class, right-click the name of the containing class in Class Outline. To add a top-level class, right-click any class or the Class Outline window itself.

2. On the shortcut menu, click **Add Class**.

3. In the **Add Class** dialog box, enter the name of the class in the **Class Name** box.

4. To make this class a nested (or inner) class of the class that is selected in Class Outline, select the **Create a nested class** option. For information about nested classes, see "Inner Classes" in the *Java Language Specification*.

5. Select an access modifier from the **Access** drop-down list. Top-level classes can be declared as public or default. Nested classes can be declared as public, protected, private, or default (package).

6. Select additional modifiers, such as abstract, final, or static. (Only nested classes can be declared as static.)

7. To insert Javadoc comments for the class, enter the comment text in the **Javadoc comment** box.

8. Click **Add** to insert the class declaration into your file. Class Outline is automatically updated to display the new class.

Adding Declarations for Interface Methods

Using Class Outline, you can automatically insert method declarations for the interfaces that your class implements.

To add declarations for interface methods

1. In Class Outline, expand the **Implemented Interfaces** node.

2. Right-click the name of the interface, and then click **Add Method Stubs** on the shortcut menu.

Class Outline adds a declaration for each method in the interface. You can then define your implementation.

Deleting a Definition

Using Class Outline, you can quickly delete a definition from your .java file.

To delete a definition

1. In Class Outline, right-click the item to be deleted.

2. On the shortcut menu, click **Delete**. The definition is removed from the source file.

   Note   If you use the Text editor to delete a definition, the associated item in Class Outline is automatically removed.

Moving or Copying a Definition

Using Class Outline, you can easily move or copy the definition of a method, member variable, or class.

To move or copy a definition

1. In Class Outline, right-click the name of the item that you want to move or copy.

2. To move the item, click **Cut** on the shortcut menu; to copy the item, click **Copy**.

3. Right-click the item that indicates where you want to insert the definition:

   - To insert a method or member variable definition at the end of a class, right-click the name of the class.

   - To insert a method or member variable definition before another item within a class, right-click the name of that item.

   - To insert a class definition, right-click the name of another class in the file before which you want to insert the definition.

4. On the shortcut menu, click **Paste**.

   Note   If you use the Text editor to move or copy a definition, the associated item in Class Outline is automatically moved or copied.

Overriding a Method

Class Outline displays all the methods that a class inherits from its superclass as well as from the other classes in the inheritance hierarchy. Using Class Outline, you can quickly add a definition to override an inherited method.

   Note   You cannot override a method that is marked as static or final.

To override an inherited method

1. In Class Outline, expand the **Inherited Members** node of the class. This node displays both methods and member variables; however, only methods can be overridden.

2. Right-click the method that you want to override. On the shortcut menu, click **Override method**.

3. A declaration for the method is inserted into the .java file, where you can add your implementation.

Setting a Breakpoint

You can use Class Outline to quickly set a breakpoint on a method for use in the integrated debugger.

To set a breakpoint

1. In Class Outline, right-click the method that you want to set a breakpoint on.

2. On the shortcut menu, click **Insert Breakpoint**. To verify that a breakpoint was set, double-click the method in Class Outline to go to the definition in the source file. Observe that a breakpoint glyph appears in the margin.

3. To clear the breakpoint, right-click the method and click **Remove Breakpoint** on the shortcut menu.

For more information about breakpoints and debugging, see Chapter 6, "Debugging Applications."

Modifying Components with the WFC Component Builder

The WFC Component Builder is a tool that assists you in adding properties and events to your WFC-based components. This builder adds the necessary member variables and methods to your code and modifies your component's ClassInfo class.

Use the WFC Component Builder to:

- Add and delete properties

- Add and delete events

For more information about WFC, see Chapter 11, "Introduction to WFC Programming," and Chapter 12, "WFC Programming Concepts." For more information about the wizards and builders included with Visual J++, see Chapter 5, "Introducing Wizards and Builders."

Adding and Deleting Properties

Using the WFC Component Builder, you can easily add and delete property definitions in your WFC-based components. A property is typically associated with a private member variable that holds the current property value. Your component then provides public get<*PropertyName*> and set<*PropertyName*> methods to retrieve and set the value of the member variable. (A read-only property does not have an associated set<*PropertyName*> method.) For more information about WFC properties, see Chapter 12, "WFC Programming Concepts."

When you add a property with the WFC Component Builder, the associated member variable and methods are added to your class. The builder also adds the property information to your component's ClassInfo class. ClassInfo allows information about your component to be publicized in a property browser, such as the Properties window.

> **Note** If your component does not contain a ClassInfo definition, the WFC Component Builder inserts one into your class.

When you delete a property with the WFC Component Builder, the associated ClassInfo entry, member variable, and methods are automatically deleted from your class.

To open the WFC Component Builder

1. Open your component's source file in the Text editor.

2. In Class Outline, right-click the name of your class, and then click **WFC Component Builder** on the shortcut menu.

To add a property

1. In the Properties pane of the WFC Component Builder, click **Add**.

2. In the **Property Name** box, type the name of the property.

3. In the **Data Type** drop-down list, select a data type . (You can enter a class type that is not in the list if the class is on the classpath or available in the Java Package Manager.)

4. In the **Category** drop-down list, you can optionally select a category. Categories allow you to group related properties in the Properties window.

5. Type any description text in the **Description** box. Property descriptions are displayed in the Properties window.

6. To make the property read-only, select **Read-only Property**. (A set<*PropertyName*> method will not be added to your class.)

7. To add the associated member variable, select **Declare Member Variable**. The **Associated Member Variable** box displays the name for the member variable.

8. Click **Add**.

9. To add another property, repeat the previous steps. (When adding or deleting multiple items in the WFC Component Builder, periodically click **Apply** to ensure your changes are saved.)

10. Click **OK** to close the WFC Component Builder.

To delete a property

1. In the Properties pane of the WFC Component Builder, select the property you want to delete.

   Note   Deleting a property deletes all associated methods, member variables, and ClassInfo information. Any code that you have added to the methods will be lost. However, you can undo multiple levels of deletion from the Text editor, after the WFC Component Builder is closed. On the Edit menu, click Undo for each deleted item that you want to restore.

2. Click **Delete**.

3. To delete another property, repeat the previous steps. (When adding or deleting multiple items in the WFC Component Builder, periodically click **Apply** to ensure your changes are saved.)

4. Click **OK** to close the WFC Component Builder.

Adding and Deleting Events

Using the WFC Component Builder, you can easily add and delete event definitions in your WFC-based components. Because an event uses a delegate to invoke its event handler, your component provides public addOn<*EventName*> and removeOn<*EventName*> methods to add and remove the delegate. Your component also defines a protected on<*EventName*> method that triggers the event. For more information about WFC events, see Chapter 12, "WFC Programming Concepts."

When you add an event with the WFC Component Builder, the associated methods and the member variable for the delegate are automatically added to your class. The builder also adds the event information to your component's ClassInfo class. ClassInfo allows information about your component to be publicized in a property browser, such as the Properties window.

> **Note** If your component does not contain a ClassInfo definition, the WFC Component Builder inserts one into your class.

When you delete an event with the WFC Component Builder, the associated ClassInfo entry, delegate, and methods are automatically deleted from your class.

To open the WFC Component Builder

1. Open your component's source file in the Text editor.

2. In Class Outline, right-click the name of your class, and then click **WFC Component Builder** on the shortcut menu.

To add an event

1. In the Events pane of the WFC Component Builder, click **Add**.

2. In the **Event Name** box, type the name of the event.

3. In the **Type** drop-down list, select an event type. (You can enter a type that is not in the list if classes named <*EventType*> and <*EventType*>Handler are on the classpath or available in the Java Package Manager.)

4. In the **Category** drop-down list, you can optionally select a category. Categories allow you to group related events in the Properties window.

5. Type any description text in the **Description** box. Event descriptions are displayed in the Properties window.

6. Click **Add**.

7. To add another event, repeat the previous steps. (When adding or deleting multiple items in the WFC Component Builder, periodically click **Apply** to ensure your changes are saved.)

8. Click **OK** to close the WFC Component Builder.

To delete an event

1. In the Events pane of the WFC Component Builder, select the event you want to delete.

    Note Deleting an event deletes all associated methods, delegates, and ClassInfo information. Any code that you have added to the methods will be lost. However, you can undo multiple levels of deletion from the Text editor, after the WFC Component Builder is closed. On the Edit menu, click Undo for each deleted item that you want to restore.

2. Click **Delete**.

3. To delete another event, repeat the previous steps. (When adding or deleting multiple items in the WFC Component Builder, periodically click **Apply** to ensure your changes are saved.)

4. Click **OK** to close the WFC Component Builder.

Browsing Packages and Libraries with the Object Browser

The Object Browser provides a convenient way to view the contents of Java packages and COM libraries. You can quickly browse Java or COM-based components without actually adding them to your project, even if you don't have the source code for these components.

Using the Object Browser, you can:

*   View the classes and members contained in the packages and libraries

*   Select the packages and libraries to be browsed

*   Filter the classes and members

*   Group and sort the classes and members

To open the Object Browser, point to **Other Windows** on the **View** menu and click **Object Browser**.

Viewing Classes and Members

The Object Browser provides two lists for viewing the classes and members in a package or library. The *primary* list can display either classes or members (or both). When a class is selected from the primary list, its members are displayed in the *dependent* list; when a member is selected from the primary list, all classes containing that member are displayed in the dependent list.

To set the Object Browser view

1. To toggle whether classes are displayed in the primary list, right-click the Object Browser and click **Show Classes** on the shortcut menu. You can also click the **Show Classes** button on the Object Browser's command bar.

2. To toggle whether members are displayed in the primary list, right-click the Object Browser and click **Show Members** on the shortcut menu. You can also click the **Show Members** button on the command bar.

To help distinguish classes from members, classes appear in bold. Note that by default, the Object Browser groups the items in the primary list into their respective packages or libraries, which also appear in bold. To toggle whether these items are grouped by packages and libraries, right-click the Object Browser and click **Group by Packages/Libraries** on the shortcut menu. You can also click the **Group by Packages/Libraries** button on the command bar.

Viewing Class and Member Information

You can use the Object Browser to obtain specific information about the classes and members in a package or library:

- When a class or member is selected in the Object Browser, the lower description pane displays information about the item and supports hyperlinking to other classes, packages, and libraries.

- When a class node is expanded, the following subnodes are displayed (when applicable):

    - **Implemented Interfaces**, which lists all interfaces implemented by the class.

    - **Subclasses**, which lists all classes that extend the class.

    - **Superclasses**, which lists all classes in the inheritance hierarchy.

- When a Java method is displayed in the dependent list, its signature is included. (The signatures for COM methods are not displayed.)

Viewing Definitions

If the source code for a package or library is available on your computer, you can navigate to a class or member definition from the Object Browser. Select the item and then right-click the Object Browser. On the shortcut menu, click **View Definition**.

Viewing Hidden Members

The Object Browser can show any hidden members of COM libraries. To toggle the display of hidden members, right-click the Object Browser and click **Show Hidden Members** on the shortcut menu. Hidden members appear in gray text.

Selecting Packages and Libraries

By default, the Object Browser only displays the packages and libraries that can be referenced from the current solution, which include all packages in the solution, the packages installed by the Java Package Manager (JPM), and the packages on the classpath. You can also add additional packages and libraries to the Object Browser.

To select the packages and libraries to be browsed

1. Right-click the Object Browser and click **Select Current Packages/Libraries** on the shortcut menu. You can also click the **Select Current Packages/Libraries** button on the Object Browser's command bar.

2. The **Select Packages/Libraries** dialog box shows the packages and libraries that are available for browsing. The **Solution** node lists the Java projects that belong to your solution. The **Other Libraries and Packages** node contains the following subnodes:

   - **COM Libraries**, which lists all COM components and type libraries that are available for browsing.

   - **Java Installed Packages**, which lists all packages that are on the classpath or have been installed by the JPM.

   - **Other Java Packages**, which lists other packages that are available for browsing but are not on the classpath and have not been installed by the JPM.

3. Select the packages and libraries that you want displayed in the Object Browser, and clear the items that you want removed. A package or library will be displayed in the Object Browser only if all of its parent nodes are also selected. (By default, selecting an item automatically selects all parent nodes.) A node that is selected with a gray checkmark indicates that some — but not all — of its child items are selected.

   Tip   The easiest way to identify which packages and libraries will be displayed in the Object Browser is that these items appear in bold.

4. To add items to the **COM Libraries** and **Other Java Packages** nodes, click **Add**.

   - To add COM components and libraries, click the **COM Libraries** tab in the **Add New Packages/Libraries** dialog box. All components and libraries that are currently registered on your computer are listed. (To register another component or library and add it to the list, click **Browse** to locate the file.) Select the components and libraries you want to add, and click **OK**.

   - To add other Java packages, click the **Other Java Packages** tab in the **Add New Packages/Libraries** dialog box. Click **Browse** to locate the file containing the package. After the package has been added to the list, click **OK**.

Important Adding COM components or other Java packages to the Object Browser simply allows you to browse the components or packages. To actually use a COM component in your project, you must import it. For information on how to do this, see "Importing COM Objects" in Chapter 17, "Building and Importing COM Objects."

To use a Java package from your project, you must add it to the classpath. For information about the classpath, see "CLASSPATH Environment Variable" in Chapter 9, "Compiling Applications with JVC," and see "Setting the Classpath" in Chapter 1, "Creating Projects."

5. Click **OK** to apply your selections.

The items that you select for browsing in the **Select Packages/Libraries** dialog box may persist after you close the Object Browser:

- The packages and libraries that you select under the **Other Libraries and Packages** node will persist per user, per computer. For example, if you create a new solution on the same computer, the same selected set of packages and libraries under **Other Libraries and Packages** will be displayed by the Object Browser. However, if another user logs onto the computer, a different set of packages and libraries may be initially selected.

- The projects that you select under the **Solution** node will not persist after you close the solution. The next time you reopen the solution, all Java projects in the solution will be selected by default.

Grouping and Sorting Classes and Members

The Object Browser allows you to group or sort classes and members by access or by type. By default, no grouping or sorting is applied.

To group or sort classes and members

1. Right-click the Object Browser and click **Grouping and Sorting** on the shortcut menu. You can also click the **Grouping and Sorting** button on the Object Browser's command bar.

2. To group or sort classes, select a group category from the drop-down list in the **Classes** section:

   - To group classes by their access level, select **Group by Class Access**. Public classes are grouped into the **Public Types** category; nonpublic classes are grouped into the **Package Types** category, since they are only accessible from the packages they belong to.

   - To group classes by their types, select **Group by Class Type**.

   - To remove class groupings, select **<No Grouping>**.

3. If classes are grouped, you can change the order of the group categories. Select a category from the list and click the up arrow button or the down arrow button.

4. To group or sort members, select a group category from the drop-down list in the **Members** section:

   - To group members by their access level, select **Group by Member Access**.

   - To group members by their types, select **Group by Member Type**.

   - To remove member groupings, select **<No Grouping>**.

5. If members are grouped, you can change the order of the group categories. Select a category from the list and click the up arrow button or the down arrow button.

6. To display the names of the group categories in the Object Browser, select **Group with headers in main list**.

   Note The group headers only apply to the primary list in the Object Browser. For example, suppose you have grouped members but the Object Browser is viewing only classes in the primary list. When a class is selected and its members are displayed in the dependent list, the members are grouped but the actual group headers are not included. For information about viewing classes and members in the primary and dependent lists, see "Viewing Classes and Members," earlier in this chapter.

7. Click **OK**.

CHAPTER 4

Accessing Data

Using the design tools and wizards, you can easily access data in Visual J++. By adding the WFC data controls to your form in the Forms Designer, you can quickly configure how data is retrieved and displayed. You can also run the Data Form Wizard to generate a data-bound form automatically.

Visual J++ provides controls to access data through ActiveX Data Objects (ADO), the data programming model for WFC applications. The core ADO objects include the Connection, Command, and Recordset objects, which allow you to connect to a database and retrieve a set of records. ADO also provides the DataSource component, which combines the functionality of the Connection, Command, and Recordset objects.

> **Note** The Toolbox in the Forms Designer provides only a DataSource control; the Connection, Command, and Recordset objects can be used only in code. For information about programming with the ADO objects, see the "ADO Tutorial (VJ++)" in the Visual Studio online documentation, Microsoft ActiveX Data Objects.

ADO supports *simple* data binding through the DataBinder component. This component binds a field from a Recordset or DataSource component to the property of a WFC control. Visual J++ also provides *complex* data-bound controls, such as the DataGrid and DataNavigator controls, that interact directly with a recordset. For more information about data binding, see Chapter 18, "Data Binding in WFC."

To access data on a form, you can either run the Data Form Wizard or perform the following steps in the Forms Designer:

- Retrieve a set of records

- Bind the data with the DataBinder control or the DataGrid control

- Navigate the records

For more information about ADO, see "Getting Started with ADO 2.0" in the Visual Studio online documentation, Microsoft ActiveX Data Objects. For information about the COM-based data access options available with Visual Studio, see "Choosing the Right Data Access Technology," in the Visual Studio online documentation.

Running the Data Form Wizard

Using the Data Form Wizard, you can automatically generate a form that is bound to the fields in a database. The Data Form Wizard retrieves data through ADO and supports Microsoft Access .mdb files and databases that can be accessed through ODBC.

To launch the Data Form Wizard

1. To add a data-bound form to your application with the Data Form Wizard, right-click the project or folder node in Project Explorer that will contain the form.

2. On the shortcut menu, point to **Add** and then click **Add Form**.

3. In the **Add Item** dialog box, select the **Data Form Wizard** icon

4. In the **Name** box, enter a name for your form.

5. Click **Open**.

   Note   The Data Form Wizard is also launched when you create a new, data-based application with the Application Wizard.

6. In the **Introduction** step of the Data Form Wizard, you can select a *profile* in the drop-down list. (If the profile you want to use is not listed, click the ellipsis button (**...**) to open that profile.) For more information about profiles, see Chapter 5, "Introducing Wizards and Builders."

7. Click **Next** to specify the database type.

Database Type Step

In the **Database Type** step of the Data Form Wizard, you specify the format of your database.

To specify the database format

1. Select the **Access** option for any Microsoft Access .mdb file. Click **Next** to specify the database file.

2. Select the **ODBC** option to access a database through ODBC, such as an ISAM database (dBase, FoxPro, or Paradox) or a remote data source (SQL Server or Oracle). Click **Next** to specify the ODBC connection information.

   Note   Although you can use the Microsoft Access ODBC driver to connect to an Access database, selecting the **Access** option provides better performance.

Database Step

If you selected the **Access** format in the Database Type step of the Data Form Wizard, then the **Database** step allows you to specify the .mdb file.

To specify the .mdb file

1. In the **Database name** box, enter the full path and name of the .mdb file, or click **Browse** to locate the file.

2. Click **Next** to specify details about the form to be created.

Connect Information Step

If you selected the **ODBC** format in the Database Type step of the Data Form Wizard, the **Connect Information** step allows you to specify the ODBC information, such as a data source name (DSN), database, and driver.

The following procedures show different ways of connecting to a database through ODBC.

To connect to a database using a DSN that you have created

1. In the **DSN** drop-down list, select the name of your ODBC data source. (To create a data source, use the ODBC icon in the Windows Control Panel.)

2. If a user ID and password are associated with this data source, enter the information in the **UID** and **PWD** boxes, respectively.

To connect to a database using a generic DSN

1. In the **DSN** drop-down list, select the name of the generic data source, such as **FoxPro Files**.

2. In the **Database** box, enter the full path and name of the database file.

To connect to a database using a specified driver

1. In the **Database** box, enter the full path and name of the database file.

2. In the **Driver** drop-down list, select the driver you want to use, such as **Microsoft FoxPro Driver (*.dbf)**.

To connect to a full server database

1. In the **UID** and **PWD** boxes, enter the associated user ID and password, respectively.

2. In the **Database** box, enter the name of the database.

3. In the **Driver** drop-down list, select the driver you want to use, such as **SQL Server** or **Oracle**.

4. In the **Server** box, enter the name of the server.

Once you have specified the connection information, click **Next** to specify details about the form to be created.

Form Step

In the **Form** step of the Data Form Wizard, you specify the name of the data-bound form as well as the layout of the form.

To specify form details

1. To change the name of the form, edit the text in the **Form name** box.

2. Under **Form layout**, select one of the following options:

   - **Single record**   (Default) The form displays one record at a time. Each non-Boolean field in the database is bound to an Edit control; Boolean fields are bound to CheckBox controls. A Label control is associated with each bound control and displays the name of the field.

   - **Grid (Datasheet)**   The form displays multiple records in a DataGrid control.

   - **Master/Detail**   The form displays data from two related tables (or queries), typically having a one-to-many relationship. The form displays one record at a time from the *master* table and multiple records from the *detail* table in a DataGrid control.

3. Under **Database Connection**, select one of the following options:

   - **Controls**   (Default) The form uses an ADO DataSource control to access your database. The DataSource control is compatible with the Forms Designer; if you want to change the property settings of this control after the wizard creates the form, you can make the modifications in the Forms Designer. (The DataSource control is a nonvisual control that is displayed only when your form is in design view; it is not displayed when your form is run.)

   - **Code**   The form uses the ADO Connection and Recordset components to access your database. These components are not supported by the Forms Designer; they can be used only in code.

4. Click **Next** to specify the record source for the bound controls.

Record Source Step

In the **Record Source** step of the Data Form Wizard, you select the fields that you want to bind to the controls on the form.

> **Note** If you selected the **Master/Detail** layout in the Form step, the Data Form Wizard provides **Master Record Source** and **Detail Record Source** steps. First use the following procedure for the **Master Record Source** step; then click **Next** and repeat the procedure for the **Detail Record Source** step.

To specify the bound fields

1. In the **Record source** drop-down list, select the name of a table that contains the fields you want to bind. (When defining a master record source in a **Master/Detail** form layout, select the table whose records are uniquely identified by the common field. For the detail record source, select the related table.)

2. The **Available fields** list contains the fields in the specified table. The **Selected fields** list contains the fields that will be bound to your form, in the order they are listed. Use the following buttons to move fields between the two lists:

Button	Description
>	Moves the selected field in the **Available Fields** list to the **Selected Fields** list. The selected field will be bound to a control on the form.
>>	Moves all fields from the **Available Fields** list to the **Selected Fields** list. All fields will be bound to controls on the form.
<	Moves the selected field in the **Selected Fields** list to the **Available Fields** list. The selected field will not be bound to a control on the form.
<<	Moves all fields from the **Selected Fields** list to the **Available Fields** list. No field will be bound to a control on the form.

> **Note** The Data Form Wizard cannot bind fields that have a binary data type.

3. To change the order of the bound fields, select the field in the **Selected Fields** list and click the up arrow button or the down arrow button.

4. To sort the data that will be displayed by the form, select a field in the **Column to sort by** drop-down list.

5. If your form layout is **Single record** or **Grid (Datasheet)**, click **Next** to add additional controls to the form.

    – or –

    If your form layout is **Master/Detail** and you have finished choosing the master and detail record sources, click **Next** to specify the master/detail relationship.

Record Source Relation Step

If you selected the **Master/Detail** layout in the Form step of the Data Form Wizard, the **Record Source Relation** step allows you to specify the one-to-many relationship between the master and detail record sources.

To specify the master/detail relationship

1. In the **Master** list, select the related field. This field should uniquely identify each record in the master record source.

2. In the **Detail** list, select the related field.

3. Click **Next** to add additional controls to the form.

Control Selection Step

In the **Control Selection** step of the Data Form Wizard, you can select the additional controls that you want to appear on the form. Any code that is required by these controls is automatically added to your form.

To add additional controls

1. Under **Available controls**, select the controls you want to add:

Control	Description
Add button	Allows the user to add new records to the database.
Delete button	Allows the user to delete records from the database.
Update button	Updates the database with the changes that have been made on the form.
Refresh button	Refreshes the form with the latest data from the database.
Close button	Allows the user to close the form.
Data navigator	Allows the user to navigate through the records.

2. Click **Next** to view the summary for the form.

Summary Step

In the **Summary** step of the Data Form Wizard, you can save and review your wizard settings.

To save and review the wizard settings

1. To save your settings to an existing profile, select the profile in the drop-down list. To save your settings to a new profile, click the ellipsis button (**...**) to specify a file name. (For more information about profiles, see Chapter 5, "Introducing Wizards and Builders.")

2. To review your settings, click **View Report**. To save the report, click **Save** in the **View Report** dialog box.

3. Click **Finish** to add the form to your project.

The Data Form Wizard provides a quick start to creating a form with controls bound to the fields in a database. To bind data without the wizard, you can directly use the DataBinder control or the DataGrid control.

Retrieving a Set of Records

Visual J++ provides the DataSource control to access data in the Forms Designer. This control allows you to connect to and query a database to retrieve a set of records.

Note   To retrieve a recordset in code, you can also use the Connection, Command, and Recordset components. The Forms Designer, however, supports only the DataSource component. For information about programming with the ADO components, see the "ADO Tutorial (VJ++)" in the Visual Studio online documentation, in Microsoft ActiveX Data Objects.

To retrieve data with the DataSource control

1. In Project Explorer, double-click the name of your form to open it in the Forms Designer.

2. In the Toolbox, click the **WFC Controls** tab. Click the **DataSource** control in the Toolbox, and then click your form to add the control.

   Note   Because the DataSource control only retrieves data and does not display it, the control is not visible when you run your form.

3. To connect to the database, set the **connectionString** property of the DataSource control:

   - Select the DataSource control on the form.

   - In the Properties window, click the **connectionString** property, and then click the ellipsis (**...**) button to open the **Data Link Properties** dialog box.

4. To access a named ODBC data source:

   - Click the **Provider** tab and select **Microsoft OLE DB Provider for ODBC Drivers**.

   - Click the **Connection** tab. In step 1, select **Use data source name** and select your data source in the drop-down list. In step 2, you can enter the user name and password, if needed.

   – or –

   To access a Microsoft Access .mdb file directly without using ODBC:

   - Click the **Provider** tab and select **Microsoft Jet 3.51 OLE DB Provider**.

   - Click the **Connection** tab. In step 1, enter the full path and file name of your database, or click the ellipsis (**...**) button to browse for the file. In step 2, you can enter the user name and password, if applicable.

5. Click **OK** to establish the database connection.

6. To query the database, set the **commandText** property of the DataSource control to an SQL string. For example, to retrieve all records from a table called Products, enter **Select * from Products**.

7. To make the recordset updateable, set the **lockType** property to **Optimistic**.

Now that you have retrieved a recordset, you must bind it with the DataBinder control or the DataGrid control.

Binding Data with the DataBinder Control

The DataBinder control binds a field from a recordset to the property of another control. When a property is bound, it is automatically set to the value of the field in the current record. The following procedures show how to bind the text property of an Edit control.

To associate the DataBinder control with a recordset

1. Add a DataSource control to your form to retrieve the data. For information on how to do this, see the previous section, "Retrieving a Set of Records."

2. Add an Edit control and a DataBinder control to the form.

   Note Like the DataSource control, the DataBinder control is not displayed when the form is run, because it only manages the binding and does not actually display data.

3. Select the DataBinder control on the form and set its **dataSource** property:

   - In the Properties window, click the **dataSource** property.

   - In the drop-down list, select the name of the DataSource control.

The **bindings** property of the DataBinder control identifies the bindings that have been currently defined. You can set this property using either the control's property page or its bindings editor.

To create the bindings using the property page

1. Select the DataBinder control on the form. In the Properties window, click the **Property Page** toolbar button.

2. In the **Data Field** drop-down list of the property page, select the name of the data field to be bound.

3. In the **Control** drop-down list, select the name of the Edit control.

4. In the **Property** drop-down list, select the text property.

5. Click **Add**. The text property is now bound to the data field.

6. To add other bindings, repeat the process. Click **OK** when all bindings have been added.

To create the bindings using the bindings editor

1. Select the DataBinder control on the form. In the Properties window, click the **bindings** property and then click the ellipsis (**...**) button.

2. To add a binding in the bindings editor, click **Add**. (For each binding you want to add, click **Add**.)

3. Click **OK**.

4. In the Properties window, expand the **bindings** property. Each binding is listed by its *index*, which indicates the order in which the binding was added. (The index of the first binding is 0.)

5. To define the binding, expand its indexed entry.

6. Click **fieldName**. In the drop-down list, select the name of the data field to be bound.

7. Click **target**. In the drop-down list, select the name of the Edit control.

8. Click **propertyName**. In the drop-down list, select the text property.

Once you have created the bindings, you can add a DataNavigator control to the form to navigate the records. You can also apply a data format to bindings that display numerical, date, or Boolean values.

For more information about the DataBinder control and for related programming examples, see "DataBinder Component" in Chapter 18, "Data Binding in WFC."

Binding Data with the DataGrid Control

The DataGrid control binds fields from a recordset and displays the data in a series of rows and columns. The control is automatically populated when you set its dataSource property to a DataSource control.

The data that is displayed in the DataGrid control is always synchronized with the data in the recordset, and vice versa. The **cursorType** and **lockType** properties of the recordset determine whether the data dynamically reflects the data in the database, and whether the data in the recordset can be changed.

To bind the DataGrid control to a recordset

1. Add a DataSource control to your form to retrieve the data. For information on how to do this, see "Retrieving a Set of Records," earlier in this chapter.

2. Add a DataGrid control to the form.

3. Set the DataGrid control's **dataSource** property:

   • In the Properties window, click the **dataSource** property.

   • In the drop-down list, select the name of the DataSource control.

Note that the DataGrid control displays live data in design view. The current record in the recordset is identified by a marker in the grid's corresponding row's header. To quickly navigate through the rows in the grid, you can add a DataNavigator control to the form.

For information about using the DataGrid control in code, see "DataGrid Control" in Package com.ms.wfc.data.ui in *Microsoft Visual J++ 6.0 WFC Library Reference, Part 1*, in the *Microsoft Visual J++ 6.0 Reference Library*.

Accessing Column Properties

By setting the DataGrid control's properties in the Properties window, you can quickly configure its appearance and functionality. Each column in the grid also has its own set of properties, which you can access from the grid's properties.

To access the properties of a column

1. In the Properties window, expand the DataGrid control's **columns** property. Each column is listed by its *index* in the grid, which indicates the order in which the column is displayed. (The index of the first column is 0.)

2. To display the properties of a column, expand its indexed entry.

By default, that DataGrid control contains a column for each field in the underlying recordset, and the columns are ordered according to the fields in the recordset. However, you can easily add, remove, and rearrange columns after the DataGrid control has been created. You can also apply a data format to columns that contain numerical, date, or Boolean values.

Adding, Removing, and Rearranging Columns

The DataGrid control provides a columns editor to add, remove, and rearrange the columns in the grid. By default, each field in the underlying recordset is bound to a column in the grid, and the columns are ordered according to the fields in the recordset.

To add, remove, and rearrange columns in the grid

1. To open the columns editor, click the DataGrid control's **columns** property in the Properties window. Then click the ellipsis (**...**) button.

2. To add a column, click **Add**.

    Note   The column that is added is initially unbound. To bind the column, set its boundFieldName property to the name of a field in the recordset. (For information about how to access column properties, see the previous section, "Accessing Column Properties.")

3. To remove a column, select the column in the list and click **Remove**.

    Note   If you simply want to hide the column temporarily rather than completely remove it from the grid, set its visible property to false.

4. To rearrange columns, select the column you want to move and click **Up** or **Down**.

5. Click **OK** when you have finished adding, removing, or rearranging columns.

Formatting Data

When you bind data with the DataBinder control or the DataGrid control, you can format the display of numerical, date, and Boolean values. Each binding managed by a DataBinder control, and each column in a DataGrid control, has a **dataFormat** property that allows you to specify the format.

To access the dataFormat property

1. If you are using a DataBinder control, expand its **bindings** property in the Properties window.

    – or –

    If you are using a DataGrid control, expand its **columns** property in the Properties window.

2. Each binding or column is listed by its *index*, which specifies its order within the parent control. (The index of the first binding or column is 0.)

3. Expand the indexed entry of the binding or column you want to format, and then click **dataFormat**.

To format numerical values

1. Set the **dataFormat** property to **NumberDataFormat**.

2. Expand **dataFormat**, and then set the **format** property to a numerical format string. For information about possible format strings, see "NumberDataFormat.setFormat," in Package com.ms.wfc.data in *Microsoft Visual J++ 6.0 WFC Library Reference, Part 1* in the *Microsoft Visual J++ 6.0 Reference Library*.

To format date (or time) values

1. Set the **dataFormat** property to **DateDataFormat**.

2. Expand **dataFormat**. To specify the date format, click the **format** property and select one of the following values in the drop-down list:

Format	Description
Long	The dates are formatted using the Long Date setting in the Regional Settings section of the Windows Control Panel. (The default setting for a long date appears as Monday, March 9, 1998.)
Short	(Default) The dates are formatted using the Short Date setting in the Regional Settings section of the Windows Control Panel. (The default setting for a short date appears as 3/9/98.)
Time	The times are formatted using the Long Time setting in the Regional Settings section of the Windows Control Panel. (The default setting for a long time appears as 2:45:05 P.M.)
Custom	The dates or times are formatted using a custom format. Set the **customFormat** property to the custom format string. For information about possible format strings, see DateDataFormat.setCustomFormat, in Package com.ms.wfc.data.ui in *Microsoft Visual J++ 6.0 WFC Library Reference, Part 1*, in the *Microsoft Visual J++ 6.0 Reference Library*.

Note   The setting of the customFormat property is applied only when the format property is set to Custom. If the format property is set to Short, Long, or Time, any setting for the customFormat property is ignored.

To format Boolean values

1. Set the **dataFormat** property to **BooleanDataFormat**.

2. Expand **dataFormat** and set the following properties:

   - **falseValue**   Specifies the string to be displayed when the value is false. The default string is False.

   - **nullValue**   Specifies the string to be displayed when the value is null. The default string is (null).

   - **trueValue**   Specifies the string to be displayed when the value is true. The default string is True.

Navigating Records

The DataNavigator control allows you to change the current record in a recordset. Use the DataNavigator control in conjunction with another data-bound control, such as the DataBinder control. The DataBinder control binds a property of another control to a field in a recordset. This property obtains data from the recordset's current record, which is initially the first record. To move to another record, use a DataNavigator control that is bound to the same recordset.

To navigate a recordset with the DataNavigator control

1. Add a DataSource control to your form to retrieve the data. For information on how to do this, see "Retrieving a Set of Records," earlier in this chapter.

2. Use a DataBinder control and an Edit control to bind data from the recordset associated with the DataSource control. For information on how to do this, see "Binding Data with the DataBinder Control," earlier in this chapter.

3. Add a DataNavigator control to the form.

4. Set the DataNavigator control's **dataSource** property to the name of the DataSource control.

5. Use the buttons on the DataNavigator control to navigate the data:

Button	Navigation Direction
<<	Move to the first record.
<	Move to the previous record.
>	Move to the next record.
>>	Move to the last record.

For information about using the DataNavigator control in code, see "DataNavigator Control," in Package com.ms.wfc.data.ui in *Microsoft Visual J++ 6.0 WFC Library Reference, Part 1*, in the *Microsoft Visual J++ 6.0 Reference Library*.

CHAPTER 5

Introducing Wizards and Builders

Visual J++ provides several wizards and builders to help you develop your applications. A wizard adds a new file to your project by guiding you through a series of steps. Each step contains Back and Next buttons to navigate through the steps. The Cancel button cancels all settings you've made and closes the wizard. The Finish button accepts the selections you've currently entered and uses the default settings for any remaining steps. (The Finish button is available once you make enough choices for the wizard to complete the task.)

Note When you run a wizard, you can typically save your settings to a *profile*. The next time you run the wizard, you can load this profile to reuse the settings.

While a wizard creates a new file through a step-by-step process, a builder assists you in modifying the existing files in your project. Visual J++ provides the following wizards and builders:

Wizard or Builder	Description
Application Wizard	Automatically creates a WFC application containing a form. You have the option of binding the form to the fields in a database. For more information, see "Creating a Windows Application with the Application Wizard," in Chapter 1, "Creating Projects."
WFC Component Builder	Modifies your WFC components by adding and removing properties and events. For more information, see "Modifying Components with the WFC Component Builder," in Chapter 3, "Editing Code."
Data Form Wizard	Automatically generates a form that is bound to the fields in a database. The Data Form Wizard supports Microsoft Access .mdb files and databases that can be accessed through ODBC. For more information, see "Running the Data Form Wizard," in Chapter 4, "Accessing Data."
J/Direct Call Builder	Inserts Java definitions for the Win32 API functions into your code, along with the appropriate @dll.import tags. For more information, see "J/Direct Call Builder," in Chapter 19, "Writing Windows-Based Applications with J/Direct."

CHAPTER 6

Debugging Applications

When syntax errors occur in your code, the Visual J++ compiler alerts you to these errors by displaying a message that indicates that your application was not successfully updated, and by displaying a list of errors in the Visual J++ task list.

However, often the errors that occur within your code are not language syntax errors, but are instead errors in logic — infinite loops, for example. To address bugs like these, you use the features supported by the Visual J++ debugger.

See "Basic Debugging Procedures," later in this chapter, to learn more about using the integrated debugger with Visual J++ projects. These procedures show you how to set breakpoints, step through code, view run-time values of member variables, and much more.

The online documentation also provides scenarios that have been created to show you how to use the debugger's features with specific types of Visual J++ projects. Details for recreating example projects can be found throughout the procedures in the following scenarios:

- Debugging a WFC Application
- Debugging a Console Application
- Debugging Multithreaded Applications
- Debugging a Java COM Object
- Debugging a Java Applet

The Debugging Process

Visual J++ debugging support includes breakpoints, break expressions, watch expressions, thread control, and exception handling. You can also step through your code one statement or method at a time and view the values of variables and properties.

There are no magic tricks to debugging, and there is no fixed sequence of steps that works every time. Basically, debugging helps you understand what's happening when your application runs. Debugging tools give you a snapshot of the current state of your application, including:

- The appearance of your application's user interface

- Values of member variables, expressions, and properties

- Active method calls

Basic Debugging Procedures

After you have debugged several applications, you'll find certain tasks may apply to debugging almost any program.

Entering Command-line Arguments

When using an executable that requires startup arguments to debug, you can type these arguments at the command line, or from within the development environment.

The following explains how to use the Custom options in the environment's Launch tab of the project's Properties dialog box. The Properties dialog box for an open project can be accessed from the Project menu.

To enter command-line arguments

1. From **Project Explorer**, double-click a .java file to load it into the Text editor.

2. On the **Project** menu, click *<Project name>* **properties** to display the **Properties** dialog box.

3. On the **Launch** tab, click the **Custom** radio button.

    The **Custom** options on this tab provide a place to enter the command line arguments for your application.

4. In the **Arguments** text box type the information you want to pass to your program.

    For example, if your program accepted a date in the format of MM DD YY, July 10, 1997 would be entered as 7 10 1997.

Note   The **Arguments** text box may have some viewer options displayed. If you have a specific reason to change these preset options, do so now and enter the date after them.

Now you are ready to debug your application. Setting a breakpoint before starting the integrated debugger is one way to start this process.

Displaying the Debug Toolbar

You can access the debugger's most commonly used commands and windows through the Debug Toolbar.

To display the Debug Toolbar

- On the **View** menu click **Toolbars** and then select **Debug**.

Setting Breakpoints

A breakpoint designates a location in your code at which process execution is stopped to allow you to examine the process's code, variables, and (in some cases) register values. In addition, you can, as necessary, make changes to your code, and then continue or terminate process execution.

This section explains how to set breakpoints.

Setting a Breakpoint Before Starting the Debugger

After you have created and built your Visual J++ project, you can set breakpoints in your code. A breakpoint designates a location in your code at which the code temporarily stops executing so that you step through your code line by line, examining variable values, examining application behavior. Where a bug occurs in your application, you can set a breakpoint that enables you to halt your program just before the unexpected behavior occurs.

To set a breakpoint and start the debugger

1. With your source code file open in the editor, place the cursor on any executable code in your application, applet, or component.

2. Click the right mouse button and select **Insert Breakpoint** from the shortcut menu.

   A solid red circle is placed in the margin of the editor indicating a breakpoint was set on the statement you just selected.

3. On the **Debug** menu, click **Start** or use the keyboard shortcut, F5.

   The program runs and stops (breaks) just before it executes the line on which you've set the breakpoint. The yellow arrow in the margin indicates the next statement to be executed.

When your program is in break mode, you can:

- Set another breakpoint

- Examine one or more debug windows to view the values of your program's member variables.

To resume the debugging session

- On the **Debug** menu, click **Continue**.

  – or –

  Press the keyboard shortcut, F5 to run to the next breakpoint.

  – or –

  Press F11 to step into the next statement.

To end the debugging session

- On the **Debug** menu, click **End**.

  For more information about how to end a debugging session, see "Ending a Debugging Session" in the Visual Studio online documentation.

Setting a Breakpoint from the Breakpoints Dialog Box

Up to this point, you have been adding and removing breakpoints by selecting options from the shortcut menu. You can also disable and enable breakpoints as well as change a breakpoint's properties from this same menu. The integrated debugger also provides a Breakpoints dialog box that gives you even more control to manage your application's breakpoints.

Examining Information with Debug Windows

The following subjects discuss the debug windows separately and include the purpose of each window. In these subjects you will also find specific procedures for accessing and using each debug window.

Viewing Information in the Auto Window

The Auto window displays the values of all variables within the scope of currently executing methods. Where the Locals window shows variables for a single thread, the Auto window shows variables for all threads. This window allows you to learn about the changes to a variable that may be caused by code executing on a different thread. A variable remains visible as long as it is in scope, reflecting any changes to its value. When the variable goes out of scope it is removed from the Auto window.

The Auto window is updated only when execution is suspended. For example, the Auto window is updated when you add a new watch variable, when you change the value of a variable, or when you switch between decimal and hexidecimal modes from the shortcut menu. Values that have changed since the last suspension are displayed in red.

To display the Auto window

- On the **View** menu, click **Debug Windows**, and then select **Auto**.

    – or –

    Press the key combination, CTRL+ALT+A.

    – or –

    Click the **Auto** button on the Debug toolbar.

To copy a variable from the Auto window to another window

- Drag a selected variable to the **Immediate** window or the **Watch** window.

To change the value of a variable

- Click a value and edit it.

To view or hide class member variables and array elements

- Expand or collapse class and array member variables to view or hide their elements.

    See "Navigation Keyboard Shortcuts for the Auto, Locals, and Watch Windows," later in this chapter, for additional information on how to move around in these windows, and expand and collapse class member variables and array elements.

See "Viewing Variables in the Auto Window," in the Visual Studio online documentation, for more information about the Auto debug window.

Viewing Information in the Locals Window

The Locals window displays the class member variables and their values for each method in the current stack frame. As the execution switches from method to method, the contents of the Locals window changes to reflect the local variables applicable to the current method.

The Locals window contains fields for the Name, Value, and Type for each member variable. The value of a given variable will be displayed after it has been declared in your program. If a variable is not in scope when you display the Locals window, a message appears in the Value field next to the variable's name. You will need to step through more code before you'll see values for these variables. The Locals window is updated only when execution is suspended. Values that have changed since the last suspension are displayed in red.

To display the Locals window

- On the **View** menu, click **Debug Windows**, and then select **Locals**.

  – or –

  Press the key combination, CTRL+ALT+L.

  – or –

  Click the **Locals** button on the Debug toolbar.

To change class information in the Locals window

- From the drop-down list box at the top of the **Locals** window, select another class.

  Note   When you've defined more than one class for your program, you may want to see values for variables in all these classes. The **Locals** window always displays the member variables for the class that contains your program's entry point (main() or init()). Once you've either stepped into or stopped on a breakpoint in a different class, use the drop-down list box at the top of the **Locals** window to select this class and view its member variables.

To copy a variable from the Locals window to another window

- Drag a selected variable to the **Immediate** window or the **Watch** window.

To change the value of a variable

- Click a variable to edit its value.

To view or hide class member variables and array elements

- Expand or collapse class and array member variables to view or hide their elements.

  See "Navigation Keyboard Shortcuts for the Auto, Locals, and Watch Windows," later in this chapter, for additional information on how to move around in these windows and expand, and collapse class member variables and array elements.

See "Viewing Local Variables in the Locals Window," in the Visual Studio online documentation, for more information about the Locals debug window.

Viewing Information in the Watch Window

The Watch window allows you to monitor the values of variables, properties, and expressions at run time. Many debugging problems aren't immediately traceable to a single statement, so you may need to use a watch expression to observe the behavior of a variable or expression throughout a procedure.

The development environment automatically monitors the watch expressions you define. When the application enters break mode, these watch expressions appear in the Watch window, where you can observe their values.

To display the Watch window

- On the **View** menu, click **Debug Windows**, and then select **Watch.**

  – or –

  Press the key combination, CTRL+ALT+W.

  – or –

  Click the **Watch** button on the Debug toolbar.

The Watch window keeps track of member variables that may change at various times or locations in an application.

To add a watch expression at design time or in break mode

- Drag an expression or variable from the Text editor, the **Locals** window or **Immediate** window to the **Watch** window.

To change the value of a variable

- Click a variable to edit its value.

To view or hide class member variables and array elements

- Expand a class or array member variable to view their elements.

- Collapse a class or array member variable to hide their elements.

  See "Navigation Keyboard Shortcuts for the Auto, Locals, and Watch Windows," later in this chapter, for additional information on how to move around in these windows, and expand and collapse class member variables and array elements.

See "Inspecting Variables and Properties with the Watch Window," in the Visual Studio online documentation, for more information about the Watch debug window.

Navigation Keyboard Shortcuts for the Auto, Locals, and Watch Windows

You can use the following keys to view or hide member variables of a selected class or array or to move around in the Auto, Locals, or Watch windows:

To	Use the
Collapse the member variables list	LEFT ARROW key
View the member variables	RIGHT ARROW key
Toggle between hiding and viewing the variables	ENTER key
Move upward in the member variables list	UP ARROW key
Move downward in the member variables list	DOWN ARROW key *(continued)*

(continued)

To	Use the
Move up an expanded list	LEFT ARROW key
Move down an expanded list	RIGHT ARROW key

Note   You can change the size of a column by dragging the border of the column header to the right to make the column larger or to the left to make it smaller.

Viewing Information in the Immediate Window

To view and change values, you use the Immediate window. You can evaluate any expression, variable, or object in the window and see the value that is returned, or you can see the effects of commands you enter (which must be in the language of the code that is currently executing).

Once you're in break mode, you can move the focus to the Immediate window to examine data. You can evaluate any valid expression in the Immediate window, including expressions involving properties or variables. The currently active form or class determines the scope.

To display the Immediate window

- On the **View** menu, click **Debug Windows**, and then select **Immediate**.

  – or –

  Press the key combination, CTRL+ALT+I.

  – or –

  Click the **Immediate** button on the Debug toolbar.

You can enter expressions into the Immediate window to display or change the value of variables, properties, and expressions.

To add an expression or variable to the Immediate window

- Drag a variable or expression from the Text editor or from the **Locals**, or **Watch** window into the **Immediate** window.

To evaluate an expression or variable in the Immediate window

1. In the **Immediate** window, move the insertion point to the variable or expression you wish to evaluate.

   Note   To examine variables or expressions that contain scripting code, insert a question mark, "?," before the variable or expression to display its value.

2. Press Enter.

    If, you select a variable for evaluation, the **Immediate** window will return its current value; for expressions, the evaluated results are returned.

To execute a statement again

1. Move the insertion point back to the statement you want to execute again.

2. If you wish, you can edit the current statement to alter its effects.

3. Press ENTER.

To move around in the Immediate window

*   Use the mouse or the arrow keys.

        Tip   Don't press ENTER unless you are at a statement that you want to execute.

See "Executing Commands and Evaluating Expressions in the Immediate Window," in the Visual Studio online documentation, for additional information on the Immediate debug window.

Viewing Information in the Threads Window

For multithreaded applications, the Threads window allows you to change the current thread of execution or view the threads in any attached process. The contents of the other debugging windows change to reflect the selected thread. For more information, see "Threads Window" and "Controlling Threads," in the Visual Studio online documentation.

Displaying the Threads Debug Window

To display the Threads debug window

*   On the **View** menu, click **Debug Windows**, and then select **Threads**.

    – or –

    Press the key combination, CTRL+ALT+H.

    – or –

    Click the **Threads** button on the Debug toolbar.

Observing Thread Activity in the Threads Debug Window

The application example for this procedure creates two threads in the `main()` method and displays output to a JVIEW console window. This procedure refers to code created in the "Multithreaded Beverages Application." If you'd like to create this project to complete the following exercises, do so now. You may also use the following procedure to observe thread activity of any multithreaded application.

To observe thread activity in the Threads debug window

1. Set a breakpoint in the Coffee class on the following statement:

   ```
   System.out.println("I Like Coffee" + " " + i);
   ```

2. Set a breakpoint in the Tea class on the following statement:

   ```
   System.out.println("I Like Tea" + " " + i);
   ```

3. In Class1's main() method, place the insertion point on the following statement:

   ```
   Coffee m_Coffee = new Coffee();  //creates Coffee object
   ```

4. Click the right mouse button and select Run To Cursor from the shortcut menu.

5. When your application enters break mode, open the Threads debug window.

   Notice the main() thread is currently the only thread running in this window.

6. Press F5 to run to the breakpoint set in the Coffee class.

   More information appears in the **Threads** debug window to identify the names, location in the code, and suspension status for the application's three threads, **main**, **Thread-0**, and **Thread-1**. The yellow arrow indicates which thread is currently running, in this case it is **Thread-0** of Coffee.run(). Notice the main() method's thread is no longer running, because it has passed control to the threads of the Coffee and Tea classes.

   > **Note** Although this scenario suggests the Coffee thread will be the first thread to run, this may not always be the case. The operating system will ultimately determine the processing order of the threads in a given application unless there are statements in the code to specify conditions under which to create and run a new thread.

7. Press F11 to execute the current statement.

8. Switch to JVIEW's console window and the following output appears:

   ```
   I Like Coffee 0
   ```

9. Press F5 to run to the breakpoint set in the Tea class.

10. Press F11 to execute the current statement and the following output appears in JVIEW's console window:

    ```
    I Like Tea 0
    ```

11. Continue pressing F5 and F11 alternately until one of the following output statements appears in JVIEW's console window:

```
I Like Coffee 9
```

– or –

```
I Like Tea 9
```

Notice when a thread is destroyed information about that thread no longer appears in the Threads debug window.

In the process of observing each of your application's threads, you may observe that a particular thread's behavior is not what you had expected. To isolate a given thread by suspending other threads, see the next section, "Suspending and Resuming Threads from the Threads Debug Window."

Suspending and Resuming Threads from the Threads Debug Window

The application example for this procedure creates two threads in the `main()` method and displays output to a JVIEW console window. This procedure refers to code created in the Multithreaded Beverages Application. If you'd like to create this project to complete the following exercises, do so now. You may also use the following procedures to suspend and resume the threads of any multithreaded application.

To suspend a thread

1. Set a breakpoint in a statements that execute after your application's threads have been created. In this procedure's example, breakpoints are set in the Coffee class on the following statement:

```
System.out.println("I Like Coffee" + " " + i);
```

– and –

in the Tea class on the following statement:

```
System.out.println("I Like Tea" + " " + i);
```

2. On the **Debug** menu, click **Start**, or press the keyboard shortcut, F5 to run your application, and start the debugger.

3. When your application enters break mode, open the Threads debug window.

   Note The operating system will ultimately determine the processing order of the threads in a given application unless there are statements in the code to specify conditions under which to create and run a new thread.

4. In the **Threads** debug window, highlight one of the threads. For this example, highlight **Thread-1** of **Tea.run**.

5. Click the right mouse button, and select **Suspend** from the shortcut menu.

    Notice the **Suspension Count** for **Thread-1** changes from **0** to **1**.

6. Continue to run your application with at least one of the threads suspended by pressing the F5 or F11 keys.

    If you are using the application created for this procedure, you'll see that only the output from the non-suspended thread appears in JVIEW's console window.

At some point in the debugging of a multithreaded application you may want to restart the suspended thread. Follow these steps to resume a suspended thread:

Note   This procedure requires that you have:

- Opened the Threads debug window

- Have suspended a thread in this window

To resume a suspended thread

1. In the **Threads** debug window, highlight a suspended thread. For this example, highlight **Thread-1** of **Tea.run**.

2. Click the right mouse button, and select **Resume** from the shortcut menu.

    Notice the **Suspension Count** for **Thread-1** changes from **1** to **0**.

Viewing Information in the Call Stack Window

The Call Stack window displays a list of all active procedures or stack frames for the current thread of execution. Active procedures are the uncompleted procedures in a process.

To display the Call Stack window

- On the **View** menu, click **Debug Windows**, and then select **Call Stack**.

    – or –

    Press the key combination, CTRL+ALT+C.

    – or –

    Click the **Call Stack** button on the Debug toolbar.

To change the active thread from the Call Stack window

- Change the active thread by selecting it from the threads list.

See "Viewing the Call Stack," in the Visual Studio online documentation, for information about the specific elements of this window.

Viewing Information in the Running Documents Window

The Running Documents window displays a list of documents that are currently loaded into the process you are running. For example, if you add an HTML frameset to your project, the Running Documents window shows you which pages are currently loaded in the browser.

To display the Running Documents window

- On the **View** menu, click **Debug Windows**, and then select **Running Documents**.

  – or –

  Press the key combination, CTRL+ALT+R.

  – or –

  Click the **Running Documents** button on the Debug toolbar.

To open a document from the Running Documents window

- Double-click on a document to open it in an editor.

To view or hide documents within the top-level documents

- Expand or collapse the list to see or hide the pages or documents within the top level documents.

Stepping Through the Code

The application example for this scenario accepts a date passed from the command line and converts it to a Julian calendar date. The application used in this scenario was built in "Creating a Console Application" in Chapter 1, "Creating Projects." If you'd like to create this project to complete the following exercises, do so now.

You have entered a date for conversion, stopped on a breakpoint you've set, and used the debug windows to examine some of your program's variables. You have an idea of what the problem may be, but you'd like to step through the statements of your code to get a better understanding of what's really happening. The following procedure shows you how to trace through your program's execution.

To step through your program when in break mode

1. Place the cursor in the margin next on the line of code where you would like to begin stepping through your code.

   Tip   Choose a line that will be executed before the application ends.

2. If you are following the scenario for debugging a Console application, place the cursor next to the following code:

   ```
   for(int nCount=1; nCount < m_nMonth; nCount++)
   ```

3. Click in the margin.

   A red dot appears in the margin indicating the line on which the breakpoint was set.

4. Press F5 and the debugger runs your application and breaks on your new breakpoint.

   The yellow arrow in the margin points to the next instruction to be processed.

5. Continue to step through your program by pressing F11, paying attention to the line of code being executed and information displayed in any open debugging windows.

   In the open debug windows, values for member variables display in red whenever these values change. If you're following the debugging scenario for a Console application, continue stepping through your application's source code until the values for m_nDayOfYear and nCount change to red in the open debug windows.

   For more information about stepping through your program's code with the debugger, see "Stepping Through Code to Trace Execution," in the Visual Studio online documentation.

To terminate the debugging session

- On the **Debug** menu, click **End**.

  For more ways to stop a debugging session, see "Ending a Debugging Session," in the Visual Studio online documentation.

When your program enters break mode, you may want to set another breakpoint or examine one or more Debug Windows to view the values of your program's member variables.

See "Basic Debugging Procedures," earlier in this chapter, for additional information on using the features of the integrated debugger.

Debugging a WFC Application

If you've created a Windows Foundation Classes for Java (WFC) application and noticed peculiar behavior when it runs, these procedures will help you debug your application.

> **Note** The application example for this scenario was built in "Creating a Windows Application with WFC," in Chapter 1, "Creating Projects." If you'd like to create this project to complete the following exercises, do so now.

The application in this scenario accepts a calendar date and converts it to a Julian date. Once the date's been entered, you'll set a breakpoint and start debugging the application. You'll also examine the value of some member variables with the debugger's windows. Although there may be references to specific code statements in the Julian Date Conversion application, you can substitute code from your application and still find the procedures in this scenario helpful.

After you've entered the date you want converted to a Julian date, see "Setting a Breakpoint Before Starting the Debugger," earlier in this chapter, to begin the debugging session.

When execution of your application stops on a break point, view current values for your application's member variables in the Auto, Locals, Watch, and Immediate debug windows. This gives you a snapshot of what's happening with your program up to the place where it entered break mode.

Now that you've had a chance to look at the state of your program up to where it entered break mode, you may want to set another breakpoint, and then continue stepping through the code.

This concludes the scenario for debugging a WFC application. See "Basic Debugging Procedures," earlier in this chapter, for additional information on using the features of the integrated debugger.

Debugging a Console Application

If you've created a Java console application and noticed peculiar behavior when it runs, these procedures will help you debug your application.

Note   The application example for this scenario was built in "Creating a Console Application," in Chapter 1, "Creating Projects." If you'd like to create this project to complete the following exercises, do so now.

The application in this scenario accepts a calendar date passed from the command line and converts it to a Julian date. Once the date's been entered, you'll set a breakpoint and start debugging the application. You'll also examine the value of some member variables with the debug windows. Although there may be references to specific code statements in the Julian Date Conversion application, you can substitute code and member variables from any application and still find the procedures in this scenario helpful.

Running the application requires that a date be entered from the command line before this program runs. The steps in the procedure for "Entering Command-line Arguments," earlier in this chapter, shows you how to pass this information to the application from the development environment's Launch tab. After you've entered command-line arguments for your program, see "Setting a Breakpoint Before Starting the Debugger," earlier in this chapter, to begin the debugging session.

When execution of your application stops on a break point, view current values for your application's member variables in the Auto, Locals, Watch, and Immediate debug windows. This gives you a snapshot of what's happening with your program up to the place where it entered break mode.

Now that you've had a chance look at the state of your program up to where it entered break mode, you may want to set another breakpoint, and then continue stepping through the code.

This concludes the scenario for debugging a console application using the Julian Date Conversion application. See "Basic Debugging Procedures," earlier in this chapter, for additional information on using the features of the integrated debugger.

Debugging a Multithreaded Application

A process is a collection of virtual memory space, code, data, and system resources, while a thread is code that is to be serially executed within a process. A processor executes threads, not processes, so each 32-bit application has at least one process and one thread. Prior to the introduction of multiple threads of execution, applications were all designed to run on a single thread of execution.

If you have created a multithreaded application or component and noticed peculiar behavior when it runs, you may need to debug the code running on a specific thread to find the source of the problem. The procedures is this scenario are designed to show you how to use the debug Threads window in conjunction with setting breakpoints and viewing information in other debug windows.

If you do not have an application that supports multiple threads and would like to walk through the following procedures, complete the procedures in the next section, "Multithreaded Beverages Application," that create a multithreaded console application.

Multithreaded Beverages Application

The following scenario creates an console application that supports two threads. The application consists of three classes: Class1, Coffee, and Tea. Class1 contains the application's `main()` method and code to start two threads — one to run the code for the Coffee class and one for the Tea class.

To create a multithreaded console application

1. On the **File** menu, click **New Project** to display the **New Project** dialog box.

2. Expand the folders for **Visual J++ Projects** and then **Applications**.

3. Single-click the **Console Application** icon.

4. In the **Name** text box, type a unique name for your project.

5. In the **Location** text box, enter or **Browse** to the location where you want to save your project.

6. Click **Open** and your project appears in Project Explorer.

7. In **Project Explorer**, expand your project's icon and double-click on the Class1.java file.

   Your .java file is now loaded in the Text editor and ready for modifications.

To add the Coffee and Tea classes to Class1.java file

1. At the end of the file, after Class1's closing brace, "{", enter the code found in the next section, "Coffee and Tea Source Code."

2. Between the braces of Class1's main() method, insert the following code:

```
Coffee m_Coffee = new Coffee();   //creates Coffee object
m_Coffee.start();                 //creates thread for Coffee object
new Tea().start();                //creates Tea object and its thread
```

Coffee and Tea Source Code

The following code snippet supports the creation of the multithreaded beverages application. The following Coffee and Tea classes extend the Thread class which allows them to run on separate threads.

```
class Coffee extends Thread
{
    public void run()
    {
        for(int i = 0; i < 10; i++)
        {
            System.out.println("I Like Coffee" + " " + i);
            yield();
        }
    }
}

class Tea extends Thread
{
    public void run()
    {
        for(int i = 0; i < 10; i++)
        {
            System.out.println("I Like Tea" + " " + i);
            yield();
        }
    }
}
```

Debugging a Multi-Process Application

A process is a collection of virtual memory space, code, data, and system resources, while a thread is code that is to be serially executed within a process. A processor executes threads, not processes, so each 32-bit application has at least one process and one thread. Prior to the introduction of multiple threads of execution, applications were all designed to run on a single thread of execution. Processes communicate with one another through messages, using RPC to pass information between processes. There is no difference to the caller in a call coming from a process on a remote machine, and a call from another process on the same machine.

When you are debugging an application that requires more than one process to run, you may want to watch activity across all processes. The following procedure shows you how to select a different process when your are debugging your application.

To select a process from the Threads debug window

1. Open the Threads debug window.

2. From the drop-down list box at the top of the **Threads** window, select the process you want to observe.

Once you have selected a process to debug see "Basic Debugging Procedures," earlier in this chapter, for specific procedures for:

- Displaying the Debug Toolbar

- Setting Breakpoints

- Examining Information with Debug Windows

- Stepping Through the Code

- Debugging a Multithreaded Application

Debugging a COM Object

A Component Object Model (COM) server is a dynamic-link library (DLL) or executable file that implements one or more classes, each of which implements one or more *interfaces*. A COM interface is a group of semantically related functions, and all access to an object's capabilities occurs through the various interfaces that the object supports.

Debugging a COM server differs considerably from debugging an executable or an applet, primarily because a COM server is not intended to run as a stand-alone application. Instead, it exists to provide services to clients. Such clients can be either executable files, Active Server Pages (ASP), or other dynamic-link libraries.

Consequently, to debug a COM server, you'll typically load the project into Visual J++, and then configure the Visual J++ environment to launch your debugging client. Next, you'll set breakpoints in your object code, so that when the Visual J++ environment starts your debug client, the execution of your object code will stop at a specified point. After a breakpoint is triggered, you can step through your server object code, just as you would if you were debugging an executable or an applet.

The approach that you take to debugging your object depends primarily on two factors: the types of debugging clients that will access your object's services, and the environment in which your object is designed to operate.

This section explains three approaches that you can take to debugging a COM server. These approaches are distinguished from one another based on the client type. Subjects covered include:

- Using an Active Server Pages (ASP) Debugging Client. An object designed specifically to be used in the Active Server Pages environment is typically referred to as a *server-side component*. This section explains how to debug a server-side component that uses an ASP client. For more detailed instructions about debugging script, see "The Script Debugging Process," in the Visual InterDev online documentation.

- Using an Executable Debugging Client. This section explains how to configure the Visual J++ environment to launch the executable program that will use your object's services.

- Using the Microsoft Transaction Server (MTS). Debugging an MTS component involves the interaction of the MTS itself and of a debugging client. This section explains how to debug an MTS-enabled component.

Using an Active Server Pages (ASP) Debugging Client

Before you can begin to debug a server-side component, make sure you have:

- Created an ASP to run your server-side component.

- Installed Microsoft Internet Information Server (IIS) on your computer or on a Web server, where IIS is configured for debugging a Java server-side component.

- Deployed your component to IIS.

- Internet Explorer (version 4.0 or later).

This scenario uses the project built in "Creating a COM DLL," in Chapter 1, "Creating Projects." However, the following procedures provide information you'll need to prepare any server-side component for debugging.

Preparing the Environment for Debugging a Java Server-Side Component

To prepare the environment for debugging a Java server-side component

1. On the **Tools** menu, click **Options** and highlight the Debugger node in the tree view of the **Options** dialog box.

   The property page for **Debugger** options appears.

2. In the **Java** and **Script** sections of this property page, select the option to **Attach to running program**.

3. Reboot your machine to enable these options.

4. Start **Internet Explorer** and point the browser to your project's .asp page at the http:// server location where you've deployed your Java server-side component.

   The contents of your .asp page appear in the Web browser.

After you have configured IIS and prepared the Visual J++ environment, you are now ready to begin the debugging of your Java server-side component.

Starting a Java Server-Side Component Debugging Session

To debug a Java server-side component

1. Start Visual J++.

2. On the **File** menu, click **Open Project**.

3. On the **Existing** tab of the **Open Project** dialog box, select your server-side component project.

4. In Project Explorer, expand your project's node, and double-click your component's .java file to load it into the Text editor.

5. On the **Debug** menu, click **Processes** to display the **Processes** dialog box.

6. In the **Processes** section of the dialog box, select **Microsoft Active Server Pages.**

7. Click **Attach**.

   This puts your project in run mode and loads the debugger.

8. From within the Text editor, set a breakpoint within a public method of your component's class.

9. From **Internet Explorer**, set a breakpoint after the script calls the server-side component in your .asp page.

10. From **Internet Explorer**, click **Refresh**.

The scripting code calls the component and breaks on the line where you've set the breakpoint.

The environment and your project are now ready for you to continue debugging your component with the debugger's windows and general features for setting breakpoints, stepping through code, and continuing after an error.

Using an Executable Debugging Client

From within your server-side component project, you can specify and configure a debug executable, an application that triggers a breakpoint within your component.

To configure a client executable

1. On the **Project** menu, click *<Project Name>* **Properties**, where *<Project Name>* is the name of the currently loaded project.

2. On the **Launch** tab of the **Properties** dialog box, click **Custom**.

3. In the **Program** box, type the path to the executable that calls into your component.

4. In the **Arguments** box, type any arguments that you want to pass to the application specified in the **Program** box.

5. Click **OK**.

6. In your component's class code, place your cursor at the location at which you want to set a breakpoint.

7. On the **Debug** menu, click **Start** to launch the executable you specified as your debug client.

When the Visual J++ debugger breaks into your component's code at the specified breakpoint, you can use the debugger's step commands on the Debug menu (Step Over, Step Into, and Step Out) to navigate your component's source.

Using the Microsoft Transaction Server (MTS)

If you design your component to support MTS transactions, you use both the MTS and a client executable to debug your component's code.

To configure MTS debugging

1. On the Windows NT Server on which you have MTS installed, shut down the server processes. To do this, right-click **My Computer** on the Windows NT desktop to display a shortcut menu, and then click **Shutdown Server Process**.

2. In the Visual J++ environment, click the **Project** menu, then click *<Project>* **Properties**, where *<Project>* is the name of your component project.

3. Click the **Launch** tab, and then click **Custom**.

4. In the **Program** box, type the path to the MTx.exe. By default, this executable resides in your Windows NT System32 directory.

5. In the **Arguments** box, type /p:"*MTS Package Name*", where *Package Name* is the name of the MTS package containing your component. Also, make sure that there are no spaces in this argument.

6. Set a breakpoint in your component code.

7. On the **Debug** menu, click **Start**.

8. Manually start the client executable that calls into your component. When the client calls into the section of code in which you've set a breakpoint, execution halts, and you can step through your component code.

Debugging a Java Applet

Once you have started your applet in JVIEW or the Internet Explorer, see "Basic Debugging Procedures," earlier in this chapter, for specific procedures to follow during your debugging session.

Debugging an Applet Running in JVIEW

The environment and your project are now ready for you to continue debugging your applet with the debugger's windows and general features for setting breakpoints, stepping through code, and continuing after an error.

Debugging an Applet Running in Internet Explorer

The environment and your project are now ready for you to continue debugging your applet with the debugger's windows and general features for setting breakpoints, stepping through code, and continuing after an error.

CHAPTER 7

Packaging and Deploying Projects

When you are ready to distribute your application, the Visual J++ development environment includes all you need to package and deploy your projects.

You can package your Visual J++ project in any of the following output formats:

- COM DLL
- Self-extracting setup (.exe)
- Windows EXE
- Zip archive (.zip)
- Cabinet archive (.cab)

You can use the Output Format tab of the Project Properties dialog box to specify what type of package you want to create when you build your project.

If you package your project as a cabinet archive file or as a self-extracting setup file, you can sign the project for added security by clicking Advanced in the Project Properties dialog box. (If you don't make changes here, cabinet files will be signed according to the default authentication settings you specify in the Security section of the Options dialog box.)

When you are ready to distribute your project, the Visual J++ development environment allows you to deploy the project to Web sites and Web servers for testing and production.

Note You can set limited packaging and deployment options when you create a project using the Application Wizard.

For detailed information about packaging and deploying projects, see the following topics in the Visual Studio documentation:

- Solution Building and Packaging Concepts
- Solution Building and Packaging User Interface Reference
- Solution Building and Packaging Common Tasks
- Solution Deployment Concepts
- Solution Deployment Common Tasks
- Solution Deployment User Interface Reference

CHAPTER 8

Managing Projects with Source Code Control

The Visual J++ environment integrates source control systems (such as Visual SourceSafe) into the **Project Explorer** and other menus and windows. You can use source control to manipulate source file (item) locations and versions, set up your source control project hierarchy to match your development directory tree, and more effectively manage team projects by delaying additions, deletions, and renames to the source control database. To learn more about using an integrated source control system to manage Visual J++ projects, see the following topics in the Visual Studio online documentation:

- Source Code Control Concepts

- Source Code Control Common Tasks

- Source Code Control User Interface Reference

CHAPTER 9

Compiling Applications with JVC

JVC.EXE (JVC) is the Microsoft compiler for Java. By default, the compiler produces (.class) files that run on any virtual machine for Java. However, JVC also builds applications optimized for the Windows platform. See Chapter 19, "Writing Windows-Based Applications with J/Direct," for more information about creating Windows applications with Visual J++.

You may select your project's compiler options on the **Compile** tab of the project's **Properties** dialog box; options may also be typed into the **Additional compiler options** text box of the same tab. Access the **Compile** tab from the **Project** menu's **Properties** dialog box. Each of the options on the **Compile** tab is described in "Setting Compiler Options."

For an alphabetic reference of the JVC command-line options, see "JVC Command-Line Options," later in this chapter.

Description of JVC Syntax

The JVC.EXE (JVC) command line uses the following syntax:

JVC [*options*] <*filename*>

The following table describes input to the JVC command.

Entry	Meaning
option	One or more JVC options. See "Setting Project Options" in Chapter 1, "Creating Projects," and "JVC Command-Line Options," later in this chapter, for more information.
	Note All options apply to all specified source files.
filename	The name of one or more source files. For more information about valid filenames, see "Filename Syntax," later in this section.

You can specify any number of options and filenames, as long as the number of characters on the command line does not exceed 1,024 or the limit dictated by the operating system.

Note   There is no guarantee that future releases of Microsoft Windows NT (version 4.0 and later) and Microsoft Windows 95 will have the same input limit of 1,024 characters for the command line.

Any options you wish to pass to JVC must be supplied before the name of the .java file(s).

Filename Syntax

JVC recognizes the following filename syntax:

- JVC accepts files with names that follow FAT or NTFS naming conventions.

- Any filename can include a full or partial path.

   A full path includes a drive name and one or more directory names. JVC accepts filenames separated either by backslashes (\) or forward slashes (/).

   A partial path omits the drive name, which JVC assumes to be the current drive. If you don't specify a path, JVC assumes the file is in the current directory.

   Note   If a filename does not have an extension, JVC assumes the extension of .java when it reads the file.

Compiling with JVC.EXE

You can use JVC.EXE (JVC) to compile specified .java source files into .class files that are run by the virtual machine for Java. To check your code for syntax errors only, without producing .class files, use the /nowrite option.

You can specify JVC options on the command line, or in the development environment. If you are compiling your Java project from within the development environment, specify the JVC options you wish to use in the **Compile** tab's **Additional compiler options**. Access the **Compile** tab from the **Project** menu's **Settings** dialog box.

If you are compiling your Java project from the command line, place the JVC options before the name of the .java file or files on the command line.

Order of JVC Options

Command-line options must appear before .java source file names on the JVC.EXE (JVC) command line. JVC reads the command line from left to right processing options in the order it encounters them. Each option applies to all files on the command line. If JVC encounters conflicting options, it uses the rightmost option.

JVC Command Files

A command file, also referred to as a response file, is a text file that contains a list of filenames you would otherwise type on the command line. JVC accepts a command file as an argument on the command line. The command file allows you to compile multiple source files.

The criteria listed below should be followed when using command files:

- A command file may contain only filenames.

- A command file must not invoke the JVC command.

- A command file must not contain any JVC compiler options.

A command file is specified by an "at" sign (@) followed by a filename; the filename can specify an absolute or relative path.

CLASSPATH Environment Variable

The **CLASSPATH** environment variable specifies the system's default location for .class files. Java compilers (JVC), application viewers (JVIEW and WJVIEW), and virtual machines use the information stored in the **CLASSPATH** environment variable when compiling and running Java programs. When compiling from the command line, use the /cp:p and /cp:a to add information to the **CLASSPATH** environment variable.

Note   The option settings for JVC, JVIEW, and WJVIEW apply only to the current compilation and must be entered each time these tools run.

Setting the **CLASSPATH** environment variable from the command line changes it permanently until the system shuts down. However, the /cp, /cp:p, and /cp:a options of JVC, JVIEW, and WJVIEW can replace or modify the **CLASSPATH** environment variable when compiling and viewing your Java programs.

Note   The directories in the **CLASSPATH** environment variable are separated by semicolons on a Microsoft Windows system.

The following syntax sets the **CLASSPATH** environment variable from the command line:

SET CLASSPATH = <path>

CLASSPATH and the Java Package Manager (JPM)

When the VM installs, it registers information about all Java packages with the Java Package Manager (JPM) and enters the following **CLASSPATH** values into the **HKEY_LOCAL_MACHINE\Software\Microsoft\Java VM\Classpath** registry key:

Windows 95   C:\WIN95\java\classes\classes.zip; C:\WIN95\java\classes;.;

Window NT   C:\WINNT\java\classes\classes.zip; C:\WINNT\java\classes;.;

When a Java programs runs, the VM searches for .class files by gathering information from the following sources in the order listed:

1. Command-line provided paths

    Note   Use the **/cp**, **/cp:p**, and **/cp:a** options to specify **CLASSPATH** information when running JVC, JVIEW, and WJVIEW.

2. The **DevClasspath** registry key

    Note   The **DevClasspath** registry key allows developers who are working on packages to supercede packages that may be installed in the Java Package Manager's (JPM) database. With this key, developers can build their packages into a specified directory and JPM's installed packages will not shadow it. For more information about the Java Package Manager, see the Java Package Manager documentation.

3. Java Package Manager (JPM) database

    Note   When your program runs from within the Visual J++ development environment, the VM includes the information entered into the **Java Packages** tab of **Settings** dialog box when searching for .class files. Access the **Java Packages** tab from the **Project** menu's **Settings** dialog box. For more information on using the Java Package Manager, see the Java Package Manager documentation.

4. The **TrustedClasspath**, **TrustedLibsDirectory**, **Classpath**, and **LibsDirectory** registry keys

5. The **CLASSPATH** environment variable

JVC Command-Line Options

This subject is an alphabetic reference to all the JVC command-line options. These options are listed in the following table.

If a command-line option can take one or more arguments, its syntax is shown under a Syntax heading before its description. Click any option in the following table for information on that option.

JVC Options Set from the Command Line

/cp — Set CLASSPATH Option	/g — Generate Debugging Information Option	/nowrite — Compile Only Option	/verbose — Display Compiler Messages Option
/cp:o — Display CLASSPATH Option	/g:l — Generate Line Number Information Option	/O — Enable Optimizations Option	/w — Set Warning Level Option
/cp:p — Prepend CLASSPATH Option	/g:t — Generate Debug Tables Option	/O:I — Inline Methods Optimization Option	/x — Disable Language Extensions Option
/d — Output Directory Option	/nologo — Suppress Copyright Banner	/O:J — Optimize Bytecode Jumps Option	/? — Online Help Option
/D — Define Conditional Compilation Symbol	/nowarn — Suppress Warning Messages	/ref — Recompile Referenced Classes	

All options listed in this table may be typed into the **Compile** tab's **Additional compiler options** text box. Access the **Compile** tab from the **Project** menu's **Settings** dialog box. These options can also be used typed onto the command line before the source filenames.

/cp — Set CLASSPATH Option (JVC)

Syntax

/cp classpath

Use the **/cp** option to set the **CLASSPATH** information for the current compilation. Using this option specifies the path where the JVC can find system and user-defined classes. The virtual machine for Java uses the CLASSPATH environment variable and the Java Package Manager to find system classes. For more information on using the Java Package Manager, see the Java Package Manager documentation in the Microsoft SDK for Java documentation in the online documentation.

> **Note**   The directories in the **CLASSPATH** environment variable are separated by semicolons on a Microsoft Windows system.

Example

When compiling myClass.java on Windows NT (version 4.0 or later), the class path might be:

```
JVC /cp x:.;x:\java\classes myClass.java
```

In this example JVC searches in and beneath the current directory and the x:\java\classes directory for system and user-defined classes.

/cp:o — Display CLASSPATH Option (JVC)

This option prints the class path to standard output. This option is especially useful for troubleshooting errors, such as "class not found," when compiling from the command line.

Example

The following example prints the class path to the screen:

```
JVC /cp:o
```

/cp:p — Prepend CLASSPATH Option (JVC)

Syntax

/cp:p path

This option prepends the information found in the **CLASSPATH** environment variable and inserts a semicolon between directory paths. When multiple **/cp:p** options are entered, the paths are concatenated.

> **Note**   The **CLASSPATH** environment variable or the **/cp** option supply the location of the .class files. For a full description of the **CLASSPATH** environment variable, see "CLASSPATH Environment Variable," earlier in this chapter.

Example

The following command prepends the directory of myproj to the existing class path:

```
JVC /cp:p myproj
```

The following commands concatenate the directories, myproj1 and myproj2, and prepends the resulting path to the existing **CLASSPATH** information:

```
JVC /cp:p myproj1 /cp:p myproj2
```

/d — Output Directory Option (JVC)

Syntax

/d directory

When compiling .java files, use the **/d** option to specify an output directory other than the current directory for the .class files. If the directory does not exist, JVC will create it. If this option is not specified, JVC will write the .class files to the directory containing the corresponding .java files.

Example

The following command compiles the `myClass.java` file into a `myClass.class` file and writes this file into the `classdir` directory:

```
JVC /d c:\classdir myClass.java
```

> **Caution** The virtual machine for Java depends upon specific directory locations for .java classes based on the names of the Java packages that contain the .class files. Using this option could cause execution to fail if the VM can't find the classes it needs to run a Java program. For an explanation of how the VM searches for .class files, see "CLASSPATH Environment Variable," earlier in this chapter.

/D — Define Conditional Compilation Symbol

Syntax

/D *identifier*

This option tells the compiler to consider the identifier as a defined symbol for conditional compilation on all files being compiled. The symbol can be tested in a .java source file by using the **#if** directive to test if a symbol is defined. See "Conditional Compilation" for more information.

Example

The following command compiles the myClass.java file, with the **WINDOWS** and **DEBUG** preprocessing symbols defined:

```
JVC /D WINDOWS /D DEBUG myClass.java
```

/g — Generate Debugging Information Option (JVC)

Syntax

/g[–]

The **/g** option generates all debugging information. No debugging options are set by default. The effect of using the **/g** option is the same as using the following options together:

Option	Action
/g:l	Generate line number information
/g:t	Generate debug tables

> **Note**   To disable this option, use a dash (–) after the option on the command line.

Example

The following command creates a .class file called `myClass.class` that contains debugging information:

```
JVC /g myClass.java
```

/g:l — Generate Line Number Information Option (JVC)

Syntax

/g:l[–]

This option generates line numbers that are used when debugging a program. No debugging options are set by default.

> **Note**   To disable this option, use a dash (–) after the option on the command line.

Example

The following command instructs JVC to generate line-number information for the resulting `myClass.class` file:

```
JVC /g:l myClass.java
```

/g:t — Generate Debug Tables Option (JVC)

Syntax

/g:t[–]

This option generates debug tables that are used when debugging a program.
No debugging options are set by default.

> **Note**   To disable this option, use a dash (–) after the option on the command line.

Example

The following command instructs JVC to generate debug-table information for the
resulting `myClass.class` file:

```
JVC /g:t myClass.java
```

/nologo — Suppress Copyright Banner

Syntax

/nologo

When compiling files from the command line, this option suppresses the display of the
compiler version number and copyright information.

Example

The following command compiles the myClass.java file without displaying the compiler
copyright notice:

```
JVC /nologo myClass.java
```

/nowarn — Suppress Warning Messages

Syntax

/nowarn

This option causes the compiler to not emit any warning messages, only error messages.

Example

The following command compiles the myClass.java file without displaying any warning
messages:

```
JVC /nowarn myClass.java
```

/nowrite — Compile Only Option (JVC)

Syntax

/nowrite

The **/nowrite** option tells JVC to compile a .java file and to suppress the writing of the .class file. This option is useful for checking your source code for syntax errors only, without producing .class files.

Example

The `myClass.java` file is compiled, errors and warnings are reported, but no corresponding `myClass.class` file is produced:

```
JVC /nowrite myClass.java
```

/O — Enable Optimizations Option (JVC)

Syntax

/O

The **/O** option combines optimizing options to produce a more efficient program. The effect of using this option is the same as using the following options together:

Option	Action
/O:I	Optimize by inlining methods when appropriate.
/O:J	Optimize bytecode jumps. Default optimization setting.

> **Note**   To disable any optimization option, use a dash (–) after the option on the command line.

Example

The following command fully optimizes the code for the `myClass.class` file that is produced:

```
JVC /O myClass.java
```

/O:I — Inline Methods Optimization Option (JVC)

Syntax

/O:I

The **/O:I** option tells the compiler it may inline methods to produce more efficient code. Code that is inlined does not have the overhead associated with a method call. Since there is no mechanism in the Java language to request inlining of methods, use this option when you want the compiler to inline your code.

Note To disable this option, use a dash (–) after the option on the command line.

Example

The following example evaluates the source code in the `myClass.java` file and inlines methods where possible. The resulting `myClass.class` file contains the optimized code:

```
JVC /O:I myClass.java
```

/O:J — Optimize Bytecode Jumps Option (JVC)

Syntax

/O:J

The **/O:J** option causes JVC to optimize the bytecode jumps in the compiled .class file. This option tells the compiler to generate code that jumps to another place in the code. This option is the compiler's default optimization setting.

Note To disable this option, use a dash (–) after the option on the command line.

Example

The following example evaluates the source code in the `myClass.java` file and optimizes the bytecode jumps to produce more efficient code. The resulting `myClass.class` file contains the optimized code:

```
JVC /O:J myClass.java
```

/ref — Recompile Referenced Classes

Syntax

/ref[–]

The option causes the compiler to check for a matching .java source file when loading class information from a class file on the class path. If this option is set, whenever the compiler is about to load class information from a .java class file, it checks for a presence of a .java source file of the same base name in the same directory. If such a source file is found, and the source file has a modification date later than that of the .java class file, the .java source file is compiled instead of reading the .java class file.

If this option is not set, the compiler will always read the .java class file, regardless of the presence of a source file.

This option is on by default when compiling from the command line; use **/ref–** to turn it off. This option is off by default when compiling from the integrated development environment.

> **Caution**   It is recommend that you do not turn this option on in the integrated development environment; doing so may cause the build operation to fail to perform as designed.

Example

The following command compiles the myclass.java files, and tells the compiler not to recompile any referenced classes:

```
JVC /ref- myClass.java
```

/verbose — Display Compiler Messages Option (JVC)

Syntax

/verbose

This option instructs JVC to display all messages while compiling a file or project. These messages give useful information about the progress of the compilation.

/w — Set Warning Level Option (JVC)

Syntax

/w0
/w1
/w2
/w3
/w4
/wx

These options control the output of warning messages produced by the compiler. The compiler determines which warnings to display based upon their severity. They affect only source files named on the command line.

Compiler warning message numbers begin with J5. The documentation describes the warnings, indicates each warning's level, and indicates potential problems (rather than actual coding errors) with statements that may not compile as you intend.

The meaning of these options is as follows:

Option	Description
/w0	Turns off all warning messages.
/w1	Displays severe warning messages.
/w2	Displays a less severe level of warning message than /w1. This is the default warning level setting.
/w3	Displays a less severe level of warning than /w2, including use of methods with no declared return type, failure to put return statements in methods with non-void return types, and data conversions that would cause loss of data or precision.
/w4	Displays the least severe level of warning messages.
/wx	Forces warnings to errors. Any warning will cause the compiler to emit an error and fail the compilation. This option can be combined with one of the warning level options above.

/x — Disable Language Extensions Option (JVC)

Syntax

/x[–]

The Visual J++ compiler supports the Java language specification. In addition, it may offer a number of features beyond those required by this specification. These features are available by default, but are not available when the **/x** option is specified.

Use the **/x** option if you plan to port your program to other environments. The **/x** option tells the compiler to treat extended keywords as simple identifiers and to disable the other Microsoft extensions.

Note To disable this option, use a dash (–) after the option on the command line.

Example

The following command ignores any Visual J++ extensions used in the myClass.class file:

```
JVC /x myClass.java
```

/? — Online Help Option (JVC)

Syntax

/?

This option displays a listing of compiler options to standard output.

CHAPTER 10

Viewing Applications with JVIEW and WJVIEW

Viewing Applications with JVIEW

JVIEW.EXE (JVIEW) is a tool used to view Java applications and applets. JVIEW provides console window where your Java programs can run. JVIEW supports both debug and retail versions of your applications and applets.

If your Java project is an application, that is, has a **public static void main(String args[])** method, JVIEW will run the application in JVIEW's console window without additional command-line options. If your Java project is an applet, that is, has a **public void init()** method, use JVIEW's **/a** option.

For an alphabetic reference of the JVIEW options see "JVIEW Command-Line Options," later in this chapter.

Description of JVIEW Syntax

The JVIEW.EXE (JVIEW) command line uses the following syntax:

JVIEW [options] <classname> [arguments]

The following table describes input to the JVIEW command.

Entry	Meaning
Options	One or more JVIEW options. See "JVIEW Command-Line Options," later in this chapter, for more information.
Classname	The name of the class to execute. Do not include the .class extension of this filename. For example, use **HelloWorldApp** and not **HelloWorldApp.class**.
	Note You may also specify a fully-qualified class name, without the .class extension, such as, **C:\My Documents\Visual Studio Projects\HelloWorldApp\ HelloWorldApp.**
Arguments	Command-line arguments to be passed to the class identified by classname.

Note   Any options that you wish to supply to JVIEW must be supplied before the name of the .class file or they will be interpreted as command-line arguments to the .class file.

Running JVIEW.EXE

You can specify JVIEW.EXE (JVIEW) options on the command line or in the development environment. By default, Visual J++ chooses WJVIEW as its application and applet viewer. Within Visual J++, to run JVIEW without specifying additional command-line options, select the **Launch as a console application** check box in the **Default** group box of the **Launch** tab. Access the **Launch** tab from the **Project** menu's **Settings** dialog box.

You can pass more than the default options to JVIEW if you are running your program from the command line or from within the development environment.

To pass more than the default options to JVIEW from within Visual J++:

1. From the **Project** menu, select **Settings**.

2. From the **Launch** tab on the **Settings** dialog box, select the **Other executables** group box.

3. Type JVIEW.EXE in the **Other executables** group's **Program** text box.

4. Type the JVIEW options for your program into the **Other executables** group's **Arguments** text box.

When you run JVIEW from the command line, enter the options you wish to pass to JVIEW before the name of your class file(s) on the command line.

JVIEW Command-Line Options

This section is an alphabetic reference of the JVIEW command-line options. These options are listed in the following table.

If a command-line option can take one or more arguments, its syntax is shown under a Syntax heading before its description.

JVIEW Command-line Options

/a — Applet Viewer Option	/d: — System Property Option
/cp — Set CLASSPATH Option	/p — Pause Viewer Option
/cp:a — Append CLASSPATH Option	/v — Class Verification Option
/cp:p — Prepend CLASSPATH Option	/? — Online Help Option

See "Running JVIEW.EXE," earlier in this chapter, for information on how to specify these options from within the development environment or on the command line.

/a — Applet Viewer Option (JVIEW/WJVIEW)

Use the **/a** option to invoke an applet viewer — a browserless environment for viewing applets. Applets that are run within the applet viewer behave in the same manner as those hosted within a browser, including loading, sound, and security. The applet viewer accepts applet parameters and class names, in addition to URLs and HTML filenames.

The **/a** option directs JVIEW or WJVIEW to run an applet and requires your Java project to have an **public void init()** method. If your Java project has a **public static void main(String args[])** method, use JVIEW or WJVIEW without the **/a** option to run it as an application.

> **Note**   When the **/a** option is used, any remaining command-line tokens become parameters for the applet viewer.

Examples

The following command-line statements run the **HelloWorld** applet in an applet viewer for JVIEW or WJVIEW, respectively:

```
JVIEW /a HelloWorld
```

– or –

```
WJVIEW /a HelloWorld
```

You can load an applet either by using an HTML file to specify parameters or by loading parameters directly from the command line. The following example shows how to load the **HelloWorld** applet from an HTML source file with the applet tag:

```
<applet code=MyApplet.class width=100 height=200>
            <param name=SomeName value=SomeValue></applet>
```

The same **HelloWorld** applet can run in JVIEW or WJVIEW with the following command-line information:

```
JVIEW /a width=100 height=200 SomeName=SomeValue HelloWorld
```

– or –

```
WJVIEW /a width=100 height=200 SomeName=SomeValue HelloWorld
```

The following examples show how to run more than one applet at a time from the command line:

```
JVIEW /a width=200 height=400 HelloWorld height=300 SpinningWorld
```

– or –

```
WJVIEW /a width=200 height=400 HelloWorld height=300 SpinningWorld
```

The results of the previous commands display the **HelloWorld** applet in a 200 x 400 frame and the **SpinningWorld** applet in a 200 x 300 frame.

Note   If no height and width are specified, the applets's default size is one-third the size of the screen.

Any parameter, including HTML files, will be loaded from directory and .zip file locations specified by CLASSPATH information and the Java Package Manager (JPM) database. For example:

```
JVIEW /a /cp \src\bvt\HelloWorld.html
```

– or –

```
WJVIEW /a /cp \src\bvt\HelloWorld.html
```

/cp — Set CLASSPATH Option (JVIEW/WJVIEW)

Syntax

/cp classpath

Use the **/cp** option to set the **CLASSPATH** environment variable for the current compilation. Using this option specifies the path where JVIEW and WJVIEW can find system and user-defined .class files. The virtual machine for Java uses a platform-dependent default location, the CLASSPATH Environment Variable, and the Java Package Manager (JPM) database to find system classes. For more information on using the Java Package Manager, see the Java Package Manager documentation in the Microsoft SDK for Java documentation.

> **Note**   The directories in the **CLASSPATH** environment variable are separated by semicolons on a Microsoft Windows system.

Examples

On Windows NT, the following commands provide **CLASSPATH** information for JVIEW and WJVIEW:

```
JVIEW /cp X:.;X:\WINNT\java\classes\classes.zip;X:\WINNT\java\classes\
```

– or –

```
WJVIEW /cp X:.;X:\WINNT\java\classes\classes.zip;X:\WINNT\java\classes\
```

In this example JVIEW and WJVIEW search in and beneath the current directory and the x:\java\classes directory for system and user-defined classes.

> **Note**   In the previous examples, X: designates the drive letter where the class or .zip files reside.

/cp:a — Append CLASSPATH Option (JVIEW/WJVIEW)

Syntax

/cp:a path

The **/cp:a** option appends the path entered to the end of the **CLASSPATH** information and inserts a semicolon between the directories. When multiple **/cp:a** options are entered, the paths are concatenated.

Note   The **CLASSPATH** environment variable or the **/cp** option supplies the location of the .class file and .zip file directories. The virtual machine for Java uses a platform-dependent default location, the CLASSPATH Environment Variable, and the Java Package Manager (JPM) database to find system classes. For more information on the JPM, see the Java Package Manager documentation in the Microsoft SDK for Java documentation.

Examples

The following commands append the directory of myproj to the existing **CLASSPATH** information:

```
JVIEW /cp:a myproj
```

– or –

```
WJVIEW /cp:a myproj
```

The following commands concatenate the directories, myproj1 and myproj2, and append the resulting path to the existing **CLASSPATH** information:

```
JVIEW /cp:a myproj1 /cp:a myproj2
```

– or –

```
WJVIEW /cp:a myproj1 /cp:a myproj2
```

/cp:p — Prepend CLASSPATH Option (JVIEW/WJVIEW)

Syntax

/cp:p path

The **/cp:p** option prepends the path entered to the beginning of the **CLASSPATH** information and inserts a semicolon between the directories. When multiple **/cp:p** options are entered, the paths are concatenated.

Note   The **CLASSPATH** environment variable or the **/cp** option supply the location of the .class file and .zip file directories. The virtual machine for Java uses a platform-dependent default location, the CLASSPATH Environment Variable, and the Java Package Manager (JPM) database to find system classes. For more information on using the Java Package Manager, see the Java Package Manager documentation.

Examples

The following commands prepend the directory of `myproj` to the existing **CLASSPATH** information:

```
JVIEW /cp:p myproj
```

– or –

```
WJVIEW /cp:p myproj
```

The following commands concatenate the directories, `myproj1` and `myproj2`, and prepend the resulting path to the existing **CLASSPATH** information:

```
JVIEW /cp:p myproj1 /cp:p myproj2
```

– or –

```
WJVIEW /cp:p myproj1 /cp:p myproj2
```

/d: — System Property Option (JVIEW/WJVIEW)

Syntax

/d:property=string value

Use the **/d:** option to set a system property for a Java program. Java programs can read system properties by using the **Java.lang.System.getProperties** methods. See these methods' documentation for descriptions of system properties.

Examples

The following commands set the `user.dir` property to some arbitrary value:

```
JVIEW /d:user.dir=c:\java\test HelloWorld.
```

– or –

```
WJVIEW /d:user.dir=c:\java\test HelloWorld.
```

You can also set user-defined properties. The following commands set the property called "myprop":

```
JVIEW /d:myprop=12 HelloWorld
```

– or –

```
WJVIEW /d:myprop=12 HelloWorld
```

/p — Pause Viewer Option (JVIEW/WJVIEW)

The **/p** option forces JVIEW and WJVIEW to pause before exiting if an error occurs. You can use this command-line option to determine the user interface state just prior to the error when debugging an application.

Example

Use the following commands to pause before exiting JVIEW or WJVIEW if an error occurs in the `HelloWorld` application:

```
JVIEW /p HelloWorld
```

– or –

```
WJVIEW /p HelloWorld
```

/v — Class Verification Option (JVIEW/WJVIEW)

The **/v** option causes JVIEW and WJVIEW to verify all invoked methods. Without this option, only methods from untrusted loaders are verified. Verification is a process applied to the bytecode loaded from the .class files to ensure that it does not pose a security threat. Verification enforces this so that if one of your .class files attempts to do anything that violates the security model, that file is rejected.

> **Note** On Microsoft's virtual machine for Java only a subset of the total functionality of this option is possible with the bytecode language for .class files that are loaded remotely.

For performance reasons, the local system classes are not normally verified. The **/v** option forces the verifier to process these files. You can use this option to ensure that a set of .class files will pass the verifier.

Example

Use the following JVIEW or WJVIEW command to insure the .class files of the `SpinningWorld` application do not pose a security problem:

```
JVIEW /v SpinningWorld
```

– or –

```
WJVIEW /v SpinningWorld
```

/? — Online Help Option (JVIEW/WJVIEW)

Syntax

/?

This option displays a listing of command-line options for JVIEW and WJVIEW.

Example

Use the following commands to display online help for JVIEW or WJVIEW, respectively:

```
JVIEW /?
```

– or –

```
WJVIEW /?
```

Viewing Applications with WJVIEW

WJVIEW.EXE (WJVIEW) is a tool used to view window-based Java applications from the command line. Unlike JVIEW, WJVIEW spawns a separate window process. WJVIEW provides an environment where your window-based programs can run and supports both debug and retail versions of your applications.

Note Use WJVIEW to run window-based Java applications. WJVIEW has the same functionality and command-line options as JVIEW. WJVIEW runs your window-based Java application in a separate graphical user interface (GUI) process and does not use or require a console window. Consequently, do not use WJVIEW for Java applications that require output to or input from the console window.

For an alphabetic reference to the WJVIEW options, see "WJVIEW Command-Line Options," earlier in this chapter.

Description of WJVIEW Syntax

The WJVIEW.EXE (WJVIEW) command line uses the following syntax:

WJVIEW [options] <classname> [arguments]

The following table describes input to the WJVIEW command.

Entry	Meaning
Options	One or more WJVIEW options. See "WJVIEW Command-Line Options," earlier in this chapter, for more information.
Classname	The name of the class to execute. Do not include the .class extension of this filename. For example, use **HelloWorldApp** and not **HelloWorldApp.class**.
	Note You may also specify a fully-qualified class name, without the .class extension, such as, **C:\My Documents\Visual Studio Projects\HelloWorldApp\ HelloWorldApp.**
Arguments	Command-line arguments to be passed to the class identified by classname.

Note   Any options that you wish to supply to WJVIEW must be supplied before the name of the class file or they will be interpreted as command-line arguments to the class file.

Running WJVIEW.EXE

You can specify WJVIEW.EXE (WJVIEW) options on the command line or in the development environment. By default, Visual J++ chooses WJVIEW as its application and applet viewer.

You can pass more than the default options to WJVEIW if you are running your program from the command line or from within the development environment.

To pass more than the default options to WJVIEW from within Visual J++:

1. From the **Project** menu, select **Settings**.

2. From the **Launch** tab on the **Settings** dialog box, select the **Other executables** group box.

3. Type WJVIEW.EXE in the **Other executables** group's **Program** text box.

4. Type the WJVIEW options for your program into the **Other executables** group's **Arguments** text box.

When you run WJVIEW from the command line, enter the options you wish to supply to WJVIEW before the name of your class file on the command line. See "WJVIEW Command-Line Options," earlier in this chapter, for details about specific options.

WJVIEW Command-Line Options

This section is an alphabetic reference to the WJVIEW command-line options. These options are listed in the following table.

If a command-line option can take one or more arguments, its syntax is shown under a Syntax heading before its description.

WJVIEW Command-line Options

/a — Applet Viewer Option	/d: — System Property Option
/cp — Set CLASSPATH Option	/p — Pause Viewer Option
/cp:a — Append CLASSPATH Option	/v — Class Verification Option
/cp:p — Prepend CLASSPATH Option	/? — Online Help Option

See "Running WJVIEW.EXE," earlier in this chapter, for information on how to specify these options from within the development environment or on the command line.

PART 2

Programming with Visual J++

CHAPTER 11

Introduction to WFC Programming

Windows Foundation Classes for Java (WFC) is a set of class libraries that works seamlessly with the Rapid Application Development (RAD) tool Visual J++. The combination of this class framework and RAD tool make it easy to build fast and powerful applications and components for the Microsoft platform using the Java language. WFC brings the Java language to the Win32 platform and the Dynamic HTML (DHTML) object model, which is a W3C standard supported by Internet Explorer 4.0. This means you can use Java to solve real problems today and know that you have a smooth migration path into the future.

A goal of WFC is to provide complete and compelling component and programming models for Java. Because Java provides a unique set of advantages in terms of language features, it is the language of choice for developing Windows and DHTML applications using this new programming model.

WFC enables developers to quickly build rich Win32 applications and ActiveX controls in Java by using the Visual J++ Forms Designer to drag and drop controls onto a form, set properties, and generate event handlers. Developers can also easily access data on a server from their applications and deploy their applications as Windows .EXE files or Internet URLs. Moreover, they can build their own WFC components by using the designer or writing code directly in the editor. Finally, developers can access the DHTML object model using Java classes.

The rich application model takes advantage of the J/Direct technology to access the Win32 API. However, it makes it much easier to program by taking care of details like Window message-handling procedures, message pumps, messages, window handles, and so forth. The application model is open, so experienced Win32 programmers can intermix J/Direct calls with WFC classes to add any functionality available on the Win32 platform.

If you are looking for a quick "hands-on" introduction to using Visual J++ to develop a WFC application, take a few minutes to walk through "Creating a Windows Application with WFC," in Chapter 1, "Creating Projects," which steps you through building and running a simple WFC application.

Getting Started with Controls and Templates

One of the strengths of the WFC component model is that the Visual J++ development environment provides most of the components, forms, menus, and dialog boxes that you typically need. These components can either be extended for your own needs or you can author your own controls. Because Visual J++ provides controls typically used in the Win32 environment, you'll feel at home with the visual components available from the Visual J++ design environment.

The Visual J++ development environment is tightly integrated with the WFC classes, so most of what you need to know to get started using controls, forms, and menus can be found in Using Visual J++.

Starting with a Form

Most application windows are represented in WFC programming as forms. A form is used wherever you want a separate overlapping, graphical component, such as a main application window or dialog box. Forms act as containers for controls, allowing you to visually compose applications. Forms have their own properties, which can be set in the Properties window. Syntactically, a form is a Java class derived from the com.ms.wfc.ui.Form class. The Form class extends the com.ms.wfc.ui.Control class, as do the controls that you place on a form. Control encapsulates a Win32 window.

When you create a new project, and choose Windows Application from the New Projects dialog box, a form is automatically created for you. You can add other forms by choosing either Add Item or Add Form from the Project menu.

Once a form is added to your project, the form can be viewed either in design mode or in the Text editor. You can use the Forms Designer to size it and set properties by choosing View Designer from the shortcut menu of the form in Project Explorer. Each form belongs to a nonvisual Application object that contains the main thread of the application. Forms and controls represent the visual Windows components. The integration of the visual and nonvisual aspects of the window are handled completely by WFC framework.

When you open the Text editor on a new form, you'll see the template-based class created for you that contains the necessary syntax of the Form class, including a constructor and a main() method with code that instantiates your form. When you work in design mode, adding controls, setting properties, and so forth, the Forms Designer inserts and modifies a section of this class. See "Creating a Form" in Chapter 2, "Designing Forms," to learn about adding forms to your project.

Adding Controls

Controls are added by dragging them from the Toolbox onto the form, sizing them, and setting their properties in the Properties window. You can drag and drop both ActiveX and WFC controls onto your forms in Visual J++. See "Adding Controls to a Form" in Chapter 2, "Designing Forms," to learn about adding controls from the Toolbox to a form.

WFC controls can be grouped into three categories, although there is no distinction between categories in the way you use them:

- **Intrinsic controls**. The basic Windows controls such as buttons, check boxes, edit boxes, list boxes, and so on.

- **Common controls**. The Win32 common controls found in comctl32.dll. These include controls such as animations, toolbars, tabs, status bars, and Tree view controls.

- **WFC controls**. Custom controls written specifically for the WFC framework.

All existing WFC controls are Java classes found in the com.ms.wfc.ui package.

If you want, you can create your own controls using the WFC packages, either by extending existing controls or writing your own from scratch, and adding them to the Toolbox. The WFC component model makes it easy to expose information about your control's properties and events, enabling your control to work seamlessly with the Visual J++ Forms Designer.

Adding Menus

Menus are added in a manner similar to controls and appear in the Toolbox as simply another control. To add a menu, you drag the MainMenu control from the Toolbox onto the form. Once the menu is enabled on the form, the Forms Designer lets you add submenus and menu items by simply typing them in. Each menu item has an event handler that can be hooked up in the coding phase of development. And, as with controls, all implementation code for the menus and menu items is created automatically for you as you visually create the menu. See "Creating Menus for Forms" in Chapter 2, "Designing Forms," for more information on adding menus to a form.

Adding Code

The Forms Designer helps you to create your initial form class and even provides much of the skeleton code for things like event handlers. However, at some point you need to actually write code to make your application do what you want it to.

Event handler methods are called when an event is triggered from a user-interface element on the form, such as a mouse click on a control. The Forms Designer creates skeleton code for these, so it's mostly a matter of filling in the code you want run when the event occurs. The WFC component model employs a new delegate keyword in the Visual J++ compiler that is the basis of all event handling. While delegates are transparent when using the Forms Designer to hook up handlers for events, they can be used directly for more advanced scenarios, such as sourcing your own events. Since they are essentially the same as a function pointer in other languages, they are useful in a number of ways.

In addition to controls and event handlers, there are many other parts of the WFC library that you will find useful.

- **Graphics support**. Several classes in the com.ms.wfc.ui package, including the Graphics class, provide support for accessing Windows graphical services.

- **Dynamic HTML support**. The com.ms.wfc.html package provides an extensive set of classes that provide access to the DHTML object model implemented by Internet Explorer (versions 4.0 and later).

- **Data binding support**. WFC is designed to use the ActiveX Data Objects (ADO) components to support both simple and complex data binding. Using the DataBinder component, you can bind a field from a recordset to the property of any WFC component. WFC also provides other complex-bound components that interact directly with a recordset.

- **Localization support**. WFC provides support for localizing your code much easier by letting you store your resource elements, such as strings, fonts, and bitmaps, in a resource file matching a specific international locale. This simplifies the job of translating user interfaces for multiple languages.

- **Direct Win32 API support**. The J/Direct technology provided with Visual J++ enables you to call any dynamic-link library (DLL) from your Java code. WFC is built upon a layer of J/Direct calls to Win32 libraries (implemented in the com.ms.wfc.Win32 and com.ms.wfc.OLE32 packages). Consequently, if you are comfortable with standard Windows programming and want to access those libraries directly, WFC provides the underlying elements (such as device contexts and window handles) to give you ultimate control. While this may be desirable for some specialized applications, most programmers will find the basic services of WFC sufficient.

A Sample Walkthrough

This section contains a brief overview of a simple Visual J++ application called MyNotepad, which is based on the Windows Notepad application. MyNotepad is a Text editor with a File menu containing New, Open, Save, Save As, and Exit menu items. It covers the most primitive functions of an editor, allowing the user to open a file, edit it, and save it to the same file or to a different file.

Note that this application is similar to the JPad application generated using the Visual J++ Application Wizard. However, MyNotepad was not constructed using the Application Wizard; it was written specifically to demonstrate a few basic concepts as clearly as possible. After walking through MyNotepad, the code generated by the Application Wizard should be much easier to understand, since it uses most of the same principles.

MyNotepad is essentially a single form (MyNotepad.java) with an edit control and a menu. A second form (NewDialog.java) represents the modal dialog box that prompts the user to save when opening a new file or closing the current file. You can find a complete listing of the code for both these files at the end of this topic.

This application was designed and coded using the Visual J++ Forms Designer and Text editor. Much of the code was automatically generated by the designer. This walkthrough points out what the Forms Designer does for you, the code automatically generated by the designer to create this application, and a few basic concepts for programming a WFC application. Specifically, it describes:

- Using the Forms Designer to create the applications forms

- How to start and stop an application

- The anatomy of a Visual J++ Form template

- How to handle events

- How to open a modal dialog box and retrieve user results

- How to use OpenFileDialog and SaveFileDialog classes to work with files

- How to use the File stream class for file input/output (I/O)

The Sample Walkthrough ends with:

- Sample Walkthrough Summary

- Code Listings

Creating the Application Using Visual J++

This section walks through the steps required to create the MyNotepad application in Visual J++. It's helpful to look at the steps in the design environment before jumping into the code generated by the designer for those steps.

1. Create the main form.

   To create the main form, use the New Project dialog box that appears when you first open Visual J++ or select New Project from the File menu. Select the Windows Application icon, type in the name of your application form (MyNotepad in this case), and choose Open, and Visual J++ creates a project with that name.

   The project contains a form called Form1.java by default, which will be renamed to MyNotepad.java in a later step.

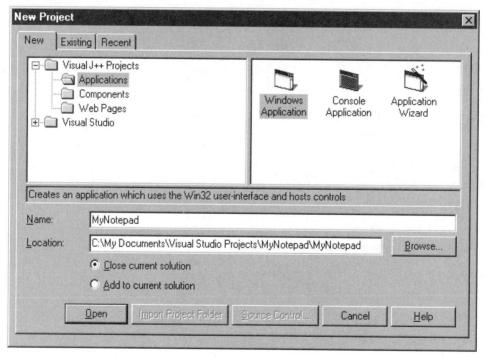

2. Add controls and menus to the form.

The Visual J++ Forms Designer makes it easy to lay out the form. To open the form in design mode, select Form1.java in the Project Explorer and then choose Designer from the View menu (or choose View Designer from the shortcut menu). With the form displayed, you can add controls from the toolbox. To access the WFC controls in the toolbox, click on the Toolbox tab or choose Toolbox from the View menu, and click the WFC Controls button in the toolbox to display those controls.

For this sample, an edit control was added to the form from the toolbox.

Adding a menu is just as easy: drag the MainMenu control from the toolbox onto the form and place it anywhere; then begin typing in the first box and continue adding menu items in the boxes below or to the right.

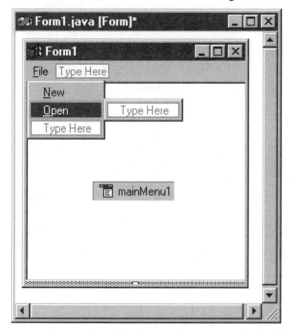

Note that you can create an accelerator key on the menu by entering an ampersand (&) before the desired character. This becomes underlined on the menu.

3. Set properties on the form and controls.

To set properties, use the Properties window. In this case, most properties were left with default values for the sake of simplicity. The following properties on the edit control were changed: the multiline property was set to true, the doc property to was set to Fill, the scrollBars property was set to Vertical, and the font name property was set to Fixedsys to better emulate Notepad. There may be other properties you'll want to set as well on the form and controls.

You'll probably want to rename some of the components to make more sense programmatically. Renaming is done by selecting the form or control and setting the name property. In the case of MyNotepad, the following name changes were made:

Default Name	New Name
Edit1	EditBox
MainMenu1	Menu
MenuItem1	FileMenu
MenuItem2	FileMenuNew
MenuItem3	FileMenuOpen
MenuItem4	FileMenuSave
MenuItem5	FileMenuSaveAs
MenuItem6	FileMenuExit
MenuItem7	HelpMenu
MenuItem8	HelpMenuAbout

4. Change the name of Form1.java.

You may want the main form to have a different name than Form1.java. To do this, select Form1.java in the Project Explorer, right-click and choose Rename from the shortcut menu, and type the new name (in this case, MyNotepad.java).

If you do change the name, remember that you must change all occurrences of Form1 in the source code. To do this, first close the Forms Designer. Then open the source by choosing View Code from the shortcut menu. Choose Find and Replace from the Edit menu, and replace all instances of Form1 with the new name (for example, replace Form1 with MyNotepad).

5. Create a dialog box.

The NewDialog dialog box is just another form in the project. To create additional forms, choose Add Form from the Project menu, select Form in the Add Item dialog box, type the name of the new form (NewDialog.java, in this case) and click Open.

In this case, three buttons were added and named YesButton, NoButton, and CancelButton, with appropriate labels (&Yes, &No, and &Cancel). The button control has a dialogResult property, which is useful when the buttons are used on a modal dialog box. For example, if the YesButton control's dialogResult property is set to Yes and the user clicks this button, the dialog box closes and returns DialogResults.Yes. In this case, the dialogResult properties were set as follows:

Control	dialogResult Property
YesButton	Yes
NoButton	No
CancelButton	Cancel

One note of interest here is that the Form class has an acceptButton property that determines which button is clicked when the user presses ENTER. In this case the acceptButton property was set to the YesButton control. The Form class also has a cancelButton property that determines which button to click when the ESC key is pressed; this was set to the CancelButton control.

Likewise, the accelerator (&) characters in the button labels were used to map a specific key to each button (for example, because the label for the YesButton button is "&Yes," pressing Y clicks that button).

Two additional label controls were then added to display the message text of the dialog box. Finally, the PictureBox control was added to the form and that control's image property was set to a bitmap containing an exclamation graphic.

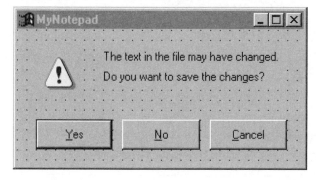

Because an image was added to the form, Visual J++ automatically created a resource file (called NewDialog.resources) and serialized the image to this file when the form was saved. The resource file provides a mechanism for localizing the form to different languages, although in this case it is mostly used for packaging. You can also set the localizable property of a form to true to cause a resource file to be added to your project, in which case all resources, including strings are added to the resource file.

Starting and Stopping an Application

The com.ms.wfc.app package includes the static Application class, which takes care of all the Win32 window processing, such as registration, instantiation, handling the message loop, and so on. The main application window is created by calling the Application.run method and passing it your Form-derived object that makes up the visual aspect of the window. This call occurs in the main() method in the Form-based template class generated by Visual J++. The following code was generated for the MyNotepad application:

```
public static void main(String args[])
{
    Application.run(new MyNotepad());
}
```

By default, the basic application created by a Visual J++ template is closed using the Window's exit (X) button in the top-right corner of the application. However, you can programmatically quit the application anywhere in the code by calling the Application.exit method. For example, this application is closed when Exit on the File menu is clicked:

```
private void FileMenuExit_click(Object sender, Event e)
{
    // Call the new file handler to invoke NewDialog
    // to ask if user wants to save current data
    this.FileMenuNew_click(sender, e);
    Application.exit();
}
```

Having described the code that is invoked when an application is run, it is worth mentioning how a user runs your application. Visual J++ has rich deployment features, one of which is to create a Windows executable (.exe) file enabling users to run your WFC applications in a similar manner to other Windows application, assuming the WFC classes are installed on the user's computer. WFC classes are included with the latest Virtual Machine for Java which can be redistributed.

Anatomy of a Visual J++ Form Template

A basic WFC form is a public class extending the Form class with a default constructor and an initForm method. When the Form class is instantiated, the class constructor calls the initForm method, which is where the Forms Designer puts all the code used to initialize the form and control properties. Other code specific to your application follows the call to initForm in the constructor. In the MyNotepad application, the title for the application is set here (although it could have just as well been set in the form's Properties window). The constructor for the MyNotepad application is:

```
public MyNotepad()
{
    // Required for Visual J++ Form Designer support
    initForm();
    this.setBounds(100, 100, 300, 300);
    this.setText("Untitled - MyNotepad");
}
```

The Visual J++ Forms Designer adds declarations for any added controls in the main body of the class just before the initForm method. For example, here are the declarations for the objects that make up the MyNotepad.java form:

```
/**
 * NOTE: The following code is required by the Visual J++ Forms
 * Designer. It can be modified using the Form editor. Do not
 * modify it using the Text editor.
 */

Container components = new Container();
MainMenu Menu = new MainMenu();
MenuItem FileMenu = new MenuItem();
MenuItem FileMenuNew = new MenuItem();
MenuItem FileMenuOpen = new MenuItem();
MenuItem FileMenuSave = new MenuItem();
MenuItem FileMenuSaveAs = new MenuItem();
MenuItem FileMenuExit = new MenuItem();
MenuItem HelpMenu = new MenuItem();
MenuItem HelpMenuAbout = new MenuItem();
Edit editbox = new Edit();

private void initForm()
{
    . . .
```

The Visual J++ Forms Designer creates this declaration code as well as the code in the initForm method that sets properties of the form and the controls placed on the form. The infrastructure for handling events is also tightly integrated with the Forms Designer, which can generate event handler mappings in the initForm method.

The first two statements in the initForm method demonstrate how the Forms Designer sets properties on an object (in this case setting the menu item Text property to "&New") and uses the object's addOnClick method to establish a click event handler for the object.

```
private void initForm()
{
    FileMenuNew.setText("&New");
    FileMenuNew.addOnClick(new EventHandler(this.FileMenuNew_click));
```

Handling Events

Most of the code in the MyNotepad application occurs in the event handler methods that are called when menu items are clicked. The Forms Designer makes it easy to create the skeleton event handlers for events generated by controls on the form. For example, to add a handler method for menu click events, you just double-click the menu item on the form. (While double-clicking directly on a button or a menu item produces the click event handlers, you can just as easily create hander skeleton code for other events by using the Events tab in the Properties window).

The Forms Designer then adds a skeleton event handler method, in which you can add code, to your form's class, and inserts a MenuItem.addOnClick call for the appropriate MenuItem class in initForm.

For example, when you click a menu item named FileMenuNew, the following line is added to initForm and a method called FileMenuNew_click is added to your class:

```
FileMenuNew.addOnClick(new EventHandler(this.FileMenuNew_click));
```

The MenuItem.addOnClick method takes an EventHandler object. The EventHandler object is created with a reference to the method to call when that menu item is clicked. Essentially, the MenuItem object monitors mouse clicks and calls each event handler added to it, using the delegate, when the event occurs.

All event handler objects are delegates; the difference between them is the event object they pass to the handler. An EventHandler delegate passes an Event object, which contains information about the event. But a KeyEventHandler, for example, passes a KeyEvent object that extends Event for keydown and keyup events. (KeyEvent contains an extra field specifying the UNICODE character and whether it was combined with a CTRL, SHIFT, or ALT key.)

Most WFC programmers need to know little about delegates because event handlers already exist in the WFC packages for the events they care about and the code to add them is generated by the Forms Designer for the most part.

The following is the event handler in the MyNotepad application that handles the selection of this particular menu item:

```
private void FileMenuNew_click(Object sender, Event e)
{
    // If edit control contains text, check if it should be saved
    if (editbox.getText().length() != 0) {
        // Open NewDialog class as a modal dialog
        int result = new NewDialog().showDialog(this);
        // Retrieve result
        // If Yes button was clicked open Save As dialog box
        if (result == DialogResult.YES)
            this.FileMenuSaveAs_click(sender, e);
```

```
    // If No button was clicked clear edit control and set title
    else if (result == DialogResult.NO) {
        editbox.setText("");
        this.setText("Untitled - MyNotepad");
    }
  }
}
```

Of course, the Forms Designer creates just the skeleton event handler. The code that opens the custom modal dialog box was added manually.

Implementing a Modal Dialog Box

In the MyNotepad application, when a user clicks New on the File menu, the code in this event handler determines if there is text in the edit control. If so, it opens a modal dialog box that displays a message asking the user if they want to save the text. If the user clicks the Yes button, the MyNotepad.FileMenuSaveAs_click method is called, which allows the user to choose a file and save the current text. If the user clicks No, the edit control is cleared, and the title displayed on the main form becomes "Untitled – MyNotepad."

In the FileMenuNew_click method, the invocation of this dialog box and retrieval of the dialog result is done in one line as follows:

```
int result = new NewDialog().showDialog(this);
```

While the modal dialog box is open, the dialog result value can be set from within the dialog form. The DialogResult class contains integer constants used for this purpose, but any integer can be returned. The button's dialogResult properties were used in this case, which accomplishes the same purpose of setting the DialogResult value.

As an example, clicking the yesButton control sets DialogResult.Yes. This result is then returned from the showDialog method in the owner class when the dialog box is closed. The integer result returned by showDialog is then used to determine what action to take.

The NewDialog.java form was created as a new form using the same Form template used by the main application form. Note the main method is not required for modal dialog boxes and was removed from this example (leaving it in does not cause errors, but is not considered good practice). Also, extraneous template comments for this method were removed.

Using a Message Box as a Modal Dialog Box

You can also use a message box instead of a custom modal dialog box for simple cases. The click event handler for the About MyNotepad menu item on the Help menu uses a MessageBox object as follows:

```
private void HelpMenuAbout_click(Object sender, Event e)
{
MessageBox.show("Version: Visual J++ 6.0", "MyNotepad");
}
```

Implementing File Dialog Boxes and File I/O

The remaining code of interest in this application has to do with file I/O and using File Open and File Save dialog boxes. It demonstrates how the WFC classes simplify the job of locating, opening, reading from, and writing to files. The following is a brief summary of the WFC classes used for doing this.

In the WFC class hierarchy, both the com.ms.wfc.ui.OpenFileDialog and com.ms.wfc.ui.SaveFileDialog classes extend com.ms.wfc.ui.FileDialog. FileDialog extends CommonDialog, which is a wrapper for the Win32 common dialog API. All common dialogs are set up with properties such as setTitle and setFilter, and are run by calling the showDialog method. These dialog boxes enable users to choose a file name for opening or saving a file.

The com.ms.wfc.io package contains stream-based I/O classes. The File class, which extends DataStream, contains methods for file I/O. In the case of the MyNotepad application, all that is needed is to open a file, read all of it into the edit control (or write the contents of the edit control to the file), and then close the file.

In the MyNotepad application, all I/O and file dialog code is in the event handler methods for the Open, Save, and Save As items on the File menu. We'll look at just one of these, the Open menu event handler, because it encapsulates the common dialog and File I/O functionality. The code for FileMenuOpen_click is:

```
private void FileMenuOpen_click(Object sender, Event e)
{
    // Create an Open File dialog box
    OpenFileDialog ofd = new OpenFileDialog();
    // Set up filters and options
    ofd.setFilter("Text Docs (*.txt)|*.txt|All Files (*.*)|*.*");
    ofd.setDefaultExt("txt");
    // Run the Open File dialog box
    int OK = ofd.showDialog();
    // Check result of dialog box after it closes
    if (OK == DialogResult.OK) {
        // Retrieve the filename entered
        fileName = ofd.getFileName();
        // Open a File stream on that filename
        currentDoc = File.open(fileName);
        // Retrieve the length of the file
        int ilength = (int)currentDoc.getLength();
        // Read in ANSI characters to edit buffer
        editbox.setText(currentDoc.readStringCharsAnsi(ilength));
        // Close the file handle
        currentDoc.close();
        fileOpen=true;
        // Set the application's caption
        this.setText(File.getName(fileName) + " - MyNotepad");
    }
}
```

When a user clicks Open on the File menu, the FileMenuOpen_click event handler method is called. The first three lines of code in this method create an OpenFileDialog object and set the filters and extensions used by the dialog box. While these lines are manually coded here, you can do the same thing using the Forms Designer by adding an OpenFileDialog object to the form and setting its properties (the initialization code is then placed in the initForm method).

Finally, the OpenFileDialog.showDialog method is called to open the dialog box. When the dialog box closes, this method returns an integer equivalent to DialogResult.OK if the user clicks the OK button, and DialogResult.Cancel if the user clicks the Cancel button. If OK was clicked, the file name is retrieved from the OpenFileDialog object and passed to the File.open method, which returns a File stream opened on the file as read-write access to the file. File.open is a utility function that does the same thing as creating a File object with the following constructor:

```
File(fileName, File.OPEN, FileAccess.READWRITE, FileShare.NONE);
```

Sample Walkthrough Summary

A brief tutorial such as this cannot hope to cover every concept of a useful application, even one as simple as the MyNotepad application. However, the concepts of event handling, working with dialog boxes, and simple file I/O are common to most applications, and have been the main focus.

In this walkthrough we haven't touched on the code in the event handlers for the Save and Save As menu items. However, this code uses the same principles discussed elsewhere, so there should be no surprises when you look at the listings.

It's noteworthy that besides java.lang, none of the other standard Java packages were used in this application. Instead, packages such as com.ms.wfc.io and com.ms.wfc.ui were used to access the underlying power of the Windows API. This provides immense performance and usability gains when you know that your target environment will be a Win32 operating system.

Keep in mind the MyNotepad application was written as a demonstration vehicle. To keep it short and to the point, it doesn't provide much error checking or many of the features of Notepad or even JPad. However, with this quick tour completed you should be well on your way to creating your own Windows applications using Visual J++ and WFC.

Code Listings

The following code listings are provided for the two form-based classes in the MyNotepad application.

MyNotepad.java

```
/*********************************************************************
MyNotepad.java
This sample is provided as a companion to the Introduction to WFC
Programming topic in the Visual J++ documentation. Read the section
titled MyNotepad Sample Walkthrough in conjunction with this sample.

*********************************************************************/

import com.ms.wfc.app.*;
import com.ms.wfc.core.*;
import com.ms.wfc.ui.*;
import com.ms.wfc.io.*;

public class MyNotepad extends Form
{

    private File currentDoc; // the I/O file stream
    private String fileName; // the most recently-used file name
    private boolean fileOpen = false; // set true after file opened

    public MyNotepad()
    {
        // Required for Visual J++ Forms Designer support
        initForm();
        this.setBounds(100, 100, 300, 300);
        this.setText("Untitled - MyNotepad");
    }

    private void HelpMenuAbout_click(Object sender, Event e)
    {
        MessageBox.show("Version: Visual J++ 6.0", "MyNotepad");
    }

    private void FileMenuNew_click(Object sender, Event e)
    {
        // If edit control contains text, check if it should be saved
        if (editbox.getText().length() != 0) {
            // Open NewDialog class as a modal dialog
            int result = new NewDialog().showDialog(this);
            // Retrieve result
```

```
      // If Yes button was clicked open Save As dialog box
      if (result == DialogResult.YES)
         this.FileMenuSaveAs_click(sender, e);
      // If No button was clicked clear edit control and set title
      else if (result == DialogResult.NO) {
         editbox.setText("");
         this.setText("Untitled - MyNotepad");
      }
   }
}

private void FileMenuOpen_click(Object sender, Event e)
{
   // Create an Open File dialog box
   OpenFileDialog ofd = new OpenFileDialog();
   // Set up filters and options
   ofd.setFilter("Text Docs (*.txt)|*.txt|All Files (*.*)|*.*");
   ofd.setDefaultExt("txt");
   // Run the Open File dialog box
   int OK = ofd.showDialog();
   // Check result of dialog box after it closes
   if (OK == DialogResult.OK) {
      // Retrieve the filename entered
      fileName = ofd.getFileName();
      // Open a File stream on that filename
      currentDoc = File.open(fileName);
      // Retrieve length of file
      int ilength = (int)currentDoc.getLength();
      // Read in ANSI characters to edit buffer
      editbox.setText(currentDoc.readStringCharsAnsi(ilength));
      // Close the file handle
      currentDoc.close();
      fileOpen=true;
      // Set the application's caption
      this.setText(File.getName(fileName) + " - MyNotepad");
   }
}

private void FileMenuSave_click(Object sender, Event e)
{
   // If there has been a file opened or saved
   if (fileOpen){
      // Open the current file again
      currentDoc = File.open(fileName);
      // Write edit control contents to file
      currentDoc.writeStringCharsAnsi(editbox.getText());
      // Close file handle
      currentDoc.close();
   }
```

```
        else
            this.FileMenuSaveAs_click(sender, e);
    }

    private void FileMenuSaveAs_click(Object sender, Event e)
    {
        SaveFileDialog sfd = new SaveFileDialog();
        // Set the options
        sfd.setFileName (fileName);
        sfd.setTitle("Save Text File");
        sfd.setFilter("Text Docs (*.txt)|*.txt|All Files (*.*)|*.*");
        sfd.setDefaultExt("txt");
        // Run the dialog box
        int result = sfd.showDialog();
        if (result == DialogResult.OK ) {
            // Retrieve the filename entered in the dialog box
            fileName = sfd.getFileName();
            // Open a File stream with ability to create a file if needed
            currentDoc = new File(fileName, FileMode.OPEN_OR_CREATE);
            // Write the contents of the edit control to the file
            currentDoc.writeStringCharsAnsi(editbox.getText());
            // Close the file handle
            currentDoc.close();
            fileOpen = true;
            // Set the app's caption using the filename minus its path
            this.setText(File.getName(fileName) + " - MyNotepad");
        }
    }

    private void FileMenuExit_click(Object sender, Event e)
    {
        // Call the new file handler to invoke NewDialog
        // to ask if user wants to save current data
        this.FileMenuNew_click(sender, e);
        Application.exit();
    }

    /**
     * NOTE:  The following code is required by the Visual J++ Forms
     * Designer. It can be modified using the Form editor. Do not
     * modify it using the Text editor.
     */

    Container components = new Container();
    MainMenu Menu = new MainMenu();
    MenuItem FileMenu = new MenuItem();
    MenuItem FileMenuNew = new MenuItem();
    MenuItem FileMenuOpen = new MenuItem();
    MenuItem FileMenuSave = new MenuItem();
```

```
MenuItem FileMenuSaveAs = new MenuItem();
MenuItem FileMenuExit = new MenuItem();
MenuItem HelpMenu = new MenuItem();
MenuItem HelpMenuAbout = new MenuItem();
Edit editbox = new Edit();

private void initForm()
{
    FileMenuNew.setText("&New");
    FileMenuNew.addOnClick(new EventHandler(this.FileMenuNew_click));

    FileMenuOpen.setText("&Open");
    FileMenuOpen.addOnClick(new EventHandler(this.FileMenuOpen_click));

    FileMenuSave.setText("&Save");
    FileMenuSave.addOnClick(new EventHandler(this.FileMenuSave_click));

    FileMenuSaveAs.setText("Save &As");
    FileMenuSaveAs.addOnClick(new
        EventHandler(this.FileMenuSaveAs_click));

    FileMenuExit.setText("E&xit");
    FileMenuExit.addOnClick(new EventHandler(this.FileMenuExit_click));

    FileMenu.setMenuItems(new MenuItem[] {
                        FileMenuNew,
                        FileMenuOpen,
                        FileMenuSave,
                        FileMenuSaveAs,
                        FileMenuExit});
    FileMenu.setText("&File");

    HelpMenuAbout.setText("&About MyNotepad...");
    HelpMenuAbout.addOnClick(new
        EventHandler(this.HelpMenuAbout_click));

    HelpMenu.setMenuItems(new MenuItem[] {
                        HelpMenuAbout});
    HelpMenu.setText("&Help");

    Menu.setMenuItems(new MenuItem[] {
                    FileMenu,
                    HelpMenu});

    this.setText("MyNotepad");
    this.setVisible(false);
    this.setAutoScaleBaseSize(13);
    this.setClientSize(new Point(302, 314));
    this.setMenu(Menu);
```

```
        editbox.setDock(ControlDock.FILL);
        editbox.setFont(new Font("Fixedsys", 8.0f,
            FontSize.POINTS, FontWeight.NORMAL, false, false, false,
            CharacterSet.DEFAULT, 0));
        editbox.setSize(new Point(302, 314));
        editbox.setTabIndex(1);
        editbox.setText("");
        editbox.setMultiline(true);
        editbox.setScrollBars(ScrollBars.VERTICAL);

        this.setNewControls(new Control[] {
                            editbox});
    }


    /**
     * The main entry point for the application.
     *
     * @param args Array of parameters passed to the application
     * via the command line.
     */
    public static void main(String args[])
    {
        Application.run(new MyNotepad());
    }
}
```

NewDialog.java

```
/*********************************************************************
NewDialog.java
This sample is provided as a companion to the Introduction to WFC
Programming topic in the Visual J++ documentation. Read the section
titled MyNotepad Sample Walkthrough in conjunction with this sample.

This form represents a simple modal dialog box.

*********************************************************************/


import com.ms.wfc.app.*;
import com.ms.wfc.core.*;
import com.ms.wfc.ui.*;

public class NewDialog extends Form
{
```

```
public NewDialog()
{
   // Required for Visual J++ Forms Designer support
   initForm();
}

/**
 * NOTE: The following code is required by the Visual J++ Forms
 * Designer. It can be modified using the Form editor. Do not
 * modify it using the Text editor.
 */

Container components = new Container();
Label label1 = new Label();
Label label2 = new Label();
Button yesButton = new Button();
Button noButton = new Button();
Button cancelButton = new Button();
PictureBox pictureBox1 = new PictureBox();

private void initForm()
{
   // NOTE:  This form is storing resource information in an
   // external file. Do not modify the string parameter to any
   // resources.getObject() function call. For example, do not
   // modify "foo1_location" in the following line of code
   // even if the name of the Foo object changes:
   // foo1.setLocation((Point)resources.getObject("foo1_location"));

   IResourceManager resources = new
           ResourceManager(this, "NewDialog");
   label1.setLocation(new Point(90, 20));
   label1.setSize(new Point(210, 20));
   label1.setTabIndex(0);
   label1.setTabStop(false);
   label1.setText("The text in the file may have changed.");

   label2.setLocation(new Point(90, 40));
   label2.setSize(new Point(190, 20));
   label2.setTabIndex(1);
   label2.setTabStop(false);
   label2.setText("Do you want to save the changes?");

   yesButton.setLocation(new Point(20, 90));
   yesButton.setSize(new Point(80, 30));
   yesButton.setTabIndex(2);
   yesButton.setText("&Yes");
   yesButton.setDialogResult(DialogResult.YES);
```

```
noButton.setLocation(new Point(110, 90));
noButton.setSize(new Point(80, 30));
noButton.setTabIndex(3);
noButton.setText("&No");
noButton.setDialogResult(DialogResult.NO);

cancelButton.setLocation(new Point(200, 90));
cancelButton.setSize(new Point(80, 30));
cancelButton.setTabIndex(4);
cancelButton.setText("&Cancel");
cancelButton.setDialogResult(DialogResult.CANCEL);

this.setText("MyNotepad");
this.setAcceptButton(yesButton);
this.setAutoScaleBaseSize(13);
this.setCancelButton(cancelButton);
this.setClientSize(new Point(297, 136));

pictureBox1.setLocation(new Point(20, 20));
pictureBox1.setSize(new Point(50, 50));
pictureBox1.setTabIndex(5);
pictureBox1.setTabStop(false);
pictureBox1.setText("");

pictureBox1.setImage((Bitmap)resources.getObject
    ("pictureBox1_image"));

this.setNewControls(new Control[] {
                    pictureBox1,
                    cancelButton,
                    noButton,
                    yesButton,
                    label2,
                    label1});
    }

}
```

CHAPTER 12

WFC Programming Concepts

Windows Foundation Classes for Java (WFC) provides a framework of Java packages that support components targeted for the Windows operating system and the Dynamic HTML object model. WFC is tightly integrated with the Visual J++ development environment and provides a full set of Windows controls written in Java. Building a Java application for Windows is made much easier by this tight integration and the support of features such as IntelliSense, the Forms Designer, the Application Wizard, and the Object Browser. While these Visual J++ features put you well on your way to creating applications, you'll probably want to understand the structure and logic behind the packages and classes that make up WFC.

The purpose of this section is to provide a conceptual framework for the WFC packages and classes and to explain some of the fundamental WFC models. Many of the packages exist as infrastructure for the component model and can be ignored by developers focusing on using the WFC controls. Other packages are most easily accessed from the Visual J++ Forms Designer. When you start exploring the WFC library, you'll want to know which packages and classes are important for your particular application.

The following subjects are covered in this chapter:

- "WFC Packages" provides a high-level overview of the main packages that make up WFC.

- "Working with WFC Visual Components" describes the controls, forms, and graphical objects in WFC, which include the following:

  - Windows Visual Components

  - Dynamic HTML Visual Components

- "Handling Events in WFC" describes the use of delegates for handling events.

- "Localizing Your Application" describes the Visual J++ and WFC support and methodology for localizing your project in various languages.

- "Using WFC Application Services" describes some of the core application features and includes the following subtopics:

  - Starting and Quitting an Application

  - Handling Application Events

  - Accessing System Information

  - Performing Clipboard and Drag-and-Drop Operations

- "Using Java Threads with WFC" describes the threading model for WFC and includes the following subtopics:

  - Mixing Java and Win32 Threading Models

  - Creating and Exiting a Thread

  - Using Thread Storage

  - Working with Thread Exceptions

WFC Packages

The basic foundation blocks of WFC are Windows and Dynamic HTML. WFC is rooted firmly in the Win32 Windows programming model, enabling you to use Java to write Windows-based applications that take advantage of Windows user-interface controls, events, and system services. WFC is also rooted in the Dynamic HTML object model, which enables you to create both client and server HTML pages that use the power of Dynamic HTML directly from Java.

At the heart of these technologies are native dynamic-link libraries (DLLs) that provide the core API of the WFC infrastructure. These libraries are made available to the Java language thanks to two different technologies: the JActiveX tool and J/Direct. If the DLL represents a COM/ActiveX component, JActiveX creates wrapper classes that map the COM objects to Java objects. If the DLL is not COM-based, J/Direct is used to call directly into the DLL and to marshal the data types between Java and the native language of the DLL (such as C or C++). Both these technologies take advantage of the built-in support and synergy of the JVC compiler and the Microsoft Virtual Machine for Java.

This is mostly important to know because several WFC packages are composed entirely of either COM wrapper classes (produced by JActiveX) or J/Direct classes. These classes have methods that map directly to the underlying API; they are not documented in the WFC Reference because they are not typically called directly. However, they are discussed as support classes for other packages.

Not including the native API support packages, there are seven main packages in WFC.

Package	Description
com.ms.wfc.app	Base classes that encapsulate Windows application operations. The Visual J++ form component template uses the services of this class. In addition to the basic Windows message handling structure, there is support for Windows features such as the Clipboard, the registry, threads, window handles, system information, and so on.
com.ms.wfc.core	Base classes for the component model. This package includes support for containers, events, exceptions, properties, and the infrastructure for interoperating with features in Visual J++ such as the Forms Designer.

(continued)

Package	Description
com.ms.wfc.data	Active Data Objects (ADO) Java classes that enable data access and data binding. This package also includes com.ms.wfc.data.ui, the package that provides the base classes for the data-bound controls in WFC.
com.ms.wfc.html	Classes used to implement Dynamic HTML in Java. These classes provide both client- and server-side support.
com.ms.wfc.io	Classes used to access data streams, implementing a complete package for reading and writing serial streams, for file access, and for mapping between differing types of data streams.
com.ms.wfc.ui	Core classes for the controls that ship with WFC. These classes also provide access to the Windows Graphics API.
com.ms.wfc.util	Utility classes for various forms of sorting, implementing hash tables, and so on.

The following are the core native API support classes in WFC.

Package	Description
com.ms.wfc.ax	Provides Java wrapper classes for the ActiveX interfaces.
com.ms.wfc.html.om	Provides Java wrapper classes for the Dynamic HTML object model.
com.ms.wfc.ole32	Provides Java wrapper classes for OLE services.
com.ms.wfc.win32	Provides Java wrapper classes for Win32 API.

Working with the Visual Components of WFC

While there are some differences in the WFC visual components of Win32 and Dynamic HTML (DHTML) applications, there are many more similarities. These similarities enable the WFC component model to easily serve both types of applications. For example, both the Win32 and DHTML models include basic control types, such as edit boxes, check boxes, buttons, radio buttons, and combo boxes. For the most commonly used controls in Win32, there is usually a DHTML control with the same name prefaced by the letters "Dh" (for example, the com.ms.wfc.ui.Edit class has a corresponding com.ms.wfc.html.DhEdit class). Fonts, color constants, and most event types are also shared between the Win32 and DHTML models.

Of course, there are also components that are specific to each model, such as tables for DHTML or list view controls for Win32 components.

Probably the most notable difference between the WFC Win32 and DHTML components is that the DHTML components are not available from the Forms Designer. This means you must create, add, and modify DHTML elements in the code editor; however, the underlying Java code looks very similar in both models.

Windows Visual Components

The WFC framework is rooted in its visual components: WFC is integrated with Visual J++, a visual development tool, and sits on top of the Win32 API for the Windows operating system. The main package in WFC that supports the visible components is com.ms.wfc.ui and the base class for most visual elements in WFC is com.ms.wfc.ui.Control. Most of the WFC controls extend this class, including the Form class, which is the visual container for controls.

The Control Class

The Control class contains all the essential base properties, methods, and logic for manipulating a Win32 window. These methods can be categorized as follows:

- Methods for setting and retrieving the control's properties, such as the size of the display and client rectangles, the foreground color, background color, associated brush, cursor, text, font, position, and so on. These methods have names that start with set or get (for example, setBrush and getBrush).

- Event methods. For every event that a control generates, there are three methods implemented in the control. For example, for the move event, there is an onMove method, which triggers the event, an addOnMove method, which assigns an event handler to the move event, and a removeOnMove method, which removes the event handler. The Control object handles most basic control events.

- Methods dealing with parent/child relationships of controls. For example, the add method adds a child control, and assignParent and getParent assign and retrieve the parent control. There are also methods for handling arrays of child controls.

- Methods affecting the layout, z-order, painting, and input focus of the control, such as bringToFront, sendToBack, updateZOrder, performLayout, focus, show, hide, update, invalidate, createGraphics, and createWindowGraphics.

- Low-level event-processing methods. At the Win32 level, windows receive messages from the system. In the Control class, every input message to a control has a protected process method (for example, processCmdKey, processCmdKeyEvent, or processDialogKey). These methods are important only if a control extending this base class wants to override them to do special processing.

- Methods relating to window handles, messages, and thread invocation. These are available for programmers experienced with the Win32 programming model. For example, createHandle, destroyHandle, getRecreatingHandle, fromHandle, fromChildHandle all deal with window handles, and sendMessage and reflectMessage allow the control access to the underlying window messages. For descriptions of the thread invocation methods, see "Using Java Threads with WFC," later in this chapter.

The Control class extends com.ms.wfc.core.Component class, which is the base class for all WFC components.

Using Forms

A form is the main visual element of an application or a custom dialog box associated with an application. The com.ms.wfc.ui.Form class serves as the foundation for forms in WFC.

The Visual J++ Forms Designer starts with the Visual J++ form template, which provides a class extending com.ms.wfc.ui.Form, and helps you to set properties on the form and add controls to it. The Form-derived class adds a method called main, not found in Form. The form is run when the com.ms.wfc.app.Application.run method is called from main and passed a new instance of the Form-based class (this code already exists in the template). For more information, see "Starting and Quitting an Application" in "Using WFC Application Services," later in this chapter. A Form-based class used as a modal dialog box can be run by calling the Form.showDialog method (showDialog also runs modal dialog boxes that are based on the com.ms.wfc.ui.CommonDialog box class). A Form-based modeless custom dialog box can be opened by calling the form's show method, which makes the form visible.

The Form class extends com.ms.wfc.ui.Control, so it has all the Control methods plus many of its own for handling its role as a container for controls and as a window. These include methods used to:

- Add and remove handlers for the active, closed, closing, deactivate, inputLangChange, inputLangChangeRequest, MDIChildActivate, menuComplete, menuStart, and ownedForm events.

- Set the form's window properties, for example, to set the form's initial maximized or visible state, start position and border style; or to determine whether the form has an automatic scroll bar, a control box, or a minimize box, and whether the form's icon is in the taskbar.

- Determine the relationship of menus, controls, or other forms placed on the form, such as setting the main menu, arranging controls, supporting multiple document interface (MDI) forms, or determining whether the form receives all the control's key events.

- Set properties when the form is used as a modal dialog box and to run and retrieve results from a dialog box when the form is an application. This includes methods to set the Accept, Cancel, and Help buttons on a dialog box, to start a dialog box, and to set and retrieve the dialog result values returned by a modal dialog box.

This list is not comprehensive but provides a general idea of what a form is. One other class in the com.ms.wfc.ui package extends Form, and that is the UserControl class. UserControl is a class for creating your own composite Form-based controls that you can install in the Toolbox.

Overview of WFC Controls

All visible WFC controls reside in the com.ms.wfc.ui package. With over 240 classes in this package, it can be difficult to immediately determine which classes you want to use. Fortunately, the classes fall into several major categories, as follows:

- Classes that are controls in the Visual J++ Toolbox and directly extend the com.ms.wfc.ui.Control class or ultimately derive from the Control class.

- Classes that are controls in the Visual J++ Toolbox and use CommonDialog as a base class (this includes the CommonDialog class itself). CommonDialog wraps the Win32 CommonDialog API.

- Classes that contain constant values used by controls. These classes all extend com.ms.wfc.core.Enum.

- Classes that represent events and extend com.ms.wfc.core.Event or are event handler classes (delegates).

- Classes that represent intrinsic Windows graphical objects such as brushes, bitmaps, colors, cursors, fonts, pens, palettes, icons, regions, and images. For pointers to detailed information on using these objects, see the next section, "Accessing Graphical Services."

- Classes that, like Control, extend com.ms.wfc.core.Component but do not require the visual run time overhead of Control. Some examples are ColumnHeader, Menu (and MainMenu, ContextMenu, and MenuItem, which extend it), RebarBand, StatusBarPanel, ToolTip, and ImageList (and ImageListStreamer, which extends it).

- Miscellaneous classes that wrap other Windows interfaces; these include Help, which wraps the Windows Help engine, HTMLControl, which wraps a browser, and MessageBox, which wraps the Windows message box, among others.

The following com.ms.wfc.ui classes directly extend Control. Controls that extend these classes are listed in the description.

Class	Description
Animation	Encapsulates a Windows animation control, a rectangular control that plays an Audio-Video Interleaved (AVI) animation file.
AxHost	Wraps an ActiveX control and exposes the control as a WFC control.
Button	Encapsulates a Windows button control.
Checkbox	Encapsulates a Windows check box control, which is a labeled box that is checked or unchecked to select or clear an option.
ComboBox	Encapsulates the Windows combo box control.
DateTimePicker	Encapsulates a Windows date and time picker control, which allows users to specify date and time information.
Edit	Encapsulates a Windows edit control, which is a rectangular control that the user can enter text into.
Form	Represents the basic top-level window.
GroupBox	Encapsulates a group box control, which is a rectangle that contains other controls.
Label	Encapsulates the Windows label control, which displays a string of text that the user cannot edit.
ListBox	Encapsulates the Windows list box control, which displays a list from which the user can select one or more items. ListItem is used with this class. The CheckedListBox control extends this class.
ListView	Encapsulates the Windows list view control, which displays a collection of items, each consisting of an icon (from an image list) and a label.
MDIClient	Represents a window that contains MDI child windows.
MonthCalendar	Encapsulates a Windows month calendar control, which provides a simple calendar interface from which the user can select a date.
Panel	Represents a container you can use to parent other controls visually. The TabPage class extends Panel.
PictureBox	Encapsulates a Windows PictureBox control used to contain bitmaps.
ProgressBar	Encapsulates the Windows ProgressBar control, which dynamically tracks the progress of an operation by moving a bar.
RadioButton	Encapsulates a Windows radio button (or option button) control, which displays an option that can be selected or cleared.
Rebar	Encapsulates a rebar control, which contains other controls within moveable, resizable bands. RebarBand is used with this class.

(continued)

(continued)

Class	Description
RichEdit	Encapsulates a Windows RichEdit control.
ScrollBar	Represents the base class for scroll bar controls. HScrollBar and VScrollBar extend ScrollBar.
Splitter	Encapsulates the splitter control, which allows the user to resize docked controls at run time.
StatusBar	Encapsulates the Windows status bar control. StatusBarPanel is used with this class.
TabBase	Defines the base class that contains common functionality for Tab classes controls. TabControl (which uses TabPage) and TabStrip (which uses TabItem) extend this class.
ToolBar	Encapsulates the ToolBar custom control. ToolbarButton is used with this class.
TrackBar	Encapsulates a Windows trackbar control (also known as a slider control), which contains a slider for selecting a value in a range.
TreeView	Encapsulates a Windows tree view control. TreeNode is used with this class.
UpDown	Encapsulates the up-down control (sometimes called a spinner control).

Accessing Graphical Services

In the WFC environment, applications perform graphical operations by using the Graphics object, which encapsulates the native drawing capabilities of the Windows operating system. This object provides flexible support for the most commonly used drawing operations, including displaying images and icons and drawing lines, polygons, and text.

The Graphics object performs its work by wrapping a Windows device context, a system data structure that defines system graphical objects, their associated attributes, and the graphic modes affecting output to a device. Because you can retrieve the device context that underlies a Graphics object, you can use the Graphics object seamlessly with native Win32 drawing routines.

All WFC objects that extend the Control object support creating a Graphics object through the createGraphics method. In addition, all objects that extend the Image object, such as Bitmap, Icon, and Metafile, support the creation and retrieval of their associated Graphics object through the getGraphics method.

For more information on how to use this object, see Chapter 15, "Graphical Services."

Dynamic HTML Visual Components

Dynamic HTML elements make up the second set of visual components in WFC. The controls in com.ms.wfc.html are based on the Dynamic HTML object model. The classes in com.ms.wfc.html are used to create new elements and also to bind to existing elements on an HTML page. These components can be created and manipulated on a client browser or on a server, which sends them to a client browser. This object model exists on several platforms. Therefore, it is not fundamentally rooted in Win32, although user interface controls tend to be similar because the standard set of buttons, list boxes, radio buttons, and so on, are present on both.

Both sets of WFC controls (Win32 and Dynamic HTML) have a similar base because they both ultimately derive from com.ms.wfc.core.Component. Components are elements that can be hosted in a container and support the IComponent interface, which has methods for siting the component. How components and containers are hooked up is of little concern to most programmers using WFC; however, because elements from both com.ms.wfc.html and com.ms.wfc.ui are based on components, they exhibit similar characteristics. For example, all components are added to their parent containers using the add method.

For a better understanding of how to use the com.ms.wfc.html package, see Chapter 14, "Programming Dynamic HTML in Java."

Handling Events in WFC

The Control base class and classes that extend it, such as buttons and edit boxes, expose standard Windows events such as click, keyPress, mouseMove, dragDrop, and others. You can work with an event in your application using *delegates*. You do not have to understand delegates in great detail to write event handlers in an application. However, understanding how to create and use delegates is useful if you are building controls, working with other applications that trigger events, or are using threads with WFC components. It is also interesting if you want to understand the details of the Java code created by the Forms Designer. This section provides some background on delegates and then addresses the practical aspects of handling events.

What is a delegate? A delegate declaration defines a class that extends com.ms.lang.Delegate. The JVC compiler also recognizes delegate as a keyword, providing a shortcut for creating a delegate-based class. A delegate instance can call a method on an object and pass data to that method. Most importantly, the delegate is isolated from the object it refers to and needs to know nothing about it. Therefore, it is ideal for "anonymous invocation." In other languages, this functionality is implemented as a function pointer. However, unlike function pointers, delegates are object-oriented, type-safe, and secure.

In WFC, delegates are most often used to bind events to handler methods, such as a click event on a button control to a handler method in your class. When the event occurs, the control invokes the delegate, passing it any event information. The delegate, in turn, calls the registered handler method and passes the event data. You can also use delegates to bind one event to more than one method (called *multicasting*); when the event occurs, each delegate in the list is called in the order in which they were added. Conversely, delegates from different events can be assigned the same handler method (for example, a toolbar button and a menu item can both call the same handler).

To work with events in your application, you use a delegate to register for notification when that event occurs for a specific control. To register, call the addOn<*event*> method of a control, where <*event*> is the name of the event you want to handle. For example, to register for the click event of a button, you call the button object's addOnClick method.

The addOn<*event*> method takes as a parameter an instance of a delegate, typically an existing WFC delegate that is associated with specific event data. In the addOn<*event*> call, the delegate instance is created with a reference to the method you want to bind the event to. The following example shows how you would bind the event handler "btnOK_Click" (in the current class) to the click event of a button called btnOK.

```
Button btnOK = new Button();
btnOk.addOnMouseClick( new EventHandler( this.btnOK_Click ));
```

For most events, you can create and pass an instance of the generic EventHandler delegate, which passes a generic Event object. However, some events use special event handler classes when they include extra, event-specific information. For example, mouse movement events typically include information such as the mouse cursor location. To get this type of information, you create and pass an instance of the MouseEventHandler class, which passes a MouseEvent object to the handler. Keyboard events require the KeyEventHandler to get information about the status of SHIFT keys, and so on (this handler passes a KeyEvent object).

All WFC event handler delegate classes extend com.ms.lang.Delegate. Most of them are in the com.ms.wfc.ui package with names that end in *EventHandler*. All WFC events extend com.ms.wfc.core.Event, have names that end in *Event*, and can be found in the com.ms.wfc.ui package.

> **Tip** In the Forms Designer, you can use Events view in the Properties window to bind an event to a specific method. The Forms Designer then creates the appropriate addOn<*event*> method and the skeleton handler for you.

When the delegate calls your handler, it passes two parameters. The first parameter is a reference to the object that originated the event. The second is an event object that can contain information about the event. A handler for the delegate from the preceding example might look like this:

```
private void btnOK_Click(Object source, Event e) {
    if (source instanceof Button) {
        String buttonName = ((Button)source).getText();
        MessageBox.show("You clicked button " + buttonName);
    }
}
```

If you used the generic EventHandler class to bind to your method, the Event object
in your handler will not contain any interesting information. But if extra information is
available for the event, you can extract it from the specific event object. The following
is what the delegate and handler might look like for a mouse movement event. The
MouseEvent object exposes properties that allow you to get the mouse position.

```
// This is the request for notification
Button btnTest = new Button();
// Note that the addOn<event> method uses the MouseEventHandler class
btnTest.addOnMouseMove( new MouseEventHandler(this.btnTestMouseMove));

// This is the handler for the mouse movement event
private void btnTestMouseMove(Object source, MouseEvent e){
    edit1.setText( e.x + ", " + e.y);
}
```

If you want to handle events for multiple controls or multiple events for the same control,
you request a separate notification for each control/event combination. Multiple notifications
can specify the same handler; for example, all the buttons on a toolbar might call the same
handler for their click event. You can use the source object passed to the event handler to get
details about which button was clicked. (Typically, you cast the object passed to the handler
into the appropriate class to be able to invoke methods from the appropriate class.)

The following example shows code that defines buttons for a toolbar and requests
notification for their click events, along with the method used to handle them.

```
private void initEventHandlers() {
    Button buttonNew = new Button();
    Button buttonSave = new Button();
    Button buttonExit = new Button();
    // All events are routed to the same handler
    buttonNew.addOnClick( new MouseEventHandler( this.toolbarClick) );
    buttonSave.addOnClick( new MouseEventHandler( this.toolbarClick) );
    buttonExit.addOnClick( new MouseEventHandler( this.toolbarClick) );
}
// common event handler
private void toolbarClick( Object source, Event e){
    String buttonName;
    if (source instanceof Button) {
        buttonName = new String((Button)source).getText());
        MessageBox.show("You clicked button " + buttonName);
    }
}
```

Localizing Your Application

WFC and the Visual J++ Designer provide a simplified means for developing multilingual applications. A WFC application can be created in several localized language versions where the only difference between versions is a binary resource file. The naming convention for each resource file indicates the languages it supports, and the correct resources are loaded at run time according to the user's locale setting.

There are two parts to understanding localization concepts: design-time implementation and run time support. Certain properties of visual elements (forms and controls) are understood by Visual J++ to be localizable. At design time, Visual J++ is used to serialize these localizable properties to a binary resource file. For example, the text, font, and size of a control can change between language versions. At run time, when the application is loaded, the system loads the resources that correspond to the client thread after determining the user's locale.

To create a localized version of your application, design the visual layout using Visual J++, set the form's localizable property to true, and save the form. Visual J++ automatically creates a binary resource file and serializes all localizable properties to it.

When a form's localizable property is set to true, Visual J++ always saves resources to a single resource file with the name *Form*.resources, where *Form* is the name of the main form (for example, Form1.resources). Each version that you create will be saved to this resource file name. After creating each new version, you make a copy of this resource file and rename it to the appropriate language locale name using the standard Windows locale suffixes (for example, Form1_jpn_jpn.resources for a Japanese version) using the Windows Explorer or MS-DOS commands. The first local suffix specifies the primary language; the second specifies the secondary language.

> **Important** Be sure to save your original layout with a new name before laying out and saving any localized versions. This will be your master .resources file.

As an example scenario, assume you want to create American English, French, and Japanese versions of your application, whose main form is called Zippo.java. Also assume you start with the English version (although this is not necessary). First, lay out the form in English and set the localizable property to true. When you save the form, the file Zippo.resources is created. Now use the Windows Explorer or MS-DOS commands to make a copy of Zippo.resource and rename it as Zippo_enu_enu.resources (enu is the local suffix for American English, which is specified as the primary and secondary language.)

Next, in the Visual J++ Designer, change your default language to French, and lay out the controls with properties localized in French. When you are finished, save the form again, overwriting the previous version of Zippo.resources. Again, make a copy of Zippo.resources and rename it as Zippo_fra_fra.resources.

To test this version, in the Regional Settings dialog box in Control Panel, select the locale: French (Standard), in this case. (There is no need to restart your computer; the locale will be changed on the local thread.)

Using WFC Application Services

The com.ms.wfc.app package contains many classes that provide WFC application services. Many of these operations belong to the Application object itself. These operations have mostly to do with creating threads, starting the application, handling application events, and so on. Because understanding Java threads is important, it is discussed in its own section, "Using Java Threads with WFC," later in this chapter.

Other operations that qualify as application services pertain to those provided by the Win32 operating system. These include accessing the Windows registry, accessing Clipboard data, and retrieving system information, among other operations.

Starting and Quitting an Application

The Application.run method starts a WFC application. This is typically placed in the main method of the Form-based class that constitutes the main application form. Application.run has overloaded methods that take either no parameters or one parameter specifying the form class that represents the main window of the application. For example, the following is a typical form of this call:

```
public static void main(String args[])
{
    Application.run(new MyMainWindow());
}
```

If a form is passed to the run method, the form's visible property is automatically set to true, and an onClosed event handler is added to the form. The onClosed event handler calls the Application.exitThread method when the form is closed. If no form is passed, the application runs until Application.exit is called, shutting down all threads and windows on the application, or until exitThread is called, shutting down just the application's current thread.

Handling Application Events

You use the Application object to assign event handlers for five different events that occur in the context of the application: applicationExit, idle, settingChange, systemShutdown, and threadException. The following addOn methods can be called to define event handlers for these events.

Application Method	Description
addOnApplicationExit	Specifies a handler that is called when the application quits. You can clean up application resources here that will not be released by garbage collection. (To force the application not to quit, specify a handler for the form's closing event.)
addOnIdle	Specifies a handler that is called when the application's message queue is idle, for example, to perform background operations or application cleanup.
addOnSettingChange	Specifies a handler that is called when the user changes window settings.
addOnSystemShutdown	Specifies a handler that is called immediately before a system shutdown initiated by a user. This provides an opportunity to save data.
addOnThreadException	Specifies a handler that is called when an untrapped Java exception has been thrown, allowing the application to gracefully handle the exception. This event handler takes a com.ms.wfc.app.ThreadExceptionEvent object, which has one field that represents the exception thrown.

All these "addOn" methods have reciprocal "removeOn" methods to remove the event handler.

Accessing System Information

The Win32 system contains a large amount of information that is accessible to a WFC application or component. Most of this access is through classes in the com.ms.wfc.app package. Much of this information is stored in the Windows registry and accessed through the RegistryKey and Registry classes. Other system information, such as Windows display element sizes, operating system settings, network availability, and the hardware capabilities, are accessed using static methods in the com.ms.wfc.app.SystemInformation class. System time is available using the com.ms.wfc.app.Time class.

This section provides an overview of how a WFC application can access this system information.

Windows Registry Information

The RegistryKey class in the com.ms.wfc.app package contains methods to access the Windows system registry. Use the methods in this class to create and delete subkeys, to get the count and names of subkeys for the current key, and to retrieve, set, and delete values assigned to subkeys.

The com.ms.wfc.app.Registry class contains fields holding RegistryKey objects that represent the root keys of the registry (those starting with HKEY_). (Root RegistryKey objects can also be instantiated using the getBaseKey method.) Methods can be called on any RegistryKey object to enumerate and manipulate keys and key values in the subkey tree below the root object. For example, the following code obtains an array of subKey names under the HKEY_CURRENT_USER key and the number of names in that array:

```
int subKeyCount;
String[] subKeyNames;
subKeyNames = Registry.CURRENT_USER.getSubKeyNames();
subKeyCount = Registry.CURRENT_USER.getSubKeyCount();
```

Similarly, any subkey can be retrieved or set given its path, and subkey value names and data can be retrieved or set given the value name. The following example shows retrieving the most recently used file names in Visual Studio and displaying them in an edit box:

```
String path; // Holds the path name.
String[] valueNames; // Holds array of MRU file names in the key.
int valueCount; // The number of MRU file names in valueNames.
path = new  String("Software\\Microsoft\\VisualStudio\\6.0\\FileMRUList");
RegistryKey subKey = registry.CURRENT_USER.getSubKey( path );
// Get the file names and the number of file names.
valueNames = subKey.getValueNames();
valueCount = subKey.getValueCount();
if (valueCount > 0)
   for (int i = 0; i < valueCount; ++i){
      // Get the value, which is the actual file name.
      String value = new   String((String)subKey.getValue(valueNames[i]));
      // Concatenate the name ("1", "2", etc.) with the file name value.
      String valString = new String(valueNames[i] + "   " + value);
      // Add this to the edit box.
      edit1.setText(edit1.getText()+ valString +"\r\n");
   }
```

You can also create new keys, using the createSubKey method and set values in that key using the setValue method.

Locale Information

Locale information provides details about the language and regional settings on the user's computer. There are many characteristics about a language or region that are stored. These include the character set, international telephone codes, how monetary information is displayed, which calendar is used, the measurement system, and so on.

This information is typically set using the Regional Settings dialog box in Control Panel, but it is also available programmatically. In WFC this access is provided through the methods in the com.ms.wfc.app.Locale class and through the many subclasses of Locale that contain field constants that pertain to Locale methods. For details about setting and retrieving this information, see the methods in the Locale class.

Time Information

Another category of system information is time. The com.ms.wfc.app.Time class provides a Time object that has many capabilities, including capturing system time: the default constructor creates a Time object with the system date and time. Beyond retrieving system time information, the Time object is useful for doing many other things, such as comparing Date and Time objects, converting the time to various formats, and storing a Time object for later retrieval.

Time objects, once created, cannot be altered. However, the Time class provides many methods for creating new objects with offset time (such as addSeconds, addMinutes, addHours, addDays, and addYears). Also, there are many methods for retrieving just one of the properties of a Time object, such as the second, minute, hour, day, and so forth.

The Time object in WFC stores time as the number of hundred-nanosecond units since Jan 1, 100ad. The maximum value that can be stored in a WFC Time object is Dec 31, 10,000ad. Converting WFC Time objects to other formats (Strings, Variants, SYSTEMTIME, and so on) can cause loss of accuracy, and not all formats can store this wide of a range.

Do not confuse the Time class with another com.ms.wfc.app class called Timer. Timer is actually a control; however, it is not in the com.ms.wfc.ui package because it does not have a user interface.

Performing Clipboard and Drag-and-Drop Operations

The drag-and-drop feature in WFC is based on the Win32 (OLE) model, which implements a shortcut for copying and pasting data. When you use the Clipboard, you must perform several steps involving selecting the data, choosing Cut or Copy from the context menu, moving to the destination file, window, or application, and choosing Paste from the context menu. (The origin of the data is called the *source* and the destination is called the *target*.)

The drag-and-drop feature removes the necessity of using the context menu. Instead, it uses the action of pressing the left mouse button to capture the selected data in the source and releasing the button in the target to drop it. Drag-and-drop operations can transfer any data that can be placed on the Clipboard; consequently, the data formats for drag and drop are the same as those of the Clipboard. Data formats specify, for example, whether the data is text, bitmap, HTML, .wav, and so on. The com.ms.wfc.app.DataFormats class contains fields pertaining to each of the Clipboard formats. These field names (such as CF_TEXT) come straight from the Win32 constant names.

The data for Clipboard and drag-and-drop operations is stored in a com.ms.wfc.app class called DataObject, which implements the IDataObject interface. IDataObject defines methods for setting and retrieving the data, getting a list of data formats in the data object, and querying for the existence a specific data format.

To programmatically place data on and retrieve it from the Clipboard, use the static methods in com.ms.wfc.app.Clipboard. Clipboard.setDataObject takes an IDataObject and places it on the Windows Clipboard; Clipboard.getDataObject returns an IDataObject from the Clipboard. The target must make sure that the data format on the Clipboard is one that it can use. To do this, it should query the data object with the IDataObject.getDataPresent method, passing it a data format that it can accept; getDataPresent returns true if this type of data is present.

Implementing a Drop Source

For any WFC control component (based on com.ms.wfc.ui.Control), the Control.doDragDrop method is called to start the operation. This is typically done in response to the user's moving the mouse with the left button pressed. Therefore, the code is placed in a mouseMove event handler where the MouseEvent object is checked to see if the left button is down, indicating the start of a drag operation. For example, the following is an event handler for a list box control containing file names:

```
private void listFiles_mouseMove(Object source, MouseEvent e)
{
    //if the left button is down, do the drag/drop
    if(this.getMouseButtons()==MouseButton.LEFT)
    {
        String data = (String)listFiles.getSelectedItem();
        listFiles.doDragDrop( data, DragDropEffect.ALL);
    }
}
```

The doDragDrop method takes the data to be transferred and a com.ms.wfc.ui.DragDropEffect object. The DragDropEffect class contains the following constants that can be combined using the bitwise OR for the intended mode of the drag-and-drop operation.

DragDropEffect Method	Description
COPY	Specifies that data will not be removed from the source after the transfer.
MOVE	Specifies that data will be removed from the source after the transfer.
SCROLL	Specifies that data will be scrolled in the target after the transfer.
ALL	Specifies that data will be removed from the source after the transfer and scrolled into the target (essentially COPY | MOVE | SCROLL).
NONE	Specifies that no operation is performed.

The target that receives the data in the drag-drop operation receives the dragDrop event, which contains this DragDropEffect object, so it can easily determine the intent of the operation.

Implementing a Drop Target

The drop part of the drag-and-drop operation is handled as an event. The Control class provides the event handler infrastructure for these drag-and-drop events: dragDrop, dragEnter, dragLeave, and dragOver. You can use the following methods to specify handlers for these events.

Control Method	Description
addOnDragDrop	Specifies a handler for data that is dropped into your control or window (when the left mouse button is released).
addOnDragEnter	Specifies a handler for drop data as the cursor first enters the window.
addOnDragLeave	Specifies a handler for drop data as the cursor leaves the window.
addOnDragOver	Specifies a handler for drop data as the cursor is dragged across the window.

All these "addOn" methods have reciprocal "removeOn" methods to remove the event handler. As with all event handler addOn and removeOn methods in WFC, these methods take a delegate (in this case, DragEventHandler) that is created with the name of your handler method. For example, the following line adds the txtFile_dragDrop method as a dragDrop event handler:

```
txtFile.addOnDragDrop(new DragEventHandler(this.txtFile_dragDrop));
```

Of all the drag-and-drop events, the dragDrop event is the most commonly handled. Regardless of which of these events is handled, the code in the handler must do at least three things. It must first determine if it can accept the data format, and if so, it must then copy the data and optionally display it (or provide some user interface feedback that the data was dropped).

All data and information is passed in the DragEvent event. This contains, among other fields, a data field and an effect field. The DragEvent.data field contains an object that supports IDataObject that has methods to retrieve the data and the data formats and to query for the existence of a specific format.

Therefore, the handler must first call DragEvent.data.getDataPresent method with a format it will accept and then determine whether it holds that data type. If so, it can then call the DragEvent.data.getData method (passing in that data type) and retrieve the data. How the data is displayed is up to that control. The following example illustrates an edit control dragDrop event handler that displays text data dropped to it.

```
private void txtFile_dragDrop(Object source, DragEvent e)
{
    // If text is in the object, write it into the edit control.
    if (e.data.getDataPresent(DataFormats.CF_TEXT))
    {
        String filename=(String)e.data.getData(DataFormats.CF_TEXT);
        txtFile.setText(filename);
    }
}
```

Using Java Threads with WFC

Java is a free-threaded environment. This means that any object can call any other object, at any time, from any thread. Special care must be taken when writing objects so that their methods are atomic and thread-safe.

There are several classes that benefit from being free-threaded, and WFC has provided the locking code to make these objects thread-safe. These classes are as follows:

- com.ms.wfc.core.Component
- com.ms.wfc.core.Container
- com.ms.wfc.ComponentManager
- com.wfc.ui.Brush
- com.wfc.ui.Font
- com.wfc.ui.Pen

On the other hand, any object that derives from com.ms.wfc.ui.Control is apartment-threaded because of the Win32 window that is tied to each control. Additionally, most other objects in the com.ms.wfc.ui package are not synchronized, so they should also be considered to be apartment threaded. Likewise, the com.ms.wfc.io, com.ms.wfc.html, and com.ms.wfc.util packages are not thread-safe.

Mixing Java and Win32 Threading Models

WFC accesses native Win32 constructs (such as windows) from Java objects. The Win32 window manager is apartment-threaded, and Windows automatically marshals calls from one thread to another as needed. When a free-threaded object calls into an apartment-threaded object, the call must marshal to the object's apartment. This means that the free thread is blocked for a period of time while the apartment thread handles the request. Any other calls from free-threaded objects to the apartment call will block until the apartment call is free. Consequently, this can lead to deadlock situations.

So how do Java objects, which are inherently free thread work with WFC controls? Rather than hide when thread transitions occur, WFC makes it the programmer's responsibility to request the transition. The programmer can then design an algorithm in such a way as to prevent deadlocks. This can be done by invoking a delegate on the control's thread, which in turn calls the method specified in the delegate.

To execute a given delegate on the thread that created the control's window handle and contains the message loop, use the Control.invoke or Control.invokeAsync methods from the desired control. It is important to use the control's own thread in case the control needs to re-create its window handle for any reason. The invoke method causes the thread to call the specified callback method and wait for a return. The invokeAsync method causes the thread to call the callback method without waiting for reply. All exceptions on the invoked thread are passed on to the owning control in both cases.

You can also use the Control.createGraphics object to perform background painting and animation techniques on a ui.Graphics object. Whereas the Graphics object is apartment-threaded, the createGraphics call is entirely free-threaded. This allows one thread to create a graphics object for a control in another thread.

Creating and Exiting a Thread

Free-threaded threads can be created using the standard Java method of implementing the java.lang.Runnable interface.

This sample shows a class that implements Runnable and takes two controls (a trackbar and a label) as parameters to its constructor. From the thread's run method, it transitions to the trackbar's thread by calling the trackbar's invokeAsync method. InvokeAsync passes a delegate called tDelegate (an instance of com.ms.app.MethodInvoker) that specifies a callback method called tCallBack. Inside that method, the control's thread can safely manipulate the control's properties, in this case, changing the trackbar's tick style. This causes the trackbar's window handle to be re-created. If the thread was not transitioned as demonstrated here, the trackbar would be re-created on the new thread rather than on the thread containing the message loop; in this case, the control trackbar wouldn't receive any new messages and would fail to respond.

```java
import com.ms.wfc.app.*;
import com.ms.wfc.core.*;
import com.ms.wfc.ui.*;

/**
 * Runnable is the interface you need to implement to make a new
 * java thread
 */
public class RunnableClass implements Runnable
{
    final int SLEEP = 500;
    Label l;
    TrackBar tb;

    /**
     * This is the thread for our class.
     */
    Thread thread;

    /**
     * Makes a special delegate so WFC can call it from the control's
     * thread.
     */
    MethodInvoker tDelegate = new MethodInvoker(tCallback);

    /**
     * Make a new Java thread; tell it to begin running via the
     * start() method.
     */
    public RunnableClass (TrackBar tb, Label l)
    {
        this.l  = l;
        this.tb = tb;
        thread  = new Thread(this, "RunnableClass thread");
        thread.start();
    }
```

```java
public void run()
{
    while (true)
    {
        /**
         * Call the specified method from the label's thread.
         */
        tb.invokeAsync (tCallback);
        try
        {
            Thread.sleep (SLEEP);
        }
        catch (InterruptedException e)
        {
        }
    }
}

int nCount = 0;
int nTickStyles[] = {TickStyle.BOTH,
                     TickStyle.BOTTOMRIGHT,
                     TickStyle.NONE,
                     TickStyle.TOPLEFT};
/**
 * This code is executed on the trackbar's thread.
 */
private void tCallback()
{
    int nIndex = nCount % (nTickStyles.length);
    l.setText ("hello from tCallBack: " + nCount);
    tb.setTickStyle (nTickStyles [nIndex]);
    nCount++;

    int nValue = tb.getValue();
    if (nValue >= tb.getMaximum())
        tb.setValue(0);
    else
        tb.setValue (nValue + 1);
}

public void stopThread()
{
    thread.stop();
}
}
```

Exiting a thread in this case is just a matter of running the thread's stop method. In this example, the Form class that creates the RunnableClass object calls that object's stopThread method when it is disposed. The following code fragment demonstrates this.

```
...
import RunnableClass;

public class SimpleRunnable extends Form
{
    /**
     * This is the class that implements the Runnable interface.
     */
    RunnableClass runnableClass;

    public SimpleRunnable()
    {
        // Required for Visual J++ Forms Designer support.
        initForm();
        runnableClass = new RunnableClass (tb, 1);
    }

    public void dispose()
    {
        runnableClass.stopThread();
        super.dispose();
        components.dispose();
    }
    Container components = new Container();
    Edit eDescription = new Edit();
    TrackBar tb = new TrackBar();
    Label l = new Label();

    private void initForm()
    {
        // Code to initialize the controls omitted ...
    }

    public static void main(String args[])
    {
        Application.run(new SimpleRunnable());
    }
}
```

Alternately, to create a new application thread without having to implement the Java
Runnable interface or extend java.lang.Thread, you can use the Application.createThread
method. The createThread method takes a delegate as a parameter (MethodInvoker is often
used, but any delegate can be used). In this case, all logic can be contained in one class,
typically the Form-based class of the application. The following example code fragment
shows how this works.

```
import com.ms.wfc.app.*;
import com.ms.wfc.core.*;
import com.ms.wfc.ui.*;
```

```java
public class SimpleAppThread extends Form
{
    final int SLEEP = 700;
    Thread thread;

    // Specify the thread context to run a method on.
    MethodInvoker cbDelegate = new MethodInvoker( cbThrdCallback );

    public SimpleAppThread()
    {
        initForm();
        /**
         * Creates a new thread and runs the methodInvoker method
         * on the new thread.  The returned thread object is needed
         * so we can stop the thread when this form is closed (disposed).
         * Note that thread.start() is called automatically.
         */
        thread = Application.createThread (new MethodInvoker (this.methodInvoker));
    }

    private void methodInvoker()
    {
        while (true)
        {
            // cbThrdCallback is called on the check box's thread.
            cb.invoke (cbDelegate);
            try
            {
                Thread.sleep (SLEEP);
            }
            catch (InterruptedException e)
            {
            }
        }
    }

    int nCount = 0;
    /**
     * Thread callback that sets check box alignment property.
     * This code is to be executed on the check box's thread.
     */
    private void cbThrdCallback()
    {
        cb.setText ("threadCallback loop: " + nCount++);
        if (nCount % 2 == 0)
            cb.setTextAlign (LeftRightAlignment.LEFT);
        else
            cb.setTextAlign (LeftRightAlignment.RIGHT);
    }
```

```
public void dispose()
{
    thread.stop();
    super.dispose();
    components.dispose();
}

private void cbSuspend_click(Object sender, Event e)
{
    if (cbSuspend.getChecked())
    {
        cbSuspend.setText ("press to resume thread");
        thread.suspend();
    }
    else
    {
        cbSuspend.setText ("press to suspend thread");
        thread.resume();
    }
}

Container components = new Container();
CheckBox cbSuspend = new CheckBox();
CheckBox cb = new CheckBox();

private void initForm()
{
    // Code to initialize the controls here ...
}

public static void main(String args[])
{
    Application.run(new SimpleAppThread());
}
}
```

Here the thread is stopped by calling the thread's stop method from the form's dispose method. The thread is not in a separate class, so its methods can be called directly from the Form-based class.

The Application class also contains the Application.exitThread method, which closes the thread's message loop and shuts down all windows on the thread (note that it does not stop or exit the thread itself). By way of contrast, Application.exit closes message loops on all threads and closes all windows.

Using Thread Storage

The WFC Application class provides support for Thread Local Storage (TLS). Each thread can allocate a slot of memory for storing data that is specific to the thread. Calling Application.allocThreadStorage returns an index to that slot. To set a value in TLS, call the Application.setThreadStorage with the index and a value you want to set. To retrieve that value, call Application.getThreadStorage. Remember to free any allocated thread storage with a call to Application.freeThreadStorage.

Working with Thread Exceptions

The com.ms.wfc.app class provides a ThreadExceptionDialog class, which is automatically displayed whenever an unhandled exception occurs in a thread. You can gain control of exceptions by using the Application.addOnThreadException method to specify your own thread exception handler. The addOnThreadException method takes a ThreadExceptionEventHandler delegate, which is constructed with your event handler method and the ThreadExceptionEvent class.

Typically, a thread exception event handler queries the exception field of the ThreadExceptionEvent object passed to it to determine the next course of action. From this thread exception handler, you can run the ThreadExceptionDialog and retrieve the dialog results in the same way as any other WFC dialog box: use the Form.showDialog method to launch the dialog box, and compare the returned results with the com.ms.wfc.ui.DialogResult class fields.

CHAPTER 13

WFC Control Development

Visual J++ and WFC allow you to create controls that you can use in your Java applications, as well as in Visual Basic, Web pages, and any other host application that supports standard ActiveX controls. WFC provides classes that incorporate most of the functionality of your control, including facilities for designing and implementing properties, handling and invoking events, and so on.

Visual J++ also includes visual tools for creating composite controls — controls made up of multiple visual elements such as check boxes and list boxes. The visual tools allow you to design the layout of your control and generate the appropriate code that you can amend as required to implement the full functionality of your control.

For details about creating controls, see the sections listed in the following table.

For information about	See
The technology of controls in WFC, writing controls using code.	Writing WFC Controls
Using visual tools to create composite controls.	Creating Composite WFC Controls

Writing WFC Controls

WFC provides a rich framework to develop custom controls. The following figure shows the basic class hierarchy of visual controls in WFC.

```
...core.IComponent
  └...core.Component
     └...ui.Control
        ├...ui.Button
        └...ui.Form
           └...ui.UserComponent
```

The com.ms.wfc.ui.Control class is the base for all controls and provides most of the functionality for your control.

> **Note**   For composite controls — controls created by combining other controls and business logic — the primary WFC package you use is com.ms.wfc.ui. You can use visual tools to design composite controls. For more information, see "Creating Composite WFC Controls," later in this chapter.

When you write a control, you extend the base Control class, and then add the members you need. (Composite controls are created in the visual designer by extending UserControl.) You can also override members inherited from the Control class as needed. The following sections provide information about creating a control:

- **Creating a Basic Control**   How to subclass the Control class and expose your control in the design-time environment.

- **Defining Control Properties**   How to define and expose properties for your control, and how to specify custom editors for property values.

- **Working with Control Events**   How to create custom events for your control, and how to capture and use standard events.

- **Customizing a Control**   Managing the control's visual display, specifying verbs, and more.

- **Using Controls**   What you need to do to make your control available to host applications on other computers.

Creating a Basic Control

This section provides an overview of creating a control by walking you through the process. Here you will learn how to define a basic control and provide functionality for its base events.

Defining a Control

A custom control subclasses the WFC Control class. To make your control visible in the Toolbox inside Visual J++, you also need to extend the com.ms.wfc.ui.Control.ClassInfo class. The ClassInfo class contains metadata used to provide design-time information about a class and to browser component properties and events at run time. If you do not require that your control be visible in the Toolbox, do not extend com.ms.wfc.ui.Control.ClassInfo. However, you must still subclass Component.ClassInfo, which implements com.ms.wfc.core.IClassInfo. This inner class must be named ClassInfo.

> **Note**   The WFC Component Builder creates a skeleton control, including properties and methods, which you can fill in. The information in this section includes details about how a control is built to help you build a control manually and to explain what the builder does.

The following shows a skeleton control. If you compile it, the control is registered on your computer and becomes available in the Customize Toolbox dialog box:

```
// MyControl.java
import com.ms.wfc.ui.*;
import com.ms.wfc.core.*;

public class MyControl extends Control {

    public static class ClassInfo extends Control.ClassInfo {

    }

}
```

If you add an instance of this control to a form, you will see its properties and events in the Properties window. You can change these properties, and you can also see that the control already supports backColor, foreColor, anchor, dock, mouse events, focus, and more. The com.ms.wfc.ui.Control class defines the default implementation of these common properties and events.

Adding a Control Description

You can include a text description for controls exposed as ActiveX controls. Host applications can then query and display the description. To create a description, add a DescriptionAttribute object in the ClassInfo class. The following example shows how you can add a text description:

```
public static class ClassInfo extends Control.ClassInfo
{
    public void getAttributes(IAttributes attribs){
    super.getAttributes(attribs);
    attribs.add(new DescriptionAttribute("This describes MyControl"));
}
```

Providing Functionality for Class Events

The com.ms.wfc.ui.Control class exposes a common set of members with default functionality. For example, if you create a basic control as described earlier, a text property is available for it in the Properties window.

Typically, to add functionality to your control, you must override the members for that control exposed by the base class. Most events in WFC are exposed in their base class with a protected on<*eventname*> member, which lets subclasses override the event without having to attach event handlers. In your override code, you define the functionality you want for that event. Generally, you implement the default functionality of the member by calling the superclass's event. By placing the call to the superclass's event, you can specify the order in which the event is triggered.

Note There are additional methods for receiving events when you are not subclassing an event defined in the superclass. For more details, see "Working with Control Events," later in this chapter.

The following example illustrates how you can override the protected onPaint method to define what the control should display at run time. In the example, the superclass's event is called first to perform the superclass's own paint method. The control's own code displays the value of its text property by calling the drawString method of a Graphics object:

```
// MyControl.java
import com.ms.wfc.ui.*;
import com.ms.wfc.core.*;

public class MyControl extends Control {

    protected void onPaint(PaintEvent p) {

        super.onPaint(p);

        Graphics g = p.graphics;

        g.drawString(getText(), 0, 0);

    }


    public static class ClassInfo extends Control.ClassInfo {
    }
}
```

In this example, you display text by calling the control's getText method to retrieve the text stored in the control. When you compile and add your new version of the class, the control now contains whatever text you typed into the text property. Because com.ms.wfc.ui.Control provides a text property, there isn't really a need to create a new one.

The parameter for onPaint is a PaintEvent, which contains event-specific data. When you are subclassing a protected member, the object sending the event is implicitly known because the sender is *this* (the current instance of the class). The event data varies from event to event. In this case, the PaintEvent looks like this:

```
public class PaintEvent extends Event {
   // Graphics object with which painting should be done.
   public final Graphics graphics;

   // Rectangle into which all painting should be done.
   public final Rectangle clipRect;
}
```

The graphics member of the PaintEvent refers to a com.ms.wfc.ui.Graphics object. This is the WFC wrapper for a drawing surface, a Win32 device context. The Graphics object exposes methods to draw strings, lines, points, ellipsis, and so forth. You can change the values of the font, foreColor, and backColor properties, and these will display correctly, because the Graphics object that is passed in through the PaintEvent event is set up with the correct fonts and brushes based on the settings in the control. For more details about painting, see "Updating Visual Display," later in this chapter.

Working with Window Handles

The base Control class encapsulates a Win32 HWND (handle) through a private member that extends com.ms.wfc.app.Window. The Window class manages the subclassing of the window procedure for the HWND created for your control.

Whenever you request a handle with a call to Control.getHandle, the handle is created if needed or returned if it exists. When the handle is created, the Control class first calls the getCreateParams method to determine the correct window styles for creating the handle. If you want to specify window styles or extended window styles, you can override the getCreateParams method. Immediately after the handle is created, the createHandle event is fired. The destroyHandle event is fired immediately before the handle is destroyed. The handle is therefore valid during both the create and destroy handle events.

The lifetime of any given handle is determined by the implementation of your control. However, the lifetime of an instance of any control is not tied to the lifetime of a handle.

WFC allows you to manipulate controls in various ways that might require that the control be re-created in Windows. For example, you might be working with a control such as a ruler. When you change the ruler's units, this might result in the control being re-created, invalidating the HWND, as in the following example:

```
{
h = x.getHandle();
x.units = "points";  // change property that results in recreation
// h is now invalid
}
```

As a rule, it is safest when using a handle to get it immediately before using it.

You can request that your handle be re-created (destroyed and then immediately created again) by calling the recreateHandle method. If the recreateHandle method is called, then getRecreatingHandle will return true until the handle is created again. This allows you to place special logic in the destroyHandle event that retrieves state from the HWND during handle recreation. An example is a list box, where you might want to save all the items from the list box upon handle destruction if the handle is being re-created. If you need the window styles reapplied to the window, but you don't need the handle to be re-created, you can call updateStyles. This will call the getCreateParams method and reapply the style and extended style to the HWND.

Note that calling these functions will do nothing if the handle has not been created. This is useful in property setting methods, because you don't want to force handle creation, but might need to change the HWND if it has already been created. By convention, you should not force handle creation for simple property changes. Forcing handle creation early can be expensive because the user might set other properties that might require handle re-creation. It is best to require handle creation only to show a control visually, but not to adjust the properties.

Threading in WFC Controls

The Java language supports multithreading through a set of classes and APIs to control thread creation and execution. Win32 windows are inherently apartment threaded. That is, they can be created on any thread, but they cannot switch threads, and all function calls to that window must occur on its main thread. WFC controls (anything derived from com.ms.wfc.ui.Control) require this threading model, while most WFC components are free threaded.

The Control class provides two functions, invoke and invokeAsync, that will marshal any delegate onto the control's main window thread and execute it. If you attempt to call a function on a control that manipulates the underlying Win32 HWND, it will get marshaled to the correct thread by Windows. By calling the invoke function directly, you can batch up calls to the HWND and limit the number of expensive cross thread marshals that occur.

> **Note** The Windows message loop is tied to the thread that the HWND was created on. If the control's HWND is recreated on a new thread, the new thread won't receive messages any more. For more details, see "Using Java Threads with WFC," in Chapter 12, "WFC Programming Concepts."

Although most WFC components support free threading, most of the method calls are not synchronized. Synchronization is very expensive and should be done only when needed. For example, by synchronizing on the object and calling multiple methods, you will get substantial performance benefits.

Defining Control Properties

Most controls expose a set or properties that allow the user to determine the control's behavior and appearance. In WFC controls, you create properties as members with get and set functions. But WFC also provides classes and interfaces that help you integrate a control into design-time environments.

The following sections provide information about creating, exposing, and customizing properties in your control.

Creating and Exposing a Property

Defining a control property is similar to adding a property to any Java class. In addition, however, you add members to the ClassInfo class to make your property visible in the Properties window.

Adding a Property Definition

A property is stored in a private member variable of your control. You then provide a public get<*property*> method to expose the property value. If you intend to make the property read-write, you also provide a public set<*property*> method that takes a parameter containing the new property value.

Note   The WFC Component Builder will create property skeletons for you.

A simple integer property called myProp in the MyControl control might be implemented as in the following example:

```
public class MyControl extends Control{
    private int myProp = 0; // 0 is the default value
    public getMyProp(){
        return myProp;
    }
    public setMyProp( int newValue ){
        myProp = newValue;
    }
}
```

Note   The name used in the property definition should start with a lowercase letter, unless the first two letters are uppercase. The function names should have a capital letter immediately following the get or set. For example; text would have getText and setText, while MDIChild would have getMDIChild and setMDIChild.

Exposing a Property at Design Time

To make your property visible in the Properties window, you do the following:

- Create a static, final instance of the PropertyInfo class indicating the new property's class, name, and data type.

- Override the superclass's getProperties method, adding the superclass's existing properties and then your new property.

   Note   The getProperties method is one of several methods you can use to allow you to expose properties, events, extender, and class attributes. For details about other methods, see "Working with Control Events," later in this chapter.

The following example shows the ClassInfo class for the myProp property:

```
public static class ClassInfo extends Control.ClassInfo {
    public static final PropertyInfo myProp =
        new PropertyInfo(MyControl.class, "myProp", int.class);
    public void getProperties(IProperties props){
        // Add existing properties from parent class
        super.getProperties(props);
        props.add(myProp);   // adds custom property
    }
}
```

For more information about the use of the PropertyInfo class, see "Specifying Custom Property Attributes," later in this chapter.

Alignment Property Example

This section provides a complete example of an alignment property for a SuperLabel class, which allows users to specify how they want the text aligned inside a label: left, right, and center. The example shows how to:

- Define and expose the property.

- Use an enumerator (enum) class to define allowable values for the property.

- Provide validation for a new property value.

- Use the alignment property value when painting the control.

- Expose the property at design time.

For the sample code, see "A Complete Example," later in this chapter.

Basic Alignment Property

The basic code for creating the alignment property is as follows. In the setAlignment method, the invalidate function is called, which indirectly forces the control to repaint so that it will reflect the new property value:

```
private int align = AlignStyle.LEFT;

public int getAlignment() {
    return align;
}

public void setAlignment(int value) {
    align = value;
    invalidate();  // Repaint control when property changes
}
```

Creating an Enumerated Property Value

Because there are only three possible values for the property, you can use an enumerator (enum) to define them. Although Java does not have native support for enumeration types, WFC provides a com.ms.wfc.core.Enum class. Any class that derives from com.ms.wfc.core.Enum will be treated as an Enum object. All Enum objects conform to the standard that they contain only public static final integers that represent the valid selections. They may optionally contain a valid method that returns true if a passed value is legal in that Enum object.

Enumerator objects are recognized in the Properties window. Therefore, when you subclass the Enum class, you automatically get a drop-down list of valid items in the Properties window at design time.

The following example shows a class that defines an AlignStyle enumerator:

```
// AlignStyle.java
import com.ms.wfc.core.*;

public class AlignStyle extends Enum
{
    public static final int LEFT = 1;
    public static final int RIGHT = 2;
    public static final int CENTER = 3;

    // Optional valid method to test passed value
    public static boolean valid(int value) {
        return (LEFT <= value && value <= CENTER);
    }
}
```

Note Creating the valid method as a static member allows users to call it without having to create an instance of the class first.

Providing Property Validation

In order to test that the user has specified a legal alignment value when setting the property, you can add validation to the setAlignment method. To test the value, you can call the valid method of the AlignStyle enumerator. If there is an error, you can throw the WFCInvalidEnumException exception.

The example below shows a modified setAlignment method with validation added:

```
public void setAlignment(int value) {

    if (!AlignStyle.valid(value))

        throw new WFCInvalidEnumException("value", value, AlignStyle.class);

    align = value;
    invalidate();  // Repaint control when property changes
}
```

> **Note** For information about using invalidate to repaint a control, see "Updating Visual Display," later in this chapter.

By throwing a WFCInvalidEnumException, you get the benefit that it is a non-checked exception, and there is a predefined message associated with it. This message has been translated to multiple languages so that when you run this control in various locales, you automatically get a meaningful error message.

Using the Property Value When Painting

The alignment property affects the appearance of text in the control. Therefore, whenever the control is painted, the paint code must check the property's value and use it accordingly.

You specify paint behavior by overriding the onPaint method. The example below shows you would read the alignment property value and then use the value in the drawString method to set the alignment. The constants LEFT, RIGHT, and so on are defined in the TextFormat class in com.ms.wfc.ui:

```
protected void onPaint(PaintEvent p) {
    Graphics g = p.graphics;
    int style = 0;
    switch (align) {
       case AlignStyle.LEFT:
          style = TextFormat.LEFT;
          break;
       case AlignStyle.RIGHT:
          style = TextFormat.RIGHT;
          break;
```

```
        case AlignStyle.CENTER:
            style = TextFormat.HORIZONTALCENTER;
            break;
    }
    g.drawString(getText(), getClientRect(), style);
}
```

Exposing the Property at Design Time

To make the alignment property available at design time, you subclass ClassInfo to first define the property (by creating an instance of PropertyInfo). You then expose the property by calling the getProperties method:

```
public static class ClassInfo extends Control.ClassInfo {

    public static final PropertyInfo alignment = new PropertyInfo(

        MyControl.class, "alignment", AlignStyle.class);

    public void getProperties(IProperties props) {
        super.getProperties(props);
        props.add(alignment);
    }
}
```

Note   The third parameter passed to the PropertyInfo constructor (in this case, AlignStyle.class) is normally the data type of the property. However, because this property is an enumerated value, you pass the class you created that extends Enum.

Because AlignStyle derives from the Enum class, the Properties window uses the editor associated with the Enum class. The result is a drop-down list that allows you to set the value of the property.

Note   To create a property that is not exposed at design time (for example, a run time-only property), use the PropertyInfo object to set the BrowsableAttribute attribute to NO. For details, see "Specifying Custom Property Attributes," later in this chapter.

A Complete Example

The following example shows a complete label control with an alignment property including all the features discussed previously:

```
// SuperLabel.java
import com.ms.wfc.ui.*;
import com.ms.wfc.core.*;

public class SuperLabel extends Control {
    private int align = AlignStyle.LEFT;
```

```
public int getAlignment() {
    return align;
}

public void setAlignment(int value) {
    if (!AlignStyle.valid(value))
        throw new WFCInvalidEnumException("value", value, AlignStyle.class);
    align = value;
    invalidate();  // Repaint control when property changes
}

protected void onPaint(PaintEvent p) {
    Graphics g = p.graphics;
    int style = 0;
    switch (align) {
        case AlignStyle.LEFT:
            style = TextFormat.LEFT;
            break;
        case AlignStyle.RIGHT:
            style = TextFormat.RIGHT;
            break;
        case AlignStyle.CENTER:
            style = TextFormat.HORIZONTALCENTER;
            break;
    }
    g.drawString(getText(), getClientRect(), style);
}

public static class ClassInfo extends Control.ClassInfo {
    public static final PropertyInfo alignment = new PropertyInfo(
        SuperLabel.class, "alignment", AlignStyle.class);

    public void getProperties(IProperties props) {
        super.getProperties(props);
        props.add(alignment);
    }
}
}
```

Specifying Custom Property Attributes

When you create a property and create a PropertyInfo object to set its attributes, you can specify a variety of options to customize the property.

Note More details about using the PropertyInfo class are provided in "Defining Control Properties," earlier in this chapter.

The basic syntax for creating a PropertyInfo object is:

```
new PropertyInfo(Class owner, String name, Class dataType)
```

For example, the following is a PropertyInfo object for a property called myProp in the MyControl control:

```
public static final PropertyInfo myProp =
   new PropertyInfo(MyControl.class, "myProp", int.class);
```

You can customize the property by providing any number of additional member attributes for the PropertyInfo object. A member attribute is defined as any class that derives from com.ms.wfc.core.MemberAttribute. A certain number of attributes are available by default in the PropertyInfo class, or you can create and add your own attributes by deriving them from MemberAttribute. The following table lists pre-defined attributes in the PropertyInfo class.

Attribute	Description
BrowsableAttribute	Specifies whether the property is visible in the Properties window. The default is YES. This attribute can be used in conjunction with the PersistableAttribute attribute (see below) to define properties whose value should be saved in the control but should not be editable in the Properties window.
CategoryAttribute	Specifies what category the current property fits into in the Properties window, such as Appearance, Behavior, and so on. The default is Misc. You can either place the property in a predefined category by using one of the static members in CategoryAttribute or create a new category by constructing a new CategoryAttribute and passing in the string name that you want the category to be called.
DataBindableAttribute	Specifies that the property is a candidate for data binding. The default is .NO. When this is set to .YES, the DataBinder component lists this property in its drop-down list.
DefaultValueAttribute	The default value for simple properties. This value is used when the user resets the property value in the Properties window. The Forms Designer also compares the default value against the current value. If they match, the Forms Designer does not generate code to set the property value, which reduces the size of code generated for the form.
	Note You can also create a default value by creating a reset*<property>* method. For details, see the next section, "Specifying Dynamic Default Values and Property Persistence."
	The most common values for various data types are predefined as static values (for example, for Boolean values, the values TRUE and FALSE are already defined).

(continued)

(continued)

Attribute	Description
DescriptionAttribute	Defines text displayed in the bottom of the Properties window when the user selects the current property. The default is "".
LocalizableAttribute	Specifies that the property value is saved in a resource file if the user chooses to localize a form. The default is NO. The user can then localize the resource file and not have to modify the code.
PersistableAttribute	Specifies whether the value of the property is saved when its container is saved at design time. The default value is YES. This attribute is primarily useful when you do not want to save a property value, for example, transient property values whose values depend on state or are calculated. Normally, properties with this attribute set to NO are also not browsable (BrowsableAttribute is NO).
ValueEditorAttribute	Specifies a custom editor used by the Properties window for the current property. If no value editor is specified, the Properties window uses an editor associated with the property's data type. For more details, see "Creating a Custom Properties Value Editor," later in this chapter.

To specify an attribute, you create an instance of the attribute you want or use one of the predefined instances (such as BrowsableAttribute.NO), and then add it to the PropertyInfo definition, using syntax such as:

```
new PropertyInfo(Class owner, String name, Class dataType,
   [MemberAttribute, [MemberAttribute, ...]])
```

The following example shows how you can define a description and default value for the myProp property using predefined attributes:

```
public static final PropertyInfo myProp =
   new PropertyInfo(MyControl.class, "myProp", int.class,
   new DescriptionAttribute("Test property"),
   new DefaultValueAttribute(DefaultValueAttribute.ONE);
```

You can add up to six attributes by simply including them as parameters to the PropertyInfo constructor. If you want to specify more than five member attributes, you can use syntax for the PropertyInfo constructor that accepts an array of member attributes. For details, see "PropertyInfo" in Package com.ms.wfc.core in *Microsoft Visual J++ 6.0 WFC Library Reference, Part 1*, in the *Microsoft Visual J++ 6.0 Reference Library*.

Specifying Dynamic Default Values and Property Persistence

To set a default value for a property, you can specify a DefaultValueAttribute attribute when creating a new PropertyInfo object, as described in "Specifying Custom Property Attributes." In some cases, you might want to specify a default value dynamically — that is, a value calculated at run time. Similarly, you might want to specify that a property value is *persisted* (saved between design-time sessions) based on run-time conditions.

Setting Persistence for Property Values

By default, when a control property value is changed from the default at design time
(as in the Properties window), it is saved whenever the host control is saved. For example,
if your control is instantiated in a Visual J++ form, and if you change the value of a
property in the Properties window, the property's value is saved when you save the form.
For efficiency, if the property value matches its default value, the value is not persisted.

In rare instances you want to specify that a value is persisted based on a run time
condition. To control persistence, override the Control class's shouldPersist<*property*>
method. After testing for the condition, the method should return a Boolean value
indicating whether the custom value should be saved. To prevent the value from being
saved, return false from this method. You can also override the shouldPersist<*property*>
for properties inherited from the superclass, as in this example, which sets persistence
of the font property depending on whether the font has changed:

```
public boolean shouldPersistFont() {
    return font != null;
}
```

> **Note**   Ambient properties (whose value is inherited from the parent) such as font and
> backColor return null when compared as illustrated above to represent that they are set
> to the default values. However, explicitly getting the value of such properties — for
> example, calling the getFont method — returns the actual font information.

Calculating Dynamic Default Values

To create a default value for a property at run time, create a reset<*property*> method for
that property. The following example shows how you can implement a default value based
on today's date for a property called lastUpdate:

```
private Date dtLastUpdate;
public void setLastUpdate( Date d ){
    dtLastUpdate = d ;
    invalidate();  // Repaint control when property changes
}

public void resetLastUpdate(){
    return new Date();
}
```

You can also override the reset<*property*> methods inherited from the Control class. The
following example shows how you can override the resetFont method for your control:

```
public void resetFont() {
    Font f = new Font("Arial", 8.0f, FontSize.POINTS, FontWeight.BOLD,
        false, false, false);
    setFont(f);
}
```

Creating a Custom Properties Value Editor

The Properties window in Visual J++ 6.0 provides editing capability for the values of the properties exposed in your control. In fact, the Properties window is really just a custom editor host. You can specify a custom editor, or you can rely on the default editing capabilities of the Properties window.

The mechanism is this: the Properties window first checks to see if you have specified a custom value editor. If not, it will look for an inner class called Editor inside the class of the type of the property. If no editor is found, it traverses the type's hierarchy looking for any superclass that has an editor. Because there is an ObjectEditor class associated with java.lang.Object, an editor will always be found. The Properties window will provide a default editor for all simple types, such as a string editor, integer editor, and so forth.

You might specify a custom value editor for many reasons. Typical tasks for a custom property editor include:

- Text-to-value conversion

- Value painting

- Specifying subproperties of the value

- Displaying custom dialog boxes

- Displaying custom drop-down lists

- Participating in code generation by specifying a constant name that should be substituted for a specific value

For more information, see the next section, "Defining a Custom Value Editor."

Defining a Custom Value Editor

To create a custom value editor, you must implement com.ms.wfc.core.IValueEditor. A convenient way to do so is to extend com.ms.wfc.core.ValueEditor to provide a default implementation of all methods.

To create the value to be displayed (as a string) in the Properties window, override the getTextFromValue method. In order for the changed value to be reflected in the control and displayed in the Properties window, override the getValueFromText method.

The following example illustrates a simple custom value editor that displays a percentage value with "%" in the Properties window, but then strips out the punctuation before the value is stored. This example makes use of the Value class in com.ms.wfc.util class for conversions:

```
import com.ms.wfc.core.*;
import com.ms.wfc.util.*;

public class PercentEditor extends ValueEditor {
    // Creates string as "nn%" for display in the Properties window
    public String getTextFromValue(Object value) {
        return Value.toString(Value.toInt(value)) + "%";
    }

    // Converts string in format "nn%" to integer. This method
    // is required.
    public Object getValueFromText(String text) {
        String s = Utils.trimBlanks(text.replace('%', ' '));
        return Value.toObject(Value.toInt(s));
    }
}
```

The methods provided by com.ms.wfc.core for exchanging information with a property editor are listed in the following table.

Method	Description
editValue	Provides a user interface for editing the property value.
getConstantName	Retrieves the fully-qualified name of a constant that represents the specified value.
getStyle	Returns a bitfield of style flags.
getTextFromValue	Converts a value into a string.
getValues	Returns an array of values; typically, the Properties window displays these in a list by calling getTextFromValue in a loop.
getValueFromText	Returns a value from a string. You must implement this method.
paintValue	Paints a representation of the value in a specified rectangle.

Two additional methods — getSubProperties and getValueFromSubPropertyValues — allow you to work with properties of objects, such as a Font object, that normally are passed as part of the constructor.

The getStyle method is used to get and set flags used to specify behavior in the value editor. Valid styles are:

- STYLE_NOEDITABLETEXT   Indicates that the value editor does not support accepting arbitrary text in the getValueFromText method. It should accept text that is returned from getTextFromValue. This style will typically cause a property editor to disallow typing in the edit box for properties of the value editor's type.

- STYLE_PAINTVALUE   Indicates that the value editor implements the paintValue method. Typically, this causes a property editor to paint a representation of properties of the value editor's type.

- **STYLE_VALUES**   Indicates that the value editor implements the getValues method. Typically, this causes a property editor to display a drop-down list for properties of the value editor's type.

- **STYLE_EDITVALUE**   Indicates that the value editor implements the editValue method. Typically, this causes a property editor to display an ellipsis button for properties of the value editor's type.

- **STYLE_DROPDOWNARROW**   Indicates that if STYLE_EDITVALUE is also returned, a drop-down arrow should be shown instead of an ellipsis button. This is useful if the value editor plans to show a drop-down list in editValue as opposed to launching a modal dialog box.

- **STYLE_IMMEDIATE**   Indicates that values of this type are suitable for updating even when the new value is incomplete. Typically, this causes a property editor to update the underlying property after each change made in the editor (for example, as each character is typed in an edit box).

- **STYLE_PROPERTIES**   Indicates that values of this type can have subproperties that can be edited, such as those for a Font object.

- **STYLE_NOARRAYEXPANSION**   Indicates that if the value is an array, a property inspector should not drill down into the array.

- **STYLE_NOARRAYMULTISELECT**   Indicates that if the value is an array, a property inspector should not have an entry that selects all the elements of the array.

The following example shows how you can display a modal dialog box as the custom property editor. In this example, you can see how IValueAccess provides an abstract way to get and set a value on the component that an editor is currently editing. This is useful if more than one component might be selected. When you call the get and set value methods through IValueAccess, the Properties window can correctly set the value on multiple components. To display an ellipsis button that calls the dialog box, the example overrides the getStyle method and sets STYLE_EDITVALUE in the bitfield returned by getStyle:

```
import com.ms.wfc.core.*;
import com.ms.wfc.util.*;

public class PercentEditor extends ValueEditor {
    public void editValue(IValueAccess valueAccess) {
        PercentDialog dialog = new PercentDialog();
        int value = Value.toInt(valueAccess.getValue());
        dialog.setPercentValue(value);
        int result = dialog.showDialog();
        if (result == DialogResult.OK) {
            valueAccess.setValue(dialog.getText());
        }
    }
}
```

```
    public int getStyle() {
        // Using OR operator sets bitfield to display ellipsis button
        return super.getStyle() | STYLE_EDITVALUE;
    }
}
```

The following example illustrates how to display a drop-down dialog box. The control calls IEditorHost.dropDownDone when done editing the property. In addition, the control is responsible for calling the setValue method of IValueAccess. The Properties window will shut the drop-down list if the user cancels the drop-down dialog box in any way:

```
import com.ms.wfc.core.*;
import com.ms.wfc.util.*;

public class PercentEditor extends ValueEditor {
    public void editValue(IValueAccess valueAccess) {
        PercentControl control = new PercentControl();
        int value = Value.toInt(valueAccess.getValue());
        dialog.setPercentValue(value);

        IEditorHost host =
                (IEditorHost)valueAccess.getService(IEditorHost.class);
        control.setValueAccess(valueAccess);
        host.dropDownControl(control);
    }

    public int getStyle() {
        return super.getStyle() | STYLE_EDITVALUE | STYLE_DROPDOWNARROW;
    }
}
```

Working with Control Events

As a subclass of Control, your control automatically supports a standard set of Windows events. You can capture and process these events within your control, optionally passing them to the host application. In addition, you can define custom events unique to your control and fire them as needed.

Capturing User Interaction with a Control

Your control can capture and process standard events before they are sent to the host application. The two most common types of interactions are mouse and keyboard events.

Capturing Mouse Events

The Control class in WFC provides for most of the mouse events that you need. These include mouseMove, mouseUp, mouseDown, mouseWheel, mouseEnter, and mouseLeave. In addition, you can optionally receive the click and doubleClick events.

To receive mouse events in your control, you can override the event you want. To pass the mouse event through to the host application, call the superclass's corresponding event method.

The following example illustrates how you can override the mouseMove event. The handler indirectly displays the location of the mouse, which is available in the x and y properties of the MouseEvent object passed to the handler:

```
protected void onMouseMove( MouseEvent e){
    String sMsg = "" + e.x + ", " + e.y;
    this.setText(sMsg);
    invalidate();  // Repaint control when property changes
    super.onMouseMove( e ); // to make it visible in the host
}
```

Capturing Keyboard Events

The standard key events exposed are keyUp, keyDown, and keyPress. These events will be triggered for both normal keys and system keys (for example, F1 through F12).

All keyboard input in WFC is done using Unicode character data. When running under an operating system that doesn't support Unicode messages (like Windows 95) the WFC framework will automatically perform the needed message filtering to generate Unicode events.

The following example illustrates how you can capture keyboard events within a control. The overridden onKeyUp method here filters out numeric characters before passing the event to the host application:

```
protected void onKeyUp( KeyEvent e){
    if(e.keydata < Key.D0 && e.keyData > Key.D9){
        super.onKeyUp( e );
        invalidate();  // Repaint control when property changes
    }
}
```

Creating a Custom Event

WFC controls support a standard set of events that they inherit from the Control class, such as click, mouseDown, keyPress, and so on. Your control automatically exposes these events, and they are available in the host application without any special effort on your part unless you want to override the events to add special functionality.

Note   For information about creating event handlers — receiving events in a host application — see "Handling Events in WFC," in Chapter 12, "WFC Programming Concepts." For details about how to capture a standard event and process it within your control, see "Capturing User Interaction with a Control," earlier in this chapter.

In some instances, however, you might want to create custom events that are unique to your control. For example, you might want your control to use an event to notify the host application of a change in status, such as the completion of an initialization procedure, or to report an error condition.

Note   By convention, to indicate a change in the value of a property, you create on<*property*>Changing and on<*property*>Changed methods using the techniques described below. For additional details, see "Providing Property Change Notification," later in this chapter.

Custom events rely on Visual J++ delegate technology. To implement a custom event, you create a delegate that can bind event handlers in an application to your event.

Using Delegates for Events

The event model for WFC uses delegates to bind events to the methods used to handle them. To define an event in Visual J++, you subclass the Event class, and then create a delegate class based on com.ms.lang.Delegate that binds to it. The delegate allows other classes to register for event notification by specifying a handler method. When the event occurs (is invoked), the delegate calls the bound method.

Delegates can be bound to a single method or to multiple methods, referred to as *multicasting*. When creating a delegate for an event, you typically create a multicast event. A rare exception might be an event that resulted in a specific procedure (such as displaying a dialog box) that it would not be sensible to repeat multiple times per event.

A multicast delegate maintains an *invocation list* of the methods it is bound to. The multicast delegate supports a combine method to add a method to the invocation list and a remove method to remove it.

A control fires an event by invoking the delegate for that event. The delegate in turn calls the bound method. In the most common case (a multicast delegate) the delegate calls each bound method in the invocation list in turn, which provides a one-to-many notification. This strategy means that the control does not need to maintain a list of target objects for event notification — the delegate handles all registration, notification, and unregistration.

Delegates also allow multiple events to be bound to the same method, allowing a many-to-one notification. For example, a button click event and a menu command click event can both invoke the same delegate, which then calls a single method to handle these two separate events the same way.

The binding mechanism used with delegates is dynamic — a delegate can be bound at run time to any method whose signature matches that of the event handler. This feature allows you to set up or change the bound method depending on condition and to dynamically attach an event handler to a control.

Creating a Custom Event Class

If you want to pass event-specific data with the event (similar to the x and y properties of the Control class's mouseMove event), you must create a custom event class and define its data. To create a custom event, you subclass the Event class. To make the event a top-level public class, it must reside in a separate .java file. In your class you define members to hold the event data.

The following example shows how you can create a simple error event class that has two fields, one for an error number and another for the text of the error message:

```
// ErrorEvent.java
import com.ms.wfc.core.*;
public class ErrorEvent extends Event{
    public final int errorNumber;
    public final String errorText;
    public ErrorEvent( int eNum, String eTxt){
        this.errorNumber = eNum;
        this.errorText = eTxt;
    }
}
```

Creating a Delegate

To allow binding for your event, create a handler class which declares a delegate specifying the signature for your event. If you want to be able to bind the delegate to multiple methods, declare it as a multicast delegate. The delegate should be a top-level class, it should therefore be in a separate file.

The following example shows a handler class for the ErrorEvent class illustrated earlier:

```
// ErrorEventHandler.java
import com.ms.wfc.core.*;
public final multicast delegate void ErrorEvent(Object sender,
    ErrorEvent event);
```

Multicast delegates must return void, because they cannot return the results of more than one method.

Implementing a Custom Event

To implement a custom event in your control, you provide a way for the host application to register for the event. First create a private instance of your delegate. Then create an addOn<*event*> method that the host can call to register for an event and bind it to a specific method. If the delegate is multicast, call the delegate's combine method in your addOn<*event*> method to add the user's method to the delegate's invocation list.

The following example shows how you can perform these steps for the ErrorEvent class illustrated earlier:

```
// Create instance of delegate
private ErrorEventHandler err = null;
// Call delegate's combine method to add binding to invocation list
public final void addOnErrorEvent(ErrorEventHandler handler){
    err = (ErrorEventHandler)Delegate.combine(err, handler);
}
```

Typically, you also provide a removeOn<*event*> method so the host can unregister for the event:

```
public final void removeOnErrorEvent(ErrorEventHandler handler){
    err = (ErrorEventHandler)Delegate.remove(err, handler);
}
```

If you are using a non-multicast delegate, the syntax for the addOn<*event*> method is simpler:

```
private ErrorEventHandler err = null; // Create instance of delegate
public final void addOnErrorEvent(ErrorEventHandler handler){
    err = handler;
}
```

Note The Component class from which the control derives contains utility code to add, remove, and fire events.

Exposing the Event at Design Time

Exposing an event at design time is similar to exposing a property. First, you create an instance of the EventInfo class indicating the new event's class, name, and delegate. You then you override the superclass's getEventsEventInfo method, adding the superclass's existing events and then your new event.

Note The event name should start with a lowercase letter (for example, errorEvent), unless the first two letters are uppercase (such as MIDIChildActivated).

The following example shows the ClassInfo class for the ErrorEvent event shown earlier:

```
public static class ClassInfo extends Control.ClassInfo{
    public static EventInfo errEvt = new EventInfo(MyControl.class,
        "errorEvent", ErrorEventHandler.class);
    public void getEvents(IEvents events({
        super.getEvents(events);
        events.add(errEvt);
    }
}
```

Firing an Event

To fire the event, you create an instance of your event class, passing to it the event-specific parameters that you defined in the class. You then invoke the delegate, as in the following example:

```
// the err delegate must already exist
int errNumber = 1020;
String errText = "Invalid value."
ErrorEvent e = new ErrorEvent(errNumber, errText);
err.invoke(this, e);
```

Most events in WFC include a protected *<eventname>* member that lets subclasses override the event and determine the order in which the event is triggered through placement of the call to super.on*<eventname>*. The following shows the protected member for ErrorEvent:

```
protected void onErrorEvent(ErrorEvent event){
    if(err != null){
        err.invoke(this, event);
    }
}
```

If you include the protected member, you can fire the event within your control by calling it instead of directly calling the invoke method, as in this example:

```
if(value > 20){
    onErrorEvent(new ErrorEvent(1020, "Invalid value"));
}
```

A Complete Example

The following shows a complete, simple control that includes the ErrorEvent event
described in the preceding sections:

```
// MyControl.java
import com.ms.wfc.ui.* ;
import com.ms.wfc.core.* ;
import com.ms.lang.Delegate;

public class MyControl extends Control {
   private int myProp = 1;
   public int getMyProp(){
      return myProp;
   }
   public void setMyProp(int value){
      // Fires error event if property value exceeed 200
      if(value > 200){

         onErrorEvent(new ErrorEvent(1020, "Invalid value"));

      }
      myProp = value;
   }

   protected void onPaint( PaintEvent p){
      super.onPaint(p);
      Graphics g=p.graphics;
      g.drawString( getText(), 0, 0);
   }

   // event setup to be able to fire event "ErrorEvent"

   private ErrorEventHandler errDelegate = null;

   public final void addOnErrorEvent(ErrorEventHandler handler){

      errDelegate = (ErrorEventHandler)Delegate.combine(errDelegate,
         handler);

   }

   public final void removeOnErrorEvent(ErrorEventHandler handler){

      errDelegate = (ErrorEventHandler)Delegate.remove(errDelegate,
         handler);

   }
```

```
protected void onErrorEvent(ErrorEvent event){

    if(errDelegate != null){

        errDelegate.invoke(this, event);

    }

}


public static class ClassInfo extends Control.ClassInfo{
    public static final PropertyInfo myProp = new
        PropertyInfo(MyControl.class, "myProp", int.class);
    public void getProperties(IProperties props){
        super.getProperties(props);
        props.add(myProp);
    }

    public static EventInfo evt = new EventInfo(MyControl.class,
        "errorEvent, ErrorEventHandler.class);

    public void getEvents(IEvents events){

        super.getEvents(events);

        events.add(evt);

    }

}
}
```

Providing Property Change Notification

WFC uses a naming convention for creating events that indicate that a property value is changing or has changed:

- The *<propertyName>*Changing event indicates that the function used to change a property value has been called. Typically, you fire this event at the beginning of your set*<Property>* method. You pass it a CancelEvent object; if the host application has a *<propertyName>*Changing event handler, the handler can prevent the property from being changed by setting the CancelEvent object's cancel property to true.

- To indicate a successfully completed change, you fire a *<propertyName>*Changed event.

   Note   Data binding requires that you implement the *<propertyName>*Changed event.

These events are not designed to provide data validation, but rather to allow control over properties being edited, such as preventing a control from updating its value. Data validation is either done on the data source (for example, a recordset) or through custom properties on the control.

You implement the property change events the way you do a custom event. For each event, you provide an addOn<*property*>Changing and addOn<*property*>Changed method and corresponding removeOn methods. You also typically create protected on<*PropertyName*>Changing and on<*PropertyName*>Changed methods. The on<*PropertyName*>Changing usually uses a CancelEvent object to allow the change to be stopped. For details about creating these methods, see "Creating a Custom Event," earlier in this chapter.

The following example illustrates how you can include property notification for an alignment property:

```
public void setAlignment(int value) {
    if (alignment != value) {
        CancelEvent e = new CancelEvent();
        onAlignmentChanging(e);
        if (!e.cancel) {
            alignment = value;
            invalidate();  // Repaint control when property changes
            onAlignmentChanged(Event.EMPTY);
        }
    }
}
}


private EventHandler eAlignChanged = null;
public final void addOnAlignmentChanged(EventHandler handler){
    eAlignChanged = (EventHandler)Delegate.combine(eAlignChanged,
        handler);
}
public final void removeOnAlignmentChanged(EventHandler handler){
    eAlignChanged = (EventHandler)Delegate.remove(eAlignChanged, handler);
}
protected void onAlignmentChanged(Event event){
    if(eAlignChanged != null){
        eAlignChanged.invoke(this, event);
    }
}


private CancelEventHandler eAlignChanging = null;
public final void addOnAlignmentChanging(CancelEventHandler handler){
    eAlignChanging = (CancelEventHandler)Delegate.combine(eAlignChanging,
        handler);
}
```

```
public final void removeOnAlignmentChanging(CancelEventHandler handler){
    eAlignChanging = (CancelEventHandler)Delegate.remove(eAlignChanging,
        handler);
}
protected void onAlignmentChanging(CancelEvent event){
    if(eAlignChanging != null){
        eAlignChanging.invoke(this, event);
    }
}

public static EventInfo eiAlignChanged = new EventInfo(MyControl.class,
    "onAlignmentChanged", EventHandler.class);
public static EventInfo eiAlignChanging = new EventInfo(MyControl.class,
    "onAlignmentChanging", EventHandler.class);

public void getEvents(IEvents events){
    super.getEvents(events);
    events.add(eiAlignChanged);
    events.add(eiAlignChanging);
}
```

Customizing a Control

In addition to defining your control's members, you can define its functionality by customizing it.

Determining the Control's Display

Within your control, you can write code to determine and modify the visual representation of your control. The following sections provide background information on control display and information on how to manage it.

Control Dimensions

There are three main dimensions associated with a control: bounds, client, and display coordinates. The bounds of a control are the outer window coordinates of the control. The bounds are always expressed in parent-client coordinates, that is, with respect to the dimensions of the parent.

Client coordinates are the dimensions of the area that the control can draw into. The client area of a control is always based at (0, 0) and is sized based on the inner-client owned area of the control. The client coordinates do not encompass non-client areas such as borders applied to the windows (for example, WS_BORDER, WS_EX_CLIENTEDGE) and the title bar for top-level windows.

The display coordinates are virtual client coordinates that define the area in which child controls appear. Display coordinates can define an area larger than that defined by the client coordinates. A good example of the difference between client coordinates and display coordinates is a form with autoscrolling. When autoscrolling is enabled for a form, the display size of the form can become bigger than the client size, resulting in a virtual form larger than the physical window. When you move the scroll bars on the form, the display coordinates change.

Note   Because the bounds of controls are always in parent-client coordinates, when a form is scrolled, the child control's bounds will change to reflect their actual position relative to the client coordinates of the parent.

In most controls, you only need to work with client coordinates. Display coordinates are important only if you write a control that is going to host other controls (such as a TabControl control), and you want to enable docking or other layout mechanisms.

Location and Size

A control's layout is determined by the combination of values of several properties that the control inherits from the Control class:

- The location property contains a Point class that sets the x and y coordinates of the top leftmost corner of the control.

- The size property contains a Point class that sets the width and height of the control.

- The anchor property fixes one or more sides of the control to its container. When the container is resized, the anchored sides of the control are resized as well.

- The dock property specifies what edge of the host container a control is docked to.

These properties can be set at run time to change the location and size of the control.

If the control's location or size changes at run time, the control fires notification events. The layout event is fired when anything changes on a control that would cause it to reapply any layout. Examples include adding child controls, changing the control's boundaries, or performing some other control-specific event such as changing a property value. The resize event is fired only when the bounds of the control changes.

The default WFC layout logic is processed in Control.onLayout and Form.onLayout. The dock and anchor of a child control are applied in the layout event of the parent. Thus a panel would lay out all children, and the parent of the panel would lay out that panel.

Updating Visual Display

Any visual control must provide a representation of itself. Unless your control is subclassing another control, you must add custom paint logic to your control by overriding the onPaint method. Call the superclass's onPaint method to display the control, and then add your own logic to customize the display.

The onPaint event receives a PaintEvent object that you can use to get an instance of a Graphics object. You then call methods of the Graphics object to update the control's display. The following shows a simple example of how to display text in a control by updating the text property:

```
protected void onPaint(PaintEvent p) {
    super.onPaint(p);
    Graphics g = p.graphics;
    g.drawString(getText(), 0, 0);
}
```

The Graphics object in WFC is very rich and full featured. You can draw almost any primitive structure including arcs, ellipsis, rectangles, polygons, lines, and points. The following table lists commonly-used properties and methods of the Graphics object.

Graphics object member	Description
setPen method	Specifies a Pen object that defines how lines and borders around objects are drawn.
setBrush method	Specifies a Brush object that fills a control (for example, in the clearRect method).
setBackColor method	Specifies the color displayed behind text.
setTextColor method	Specifies the foreground color for text.
setFont method	Specifies the font with which the text will be drawn.
drawArc method	Draws an elliptical arc.
drawImage method	Draws an image.
drawString method	Displays a string; includes support for word wrapping, alignment, clipping, and so forth.

Painting in WFC uses the standard Win32 model in which a region of the control is invalidated. This effectively requests a repaint, but does not immediately perform the paint procedure. At the next free cycle, the paint event is sent asynchronously to the control. When the event reaches the control, the control first calls eraseBackground to clear the area that is about to be painted. The paint event then occurs, clipped to the invalid region.

Paint events coalesce, so the control will receive only one paint event for multiple invalidated regions of the control. The coalesced paint event that the control receives is clipped to the union of all the invalid regions.

The following example illustrates how you can call the invalidate method to request that the control repaint itself. In this instance, the invalidate method is called without a Rectangle object parameter to indicate the clipped region, so the entire control will be repainted:

```
public void setAlignment(int value) {
    if (!AlignStyle.valid(value))
        throw new WFCInvalidEnumException("value", value,
                AlignStyle.class);
    align = value;
    invalidate();  // Repaint control when property changes
}
```

Note If you modify multiple properties (or the same property twice), the control will not perform the entire paint operation twice.

To force a paint to occur synchronously, you can call the control's update method, which forces the control to perform any pending paint events immediately.

Eliminating Flicker while Painting

To eliminate flicker in your control, you should consider overriding the onEraseBackground event. The default implementation of this event clears the background of the control with the current value of the backColor property. However, it is not always necessary to repaint the entire area of the control, and doing so unnecessarily can cause flickering. This is primarily the case with controls that have a large area or complex paint logic.

In the example above, the drawString method is used to place text in the control. If the background is not cleared by the eraseBackground method, it would look as if it had never been painted, producing a "transparent" look.

Note The control is not actually transparent. However, because the old contents of that screen area are not repainted, they are still visible.

To create a control that looks solid with no flicker, avoid painting the background for areas that will be repainted again with foreground information. The easiest way to do this is to ensure that the onPaint method accounts for the entire clientRect area. You can then skip background drawing completely by overriding the onEraseBackground event specifying that the event has been handled, as in the following example:

```
protected void onEraseBackground(EraseBackgroundEvent event) {
    event.handled = true;
}

protected void onPaint(PaintEvent p) {
    Graphics g = p.graphics;
    g.clearRect(getClientRect());
    g.drawString(getText(), 0, 0);
}
```

This is a small example with simple code in the onPaint method. You might therefore not see much benefit from overriding the onEraseBackground event in this case. However, in your own control where the paint code might be more complex, using the illustrated technique greatly reduces flicker.

Another technique to increase the visual stability of a control is to double-buffer your on-screen image. In this technique, you maintain a bitmap of the entire client area, and then create a Graphics object based on that image. Performance of graphical updates against the buffer is much quicker than normal.

You should use the double-buffering technique only if you have overridden onEraseBackground and optimized your paint code already and are still experiencing flicker. Double-buffering is a resource-intensive operation, because you are maintaining an extra copy of the control's image. For large images, this can require substantial memory (the exact amount depends on the size of the image and its color depth). Maintaining the buffer can also slow performance if the buffer stores a large area.

To use a double buffer in your control, do the following:

- Specify that you are handling the onEraseBackground event.

- Override the onResize method to create a new buffer matching the new client area. It is also a good idea to dispose of the old buffer to free up resources. You should also call the invalidate method; by default, Windows will invalidate only the regions directly affected by the resize.

- In the paint code, create a Graphics object from the buffer, and perform all your draw operations on that object. You must explicitly set the backColor and pen properties for the Graphics object based on those defined for the buffer.

The following example draws a simple star pattern inside the client area of the control. If you did not include a double buffer, the control would flicker noticeably:

```
// Star.java
import com.ms.wfc.ui.*;
import com.ms.wfc.core.*;

public class Star extends Control
{
    // Create buffer
    Bitmap buffer = null;
    // Override onResize in order to recreate buffer at new size
    protected void onResize(Event e) {
        if (buffer != null) {
            buffer.dispose(); // Frees resources
            buffer = null;
        }
```

```
      Point s = getClientSize();
      buffer = new Bitmap(s.x, s.y);
      invalidate();  // Forces Windows to redraw entire control
      super.onResize(e);
   }
   protected void onEraseBackground(EraseBackgroundEvent event) {
      event.handled = true;
   }

   protected void onPaint(PaintEvent pe) {
      Graphics g = buffer.getGraphics();
      Rectangle client = getClientRect();

      // Explicitly set backColor and pen based on buffer's values
      g.setBackColor(getBackColor());
      g.setPen(new Pen(getForeColor()));
      g.clearRect(client);
      int x = 0;
      int y = 0;
      int xCenter = client.width/2;
      int yCenter = client.height/2;

      // Draws a star
      for (; x<client.width; x+=4) {
         g.drawLine(x, y, xCenter, yCenter);
      }
      for (; y<client.height; y+=4) {
         g.drawLine(x, y, xCenter, yCenter);
      }
      for (; x>=0; x-=4) {
         g.drawLine(x, y, xCenter, yCenter);
      }
      for (; y>=0; y-=4) {
         g.drawLine(x, y, xCenter, yCenter);
      }
      g.dispose();

      pe.graphics.drawImage(buffer, 0, 0);
   }

   public static class ClassInfo extends Control.ClassInfo {
   }
}
```

Adding a Bitmap for a Control

As part of the visual representation of your control, you can assign a 16-by-16-pixel bitmap to it. The bitmap is displayed in the Visual J++ Toolbox when your control is available. The bitmap is also displayed for controls that do not have a run-time representation, such as timers.

> **Note**   The bitmap is used only if the control is being used as a WFC control. If used as an ActiveX control, the control displays a standard, predefined bitmap in the toolbox.

By default, the ClassInfo object loads any bitmap that has the same file name as your control. If your control is named MyControl.java, you can associate a bitmap with it by just adding MyControl.bmp to the folder where your MyControl.class file is.

Alternatively, you can specify a particular bitmap by overriding the getToolboxBitmap method in your ClassInfo subclass. The following example shows how you can assign the bitmap Gears.bmp to your control:

```
public Bitmap getToolboxBitmap(){
    return = new Bitmap(MyControl.class, "Gears.bmp");
}
```

The bitmap you specify should be no more than 16-by-16 pixels in size, and should use 16 colors or fewer. Visual J++ can automatically resize a bitmap that is not of the correct dimensions, but this often results in a graphic that does not look good.

Creating Control Customizers

Customizers are a type of per instance design-time metadata. The ClassInfo class defines metadata that is specific to the class; in contrast, the customizer provides access to more advanced design-time functionality. By creating a Customizer object, you can add functionality to your control such as specifying design-time activation, adding control verbs, and creating design pages (custom property pages).

As with the value editors, there is a default implementation of com.ms.wfc.core.ICustomizer — com.ms.wfc.core.Customizer. You can override the getCustomizer method in ClassInfo to return an instance of a customizer.

Specifying Design-Time Activation

WFC supports design-time activation of controls, such as design-time scrolling or item expansion, through a simple hit testing scheme. When a control is selected, hit test requests will be passed to the control's customizer. If the hit test returns true then the control will be considered active at that location. This simple architecture allows for very seamless activation of regions of a control, such as the tab area of a tab strip.

The following example illustrates a simple hit testing method that allows the control to receive messages when the mouse is over the top 50 pixels of the control:

Note   A control is only activated (and the getHitTest event is fired) when it is the primary selected component.

```
import com.ms.wfc.ui.*;
import com.ms.wfc.core.*;

public class MyTabControl extends Control {

    public static class ClassInfo extends Control.ClassInfo {
        public ICustomizer getCustomzier(Object comp) {
            return ((MyTabControl)comp).new Customizer();
        }
    }

    public class Customizer extends com.ms.wfc.core.Customizer {
        public boolean getHitTest(Point pt) {
            if (pt.y < 50) {
                return true;
            }
            return false;
        }
    }
}
```

Specifying Control Verbs

Verbs allow you to define design-time actions that can be performed on an object. Verbs typically appear on the shortcut menu for the control in the designer.

To create a verb, subclass the Customizer class and then create a CustomizerVerb object, which allows you to specify the text for your verb and to create a delegate that binds the action of the verb to a method that you specify.

The following example illustrates how to create a verb called About. The About class offers one verb that reads "About" in the context menu and displays a simple message box. The method to display the results of the Action verb is included in this class:

```
// About.java
import com.ms.wfc.ui.*;
import com.ms.wfc.core.*;

public class About extends Control {
    public static class ClassInfo extends Control.ClassInfo {
        public ICustomizer getCustomizer(Object comp) {
            return ((About)comp).new Customizer();
        }
    }
```

```
public class Customizer extends com.ms.wfc.core.Customizer {
    public CustomizerVerb[] getVerbs() {
        CustomizerVerb v = new CustomizerVerb("About",
            new VerbExecuteEventHandler(About.this.showAbout));
        return new CustomizerVerb[] {v};
    }
}

private void showAbout(Object sender, VerbExecuteEvent event) {
    MessageBox.show("This control was written in WFC", "About",
        MessageBox.OK);
}
}
```

In addition to the data and the delegate, you can specify the checked and enabled state of the item and associate a bitmap with the item. Although currently Visual J++ will not display a bitmap specified in a customizer (for instance, in a shortcut menu), other hosts might support this feature.

Specifying Design Pages

Design pages are the WFC equivalent of property pages. Design pages can be edited in the design-time environment. To implement a design page, you create a class that extends DesignPage class and overrides the onReadProperty and onWriteProperty methods.

Note   Although WFC supports design pages, you are encouraged to provide functionality for your control through custom editors, verbs, and design-time activation. For details, see "Creating a Custom Properties Value Editor," earlier in this chapter.

The following example illustrates how to create a design page for an alignment property. The alignment values (left, center, right) are implemented as group of option buttons. In the onReadProperty method, the code checks for the alignment property and returns the object value of the property as it is set in the design page. In the onWriteProperty method, the code again checks for alignment and displays its value in the design page. In the handle for all the radio buttons, the setDirty method is called, which marks the design page as dirty and enables the Apply button in the Properties window:

```
// SuperLabelDP.java
import com.ms.wfc.core.*;
import com.ms.wfc.ui.*;

public class SuperLabelDP extends DesignPage {
    public SuperLabelDP() {
        initForm();
    }
```

```
private void setAlign(int value) {
    switch (value) {
        case AlignStyle.LEFT:
            radioButton1.setChecked(true);
            break;
        case AlignStyle.CENTER:
            radioButton2.setChecked(true);
            break;
        case AlignStyle.RIGHT:
            radioButton3.setChecked(true);
            break;
    }
}
private int getAlign() {
    int align = AlignStyle.LEFT;
    if (radioButton1.getChecked()) {
        align = AlignStyle.LEFT;
    }
    else if (radioButton2.getChecked()) {
        align = AlignStyle.CENTER;
    }
    else if (radioButton3.getChecked()) {
        align = AlignStyle.RIGHT;
    }
    return align;
}

private void radioClicked(Object sender, Event e) {
    setDirty();
}

protected Object onReadProperty(String name) {
    if (name.equals("alignment")) {
        return new Integer(getAlign());
    }
    return null;
}

protected void onWriteProperty(String name, Object value) {
    if (name.equals("alignment") && value instanceof Integer) {
        setAlign(((Integer)value).intValue());
    }
}

Container components = new Container();
GroupBox groupBox1 = new GroupBox();
RadioButton radioButton1 = new RadioButton();
RadioButton radioButton2 = new RadioButton();
RadioButton radioButton3 = new RadioButton();
```

```
private void initForm() {
    this.setText("Alignment");
    this.setAutoScaleBaseSize(13);
    this.setBorderStyle(FormBorderStyle.NONE);
    this.setClientSize(new Point(307, 131));
    this.setControlBox(false);
    this.setMaxButton(false);
    this.setMinButton(false);

    groupBox1.setLocation(new Point(8, 8));
    groupBox1.setSize(new Point(128, 112));
    groupBox1.setTabIndex(0);
    groupBox1.setTabStop(false);
    groupBox1.setText("Alignment ");

    radioButton1.setLocation(new Point(8, 16));
    radioButton1.setSize(new Point(112, 25));
    radioButton1.setTabIndex(0);
    radioButton1.setTabStop(true);
    radioButton1.setText("Left");
    radioButton1.setChecked(true);
    radioButton1.addOnClick(new EventHandler(this.radioClicked));

    radioButton2.setLocation(new Point(8, 48));
    radioButton2.setSize(new Point(112, 25));
    radioButton2.setTabIndex(1);
    radioButton2.setText("Center");
    radioButton2.addOnClick(new EventHandler(this.radioClicked));

    radioButton3.setLocation(new Point(8, 80));
    radioButton3.setSize(new Point(112, 25));
    radioButton3.setTabIndex(2);
    radioButton3.setText("Right");
    radioButton3.addOnClick(new EventHandler(this.radioClicked));

    this.setNewControls(new Control[] {
        groupBox1});
    groupBox1.setNewControls(new Control[] {
        radioButton3,
        radioButton2,
    radioButton1});
    }
}
```

Using Controls

After creating a WFC control, you can use it in a host environment the way you would any control.

Registering a Control

Controls must be registered on the computer where they will run. The control must include information that the registration process can read that identifies the control, and that is then placed in the Windows registry of the computer where the control will run. By reading the registration information, applications can find and load the control.

Note If you are using the control on the computer where you built the control project, you do not need to register the control; the build process registers the control automatically. If you are using the control in Visual J++, you do not need to explicitly include registration information.

The host application also requires a type library (.tlb file) for your control, which includes information about the control's members. The application reads the information in the type library to know what properties, events, and methods your control supports. Visual J++ can automatically generate a type library for your control during the build process.

Specifying Registration and Type Library Information

Registration requires the following information:

- A class ID (clsid), which is a GUID (globally-unique ID) that uniquely identifies your control. You need a class ID for both the control itself and for its type library.

- A program ID (progID), which is the name used in the host application when creating an instance of the control, such as MyProject.MyControl.

If you have used the WFC Component Builder to create your control, class IDs are generated for you automatically. You can also have Visual J++ create class IDs for you automatically during the build process by specifying that your control is a COM DLL. You can select this option in the COM Classes tab of the project's Properties window. For details about building a DLL, see Chapter 17, "Building COM Objects."

Finally, you can create and include class IDs for your control manually. You might do this if you want to guarantee that the class ID remains the same for your control, or if you have to know the classID for some other purpose and do not want to let Visual J++ generate it for you. You can generate a GUID with a program such as Uuidgen.exe, a utility freely available on the Microsoft Web site. You must provide two class IDs in all — one for the control and a second one for its type library.

To make the manual registration information visible to the registration program, you include it in a directive embedded comment in your control's .java file. The format is:

```
/*
 * @com.register ( clsid=guid, typelib=guid )
 */
```

For example, a registration block might look like the following (the example wraps because the class IDs are long, but should not wrap in your file):

```
/*
 * @com.register ( clsid=d0702fa0-fb3b-11d1-8f88-00aa00600a54, typelib=d3108a20-fb3b-11d1-
8f88-00aa00600a54 )
 */
```

When you build the project for your control, the build process looks for this block. If it is found, the build process generates a type library for the control. It also then registers the control and the type library on your computer.

Creating a ProgID

The registration process automatically builds a progID for your control using the following format:

```
ProjectName.ControlName
```

For example, your control project might be MyProject and the control's .java file might be MyControl.java. After registration, the control's progID would be MyProject.MyControl.

Running the Registration Process

If you intend to use the control on the computer where you built it, you do not need to register it — the build process automatically registers it for you. However, if you are distributing the control to another computer, you must register it there.

If you have built your control as a COM DLL, you can register it as you do any control, using the Windows Regsvr32.exe program. In a Command window use the following syntax:

```
Regsvr32.exe path/controlName
```

If your control is simply compiled as a .class file, you use a command-line utility called Vjreg.exe that is included with Visual J++. (You cannot use Regsvr32.exe to register your control because that utility is not designed to register .class files.) Register your control in a Command window using the following syntax:

```
Vjreg path/controlName
```

When you run this command, it registers the Msjaval.dll as the control's server, with the name and path of your control as a parameter.

Working with a Control in a Host Application

You can work with your control in a host application, such as Visual J++, Visual Basic, or Internet Explorer, as you would with any control. To run any control created in Visual J++, the following must reside on the host computer:

- The Microsoft Virtual Machine for Java (VM) available with Visual J++ 6.0. A redistributable VM is available as the file Msjavx86.exe. This version of the VM is compatible with both Internet Explorer 3.02 and 4.0, but some control features might not be available under version 3.02.

In addition, for each control you must distribute the following files:

- The .class files for all the classes in your control's project.

- The type library (.tlb file) generated for your project during the build process.

- The .dat files generated during the build process for your control.

- The VJPROJS.SRG file, which contains registration information.

  Note If you are running the control on the computer where you built the control project, all of these files are already available.

After installing the files on the host computer, you must register the control as described in "Registering a Control," earlier in this chapter. You can then create instances of the control. In many host applications, you can add the control to a toolbox. For example, in Visual Basic, you can right-click the Toolbox, choose Components, and then select your control.

Using a Control in Internet Explorer

To use a control in Internet Explorer, create an <OBJECT> element. In the CLASSID attribute, identify your control in one of the following ways:

- **By progID**   Use a CLASSID attribute such as the following:

```
<OBJECT CLASSID="progid:MyProject.MyControl">
</OBJECT>
```

- **By ClassID**   Use a CLASSID attribute such as the following:

```
<OBJECT CLASSID="clsid:d0702fa0-fb3b-11d1-8f88-00aa00600a54">
</OBJECT>
```

- **Using your control's class name**   This syntax requires the version of the Microsoft Virtual Machine for Java that ships with Visual J++ 6.0 or later. Use a CLASSID attribute that includes the JAVA moniker, as in the following example:

```
<OBJECT CLASSID="JAVA:MyControl">
</OBJECT>
```

Creating Composite WFC Controls

You can use the Windows Foundation Classes for Java (WFC) component model to create two types of controls: *custom* and *composite*.

Custom controls derive from the com.ms.wfc.ui.Control class. You can design a custom control in its entirety or subclass an existing WFC control. For more information on creating custom controls, see "Writing WFC Controls," earlier in this chapter.

Composite controls are controls that include other controls. All composite controls are derived from the com.ms.wfc.ui.UserControl class. Because the UserControl class is a subclass of the com.ms.wfc.ui.Form class, you can use the Forms Designer to lay out the controls that define your composite control.

By creating the control in this section, you will learn how to:

- Use the Forms Designer to define the layout of your control.

- Add properties and events using the WFC Component Builder.

- Add supporting code for a control.

Creating a Control Project

The Visual J++ Control template provides a head start in creating a WFC control. The template provides a class that is derived from com.ms.wfc.ui.UserControl and that contains a ClassInfo class that is derived from UserControl.ClassInfo.

Note Before you start the following procedure, close any open projects. (On the **File** menu, click **Close All**.)

To create a control project with the Control template

1. On the **File** menu, click **New Project**.

2. On the **New** tab, expand the **Visual J++ Projects** folder, click **Components**, and then select the **Control** icon.

3. In the **Name** box, type a name for your project.

   For this scenario, type **GroupCheck**.

4. In the **Location** box, type the path where you want to save your project, or click **Browse** to navigate to a directory.

5. Click **Open**.

   A collapsed view of your project appears in Project Explorer.

6. In Project Explorer, expand the project node.

    A file with the default name **Control1.java** is added to your project.

7. To rename the control source file to **GroupCheck.java**, right-click the file name in Project Explorer, and then click **Rename**.

    Note   Renaming this file does not rename the associated class in the source code and vice versa. You must manually change all instances of the old name. (You can create an empty project and then add a control class to the project. You can then name the control before it is created.)

The next step is to design the layout of your control.

Designing the Layout of the Control

Use the Forms Designer to design the layout of a composite control. This process is identical to designing the layout of a form. You can add controls from the Toolbox, move and size controls on the surface of the UserControl, specify properties, and create event handlers.

This scenario demonstrates how to create a composite control that contains a GroupBox control and a CheckBox control in the upper-left corner of the GroupBox control. When the composite control is placed on a form, you can add controls within the GroupBox portion of the control. When the CheckBox control is unchecked, the controls within the composite control are disabled; when the CheckBox control is checked, the controls within the composite control are enabled.

To add controls to the UserControl

1. To open your control in the Forms Designer, double-click **GroupCheck.java** in Project Explorer.

2. In the Toolbox, select the **WFC Controls** tab.

    If the Toolbox is not displayed, click **Toolbox** on the **View** menu.

3. To add a GroupBox control to the UserControl, click the GroupBox control in the Toolbox, and then click the UserControl design surface.

    A GroupBox control is added with the default name of **groupBox1**.

4. To add a CheckBox control to the UserControl, click the CheckBox control in the Toolbox, and then drag the control over the upper-left corner of the GroupBox control you added previously.

    A CheckBox control is added with the default name of **checkBox1**. Ensure that the CheckBox control is contained within the GroupBox control.

To save screen space, it is important that you resize the UserControl. Because the UserControl can be resized, it is also important for the controls within the UserControl to resize when the dimensions of the UserControl change.

To set the size of the controls

1. Resize the UserControl's design surface around the GroupBox and CheckBox controls to eliminate extra space. (To resize the design surface, select it and drag the resize handles.)

   The size of the UserControl's design surface is the default size of the control when it is added to a form.

2. To allow the GroupBox control to be resized when the UserControl is resized, select the GroupBox control in the Forms Designer and set the anchor property to **Top**, **Left**, **Right**, **Bottom**.

   The GroupBox control is now anchored to the borders of the UserControl.

3. To provide the user of the GroupCheck control with a correct display, modify the properties of the GroupBox and CheckBox controls that were added to the UserControl.

To set the properties of the controls

1. To remove the default caption of the GroupBox control, in the Properties window, select the **text** property and clear its contents.

2. To set the default state of the CheckBox control to be checked, select the control in the Forms Designer, and set the **checked** property in the Properties window to **true**.

The next step is to add a property to your control.

Adding a Custom Property with the WFC Component Builder

Use the WFC Component Builder to add and delete custom properties from your controls. By using the WFC Component Builder, you can get a head start in defining properties for your controls.

To add a property using the WFC Component Builder

1. In Project Explorer, right-click your control's source file, and then click **View Code**.

   The Text editor opens and displays the source for your control.

2. In Class Outline, right-click your control's class name and click **WFC Component Builder**. (To display Class Outline, on the **View** menu, point to **Other Windows**, and then click **Document Outline**.)

3. In the **Properties** section of the WFC Component Builder, click **Add**.

4. In the **Add WFC Property** dialog box, define the **checked** property for the GroupCheck control according to the following table, and then click **OK**.

Field	Value
Name	checked
Data Type	Boolean
Category	Behavior
Description	Determines whether the control's check box is checked.
Read-only Property	unchecked
Declare Member Variable	unchecked

5.   In the WFC Component Builder, click **OK**.

The WFC Component Builder adds the `getChecked` and `setChecked` methods to the code and a property definition to the control's ClassInfo class.

The next step is to add code to the getChecked and setChecked methods.

Adding Code to Property Methods

The WFC Component Builder creates the methods and fields needed to define and implement your custom properties. Typically, you modify this code to provide your own implementation.

To add code to your property methods

1.   For the `getChecked` method to return the checked state of the CheckBox control, replace the code that was added by the WFC Component Builder with the following line of code:

```
return checkBox1.getChecked();
```

2.   For the `setChecked` method to set the checked state of the CheckBox control, as well as call other methods that this scenario needs, replace the code that was added by the WFC Component Builder with the following lines of code:

```
checkBox1.setChecked(value);
onCheckedChanged(Event.EMPTY);
enableControls(this, value);
```

This code sets the checked state of the CheckBox control based on the value that is passed to the property's method. The code also calls the `onCheckedChanged` method and makes a call to the `enableControls` method. The call to the `onCheckChanged` method triggers a custom event, `checkedChanged`, which will be added later in this scenario.

The `Event.EMPTY` value passed to `onCheckedChanged` defines an empty Event object to be assigned to the `checkedChanged` event. The call to the `enableControls` method is used to enable or disable controls that are added to the GroupCheck control. This method will also be added later in this scenario.

The next step is to add an event to your control.

Adding Events with the WFC Component Builder

Use the WFC Component Builder to add and delete custom events from your controls. You can then avoid manually defining events in your control's ClassInfo class.

To add an event using the WFC Component Builder

1. In Class Outline, right-click your control's class name, and then click **WFC Component Builder**. (To display Class Outline, on the **View** menu, point to **Other Windows** and then click **Document Outline**.)

2. In the **Events** section of the WFC Component Builder, click **Add**.

3. In the **Add WFC Event** dialog box, define the **checkedChanged** event for the GroupCheck control according to the following table, and then click **OK**.

Field	Value
Name	checkedChanged
Type	Event
Category	Action
Description	Occurs when the control's check box check state is changed.

4. In the WFC Component Builder, click **OK**.

   The WFC Component Builder adds the `addOnCheckedChanged`, `removeOnCheckedChanged`, and `onCheckedChanged` methods to the code and adds an event definition in the control's ClassInfo class. The WFC Component Builder also adds an instance of the EventHandler delegate, which is used by the event.

The next step is to override inherited methods.

Overriding the UserControl's Methods

Use Class Outline to easily override methods in your control's inherited classes. The overridden method code that is created by Class Outline provides a head start in implementing the method in your control's class. You can use the comments provided by Class Outline in your overridden method code to quickly determine where to add your own code.

To override a method using Class Outline

1. In Class Outline, expand the class node.

2. Expand the **Inherited members** node, and right-click the method name that you want to override.

   If the method can be overridden, the shortcut menu displays **Override Method**.

3. Click **Override Method**.

   Class Outline adds a method definition for the specified method to your source code.

4. For the GroupCheck control, create overridden methods for the `add`, `getControl`, `getControlCount`, `getControls`, `remove`, and `setText` methods.

The next step is to add code to the overridden methods.

Adding Code to Overridden Methods

After you have created overridden methods using Class Outline, you provide your implementation code to the method definitions. Depending on how you implement the overridden method, you can either retain or remove the call to the superclass version of the method.

Adding Code to the add Method

To add controls to the GroupCheck control's GroupBox control, you add code to the GroupCheck's `add` method that calls the GroupBox's `add` method. This causes the GroupBox control, instead of the GroupCheck control, to parent the control being added.

To add code to the add method

1. Before adding code to the add method, you add a private member variable to the GroupCheck class to determine whether controls can be added. Add the following line of code to the GroupCheck class:

    ```
    private boolean m_bReady = false;
    ```

2. Inside the definition of the add method, add the following code:

    ```
    if(m_bReady){
        control.setEnabled(checkBox1.getChecked());
        groupBox1.add(control);
    }
    else
        super.add(control);
    ```

    This code determines whether the m_bReady member variable is set to true. This check is made to prevent the control's GroupBox control from being added to itself. If the value of m_bReady is true, the code calls the setEnabled method of the control passed as a parameter to the method. The setEnabled method is passed the checked state of the GroupCheck control's CheckBox control. Because controls can be added to the GroupCheck control when it is unchecked, it is important that controls be enabled or disabled properly when added.

    The code then calls the GroupBox control's add method and passes the control parameter to have the control added to the GroupBox control instead of the UserControl. If the m_bReady member variable is set to false, a call is made to the superclass version of the add method with the control passed as a parameter.

Adding Code to Control-Related Methods

So that the user can access the controls within the GroupBox control, you provide code in the getControl, getControlCount, and getControls methods that calls the GroupBox control's implementation of these methods.

To add code to control-related methods

1. Inside the definition of the getControl method, type the following code to replace the code that was added by Class Outline:

    ```
    return groupBox1.getControl(index);
    ```

2. Inside the definition of the getControlCount method, type the following code to replace the code that was added by Class Outline:

    ```
    return groupBox1.getControlCount();
    ```

3. Inside the definition of the getControls method, type the following code to replace the code that was added by Class Outline:

    ```
    return groupBox1.getControls();
    ```

Adding Code to the remove Method

So that controls can be deleted from the GroupCheck control, you provide code in the `remove` method for the GroupCheck control that calls the GroupBox control's `remove` method.

To add code to the remove method

- Inside the definition of the `remove` method, type the following code to replace the code that was added by Class Outline:

```
if(m_bReady) {
    groupBox1.remove(c);
}
else {
    super.remove(c);
}
```

This code determines whether the `m_bReady` variable is true. If it is, the code calls the GroupBox control's version of the `remove` method with the control that is passed to the method as a parameter. The check for `m_bReady` being true is performed to prevent the CheckBox or GroupBox controls from being removed. If `m_bReady` is false, the code calls the superclass version of the method to ensure that the control being removed is handled properly.

Adding Code to the setText Method

The GroupBox control does not provide a way to autosize the text portion of the control to the amount of text being displayed. For the GroupCheck control to display its text properly, override the `setText` method to determine the correct width of the control based on the size of the text to display.

To add code to the setText method

- Inside the definition of the `setText` method, type the following code to replace the code that was added by Class Outline:

```
Graphics g = checkBox1.createGraphics();
checkBox1.setWidth(g.getTextSize(value).x + 20);
g.dispose();
checkBox1.setText(value);
super.setText(value);
```

This code uses the Graphics class methods to determine the size of the text that is being specified. When the size of the text is determined, it is increased by a value of 20 to compensate for the size of the check box and the space between the check box and the text portion of the CheckBox control. The code then calls the `dispose` method of the Graphics class to free any resources that were allocated, sets the text property of the CheckBox control, and calls the superclass version of the `setText` method.

The next step is to add a new method to the control.

Adding Methods to the Control

When you are developing a control, you must often provide methods to perform actions in your control. For the GroupCheck control, you add a method that disables or enables the controls contained within the GroupBox control based on the checked state of the CheckBox control. The method is called from the setChecked method.

To add a method to a control

- Add the following method definition to the GroupCheck control's source code:

```
public void enableControls(Control start, boolean enable) {
    for(int i = 0; i < start.getControlCount(); i++) {
        Control c = start.getControl(i);
        if(c == groupBox1 || c == checkBox1) {
            continue;
        }
        c.setEnabled(enable);
        enableControls (c, enable);
    }
}
```

The enableControls method accepts a control and a Boolean value that determines whether the contained controls should be enabled or disabled. When this method is called by the setChecked method, it is passed the current instance of the GroupCheck control.

The enableControls method begins by looping through all the controls that are contained in the start control parameter. Within the for loop, the code obtains a contained control using the getControl method with the for loop's current index. If the control is not the GroupCheck control's GroupBox or CheckBox controls, the code enables or disables the specified control based on the value of the enable parameter. Any controls that are contained within this control are then enabled or disabled through a recursive call to enableControls.

The next step is to add code to the constructor.

Adding Code to the Constructor

To provide initial settings for your control, you add code to the constructor. For the
GroupCheck control, you add code that sets the control properly when it is added
to a form.

To add code to the constructor

- Replace the code in the constructor for the GroupCheck control with the following
  lines of code:

```
super();

initForm();

setStyle(this.STYLE_ACCEPTSCHILDREN, true);
m_bReady = true;
```

  This code sets the style of the GroupCheck control to one that accepts child
  controls. The code also sets the private member variable m_bReady to true so that
  the GroupCheck control's add method knows that the control is finished initializing
  and can accept controls to be added to the GroupBox control.

  The next step is to build the control.

Building the Control

To use your control, you must build it. When the control has been built, you can then
add it to the Toolbox.

To build the control

1. On the **Build** menu, click **Build**.

   Any compilation errors or messages appear in the Task List. (Double-clicking an error
   in the Task List moves the insertion point in the Text editor to the code that caused
   the error.)

2. Correct the errors and rebuild your control.

The final step is to debug the control.

Debugging the Control

After you have built your control, you test and debug the control to ensure that it operates as you designed it. To do this, add your control to the Toolbox, add a form to the project, and then add the control to the form. For the GroupCheck scenario, you also add controls to the GroupCheck control, add an event handler for the control's custom events, and then build and run the control.

Adding the Control to the Toolbox

After you have built your control, you add it to the Toolbox in order to use it.

To add the control to the Toolbox

1. Right-click the ToolBox, and click **Customize Toolbox**.

2. Click the **WFC Controls** tab, and select the name of your control.

   For this scenario, click the **GroupCheck** control.

3. Click **OK**.

Adding a Form to the Project

To test and debug your control, you add a form to your project.

To add a form to your project

1. In Project Explorer, right-click the name of your project, point to **Add**, and then click **Add Form**.

2. Click the **Form** icon.

3. In the **Name** box, type a name for the form.

   Ensure that the name of the form is not **GroupCheck** so that the form's source file does not conflict with the name of your control.

4. Click **Open**.

   A form is added to your project with the name that you specified and is opened in the Forms Designer.

Adding the Control to the Form

To test the control, you add the control to a form.

To add your control to a form

1. Select the form.

2. In the Toolbox, double-click your control.

   The control is added to the center of the form.

Adding Controls to the GroupCheck Control

To ensure that the GroupCheck control is properly parenting controls that are added to it, you add other WFC controls to the GroupCheck control.

To add other controls to the GroupCheck control

1. On the form, select the **GroupCheck** control.

2. In the Toolbox, double-click a control to add the specified control to the center of the **GroupCheck** control.

Creating Event Handlers

The GroupCheck control contains a custom event called checkedChanged. This event is triggered when the CheckBox control that is contained in the GroupCheck control is either checked or unchecked. To determine whether the event is being triggered properly, you add an event handler for the checkedChanged event to your form.

To add an event handler for the checkedChange event

1. In the Properties window, click the **Events** toolbar button.

2. To display the events of the GroupCheck control, select either the GroupCheck control on the form or the name of the control in the Properties window.

3. Double-click the **checkedChanged** event to create an event handler with the default method name.

   The Text editor opens to an empty event handler.

To determine whether the checkedChanged event is being triggered, add code to the event handler for the form that displays a message box each time the event is triggered.

To add code for the event handler

- Inside the definition for the event handler, add the following line of code:

```
MessageBox.show("The checkedChanged event was triggered.");
```

Building and Testing the Control

After you have added the control to a form, added controls to the GroupCheck control, and added an event handler for the control's checkedChanged event, you build and run the project.

To build and run the form

1. On the **Build** menu, click **Build**. (If you receive any compilation errors or messages, correct the errors and rebuild your project.)

2. To run the form, click **Start** on the **Debug** menu.

   Because you are running your project for the first time and because your project contains two .java files, the **Project Properties** dialog box is displayed.

3. On the **Launch** tab, select the **Default** option button.

4. Specify that **Form1** should load when the project runs, and click **OK**.

   For more information about project properties, see "Setting Project Options" in Chapter 1, "Creating Projects."

While the project is running, you can manipulate the control to determine whether it operates properly.

To test the control at run time

- Click the check box in the GroupCheck control.

  A message box is displayed notifying you that the checkedChanged event was triggered. This event occurs each time the check box's checked state changes. The controls contained in the GroupCheck control are either enabled or disabled depending on the checked state of the control.

For information on exporting a WFC control as an ActiveX control see "Building ActiveX Controls" in Chapter 16 "Building and Importing ActiveX Controls."

CHAPTER 14

Programming Dynamic HTML in Java

With Microsoft Internet Explorer 4.0, Microsoft introduced its implementation of a revolutionary HTML object model that content providers can use to effectively manipulate HTML properties on the fly. Until now, this object model has primarily been accessed using script technology. The com.ms.wfc.html package of the Windows Foundation Classes for Java (WFC) framework now lets you access the power of Dynamic HTML (DHTML) on a Web page directly from a Java class.

The following subjects are covered in this section:

- Introduction to the com.ms.wfc.html Package
- Using the initForm Method
- Understanding the DhElement Class
- Working with Containers
- Handling Events
- Using Dynamic Styles
- Working with Dynamic Tables
- Using the com.ms.wfc.html Package on the Server

Quick Start

To help you get up and running using the com.ms.wfc.html package to implement Java and DHTML, here are the basic steps you can perform to create a simple DHTML project and add your own dynamic behavior to it. While this is by no means the entire story, it sets the stage for the rest of this subject and for the samples. There are five basic steps when using the com.ms.wfc.html package:

1. Create a new project by choosing New Project from the File menu and selecting Code-behind HTML from the Web Pages category.

   This generates a project containing a class called Class1, which extends DhDocument. This class represents the dynamic HTML document. You add initialization code to its initForm method to control the document's contents and behavior.

   You can now extend the behavior of your document by doing the following:

2. Create new elements (such as DhButton) or create element objects that represent existing elements in the document (on the HTML page).

3. Hook event handlers into some of your elements.

4. In your Class1.initForm method, add the new elements using the setNewElements method, and bind any existing elements using the setBoundElements method.

5. Write the event handler methods you hooked up in step 3.

Your document class will look something like this:

```
import com.ms.wfc.html.*;
import com.ms.wfc.core.*;
import com.ms.wfc.ui.*;

public class Class1 extends DhDocument
{
    public Class1()
    {
        initForm();
    }

    // Step 2: create objects to represent a new elements…
    DhButton newElem = new DhButton();
    // … as well as elements that already exist in the HTML page.
    DhText existElem = new DhText();

    private void initForm( )
    {
        // Set properties to existing elements and newly added elements.
        newElem.setText("hello world");
        existElem.setBackColor(Color.BLUE);
```

```
    // Step 3: hook up an event handler to your object
    newElem.addOnClick(new EventHandler(this.onClickButton));

    // Step 2: create an object to represent an existing element
    existElem = new DhText();

    // Step 4: call setNewElements with an array of new elements
    setNewElements(new Component[] { newElem });

    // Step 4: call bindNewElements with an array of existing elements
    setBoundElements(new DhElement[]{ existElem.setBindID("Sample") });
}

// Step 5: implement your event handler
private void onClickButton(Object sender, Event e) {
    existElem.setText("Hello, world");
}
}
```

The Java portion of the exercise is complete. The other part is the HTML code. The
following example shows a simplified version of the HTML document generated by the
Code-behind HTML project template. There are two HTML elements that connect this
HTML to the code in your project:

- The <OBJECT> tag loads the com.ms.wfc.html.DhModule class, which is instantiated
  by the Virtual Machine for Java.

- The <OBJECT> tag has a parameter called CODECLASS. The value of this parameter
  is the name of the user class that extends DhDocument (for example, Class1).

```
<HTML>
<BODY>
<OBJECT classid="java:com.ms.wfc.html.DhModule"
        height=0 width=0 ... VIEWASTEXT>
<PARAM NAME=CABBASE VALUE=MyProject>
<PARAM NAME=CODECLASS VALUE=Class1>
</OBJECT>

<span id=Sample></span>
<!-- Insert your own HTML here -->

</BODY>
</HTML>
```

Open Internet Explorer 4.0, point it at your HTML file, and you can see your
application run.

Using the initForm Method

The initForm method plays a central role in the programming model for all user interface programming in WFC. When using the Visual J++ Forms Designer for Win32-based applications, initForm is found in the Form-derived class that represents your main form. In the com.ms.wfc.html package, this method is found in your DhDocument-derived class (for example, Class1 in the code-behind HTML template provided by Visual J++) and is called from the constructor of the class.

You should use the initForm method to initialize the Java components that represent the HTML elements you want to access and code to. As with the initForm method in Form-derived classes, there are certain restrictions when calling WFC methods from initForm in DhDocument. As a rule, you should call only methods in initForm that set properties. Moreover, you should bind only to elements on the HTML page using the setBoundElements method.

Specifically, this means that calling any method that resets or removes a property or element is strictly not supported in initForm. This also applies to any methods that attempt to locate elements on the existing HTML page (such as DhDocument.findElement).

The reason for this is that the document on the existing HTML page is not merged with your DhDocument-derived class until the DhDocument.onDocumentLoad method is called. You can use the onDocumentLoad method to retrieve properties and manipulate or locate elements in the existing HTML document. For information on using the initForm and onDocumentLoad methods on server-side classes, see "Using the com.ms.wfc.html Package on a Server," later in this chapter.

Understanding the DhElement Class

Elements are objects derived from DhElement, which is the superclass of all user interface elements in the com.ms.wfc.html package. There is a certain consistency you can count on when using any object derived from DhElement:

- Every element has an empty constructor. Therefore, you can instantiate any element with a new statement and then set properties, hook event handlers, and call methods consistently.

- Elements are modeless. Setting properties or calling methods always works in any order and is not conditional on some external state or circumstance.

- Every container has an add method that takes the type-safe element that is appropriate for it.

- In the browser environment, an element does not become visible to the end user until you add it (or the topmost container element in its parentage) to the document. However, this is merely an artifact and not part of the programming model. You don't have to change the way you program to elements because they work the same way whether they are visible or not.

If an element is already on the page when the DhDocument.onDocumentLoad method is called, you can call the document's findElement method and start programming to that element. You can also call setBoundElements from initForm to merge known elements on the page with elements in your DhDocument-derived class. (The findElement method has better performance but specifically requires that onDocumentLoad is called first.)

The searching routine used by findElement and setBoundElements assumes that the element you want to bind to has an ID attribute set to a particular name. Using findElement, you can also enumerate all the elements in the document until you find the one you are interested in.

Working with Containers

Containers are elements that can hold other elements. A basic example is the <DIV> element, which can contain any other HTML item. More complex examples include table cells and, of course, the document itself. In most cases, containers can be arbitrarily nested, such as having a table inside a cell of another table.

Containers are like other elements. They are created with a new statement, and many can be positioned and sized on the page. You can position and size elements within a container and set up their z-order relationships. One of the powerful features of DHTML is that you can then change any of these attributes in your code.

Of course, you can also allow elements within a container to be positioned using the normal HTML layout rules. Call either the setLocation or setBounds method of an element to set its absolute position, or call resetLocation to let the HTML layout engine position it (immediately after the last element in the HTML flow layout).

Once you have created a container element, you can add elements to it using either the setNewElements or add method. This mechanism follows the regular pattern of parent-child relationships: the elements, which can also be other containers, added to the container become its children. None is actually attached to the document until the topmost container, which is not a part of any other container, is added to the document.

You can position and size a container using its setBounds method. For example, to create a container, type:

```
DhForm myForm = new DhForm();
```

You can then set various attributes on the container, including the ToolTip that is shown when the mouse hovers over the panel:

```
myForm.setToolTip("This text appears when the mouse hovers");
myForm.setFont("Arial", 10);
myForm.setBackColor(Color.RED);
myForm.setBounds(5, 5, 100, 100);
```

Finally, you can add the container you've just created to the document in your DhDocument-derived class (such as Class1.java):

```
this.add(myForm);
```

When adding elements to the container, you can specify where they go in the z-order using one of a set of constants provided by the com.ms.wfc.html package. Elements are added with a default size and position. You can call setBounds on the elements to specify a different size.

```
DhForm myOverLay1 = new DhForm();
DhForm myOverLay2 = new DhForm();
myOverLay1.setBackColor(Color.BLACK);
myOverLay1.setBounds(10, 10, 50, 50);
myOverLay2.setBackColor(Color.BLUE);
myOverLay2.setBounds(20,25, 50, 50);
myForm.add(myOverLay1, null, DhInsertOptions.BEGINNING);
// Black on top of blue
myForm.add(myOverLay2, myOverLay1, DhInsertOptions.BEFORE);
// Blue on top of black (uncomment below and comment above )
// myForm.add(myOverLay2, myOverLay1, DhInsertOptions.AFTER);
```

You can also use the setZIndex method after the elements are added to move the elements around in the z-order. For example, the following syntax does not explicitly set a z-order on the added element but uses the default z-order (that is, on top of all other elements):

```
myForm.add(myText);
```

You can set this explicitly as follows, where **num** is an integer representing the relative z-order of the element within its container:

```
myText.setZIndex(num);
```

The element with the lowest number is at the bottom of the z-order (that is, everything else covers it). The element with the highest number is at the top (that is, it covers everything else).

Handling Events

Many elements in a DHTML program can trigger events. The com.ms.wfc.html package uses the same event model as the com.ms.wfc.ui package. If you are familiar with that mechanism, you'll find little difference between the two. A button is a good example. Suppose you want to handle the event that occurs when a user clicks a button on a page. Here's how:

```
public class Class1 extends DhDocument
{
    Class1() { initForm();}
    DhButton myButton = new DhButton();
    private void initForm()
    {
        add(myButton);
        myButton.addOnClick(new EventHandler(this.myButtonClick));
    }
    void myButtonClick(Object sender, Event e)
    {
        ((DhButton) sender).setText("I've been clicked");
    }
}
```

In this code, whenever the button triggers the onClick event (that is, when it is clicked), the myButtonClick event handler is called. The code inside the myButtonClick event handler does very little in this example. It just sets the caption on the button to new text.

Most events propagate all the way up a containment tree; this means that the click event is seen by the button's container and by the button itself. Although typically programmers handle events in the container closest to the event, this event bubbling model can be useful in special cases. It provides the programmer with the flexibility to decide the best place to code the event handlers.

Many different events can be triggered by elements in DHTML, and you can catch them all in the same way. For example, to determine when the mouse is over a button, try the following code, which catches mouseEnter and mouseLeave events for the button:

```
public class Class1 extends DhDocument
{
    DhButton button = new DhButton();
    private void initForm()
    {
        button.addOnMouseEnter(new MouseEventHandler(this.buttonEnter));
        button.addOnMouseLeave(new MouseEventHandler(this.buttonExit);
        setNewElements( new DhElement[] { button } );
    }
    void buttonEnter(Object sender, MouseEvent e)
    {
        button.setText("I can feel that mouse");
    }
}
```

```
void buttonExit(Object sender, MouseEvent e)
{
    button.setText("button");
}
}
```

All events that can be triggered (and caught) are defined in the event classes, based on com.ms.wfc.core.Event.

Using Dynamic Styles

You can think of a Style object as a freestanding collection of properties. The term style is borrowed from the word processing world where the editing of a style sheet is independent of the documents to which you apply it. The same is true for using and applying Style objects in this library.

As an example, your boss tells you that the new corporate color is red and you need to change the color of elements in your HTML pages. You can, of course, set properties directly on elements, which is the traditional model for GUI framework programming:

```
// old way of doing things...
DhText t1 = new DhText();
DhText t2 = new DhText();
t1.setColor( Color.RED );
t1.setFont( "arial");
t2.setColor( Color.RED );
t2.setFont( "arial");
```

You could, of course, use derivation to save yourself time. For example, you might consider improving this with the following code:

```
// old way of doing things a little better...
public class MyText extends DhText
{
    public MyText()
    {
        setColor( Color.RED );
        setFont( "arial" );
    }
}
```

This works fine until you decide you also want those settings for buttons, labels, tabs, documents, and so on. And you'll find yourself with even more work when you apply these to another part of your program or to another program.

The answer to this problem is a Style object. While using this library, you can instantiate a Style object and set its properties at any point:

```
// STEP 1: Create style objects.

DhStyle myStyle = new DhStyle();

// STEP 2: Set properties on style objects

myStyle.setColor( Color.RED );
myStyle.setFont( "arial" );
```

Then at any other time in the code, you can apply that style to any number of elements:

```
DhText t1 = new DhText();
DhText t2 = new DhText();

// STEP 3: Apply styles using the setStyle method.

t1.setStyle( myStyle );
t2.setStyle( myStyle );
```

When it's time to keep up with the dynamic nature of high-level policy setting at your corporation, the following line sets all instances of all elements with myStyle set on them to change color:

```
myStyle.setColor( Color.BLUE );
```

Here is the really powerful part: all this is available during run time. Every time you make a change to the Style object, the DHTML run time dynamically reaches back and updates all elements to which that Style object is applied.

For more information, see the next section, "Understanding Style Inheritance."

Understanding Style Inheritance

The HTML rendering engine can determine the style to use if conflicting styles are set on an element. For example, if an element has the color property set directly on it (DhElement.setColor), the color defined by the color property is used. However, if an element has a Style object on it (DhElement.setStyle) and that object has the color property set, that value is used. Failing to find a color or a style, the same process is used with the element's container (DhElement.getParent), and failing that, with the container of that container and so on.

The process continues up to the document. If the document doesn't have a color property set on it, the environment (either browser settings or some other environment settings) determines the color to use.

This process is called cascading styles because the properties cascade down the containment hierarchy. The underlying mechanism for DhStyle objects is called Cascading Style Sheets (CSS) by the W3C.

Working with Dynamic Tables

Working with tables is actually no different from any other part of the library; the principles and programming model apply to tables as they do to any other type of element. A table, however, is such a powerful and popular element that it is worth discussing.

To use a table, you create a DhTable object, add DhRow objects to that, and then add DhCell objects to the rows. The following are the rules for table usage:

- You can add only DhRow objects to a DhTable object.

- You can add only DhCell objects to a DhRow object.

- You can add any kind of element to a DhCell object.

While this may seem restrictive, you can easily create a simple container that emulates a gridbag with the following code:

```
import com.ms.wfc.html.*;

public class GridBag extends DhTable
{
    int    cols;
    int    currCol;
    DhRow currRow;

    public GridBag(int cols)
    {
       this.cols = cols;
       this.currCol = cols;
    }

    public void add(DhElement e)
    {
       if( ++this.currCol >= cols )
       {
          this.currRow = new DhRow();
          super.add(currRow);
          this.currCol = 0;
       }
       DhCell c = new DhCell();
       c.add(e);
       this.currRow.add( c );
    }

}
```

To use this GridBag class, you just set the number of rows and columns (they must be the same with this implementation) and then assign elements to cells. The following is an example of the code in your DhDocument-derived class that uses this GridBag:

```
protected void initForm()
{
    GridBag myTable = new GridBag(5);
    for (int i = 0; i < 25; ++i){
        myTable.add(new DhText("" + i));
    setNewElements( new DhElement[] { myTable } );
    }
}
```

One of the most powerful uses of the library is the combination of tables and Style objects. This combination enables you to create custom report generators that are powerful, professional looking, and easy to code.

Data Binding to Tables

Tables also have data binding capabilities. Using a com.ms.wfc.data.ui.DataSource object, you can bind data to your table, as shown in the following sample code.

```
.
.
.
import com.ms.wfc.data.*;
import com.ms.wfc.data.ui.*;
.
.
.
void private initForm( ){

    DhTable dataTable = new DhTable();
    dataTable.setBorder( 1 );
    dataTable.setAutoHeader( true );

    DataSource dataSource = new DataSource();
    dataSource.setConnectionString("DSN=Northwind");
    dataSource.setCommandText("SELECT * FROM Products" );
```

```
// if you would like to use the table on the server,
// call dataSource.getRecordset() to force the DataSource
// to synchronously create the recordset; otherwise,
// call dataSource.begin(), and the table will be populated
// when the recordset is ready, asynchronously.
if ( !getServerMode() ){
   dataSource.begin();
   dataTable.setDataSource( dataSource );
} else
   dataTable.setDataSource( dataSource.getRecordset() );

setNewElements( new DhElement[] { dataTable } );
}
```

If you know the format of the data that is going to be returned, you can also specify
a template (repeater) row that the table will use to format the data that is returned.
The steps to do this are as follows:

1. Create your DhTable element:

    ```
    DhTable dataTable = new DhTable();
    ```

2. Create your template row and set it into the table; you can also optionally create a
    header row. For each item in the template cell that you would like to receive data
    from the recordset, create a DataBinding for it.

    .
    .
    .

    ```
    DhRow repeaterRow = new DhRow();
    RepeaterRow.setBackColor( Color.LIGHTGRAY );
    RepeaterRow.setForeColor( Color.BLACK );
    DataBinding[] bindings = new DataBinding[3];
    DhCell  cell = new DhCell();
    DataBinding[0] = new DataBinding( cell, "text", "ProductID" );
    repeaterRow.add( cell );
    cell = new DhCell();.
    DataBinding[1] = new DataBinding( cell, "text", "ProductName" );
    cell = new DhCell();.
    cell.setForeColor( Color.RED );
    cell.add( new DhText( "$" ) );
    DhText price = new DhText();
    price.setFont( Font.ANSI_FIXED );
    DataBinding[2] = new DataBinding( price, "text", "UnitPrice" );
    cell.add( price );
    repeaterRow.add( cell );

    // set up the table repeater row and bindings
    table.setRepeaterRow( repeaterRow );
    table.setDataBindings( bindings );
    ```

```
// create and set the header row
DhRow headerRow = new DhRow();
headerRow.add( new DhCell( "ProductID" ) );
headerRow.add( new DhCell( "Product Name" ) );
headerRow.add( new DhCell( "Unit Price" ) );
table.setHeaderRow( headerRow );
```

3. Create a DataSource object, and set it to retrieve data in the format you expect.

```
DataSource ds = new DataSource();
ds.setConnectionString("DSN=Northwind");
ds.setCommandText("SELECT ProductID, ProductName,
    UnitPrice FROM Products WHERE UnitPrice < 10" );
```

4. Set the DataSource into the DhTable object.

```
table.setDataSource( ds );
ds.begin();
```

5. Add the DhTable to the document.

```
setNewElements( new DhElement[] { table } );
// alternately: add( table );
```

Your table is now populated with the data from the recordset and formatted like the template row.

Using the com.ms.wfc.html Package on a Server

The com.ms.wfc.html package can also be used on the server to provide a programmatic model for generating HTML and sending it to the client page. Unlike the client-side Dynamic HTML model, the server-side model is static because the server Java class has no interaction with the client document. Instead, the server composes HTML elements and sends them off sequentially to the client as they are encountered in the HTML template if one is specified.

Although not fully dynamic, this is still a powerful server feature. For example, you can apply DhStyle attributes to all parts of some template HTML code and then generate vastly different looking pages by just changing the DhStyle attributes. You do not have to programmatically generate all the individual style changes. Another advantage is that you can use the same model for generating dynamic HTML for both client and server applications, thereby making the HTML generation easier to learn and remember.

There are currently two modes of generating HTML on the server. Both use Active Server Pages (ASP) scripting and a class based on the com.ms.wfc.html classes. The first is the "bare-bones" approach that relies more on the ASP script. The second uses a class derived from DhDocument and is very similar to the model that you use on the client because it places more control inside the class than in the script.

ASP-Based Approach

This approach uses two ASP methods on the server page: getObject and Response.Write. The getObject method is used to instantiate a class based on the WFC com.ms.wfc.html classes; the Response.Write method writes the generated HTML string to the client. The com.ms.wfc.html.DhElement class provides a getHTML method that creates the HTML string; this string is then sent to the client page using the ASP Response.Write method.

For example, you have a class called MyServer that extends DhForm and incorporates some HTML elements. In your ASP script, you first call getObject("java:MyServer") to create a DHTML object. You can then perform whatever actions you want on the object from your ASP script, such as setting properties on the object. When you have finished, you call the object's getHTML method to generate the string and pass that result to the ASP Response.Write method, which sends the HTML to the client. The following code fragments show the relevant ASP script and Java code for creating a DhEdit control in HTML and sending it to the client.

ASP SCRIPT

```
Dim f,x
set f = getObject( "java:dhFactory" )
set x= f.createEdit
x.setText( "I'm an edit!" )
Response.Write( x.getHTML() )
Response.Write( f.createBreak().getHTML() )
.
.
.
```

JAVA CODE

```
public class dhFactory {
   public dhFactory(){ }

   public DhBreak createBreak() {
      return new DhBreak();
   }

   public DhEdit createEdit(){
      return new DhEdit();
   }
}
```

HTML-Based Approach

This approach is slightly more sophisticated and closer to the client model. It still uses an ASP script to site the DhDocument class, but the rest of the operational code is in Java. As in the client model, the DhModule class is instantiated as the Java component on the Web page and automatically calls the initForm method in your project class that derives from DhDocument.

As in the client model, you can do all your binding setup in your initForm call. The onDocumentLoad function is also called for your server-side class. In this method, you can access the IIS Response and Request objects (using the DhModule getResponse and getRequest methods) and also append new DhElement items to your document stream. However, it is important to understand that you cannot use document-level functions, such as findElement, or use enumeration operations on a server-side document, except on items that you have explicitly added to your DhDocument-derived class.

To use the HTML-based approach, follow these steps:

1. Create your server Java class (extending from DhDocument).

2. In that class, implement the initForm method as you would with a client application.

3. From ASP, call the Server.CreateObject method, passing it "DhModule" to create a DhModule object.

4. Call DhModule.setCodeClass method, passing it the name of your DhDocument-derived class.

5. Call the DhModule.setHTMLDocument method, passing it the full local file name path of your server Web page as a template if you have one.

   If you call setHTMLDocument with an empty string (""), your DhDocument class runs and outputs the HTML for any elements you have added at the location in your ASP where setHTMLDocument is called. You can then generate sections of HTML code inline.

   If you do not call setHTMLDocument, the DhDocument class outputs full HTML for the page, including the <HTML>, <HEAD>, and <BODY> tags.

The following sample shows an ASP page that uses a template:

```
<% Set mod = Server.CreateObject( "com.ms.wfc.html.DhModule" )
   mod.setCodeClass( "Class1" )
   mod.setHTMLDocument( "c:\inetpub\wwwroot\Page1.htm" )
%>
```

At run time, the framework recognizes that your class is running on a server and acts accordingly.

Once instantiated, you can add elements or text to your DhDocument-derived class. Those items will be appended to any template specified just before the </BODY> tag.

The following sample demonstrates a class that works on either the client or the server.

```
import com.ms.wfc.ui.*;
import com.ms.wfc.html.*;

public class Class1 extends DhDocument {
    public Class1(){
        initForm();
    }
    DhText txt1 = new DhText();
    DhForm sect = new DhForm();

    private void initForm() {

        // call getServerMode() to check
        // if this object is running on the server
        if ( getServerMode() ){
            txt1.setText( "Hello from the server!" );
        }else{
            txt1.setText( "Hello from the client!" );
        }

        // size the section, set its background color
        // and add the txt1 element to it
        sect.setSize( 100, 100 );
        sect.setBackColor( Color.RED );
        sect.add( txt1 );
        add( sect );
        setNewElements( new DhElement[] { sect } );
    }
}
```

If you want to bind to an existing HTML document on the page, use the DhDocument.setBoundElements method, just as you would on the client. For example, if your HTML template contains the following HTML:

```
<P>
The time is:<SPAN id=txt1></SPAN><BR>
<INPUT type=text id=edit1 value="">
</P>
```

Your initForm method looks like this:

```
DhText txt1 = new DhText();
DhEdit edit = new DhEdit();
DhComboBox cb = new DhComboBox();

private void initForm(){
    txt1.setText(com.ms.wfc.app.Time().formatShortTime());

    edit.setText("Hello, world!");
    edit.setBackColor( Color.RED );

    setBoundElements( new DhElement[]{ txt1.setBindID( "txt1" )
                                       edit.setBindID( "edit1" ) } );

    // Create a combo box to be added after the bound items
    cb.addItem( "One" );
    cb.addItem( "Two" );

    // Add the items to the end of  document.
    setNewElements( new DhElement[]{ cb });
}
```

There are very few differences between the interpretation of server and client
HTML classes. However, there is one important difference. Once elements are written
(sent to the client), they cannot be modified as they can on a client document. The
DhCantModifyElement exception, which is relevant only for server applications, is
thrown after a write has been performed on an element if an attempt is made to modify
that element again. (This underscores the fact that there is no real interoperation between
the server Java class and the client document as there is on the client between the Java
class and the document: from the server's standpoint, once written, the element is
essentially gone.)

One advantage of using the DhDocument-derived method is that you can implement
an HTML template that is embedded with attributes recognized by the com.ms.wfc.html
classes. By first decorating the HTML elements in the file with ID attributes and then
setting the corresponding IDs in the source code using the DhElement.setBindID method,
you can bind to these HTML elements, set properties on the elements, add your own
inline HTML code, and so forth. This essentially allows you to code and design separate
templates ahead of time and populate the template with dynamic data when the document
is requested from the server.

Graphical Services

The display of graphical objects in Microsoft Windows occurs through the graphics device interface (GDI), a device-independent graphics output model that processes graphical function calls from a Windows-based application and passes those calls to the appropriate device driver. The driver performs the hardware-specific functions that generate output. By acting as a buffer between applications and output devices, the GDI presents a device-independent view for the application while interacting in a device-dependent format with the device.

Application developers use the functionality of the GDI to display images, to draw controls, shapes, and text, and to create and use pens, brushes, and fonts. The Windows Foundation Classes (WFC) Graphics object coordinates with other WFC objects, such as the Pen, Font, and Brush objects, to encapsulate these capabilities as Java-based objects.

In the WFC environment, graphical output occurs through the Graphics object. After creating or retrieving a Graphics object, you associate other graphics-based objects, such as fonts, pens, and brushes with the object, and then use the object's numerous drawing methods to render output to the display. For example, to draw lines with a specific appearance, you use the Graphics object's setPen method to specify the pen that the object will use for drawing, then use the object's drawLine method to render the lines. You can modify these associations as often as you want.

Creating a Graphics Object

The Windows Foundation Classes (WFC) provide several ways in which to create a Graphics object.

Explicit object creation. You can create a Graphics object explicitly by calling the createGraphics method on any object that extends the Control class.

Implicit object creation. The Bitmap and Metafile objects support implicit Graphics object creation through a getGraphics method.

Explicit Graphics Object Creation

All classes that extend the Control class support the createGraphics method, which you can use to create a Graphics object instance. The following code fragment demonstrates how to call this method from within a Form-derived class:

```
Graphics g = this.createGraphics();
```

A second approach to explicit Graphics object creation involves using a handle to a Win32 device context (HDC). Generally, the only case in which you create a Graphics object in this fashion is when you have called a Win32 method that returns an HDC.

If you simply need graphical capabilities that are not supported natively in the Graphics object, you can use the object's getHandle method to retrieve the handle to a Win32 device context and can pass that handle transparently to the appropriate Win32 method.

If you create a Graphics object based on a previously existing handle, the Graphics object doesn't assume ownership of the handle; after you have used the object, you are responsible for freeing the handle using the appropriate Win32 function. If you use the Graphics object's getHandle method to retrieve the object's underlying handle, the object retains ownership of that handle and you should not try to free it.

For more information on Win32 handles and the Graphics object, see "Performing Handle-Based Operations," later in this chapter.

Implicit Graphics Object Creation

The Bitmap and Metafile objects support implicit Graphics object creation through their getGraphics method. In the following code fragment, the Bitmap object's getGraphics method is used to create a Graphics object that can be used to draw to the bitmap's surface:

```
Bitmap bmp = new Bitmap("c:\\MyImage.bmp");
Graphics gr = bmp.getGraphics();
```

The first time that you call getGraphics through an object, the object creates a new Graphics object instance and returns it. Subsequent calls to getGraphics through the same object results in the return of the object created through the original call.

Additionally, when you call drawing methods through a Graphics object created through an object's getGraphics method, the methods apply to the object through which they were created. For example, the x and y coordinates (0,0) specified in the call to drawText above are relative to the bitmap object, not to the control on which the bitmap is rendered.

Retrieving a Graphics Object

Within a form or control's paint event, you can retrieve and use a Graphics object instance. The paint event handler takes a PaintEvent object as a parameter, and this object contains a public graphics member. This member is a valid Graphics object instance, which you call as follows:

```
protected void onPaint(PaintEvent e){
    e.graphics.drawString("Hello, World", new Point(10, 10));
}
```

For information on how to create a Graphics object outside the paint event, see the earlier sections "Explicit Graphics Object Creation" and "Implicit Graphics Object Creation."

Graphics Object Scope

The Graphics object has *method scope*. This means that when a method in which you use the Graphics object returns, the object's dispose method is called automatically, freeing all resources that the object has allocated. After dispose has been called, attempts to use the object result in a run-time exception.

If you declare an instance of the Graphics object at the class level, you should use the Form object's createGraphics method to initialize that object in every method that uses it:

```
Public class Form1 extends Form{

    Graphics g  = new Graphics();

    Private void Form1_resize(Object sender, Event e){

        // Initialize object instance.
        g = this.createGraphics();

        // dispose automatically called…
    }

    private void Form1_click(Object sender, Event e){

        // Initialize object instance.

        g = this.createGraphics();

        // dispose method automatically called…
    }


}
```

Although the dispose method is called automatically, it is good practice to call it explicitly at the end of routines that use the Graphics object. This is particularly important on the Windows 95 platform because of a system limitation on the number of device context that can be allocated.

Maintaining the Bounding Rectangle

The area of a window in which you can draw is referred to as the window's *client area*. Within this area, a *bounding rectangle* defines the invisible rectangular region in which the Graphics object draws, and can include the window's entire client area.

When a window loses, and then regains focus, the part of the bounding rectangle covered by some other object does not automatically re-display the items that were previously rendered to it.

To ensure correct display, you must manage the repainting of your form or control. The paint event handler is the place in your Form class code in which such management typically takes place. Within this handler, you restore the bounding rectangle to its proper state.

The following example creates a Bitmap object at the class level, then it uses the paint event handler to redraw the Bitmap. Each time the client area of the form becomes invalid, Windows invokes this handler, and the image is repainted to the form:

```
Bitmap bmp = new Bitmap("c:\\MyImage.bmp");

protected void onPaint(PaintEvent e){
    e.graphics.drawImage(bmp, new Point(0, 0));
}
```

When your form is initially displayed, and each time it regains focus, the paint event handler is automatically invoked. However, if your form supports resizing, a change in the form's dimensions does not automatically trigger a repaint. Instead, you must add a resize handler to the Form-derived class and then call the object's invalidate method from within this handler. A call to invalidate trigger's the form's paint event handler:

```
protected void onResize(Event e){
    this.invalidate();
}
```

Performing Handle-Based Operations

A handle is a unique number with which some element of the operating system is identified to the computer. For example, every window on your desktop has a unique handle that enables the computer to distinguish it from other windows. Every device context, brush, pen, and font also has a unique handle.

To maintain optimal compatibility with the Win32 API, the Graphics, Pen, Brush, and Font objects support handle-based operations. For example, if you use the Win32 CreatePen function to create a pen, this function returns a handle. You can then pass this handle to the Pen object constructor, and the object is created based on the characteristics of that Win32 pen.

Even if you do not create a Pen, Brush, or Font object based on a handle that you allocate, you can retrieve the handle on which a Pen, Brush, or Font object is based. Each of these objects supports both a copyHandle and a getHandle method, and once you've used these methods to duplicate or retrieve the object's handle, you can pass that handle to any Win32 function that is intended to take such a handle as a parameter.

The following are a few important rules to keep in mind when performing handle-based operations with the Graphics object:

- If you create an object based on a handle that you've previously allocated using a Win32 method, the object does not assume ownership of that handle. For example, if you use the Win32 GetDC method to retrieve a form's device context handle (HDC), then create a Graphics object based on that HDC, then you own the handle. This means that when the Graphics object's dispose method is called, the handle is not freed in memory. Instead, you must use the appropriate Win32 routine to destroy the handle.

  Below is an example that illustrates appropriate handle management. This example uses the Win32 GetDC to retrieve the handle to the form's device context, then creates a Graphics object based on that handle. After using the Graphics object to draw a line on the form, the Graphics object's dispose method is used to destroy the Graphics object, and the Win32 ReleaseDC routine is used to free the device context handle allocated by GetDC:

```
// import the com.ms.wfc.Win32.Windows package.
import com.ms.wfc.win32.Windows;

int hDC = Windows.GetDC(this.getHandle());
Graphics g = new Graphics(hDC);

g.drawLine(new Point(0,0), new Point(100, 0));
g.dispose();

Windows.ReleaseDC(hDC);
```

  Note that while this example uses the handle to a device context, the principle illustrated here applies to pens, brushes, fonts, and bitmaps.

- Most graphical objects support a copyHandle method through which you can duplicate the handle on which the object is based. If you use the copyHandle method to duplicate an object's handle, you are responsible for freeing the handle.

- Most graphical objects also support a getHandle method, which returns the handle on which the object is based (as opposed to a copy of that handle). This method is intended to enable support compatibility between Graphics object methods and Win32 graphics routines.

  Handles retrieved through the getHandle method are not copies of an object's underlying handle. Therefore, you should never attempt to free handles retrieved through getHandle. Such handles are freed when the object is disposed.

The Graphics Object Coordinate System

A large number of the methods supported by the Graphics object depend on numerical coordinates. Such coordinates can be specified in a Rectangle object, which specifies the area in which an operation is to occur, or in a Point object, which specifies the x (horizontal) and y (vertical) coordinates at which the operation occurs.

The term *coordinate system* identifies how the coordinates specified in such objects map to the display or to a device. Suppose, for example, that you call the Graphics object's drawString method to draw text at coordinates 100, 100:

```
Graphics g = this.createGraphics();
g.drawString("Hello, WFC, new Point(100, 100));
```

The Point object in this example specifies the *x* and *y* coordinates at which to draw the string. However, the actual result of this operation depends on the coordinate system with which the Graphics object is associated.

The coordinate systems with which you can associate a Graphics object are defined in the CoordinateSystem class. The default coordinate system for a Graphics object is CoordinateSystem.TEXT, which means that as the x and y values in a Point object increase, the text (or bitmap or control) proceeds to the right horizontally and down vertically.

To associate a coordinate system with the Graphics object, use the setCoordinateSystem method, as follows:

```
Graphics gr = this.createGraphics();
gr.setCoordinateSystem(CoordinateSystem.ANISOTROPIC);
```

The following table lists the coordinate systems that you can associate with the Graphics object and describes the direction in which drawing proceeds as the x and y axes defined in a Point object increase.

Coordinate System	Increasing x-axis	Increasing y-axis
CoordinateSystem.TEXT	Right	Down
CoordinateSystem.LOMETRIC	Right	Up
CoordinateSystem.HIMETRIC	Right	Up
CoordinateSystem.LOENGLISH	Right	Up
CoordinateSystem.HIENGLISH	Right	Up
CoordinateSystem.TWIPS	Right	Up
CoordinateSystem.ISOTROPIC	User-defined	User-defined
CoordinateSystem.ANISOTROPIC	User-defined	User-defined

Setting the Coordinate Origin

The coordinate origin identifies the location from which coordinates are measured.

For example, if you create a Graphics object through your application's main form, the Graphics object's coordinate system is CoordinateSystem.TEXT and graphical coordinates are measured from the upper-left corner (0,0) of the form.

However, if you use a user-defined coordinate system, such as CoordinateSystem.ANISOTROPIC or CoordinateSystem.ISOTROPIC, you can specify the point from which coordinates are measured (both for the page and the device), using the Graphics object's setCoordinateOrigin method. Suppose, for example, that you include in your application's paint event the following code:

```
private void Form1_paint(Object source, PaintEvent e)
{
// Set the coordinate system.

e.graphics.setCoordinateSystem(CoordinateSystem.ANISOTROPIC);
e.graphics.setCoordinateOrigin(new Point(20, 20), new Point(20,20));
e.graphics.setCoordinateScale(new Point(1,1), new Point(1,1));
e.graphics.drawLine(new Point(0,0), new Point(100,100));

}
```

This code sets the coordinate system to CoordinateSystem.ANISOTROPIC and then sets the coordinate origin for both the page and device at 20,20. The call to drawLine that appears later in the code measures from the coordinate origin. Thus, the line will end at 100,100 from the coordinate origin (10,10).

Mapping Logical Coordinates to Device Coordinates

Windows provides built-in support for mapping page coordinates to a device, such as a printer or display.

For most of the coordinate systems defined by Windows, the system itself performs the conversion. For example, if you associate a Graphics object with the CoordinateSystem.HIMETRIC coordinate system, each logical unit on the object translates to .001 of an inch on the device.

However, when using the user-defined ANISOTROPIC and ISOTROPIC coordinate systems, you must use the setCoordinateScale method to tell the system how to perform the conversion, as in the following example:

```
Graphics g = this.createGraphics();
g.setCoordinateSystem(CoordinateSystem.ANISOTROPIC);
g.setCoordinateScale(new Point(1,1), new Point(2,2));
```

The call to setCoordinateScale in this example instructs the system to convert a single logical horizontal and vertical unit to two horizontal and vertical device units.

Drawing Text

The Graphics object's drawString method supports the output of text to the control to which the object belongs. This method writes the text to the location that you specify, as in the following example:

```
Graphics g = this.createGraphics();
g.drawString("Hello, World", new Point(0, 0));
```

The visual result of this call depends upon a host of factors, including the Graphics object's current text color, background color, font settings, and coordinate systems.

For information on how to set the text color, see the next section, "Setting Text Color." For information on associating fonts with the Graphics object, see "Using the Font Object," later in this chapter. For information about coordinate systems, see "The Graphics Object Coordinate System," later in this chapter.

Setting Text Color

To set the text and background color of the text, call the Graphics object's setBackColor and setTextColor before calling drawString:

```
// Set the text to white, the background to black.

g.setTextColor(new Color(0, 0, 0));

g.setBackColor(new Color(255, 255, 255));

// Draw the text...
```

The setBackColor method affects only the background color of text. To set the background or fill color for other objects, such as polygons and lines, use the setBrush and setPen methods, respectively.

Using the Font Object

A *font* is a collection of characters and symbols that share a common design. The major elements of a font include its typeface, style, and size.

In WFC, Windows fonts are encapsulated in the Font object. You can use this object in combination with other font-related objects to define a limitless variety of fonts for display on a Graphics object.

The following table lists the font-related classes supported by WFC.

Class	Description
FontDescriptor	Provides information about the font that underlies a Font object.
FontFamily	Defines a group of constants that represent the families to which a font may belong.
FontMetrics	Defines the physical characteristics of a font as it is mapped into a Graphics object.
FontPitch	Defines a font's pitch.
FontSize	Defines a group of constants that represent the units in which font sizes can be specified.
FontType	Defines a group of constants that represent the devices to which the font will be rendered.
FontWeight	Defines constants that represent the different weights that you can associate with a font.

Creating a Font Object

Creating a Font object can be very simple or complex, depending on the granularity with which you want to define the font. The following code fragment illustrates one of the simple approaches to Font object creation:

```
Font font = new Font("Times New Roman", 26);
```

This example uses a Font object constructor that requires only two items of information: the font name and size. When creating a Font object, you can also specify the font's family, its type, its weight, its orientation, and whether or not the font is boldfaced, italicized, underlined, or strikeout. However, once you've created a Font object, you cannot modify the object's attributes.

Setting the Font on a Graphics Object

The Graphics object supports the setFont method, which associates a font with the object. After you associate a Font object with the Graphics object, all text drawn within the Graphics object's bounding rectangle is drawn using that font.

The following code illustrates the process of setting the background color of the Graphics object to white, the text color to black, and the font to 26-point Times New Roman. The text is drawn to the display at a specified position:

```
Graphics g = this.createGraphics();

g.setFont(new Font("Times New Roman", 26));
g.setBackColor(new Color(255, 255, 255));
g.setTextColor(new Color(0, 0, 0));
g.drawString("Hello, World", 0, 0);
```

Enumerating Fonts

In some instances, an application must be able to enumerate and retrieve detailed information about the available fonts, and to select the font most appropriate for a particular operation.

The WFC FontDescriptor object describes a font, including the font's name, height, orientation, and so forth. For a detailed description of all the fonts available on your system, use the Graphics object's getFontDescriptors method. This method returns an array of FontDescriptor objects, in which each element in the array describes a font.

The following example illustrates how to use the getFontDescriptors method. This example retrieves an array of available fonts and then inserts a unique list of the font names into a list box:

```
Graphics g = this.createGraphics();

// Create the array.
FontDescriptor rgFonts[] = g.getFontDescriptors();

for(int i = 0; i < rgFonts.length; i++){

    if(listBox1.findString(rgFonts[i].fullName == -1){

        listBox1.addItem(rgFonts[i].fullName);
    }
}
```

Using Pens

A *pen* is a graphics tool that an application for Microsoft Windows uses to draw lines and curves. Applications that draw use pens to draw freehand lines, straight lines, and curves. Computer-aided design (CAD) applications use pens to draw visible lines, hidden lines, section lines, center lines, and so on. Word processing and desktop publishing applications use pens to draw borders and rules. Spreadsheet applications use pens to designate trends in graphs and to outline bar graphs and pie charts.

Each pen consists of three attributes: style, width, and color. While no limits are imposed on the width and color of a pen, the pen's style must be supported by the operating system.

WFC Pen Object

The capabilities of Win32 pens are encapsulated in the WFC Pen and PenStyle objects. The following code fragment demonstrates how to create a Pen object:

```
Pen p = new Pen(PenStyle.DASH);
```

The constant that you pass to the Pen object constructor is a *pen style*. The seven built-in pen styles supported on Windows are each represented by a constant defined in the PenStyle class. The PenStyle class is an enumeration class, which means that it defines a method (valid) that determines whether a value that you specify is a valid member of the PenStyle class.

The following table lists the PenStyle constants.

Constant	Description
PenStyle.DASH	Represents a dashed pen.
PenStyle.DOT	Represents a dotted pen.
PenStyle.DASHDOT	Represents a pen of alternating dashes and dots.
PenStyle.DASHDOTDOT	Represents a pen of alternating dashes and double dots.
PenStyle.INSIDEFRAME	Represents a pen that draws a line inside the frame of closed shapes produced by the Graphics object's output functions that specify a bounding rectangle (for example, drawRect, drawPie, and drawChord).
PenStyle.NULL	Represents a null pen.
PenStyle.SOLID	Represents a solid pen.

In addition, the Pen object includes a group of public members that you can use to specify the kind of pen you want to create. Each of these members is a Pen object, and is designed to enable you to simulate various native features of the Windows user-interface.

For example, the Pen class defines a WINDOWFRAME member. When you create a Pen of type WINDOWFRAME, the lines that you draw using this pen look identical to the frame of an active window:

```
Pen pen = Pen.WINDOWFRAME;
```

The following table lists the Pen objects defined as public members of the Pen class.

Object	Description
Pen.ACTIVECAPTIONTEXT	Creates a pen the color of the active window's caption text.
Pen.CONTROLTEXT	Represents a pen the color of the text on a control.
Pen.GRAYTEXT	Represents a pen the color of disabled text.
Pen.HIGHLIGHTTEXT	Represents a pen the color of highlighted text.
Pen.INACTIVECAPTIONTEXT	Represents a pen the color of the caption text of an inactive window.
Pen.INFOTEXT	Represents a pen the color of the information tooltip's text.
Pen.MENUTEXT	Represents a pen the color of menu text.
Pen.NULL	Represents a null pen. A null pen does nothing.
Pen.WINDOWFRAME	Represents a pen the color of an active window's frame.
Pen.WINDOWTEXT	Represents a pen the color of an active window's text.

Note that when you use a Pen based on a system constant, such as the color of an active window's text, a change in the system setting that the Pen reflects results in a change to the pen.

Setting the Pen on a Graphics Object

The Pen object itself contains no coloring or drawing capability. It only describes a subset of the capabilities of the GDI. Before you use a Pen to draw on a form, you associate the Pen with a Graphics object using the Graphics object's setPen method:

```
Graphics g = this.createGraphics();
g.setPen(new Pen(PenStyle.DASH));
```

After you associate a Pen with a Graphics object, all lines drawn within the Graphics object's bounding rectangle are drawn using that pen. In addition, you can call the setPen method any number of times on the same Graphics object.

The following example demonstrates how the Pen object works with the line-drawing capabilities of the Graphics object. In this example, the Pen styles defined in the Pen object are stored in an array of integers. Within the class's paint event handler, a for loop is used to iterate through this array of pen styles, drawing a single line using each style:

```
public class Form1 extends Form
{

int [] rgStyles = { PenStyle.DASH, PenStyle.DASHDOT, PenStyle.DASHDOTDOT,
                    PenStyle.DOT, PenStyle.INSIDEFRAME, PenStyle.SOLID };



    protected void onPaint(PaintEvent e)
    {
        Rectangle rc = this.getClientRect();

        rc.y += 10;

        for(int i = 0; i < rgStyles.length; i++){

            e.graphics.setPen(new Pen(Color.BLACK, i));
            e.graphics.drawLine(new Point(0, rc.y),
                            new Point(rc.width, rc.y));

            rc.y += 10;
        }
    }

// Rest of Form1 class...
```

Using Brushes

A *brush* is a graphics tool that a Win32-based application uses to paint the interior of polygons, ellipsis, and paths. Drawing applications use brushes to paint shapes; word processing applications use brushes to paint rules; computer-aided design (CAD) applications use brushes to paint the interiors of cross-section views; and spreadsheet applications use brushes to paint the sections of pie charts and the bars in bar graphs.

There are two types of brushes: logical and physical. A logical brush is one that you define in code as the ideal combination of colors and/or pattern that an application should use to paint shapes. A physical brush is one that a device driver creates based on your logical-brush definition.

Brush Origin

When an application calls a drawing function to paint a shape, Windows positions a brush at the start of the paint operation and maps a pixel in the brush bitmap to the window origin of the client area. (The window origin is the upper-left corner of the window's client area.) The coordinates of the pixel that Windows maps are called the brush origin.

The default brush origin is located in the upper-left corner of the brush bitmap at the coordinates (0,0). Windows then copies the brush across the client area, forming a pattern that is as tall as the bitmap. The copy operation continues, row by row, until the entire client area is filled. However, the brush pattern is visible only within the boundaries of the specified shape. (Here, the term bitmap is used in its most literal sense — as an arrangement of bits — and does not refer exclusively to bits stored in an image file).

There are instances when the default brush origin should not be used. For example, it may be necessary for an application to use the same brush to paint the backgrounds of its parent and child windows and blend a child window's background with that of the parent window.

Logical Brush Types

Logical brushes come in three varieties: solid, pattern, and hatched.

A *solid* brush consists of a color or pattern defined by some element of the Windows user interface (for example, you can paint a shape with the color and pattern conventionally used by Windows to display disabled buttons).

A *hatched* brush consists of a combination of a color and of one of the six patterns defined by Win32.

A *pattern* brush consists of a bitmap that is used as the basis for a pattern that fills a shape. Where the area to be filled is larger than the bitmap, the bitmap is tiled horizontally and vertically across the display. Pattern brushes enable you to create custom brushes that consist of any pattern that you define.

WFC Brush Object

The capabilities of Win32 brushes are encapsulated in the WFC Brush and BrushStyle objects, objects that you coordinate to create solid, pattern, and hatched brushes.

The Brush object defines a group of public final members, each of which is a Brush object representing a solid brush. The BrushStyle class represents hatched brushes as a group of integer constants, each of which represents a different brush style.

The following table lists the Brush object constants that represent solid brushes.

Constant	Description
Brush.ACTIVEBORDER	Represents a Brush object the color of the active window border.
Brush.ACTIVECAPTION	Represents a Brush object the color of the active caption bar.
Brush.APPWORKSPACE	Represents a Brush object that is the color of the application workspace window.
Brush.CONTROL	Represents a Brush object that is the color of controls.
Brush.CONTROLDARK	Represents a Brush object that is the color of the shadow portion of a 3D element.
Brush.CONTROLDARKDARK	Represents a Brush object that is the color of the darkest portion of a 3D element.
Brush.CONTROLLIGHT	Represents a Brush object that is the color of the highlighted portion of a 3D element.
Brush.CONTROLLIGHTLIGHT	Represents a Brush object that is the color of the lightest part of a 3D element.
Brush.DESKTOP	Represents a Brush object that is the current color of the desktop.
Brush.HALFTONE	Represents a Brush object that is the color of a standard halftone brush.
Brush.HIGHLIGHT	Represents a Brush object that is the color of the background of highlighted elements.
Brush.HOLLOW	Represents a null brush, which paints nothing.
Brush.HOTTRACK	Represents a Brush object that is the color used to indicate hot tracking.
Brush.INACTIVEBORDER	Represents a Brush object that is the color of an inactive window border.

(continued)

(continued)

Constant	Description
Brush.INACTIVECAPTION	Represents a Brush object that is the color of an inactive caption bar.
Brush.INFO	Represents a Brush object that is the color of the background of an information ToolTip.
Brush.MENU	Represents a Brush object that is the color of the menu background.
Brush.NULL	Represents a null brush.
Brush.SCROLLBAR	Represents a Brush object that is the color of a scrollbar background.
Brush.WINDOW	Represents a Brush object that is the color of the window background.

The following table lists the BrushStyle constants that represent hatched brushes.

Constant	Description
BrushStyle.BACKWARDDIAGONAL	Represents a backward diagonal brush. Parallel lines run from the lower-left corner of the brush origin to the upper-right corner.
BrushStyle.DIAGONALCROSS	Represents a cross-hatched brush.
BrushStyle.FORWARDDIAGONAL	Represents a forward diagonal brush. Parallel lines run from the lower-right corner of the brush origin to the upper-left corner.
BrushStyle.HOLLOW	Represents a hollow brush. A hollow brush is identical to a null brush.
BrushStyle.HORIZONTAL	Represents pattern consisting of evenly spaced horizontal lines.
BrushStyle.PATTERN	Represents a pattern brush.
BrushStyle.SOLID	Represents a solid brush.
BrushStyle.VERTICAL	Represents pattern consisting of evenly spaced vertical lines.

Creating a Brush Object

How you create a Brush object depends on the type of brush needed. Because solid brushes are Brush objects, you create a solid brush as follows:

```
Brush br = Brush.BLACK;
```

A pattern brush is represented by the Brush object as an integer constant and is created as follows:

```
Brush br = new Brush(Color.BLACK, BrushStyle.FORWARDDIAGONAL);
```

The following code fragment demonstrates one way to create a brush based on a bitmap:

```
Brush bmpBrush = new Brush(new Bitmap("c:\\myBitmap.bmp"));
```

This example assumes that the bitmap on which you want to base your brush pattern is stored in a file on disk. However, you can also use the Bitmap object's createBitmap method to define bitmaps at run time, and can use the bitmap you define as the basis for the brush pattern.

Setting the Brush on the Graphics Object

Like the Pen and Font objects, the Brush object contains no coloring or drawing capability. It expresses a subset of the capabilities of the GDI. Before a brush can be used to fill surfaces, it must be associated with a Graphics object using the setBrush method:

```
protected void onPaint(PaintEvent e)
{

    // Create a forward diagonal brush, and associate it with the
    // object.
    Brush br = new Brush(Color.BLACK, BrushStyle.FORWARDDIAGONAL);
    e.graphics.setBrush(br);

}
```

After you associate a Brush object with the Graphics object, all polygons that you draw using that Graphics object instance are filled with the associated brush. You can call setBrush as often as you want to associate a new brush with the Graphics object.

A Brush Object Example

A custom brush is one based on a bitmap that you load from a file or create in memory. The CustomBrush sample application demonstrates how to create and use custom brushes.

The CustomBrush application consists of two panels and two buttons. The first of the panels (panelGrid) consists of 64 squares. When the user clicks on one of these squares, the application registers the fact that the square has been clicked, paints the square black, and performs a bitwise operations on one of the members of an array of short integers. The integer that is modified depends on which square was clicked.

When the user clicks the Test button, the CustomBrush application creates a bitmap based on the array of short integers, creates a brush based on that bitmap, and then uses that brush to paint the panel (panelRect) that appears above the Test button.

Upon application startup, the CustomBrush application performs the following tasks:

- Calls the user-defined getRects method to create an array of 64 Rectangle objects, and draws these rectangles to the application's grid panel (panelGrid).

- Declares an array of short integers (bBrushBits). The value of the integers stored in this array will eventually form the basis on which a bitmap is created. When the user clicks the Test button, this bitmap is used to create the brush that paints the panel that appears above the Test button.

- Declares and initializes an array of Boolean variables (rgStates) to false. This array is intended to track the state of each of the rectangles in the panelGrid. When the user clicks on one of the rectangles in the panelGrid, the corresponding variable in this array is set to true:

```
public class Form1 extends Form
{

// Rectangles into which to divide the panel.
Rectangle [] rgRects = new Rectangle[64];

// Tracks the state of the rectangles.
boolean [] rgStates = new boolean[64];
int [] bBrushBits = new int[8];

public Form1()
{
    // Set the state array to an initial value of false.

    for(int i = 0; i < rgStates.length; i++){

        rgStates[i] = false;

    }
```

```
    // Initialize the form.
    initForm();

    // Divide the panel into 64 rectangles and paint the form.

    rgRects = getRects(panelGrid.getClientRect(), 8, 8);
    this.invalidate();

}


/**
 * This method divides a specified rectangular area into the specified
 * number of subrectangles (down and across), and returns an array
 * containing the subrectangles.
 */

private Rectangle [] getRects(Rectangle rcClient, int nAcross, int nDown){

int deltaX, deltaY;
int x, y, right, bottom;
int i;

Rectangle rgRects[] = new Rectangle[nAcross * nDown];

// Store the right and bottom of the rectangle.

right = rcClient.getRight();
bottom = rcClient.getBottom();

// Determine the height and width of each rectangle.

deltaX = (right - rcClient.x) / nAcross;
deltaY = (bottom - rcClient.y) / nDown;

// Initialize the array of cell rectangles.

for(y = rcClient.y, i = 0; y < bottom; y += deltaY){

    for(x = rcClient.x; x < (right - nAcross) && i < (nAcross * nDown);
        x += deltaX, i++){

        rgRects[i] = new Rectangle(x, y, deltaX, deltaY);

    }
}

return rgRects;

}
```

When the grid panel's paint event handler is invoked, it uses the dimensions stored in the application's Rectangle array (rgRects) and the states stored in the class-level Boolean array (rgStates) to draw a grid. If the Boolean value corresponding to a given rectangle is true, the rectangle is painted black. Otherwise, it is painted with a null brush. This enables the user to determine the appearance of the brush that is eventually created based on the pattern of the rectangles in the grid panel:

```
private void panelGrid_paint(Object source, PaintEvent e)
{

e.graphics.setPen(new Pen(Color.BLACK, PenStyle.SOLID, 1));

// Draw the grid to reflect the current state of the
// squares.

for(int i = 0; i < rgRects.length; i++){

    if(rgStates[i] == true){

        // If the square has been previously clicked, fill it.

        e.graphics.setBrush(new Brush(Color.BLACK));

    }else{

        e.graphics.setBrush(Brush.NULL);

    }

    e.graphics.drawRect(rgRects[i]);

    }

}
```

Each time the user clicks on one of the rectangles in the grid panel, the panel's click event is fired. Within the grid panel's click event handler, the application determines which rectangle was clicked, sets the corresponding Boolean state variable to true, and calls panelGrid.invalidate to force a repaint. Additionally, the application performs a bitwise operation on the appropriate member of the array of bits stored in the class-level bBrushBits variable:

```
private void panelGrid_mouseDown(Object source, MouseEvent e)
{

    Graphics gr = this.createGraphics();
    gr.setBrush(new Brush(Color.BLACK));
    Integer nBit = new Integer(0);
```

```
// Determine which cell was clicked.

for(int i = 0; i < 64; i++){

    Rectangle rc = new Rectangle(rgRects[i].x,
                    rgRects[i].y, rgRects[i].height,
                    rgRects[i].width);

    if(rc.contains(new Point(e.x, e.y))){

        // Set the appropriate boolean state variable.

        rgStates[i] = true;

        // Perform a bitwise NOT operation on the appropriate
        // integer in the array of shorts on which we'll base
        // our bitmap.

        if(i % 8 == 0)
            bBrushBits[i/8] = bBrushBits[i/8] ^ 0x80;
        if(i % 8 == 1)
            bBrushBits[i/8] = bBrushBits[i/8] ^ 0x40;
        if(i % 8 == 2)
            bBrushBits[i/8] = bBrushBits[i/8] ^ 0x20;
        if(i % 8 == 3)
            bBrushBits[i/8] = bBrushBits[i/8] ^ 0x10;
        if(i % 8 == 4)
            bBrushBits[i/8] = bBrushBits[i/8] ^ 0x08;
        if(i % 8 == 5)
            bBrushBits[i/8] = bBrushBits[i/8] ^ 0x04;
        if(i % 8 == 6)
            bBrushBits[i/8] = bBrushBits[i/8] ^ 0x02;
        if(i % 8 == 7)
            bBrushBits[i/8] = bBrushBits[i/8] ^ 0x01;

        break;

    }
}

// Repaint the grid.

panelGrid.invalidate();

}
```

Finally, when the user clicks the Test button, the test button's click event handler forces a repaint of the panel (panelRect) that appears above the Test button by calling panelRect.invalidate:

```
private void btnTest_click(Object source, Event e)
{
   panelRect.invalidate();

}
```

Within the panelRect paint handler, the application creates a bitmap based on the array of short integers (bBrushBits), creates a brush based on the bitmap, and paints the panel (panelRect) that appears above the Test button:

```
private void panelRect_paint(Object source, PaintEvent e)
{
   short [] rgShorts = new short[8];

   for(int i = 0; i < bBrushBits.length; i++){
      rgShorts[i] = (short) bBrushBits[i];
   }

   e.graphics.setBrush(new Brush(new Bitmap(8,8,1,1,rgShorts)));
   e.graphics.fill(panelRect.getClientRect());

}
```

Drawing Bitmaps

A bitmap is a drawable surface. This surface can be used to display pens, brushes, or images, including Windows bitmaps, metafiles, .gif, and .jpg images.

The Bitmap object supports creating and loading bitmaps. You can use this object to load bitmap images from files, streams, or resources, or you can use it to create bitmaps in memory. In addition, the Bitmap object supports defining transparent colors within a bitmap.

After creating a Bitmap object, you use the Graphics object's drawImage method to render a Bitmap object to the display.

The following code fragment creates a new Bitmap object and then uses the Form class's createGraphics method to create the Graphics object for drawing the image:

```
Bitmap bmp = new Bitmap("c:\\MyImage.bmp");
Graphics g = this.createGraphics();

g.drawImage(bmp, new Point(10, 10));
```

Shrinking and Expanding Images

All of the image objects supported by WFC (Metafile, Icon, Bitmap, and Cursor) support the drawStretchTo and drawTo methods. All image rendering performed by the Graphics object occurs through these methods. When you call the Graphics object's drawImage method, the object determines whether to call the drawStretchTo or the drawTo method on the image object that you pass the method.

The drawStretchTo method expands or shrinks an image to fit within a specified rectangular area. The drawTo method renders an image to a specified area also, but if the image is too large for the target area, the drawTo method clips it. In addition, both of these methods support drawing sections of an image to a specified section of the Graphics object's bounding rectangle.

You cannot call the drawStretchTo or drawTo methods directly; they are always defined as protected methods in WFC image classes. To determine which of these methods is called, you call a version of the drawImage method that takes a Boolean *scale* parameter. The following is one such method defined by the Graphics object:

public final void drawImage(Image *i*, Rectangle *r*, Boolean *scale*)

If the *scale* parameter is true, the image is stretched or shrunk to fit the clipping rectangle; otherwise, the image is clipped.

Rendering Images Transparently

The Bitmap object supports the transparent rendering of one or more colors in an image.

If you need to render a single color transparently, use the setTransparentColor and setTransparent methods. The setTransparentColor method takes a Color object parameter that specifies the bitmap color to be rendered transparently. The setTransparent method takes a Boolean value that specifies whether the designated transparent color should be rendered or not.

For example, the following code fragment designates black as the transparent color. When the Graphics object's drawImage method is called to draw the image, the black pixels in the image are not rendered:

```
protected void onPaint(PaintEvent e)
{

    Bitmap bmp = new Bitmap("c:\\MyImage.bmp");
    Bmp.setTransparentColor(Color.BLACK);
    Bmp.setTransparent(false);
    e.graphics.drawImage(bmp, new Point(0,0));

}
```

You can also achieve transparency by creating a Bitmap object based on two bitmasks, one of which is color and the other monochrome. In the color mask, each part of the bitmap to be drawn transparently should be black. In the monochrome mask, each part to be drawn transparently should be white.

Raster Operations

A raster operation applies a logical operation to the display of a GDI primitive, such as a pen, brush, image, or shape to achieve a visual effect. Raster operations that you can perform using the Graphics object are defined in the RasterOp object. When you review the methods supported by the Graphics object, you'll see that for each basic operation, such as the drawing of lines or the display of images, there's a method that takes a RasterOp as a parameter.

In their simplest incarnations, the drawing methods the Graphics object supports merely writes or copies pixels to some area of the display, overwriting what's currently displayed. Add raster operations to the equation and this overwrite becomes more complex.

Suppose, for example, that you want to draw a black rectangle to an area currently covered by an image, but you want to logically combine the black pixels with their corresponding pixels in the target image and to write the result to the display. Raster operations make such combinations possible.

The variations on the logic that the RasterOps object supports are too numerous to be covered thoroughly in this document. The following statements, however, demonstrate the basic syntax of a call using a RasterOps object. These statements set the background color of a form, and then draw a line that represents a color inversion of the background color:

```
protected void onPaint(PaintEvent e)
{
this.setBackColor(new Color(255, 255, 255);

e.graphics.drawLine(new Point(10, 10), new Point(100, 10),

RasterOp.TARGET.invert());
}
```

Drawing Shapes

The Graphics object supports the drawing of lines, rectangles, chords, arcs, arc angles, and Bezier splines.

Lines

A *line* is a set of highlighted pixels on a display, identified by two points: a starting point and an ending point. In Windows, the pixel located at the starting point is always included in the line, and the pixel located at the ending point is always excluded (these lines are sometimes called inclusive-exclusive).

An application can draw a single line by calling the Graphics object's drawLine method. This method takes two Point parameters, which specify the start and end of the line:

```
protected void onPaint(PaintEvent e){

    Rectangle rcClient = this.getClientRect();

    // Draw lines that divide the screen area equally into four squares.

    e.graphics.drawLine(new Point(rcClient.x, rcClient.height / 2),
                    new Point(rcClient.width, rcClient.height / 2));

    e.graphics.drawLine(new Point(rcClient.width / 2, rcClient.y),
                    new Point(rcClient.width / 2, rcClient.height));
}
```

Rectangles

Applications written for Microsoft Windows use rectangles to specify rectangular areas on the screen or in a window. Rectangles are used to describe the client area of a window, areas of the screen that need repaints, and areas for displaying formatted text. Your applications can also use rectangles to fill, frame, or invert a portion of the client area with a given brush, and to retrieve the coordinates of a window or the window's client area.

The dimensions of rectangular regions are described in the WFC Rectangle object. This object consists of *x*, *y*, *height*, and *width* integers that describe the Rectangle's screen position and dimensions. In addition, you can use the object's getRight and getBottom methods to retrieve the screen position of its right and bottom sides.

For more information, see the following sections, "Rectangle Operations" and "A Rectangle Example."

Rectangle Operations

The Rectangle object provides a number of methods for working with rectangles. The object's equals method determines whether two Rectangle objects are identical — that is, whether they have the same coordinates.

The inflateRect method increases or decreases the width or height of a rectangle, or both. It can add or remove width from both ends of the rectangle; it can add or remove height from both the top and bottom of the rectangle.

The overloaded contains method enables you to determine whether the area described by one rectangle exists within the area described by another, or to determine whether a given point exists within a rectangle.

The intersects and intersectsWith methods determine whether two Rectangle object's intersect.

A Rectangle Example

The example in this section illustrates how to divide areas of an application's client area into sub-rectangles, and how to work within these regions.

When the application starts, it divides the main form's client area into 16-by-16 subregions, and displays every shade of a given color within those rectangular regions. To modify the number of rectangles displayed across and down the display, you use the Dimensions menu item to display a dialog box in which you specify the new number of rectangles you'd like to see displayed.

The method that divides the screen into Rectangle objects is given in the following example. This method, getRects, takes three parameters: a rectangle that specifies the area to be divided, and two integers, which identify the number of cells to draw across and down, respectively. The method returns an array of rectangles that contain the appropriate coordinates:

```
private Rectangle[] getRects(Rectangle rcClient, int nDown, int nAcross){

    int deltaX, deltaY;   // The height and width of each cell.
    int x, y;
    int i;

    Rectangle rgRects[] = new Rectangle[nDown * nAcross];

    // Determine the height and width of each Rectangle.

    deltaX = (rcClient.getRight() - rcClient.x) / nAcross;
    deltaY = (rcClient.getBottom() - rcClient.y) / nDown;

    // Create and initialize the Rectangle array.
```

```
      for(y = rcClient.y, i = 0; y < rcClient.getBottom(); y += deltaY){
        for(x = rcClient.x; x < (rcClient.getRight() - nAcross) &&
              i < (nAcross * nDown); x += deltaX, i++){

          rgRects[i] = new Rectangle(x, y, deltaX, deltaY);
        }
      }

      // Return the initialized array.

      return rgRects;
    }
```

When the application starts, its Form class constructor initializes two class-level integers, *nAcross* and *nDown*, to 16, and calls the getRects method previously listed:

```
public Form1(){

    initForm();
    nAcross = 16;
    nDown = 16;

    // Initialize class-level array.

    rgRects = getRects(this.getClientRect(), nAcross, nDown);
}
```

After the class constructor returns, the class's paint event handler is automatically called. This event handler loops through the class-level *rgRects* array, uses the Graphics object's setBrush method to set a new color, and then calls the drawRect method to draw the array's rectangle:

```
protected void onPaint(PaintEvent e){

    for(int i = 0; i < rgRects.length; i++){

      e.graphics.setBrush(new Brush(new Color(0,0,i)));
      e.graphics.drawRect(rgRects[i]);
    }
}
```

Finally, the Form class's resize handler simply reinitializes the array and forces a repaint of the form's client area:

```
protected void onResize(Event e){

    Rectangle rcClient = this.getClientRect();
    rgRects = getRects(rcClient, nDown, nAcross);
    this.invalidate();
}
```

Chords

A *chord* is a region bounded by the intersection of an ellipse and a line segment, called a *secant*. The chord is outlined by using the current pen and filled by using the current brush. The part of the ellipse on one side of the secant is clipped.

To draw a chord, use the Graphics object's drawChord method, which has the following syntax:

drawChord(Rectangle *p1***, Point** *p2***, point** *p3* **)**

The drawChord method's Rectangle parameter designates the area into which the ellipse will be drawn. The two Point parameters identify the points at which the two ends of the secant intersect the ellipse.

The following sample makes two calls to drawChord. The first call draws a chord in the lower-left corner of the display, and the second draws a chord in the upper-right corner. Prior to each call to drawChord, a different brush is associated with the Graphics object to ensure that the two chords, which combine to form a circle, are painted black and white, respectively:

```
protected void onPaint(PaintEvent e){

    Rectangle rcClient = this.getClientRect();

    // Associate a black brush with the object and draw a chord.

    e.graphics.setBrush(new Brush(new Color(0,0,0)));
    e.graphics.drawChord(rcClient, new Point(rcClient.x, rcClient.y),
        new Point(rcClient.getRight(), rcClient.getBottom());

    // Associate a white brush with the object and draw a chord.

    e.graphics.setBrush(new Brush(new Color(255,255,255)));
    e.graphics.drawChord(rcClient, new Point(rcClient.getRight(),
        rcClient.getBottom()), new Point(rcClient.x, rcClient.y));
}
```

Arcs

An application can draw an ellipse or part of an ellipse by calling the drawArc method. This method draws a curve within the perimeter of an invisible rectangle called a bounding rectangle. The size of the ellipse is specified by two invisible radials extending from the center of the rectangle to the sides of the rectangle.

When calling the drawArc method, an application specifies the coordinates of the bounding rectangle and radials.

The following example draws an arc that fills the client area of a form, and then uses the Graphics object's drawLine method to draw a line from the top of the arc to its radius, then from its radius to the rightmost side of the ellipse:

```
protected void onPaint(PaintEvent e){

    Rectangle rcClient = this.getClientRect();

    e.graphics.drawArc(rcClient, new Point(rcClient.width /2,rcClient.y),
        new Point(rcClient.width, rcClient.height / 2));
    e.graphics.drawLine(new Point(rcClient.width / 2, rcClient.y),
        new Point(rcClient.width / 2, rcClient.height / 2));
    e.graphics.drawLine(new Point(rcClient.width, rcClient.height / 2),
        new Point(rcClient.width / 2, rcClient.height / 2));
}
```

Arc Angles

An arc angle is similar to an arc. The primary practical difference between the two is that when an application uses drawArc to draw an arc, it specifies the x and y locations of the arc's radials.

In contrast, to draw an arc angle the application uses the drawArcAngle method and specifies the degrees of the angle; the method itself takes care of locating the coordinates at which drawing starts and stops.

The drawArcAngle method has the following syntax:

public final void drawAngleArc(Point *center*, **int** *radius*, **float** *startAngle*, **float** *endAngle* **)**

The Point parameter identifies the screen location at which to place the radius, specified in the *radius* parameter. The *startAngle* specifies the number, in degrees, where the angle starts, and the *endAngle* parameter specifies how many degrees to draw, beginning at the *startAngle*.

The following example shows how to use this method. This method draws an arc angle, beginning at a start angle of 30, and extending 300 degrees from the start angle:

```
protected void onPaint(PaintEvent e){

    Rectangle rcClient = this.getClientRect();
    int x = rcClient.width / 2;
    int y = rcClient.height / 2;
    int radius = 100;
    float startAngle = 30;
    float endAngle = 300;

    e.graphics.drawAngleArc(new Point(x,y), radius, startAngle, endAngle);

}
```

Bezier Splines

A Bezier spline is defined by four points, which include two endpoints and two controlling points. Combined, these points define a curve. The two endpoints define the start and end of the curve. The control points serve to "pull" the curve away from the line segment formed by the start and end points.

To draw Bezier splines, use the drawBezier curve method. This method takes an array of Point objects as a parameter. The first four elements of this array define the starting point, two control points, and the end point of the spline.

To draw multiple splines, include three array elements for each spline after the first one. The end point of the first spline serves as the starting point for the next one, and the three array elements define the control points and the end point.

The following code uses the drawBezier method to draw a bezier curve every time the window is resized:

```
protected void onPaint(PaintEvent e)
{
    Point [] pt = new Point[4];
    Rectangle rc = this.getClientRect();
    int right = rc.getRight();
    int bottom = rc.getBottom();

    pt[0] = new Point(right / 4, bottom / 2);
    pt[1] = new Point(right / 2, bottom / 4);
    pt[2] = new Point(right / 2, 3 * bottom / 4);
    pt[3] = new Point(3 * right / 4, bottom / 2);

    e.graphics.drawBezier(pt);
}

protected void onResize(Event e)

{
    this.invalidate();
}
```

CHAPTER 16

Building and Importing ActiveX Controls

ActiveX is a technology built upon the Component Object Model (COM). In addition to creating Windows Foundation Classes for Java (WFC) components, you can use Visual J++ to build and import ActiveX controls. Because ActiveX is a built upon COM, you can incorporate ActiveX as easily as other COM objects. You can develop controls to use in other development environments, such as Microsoft Visual Basic and Microsoft Visual C++, and to provide advanced features in your HTML pages. Moreover, you can import third-party ActiveX controls to enhance your WFC applications.

In this section, you will learn:

- How to build an ActiveX control from an existing WFC component

- How to import ActiveX controls into your WFC applications

Building ActiveX Controls

Using the component model of the Windows Foundation Classes for Java (WFC), you can create ActiveX controls that can be used in WFC applications or in other development environments that support ActiveX. To create an ActiveX control from a WFC control, you register the WFC control's class as a COM class. Once the control's class has been registered as a COM class, you can package the class file for the control into a COM DLL and register it as an ActiveX control in the registry. Once the control is registered as an ActiveX control, it can be accessed from an ActiveX client.

In this scenario, you use the WFC control documented in "Creating a Control" in Chapter 1, "Creating Projects." If you have not created it, build the control documented in the section, and continue with the procedures in this section. You will learn:

- How to expose a WFC control as a COM object.

- How to package a control into a COM DLL for use by other applications.

- How to register a COM DLL as an ActiveX control.

- How to import a WFC based ActiveX control into Visual Basic.

   Note The following procedure assumes that you have an existing WFC component project opened in Visual J++.

Defining a WFC Control as a COM Object

To access your control from other ActiveX clients, you define your control as a COM object. So that a class can be exposed as a COM object, it needs to have an @com.register comment tag placed above the class definition. Visual J++ provides an automated way to generate @com.register comment tags for your classes.

Note If your control's project was created using the **Control** template, the control already contains a comment tag to register it as a COM object. Remove the forward slashes (//) to enable the comment tag.

To define a WFC component as a COM object

1. On the **Project** menu, click **<Project> Properties** (where **<Project>** is the name of your control project).

2. In the **<Project> Properties** dialog box, click the COM Classes tab.

3. In the list of classes, select your control's class.

4. Click the **Options** button.

5. (Optional) In the Type Library Options dialog box, change the name of the type library file that is created to define the interface to your control, the name of the library, the name of the control as it will be displayed to development environments, and Help file information, and click **OK**.

6. In the **<Project> Properties** dialog box, click **OK**.

   Visual J++ adds a comment tag at the top of your control's class definition that registers the class as a COM object.

   Note If you do not need to define multiple classes as COM classes, you can define a COM class in the **Class Properties** dialog box. To display the **Class Properties** dialog box, in Class Outline, right-click the name of the class, and then click **Class Properties**. In the **Class Properties** dialog box, select the **COM Class** check box.

Packaging the Control in a COM DLL

After you have defined your WFC control as a COM object, you package the control's class files into a COM DLL file. Your control must be packaged in a COM DLL file to be available as an ActiveX control. The COM DLL provides the interface that is used by ActiveX clients to access your control and its members.

Note To distribute your ActiveX controls over the Internet, you can package your control in a CAB file instead of a COM DLL.

To build a control as a COM DLL

1. On the **Project** menu, click **<Project> Properties** (where **<Project>** is the name of your control project).

2. In the **<Project> Properties** dialog box, click the Output Format tab.

3. Select the **Enable Packaging** check box.

   The other controls on the tab should now be enabled.

4. In the **Packaging type** drop-down list, select **COM DLL**.

5. In the **File name** box, type a name for your COM DLL. (A default name is created using the name of the project.)

6. In the associated drop-down list, select the **Outputs of type** and the **Java Classes & Resources** options.

7. Click **OK**.

Building the Project

After you have configured the packaging options for the project, you need to build the project. Visual J++ then adds a type library to your project that defines the COM interface for your control. The type library also contains information that the registry uses to register the COM class as a control. When the type library has been generated, Visual J++ registers the COM classes in your project in the registry using the type library file that was created. After the control's classes have been registered, Visual J++ packages the project's class files and the type library into a COM DLL.

To build the project

- On the **Build** menu, click **Build**.

Registering the COM DLL

Once you have registered your WFC control's classes as COM classes and packaged them in a COM DLL, you register the COM DLL in the system registry. To do this, you use the Regsvr32.exe program. Because the project's type library flags the WFC control's COM classes as a control, Regsvr32 registers the COM DLL as an ActiveX control. When the COM DLL has been registered, other applications can see your WFC control in the list of ActiveX controls that are registered on the system.

To register the COM DLL

1. Click the **Start** button, and then click **Run**.

2. In the **Open** box, type:

    Regsvr32.exe *<DLL path and filename>*

    where *<DLL path and filename>* is the path and file name of your control's DLL.
    For this scenario, type:

    Regsvr32 C:\Project1\Project1.dll

3. Click **OK**.

    If you receive a message that the registration failed, ensure that the path to the control's
    DLL is correct and that the file exists.

Testing the Control in Microsoft Visual Basic

To test your ActiveX control, you add the control to a programming tool or application
that supports ActiveX. For this scenario, you can use Microsoft Visual Basic version 5.0
or later to add the control and test its features.

To add a WFC based ActiveX control to a Visual Basic form

1. Run **Visual Basic**.

2. On the **File** menu in Visual Basic, click **New Project**.

3. In the **New Project** dialog box, click the **Standard EXE** icon, and then click **OK**.

4. Right-click the Toolbox, and then click **Components**.

5. In the **Components** dialog box, select your control, and then click **OK**.

    For this scenario, select the **Project1** control.

6. In the Toolbox, double-click your control to add it to the form.

    The control is added in the center of the form.

7. Press F5 to run the project.

    The form is displayed with your control.

If you are working with the control that is documented in "Creating a Control" in
Chapter 1, "Creating Projects, you can scroll the horizontal scroll bar. The text in the
control changes to reflect the position of the scroll bar.

For information on importing an ActiveX control into a WFC application, see the next
section, "Importing ActiveX Controls."

Importing ActiveX Controls

ActiveX controls can provide a number of enhancements to your Windows Foundation Classes (WFC) applications. A number of third-party ActiveX controls are available to add features, such as custom button shapes, telephony technology, charting, graphing, and spreadsheets. You can use Visual J++ to import ActiveX controls using a process similar to importing COM objects.

In this scenario, you import the Microsoft ActiveMovie control that is installed with Microsoft Internet Explorer version 4.0. You will learn:

- How to register an ActiveX control in the system registry.

- How to create a project to use when importing an ActiveX control.

- How to import the ActiveX control into a project.

- How to add an ActiveX control to a form and set its properties.

- How to build and run the project to test the ActiveX control.

Registering a Control

So that your ActiveX control is available to Visual J++, you must register it in the system registry.

Note   In this scenario, you do not need to register the ActiveMovie control because it is registered when Internet Explorer is installed.

To register an ActiveX control

1. Click the **Start** button, and then click **Run**.

2. In the **Open** box, type:

   Regsvr32.exe *<control path and filename>*

   where *<control path and filename>* is the path and file name of your control. For this scenario, type:

   Regsvr32 C:\Windows\System\AMOVIE.OCX

3. Click **OK**.

   If you receive a message that the registration failed, ensure that the path to the control is correct and that the file exists.

Creating a WFC Project

When importing an ActiveX control, Visual J++ creates package directories in your project and adds the class wrappers used to access the ActiveX control in those package directories. Therefore, you must have a valid WFC project to import an ActiveX control.

To create a WFC project

1. On the **File** menu, click **New Project**.

2. On the **New** tab, expand the **Visual J++ Projects** folder, click **Applications**, and then click the **Windows Application** icon.

3. In the **Name** box, type a name for your project.

4. In the **Location** box, type the path where you want to save your project, or click **Browse** to navigate to the folder.

5. Click **Open**.

   A collapsed view of your project appears in Project Explorer. (If Project Explorer is not visible, click **Project Explorer** on the **View** menu.)

6. In Project Explorer, expand the project node.

   A file with the default name of **Form1.java** has been added to your project.

7. To open your form in the Forms Designer, double-click **Form1.java** in Project Explorer.

Importing an ActiveX Control

After you have created the project, you can then import the ActiveX control into the project. Use the Customize Toolbox dialog box to select the ActiveX control from a list of ActiveX controls that are installed on your system.

Note Once you have added an ActiveX control to the Toolbox, the control remains in the Toolbox for all other projects until you remove it.

To import an ActiveX control

1. In the Toolbox, click the **General** tab. (If the Toolbox is not displayed, click **Toolbox** on the **View** menu.)

2. Right-click the Toolbox, and then click **Customize Toolbox**.

3. In the **Customize Toolbox** dialog box, click the **ActiveX Controls** tab.

4. In the list of ActiveX controls, select the control that you want to import. You can select multiple controls.

   For this scenario, select **ActiveMovieControl Object**.

5. Click **OK**.

   The controls that you selected are added to the Toolbox.

Adding the Control to a Form

When you add the ActiveX control to a form, Visual J++ creates one or more packages in your project directory and adds class wrappers for the control. The class wrappers are used by Visual J++ to access the classes and members of the ActiveX control. If the ActiveX control you are importing is contained in a file that contains multiple ActiveX controls, Visual J++ will provide class wrappers for all controls in the file but adds only the specified control to the Toolbox.

To add the ActiveX control to a form

- With a form displayed in the Forms Designer, double-click the control that you want to add.

  For this scenario, double-click the **ActiveMovie** control. The control is added to the center of the form.

Setting the Control's Properties

After you have added the ActiveX control to a form, you can use the Properties window to set properties and create event handlers.

To set the properties for the ActiveMovie control

1. In the Forms Designer, select the **ActiveMovie** control.

2. In the Properties window, select the **filename** property.

3. Type the path and file name of an .avi file to display in the control.

   – or –

   Click the ellipsis button in the value section of the **filename** property to display a dialog box to browse for a file on your computer.

Building the Project

After you have added the ActiveX control to a form and set its properties, you build and run the project to test the control's functionality.

To build and run the form

1. On the **Build** menu, click **Build**.

    If you receive any compilation errors or messages, correct the errors and rebuild your project.

2. To run the form, on the **Debug** menu, click **Start**.

3. When the form appears, click the play button on the control.

    The movie that you specified in the **filename** property is displayed.

CHAPTER 17

Building and Importing COM Objects

The Component Object Model (COM) is an object-oriented architecture for creating objects that can be reused from application to application. You can also use it to write objects that can be accessed from other programming environments such as Microsoft Visual Basic and Microsoft Visual C++, as well as applications such as Microsoft Office. COM provides a standard protocol for connecting objects together, even if they are designed in different programming languages. When a connection has been made, the objects communicate through a standard interface.

Visual J++ provides support for building and importing COM objects. By building COM objects in Visual J++, you can provide reusable components that can be shared by any number of applications as well as applications written in different languages. The COM import features allow you to use objects from other applications to provide additional features in your Windows Foundation Classes for Java (WFC) applications. For example, you can use the COM objects that Microsoft Office exposes to access spell checking features in Microsoft Word or mathematical functions in Microsoft Excel. By using COM in your Visual J++ projects, you provide true code reuse in your application development.

In this chapter, you will learn:

- How to build a COM object

- How to import existing COM objects into a WFC application

Building COM Objects

Visual J++ simplifies the building of COM objects by providing an easy-to-use interface for selecting classes in your project that you want to use as COM classes. Any public, non-abstract class can be used to create a COM object. Visual J++ uses the public members of a class as the interface to the COM object. When you build your project, classes that are selected as COM classes are built and registered in the system as COM objects. Once you have built your COM objects, you can package them in a COM DLL and access them from other programming environments or from applications that support COM.

In this scenario, you build a COM object, packaged in a COM DLL, that exposes sports-related, statistical functions. You will learn how to:

- Create a project with classes that can be exposed as COM objects.

- Use the COM Classes tab in the **Project Properties** dialog box to select classes in your project to expose as COM objects.

- Package the COM classes into a COM DLL for other programming languages and applications to use.

- Build the project.

Creating a Project

Visual J++ provides a COM DLL template that creates a project with a class that is already registered as a COM class. This template is also configured to package the project in a COM DLL. For more information on creating COM DLL projects using the template, see "Creating a COM DLL" in Chapter 1, "Creating Projects."

Although the COM DLL template is available, this scenario does not use the template because it is important to understand how to select a class in any project as a COM class. In this scenario, you create an empty project and add a Java class to the project that will be exposed as a COM object.

Note Before you start the following procedure, close any open projects. (On the **File** menu, click **Close All**.)

To create an empty project

1. On the **File** menu, click **New Project**.

2. In the **New** tab, select the **Visual J++ Projects** folder, and then click the **Empty Project** icon.

3. In the **Name** box, type a name for your project.

   For this scenario, type **Stats**.

4. In the **Location** box, type the path where you want to save your project, or click **Browse** to navigate to a directory.

5. Click **Open**.

   Your project appears in Project Explorer and contains no files.

To add a class to your project

1. In Project Explorer, right-click the name of your project.

2. On the shortcut menu, point to **Add** and then click **Add Class**.

3. To add an empty Java class, select the **Class** icon.

4. In the **Name** box, type a name for the Java class.

   For this scenario, name the class **Stats.java**.

5. Click **Open**.

Adding Code to the Class

For clients of your COM DLL to manipulate your COM object, you provide public methods in your COM class. Visual J++ exposes all public methods of a Java class, including those inherited from superclasses, through the interface to the COM object. For this scenario, you add two methods to the class. These methods provide sports-related statistical functions to the user of the COM object.

The first public method that the Stats COM object needs to expose is the winLossPercentage method. This method calculates the percentage of wins a team has over the total number of games that have been played by the team.

To add the winLossPercentage method

- Add the following method definition to the Stats class.

```
public float winLossPercentage(int gamesPlayed, int gamesWon)
{
    float returnValue = gamesWon % gamesPlayed * .100f;
    if (returnValue == 0.0f)
        return 1.0f;
    else
        return returnValue;
}
```

This code uses the modulus operator to obtain the remainder from a division between the number of games that were won by the team and the number of games that were played. The value is then multiplied by .100f to convert the value to the type typically used in a team standings display. After the value has been determined, the code checks to see if the value is 0.0f, which indicates that there is no remainder and that the team has won all its games. If so, the code returns the value of 1.0f. Otherwise, the code returns the regular value.

The final public method that the Stats COM object needs to expose is the goalsAgainstAverage method. This method calculates the average number of goals that are allowed by a goaltender. It determines this by dividing the number of goals allowed by the goaltender by the number of complete games the goaltender has played in.

To add the goalsAgainstAverage method

- Add the following method definition to the Stats class.

```
public float GoalsAgainstAverage(int gamesPlayed, int goalsAllowed)
{
    return (float) goalsAllowed/gamesPlayed;
}
```

This code divides the number of goals allowed by the number of games played and casts the result as a float value.

Defining a Class as a COM Class

After you have created your class and defined the public methods will be exposed through COM, you define the class as a COM class. Use the **COM Classes** tab in the **Project Properties** dialog box to select classes from your project as COM classes.

Note   If you do not need to define multiple classes as COM classes, you can define a COM class in the **Class Properties** dialog box. To display the **Class Properties** dialog box, in Class Outline, right-click the name of the class, and then click **Class Properties**. In the **Class Properties** dialog box, select the **COM Class** check box.

To define a class as a COM Class

1. On the **Project** menu, click **<Project> Properties** (where **<Project>** is the name of your control project).

2. Click the **COM Classes** tab.

3. In the **COM Classes** tab, select the **Automatically generate Type Library** option.

4. In the list of classes, select the name of the class that you want to expose as a COM object.

   For this scenario, select the **Stats** class.

5. Click **OK**.

   Visual J++ adds an @com.register comment tag to the top of your class definition. When your project is compiled, the compiler uses the information in the comment tag to register your class as a COM class in the registry.

Packaging the Project as a COM DLL

So that other applications can access your COM object, you package it in a COM DLL.

Note If you want to distribute your COM object over the Internet, you can package your control in a CAB file instead of a COM DLL.

To package your COM object in a COM DLL

1. On the **Project** menu, click **<Project> Properties** (where **<Project>** is the name of your control project).

2. Click the Output Format tab.

3. Select the **Enable Packaging** check box.

4. In the **Packaging type** drop-down list, select **COM DLL**.

5. In the **File name** box, type a name for your COM DLL. (A default name is created for you using the name of the project.)

6. Select the **Outputs of type** and the **Java Classes & Resources** options.

7. Click **OK**.

Building the Project

During the build process, Visual J++ packages your COM classes in a COM DLL and registers the DLL and the COM classes within it as COM objects. When the classes are in the registry, they are available to other applications. For more information on importing a COM object into Visual J++, see the next section, "Importing COM Objects."

To build your project

- On the **Build** menu, click **Build**. (If you receive any compilation errors or message, correct the errors and rebuild your project.)

Note To perform additional registration while your COM class is being registered, you can add a user-defined method named `onCOMRegister` to your COM class. You can use this method to perform tasks such as registering a Visual J++ add-in into the list of Visual J++ add-ins. This method is called by Visual J++ during the COM registration process for COM classes and during the registration of a COM DLL built with Visual J++. The signature of the `onCOMRegister` method must match the following signature:

```
public static void onCOMRegister(boolean register)
{
    // Add your custom registration code here
}
```

Importing COM Objects

COM objects provide a great way to encapsulate functionality and reuse it across multiple applications. You can use COM objects to expose specific functionality within your application to use in other applications or to create a set of routines that you want to use in more than one application. Because COM is not language-specific, COM objects can be easily integrated into applications developed in a variety of programming languages. You can use Visual J++ to view and import COM objects that are registered on your system. During the import process, Visual J++ creates class wrappers so that you can access COM objects just as you would other Java objects.

In this scenario, you import a COM object that was built in the "Building COM Objects" section, earlier in this chapter. You will learn how to:

- Import a COM object into a Windows Foundation Classes for Java (WFC) project.

- Access the methods of a COM object.

- Build and run the project to test the functionality of the COM object.

  Note   This section assumes that you have created the COM object in "Building COM Objects," earlier in this chpater, and that you have closed any open projects.

Creating a Project

When importing a COM object, Visual J++ creates directories within your project and adds the class wrappers to access the COM object in those directories. To import a COM object, you must have a valid Java project.

To create a project

1. On the **File** menu, click **New Project**.

2. On the **New** tab, expand the **Visual J++ Projects** folder, click **Applications**, and select the **Windows Application** icon.

3. In the **Name** box, type a name for your project.

4. In the **Location** box, type the path where you want to save your project, or click **Browse** to navigate to the folder.

5. Click **Open**.

   A collapsed view of your project appears in Project Explorer.

6. In Project Explorer, expand the project node.

   A file with the default name of **Form1.java** has been added to your project.

Importing a COM Object

After you have created a project, you can then import COM objects to that project. A COM object must be imported for each project that is to access it. When you import a COM object into a project, Visual J++ creates class wrappers that provide the interface for accessing the COM object. These class wrappers are added to packages in your project directory. (Depending on the number of objects stored in the COM DLL, Visual J++ can create multiple packages.)

Note To access a specific COM object from another project, you can avoid wrapping the object for each project by placing the COM wrapper classes in the Classpath.

To import a COM object

1. On the **Project** menu, click **Add COM Wrapper**.

   The **COM Wrappers** dialog box is displayed.

2. In the list that contains COM DLLs and type libraries that are registered on your computer, select the name of the COM object that you want to import.

   For this scenario, select the **Stats** COM object.

3. Click **OK**.

   Visual J++ adds package directories and class wrappers for each of the COM objects contained in the COM DLL that you selected.

Adding Code to Access the COM Object

After Visual J++ has created the class wrappers, you can then write code to access the methods of the COM object. For this scenario, you add code to your project's form constructor. This code creates an instance of the COM object and make calls to the two methods of the COM object. The methods are called with hard-coded values, and their results are displayed in the Output window.

To add code to the constructor of the form

1. In Project Explorer, right-click **Form1** and then click **View Code**.

   The text editor displays the source code for **Form1**.

2. Inside the **Form1** constructor below the call to `initForm`, add the following lines of code:

   ```
   statisticsobject.Stats stats = new statisticsobject.Stats();
   System.out.println("Our team has a winning percentage of " +
        stats.winLossPercentage(10, 4));
   System.out.println("Our goaltender has a Goals Against Average of " +
        stats.goalsAgainstAverage(12, 15));
   ```

This code creates an instance of the Stats COM object. The reference to statisticsobject before the Stats object is the name of the package where the class wrappers for Stats were created. After the instance of Stats is defined, the code calls its winLossPercentage and goalsAgainstAverage methods with hard coded values and sends the results to the Output window through a call the System.out.println.

Building and Running the Project

After you have incorporated calls to the COM objects methods, you build and run the project.

To build and run the project

1. On the **Build** menu, click **Build**. (If you receive any compilation errors or messages, correct the errors and rebuild your project.)

2. To run the form, click **Start** on the **Debug** menu.

After the project starts, you can see the output from the calls to the **Stats** COM object in the Output window. (To display the Output window, on the **View** menu, click **Other Windows**, and then click **Output**.)

CHAPTER 18

Data Binding in WFC

To access data from your Java project, you typically use the ActiveX Data Objects (ADO) components, which define the data programming model for WFC applications. The core ADO objects include the Connection, Command, and Recordset objects.

The Connection object allows you to connect to a database. Once a connection is established, you can query the database to retrieve a set of records. The Recordset object represents the records returned from a query. You can use either an SQL string or a Command object to specify the query.

ADO also provides the DataSource component, which combines the functionality of the Connection, Command, and Recordset objects. For information about programming with the ADO objects, see the "ADO Tutorial (VJ++)," in the Microsoft ActiveX Data Objects online documentation. The ADO classes are defined in the com.ms.wfc.data and com.ms.wfc.data.ui packages.

> **Note** The Toolbox in the Forms Designer only provides a DataSource control;
> the Connection, Command, and Recordset objects can only be used in code.

Once a recordset has been retrieved, either through a Recordset object or a DataSource component, you can bind the recordset to a WFC component. WFC supports both *simple* and *complex* data binding, described as follows:

Type of Binding	Description
Simple	Refers to the relationship between a field in a recordset and the property of a WFC component. The binding is called *simple* because the component does not need explicit knowledge about the data protocol or data provider.
Complex	Refers to the direct relationship between a recordset and a WFC component.

Note that the recordset's cursor and lock types determine whether the data in the recordset dynamically reflects the data in the database, and whether the data in the recordset can be changed.

For more information about ADO, see "Getting Started with ADO 2.0," in the Microsoft ActiveX Data Objects online documentation.

Simple Data Binding

Simple data binding refers to the relationship between a field in a recordset and the property of a WFC component. When a property is bound, data is automatically transferred between the field and the property:

- If the value of the field changes, the new value is propagated to the property.

- If a new record in the recordset is navigated to, the current field value is propagated to the property.

- If the value of the property changes and the component supports a property change notification, the new value is propagated to the field in the recordset. The recordset is updated when a new record is navigated to.

    Note   If an attempt is made to update a read-only recordset, the recordset will generate an ADO exception. You can then catch this exception and set the bound property back to its previous value; otherwise, the value of the property and the value of the field will be inconsistent.

Bindable Properties

Simple data binding in WFC is performed by the DataBinder component. This component creates and manages the binding between the field and the property. The DataBinder component can bind a property that is accessible through methods matching the following design patterns:

```
public <PropertyType> get<PropertyName>()
public void set<PropertyName>(<PropertyType>)
```

Note that if a property is also marked with BindableAttribute.YES in the component's ClassInfo, it is enumerated in the Properties window and in the DataBinder component's design page. (You can still bind a property that is not marked as bindable by manually typing the name in the Properties window or design page, or by binding the property programmatically.)

Property Change Notifications

The component of a bound property can provide a *<propertyName>*Changed event to indicate that the property's value has been changed. When this event is triggered, the DataBinder component marks the binding as dirty. Then when the user navigates to a new record or when the DataBinder.commitChanges method is called in code, the DataBinder component determines which bindings are dirty and updates those bindings on the recordset.

Note If your component does not provide a *<propertyName>*Changed event for a
property that is bound through the DataBinder component, the binding is read-only
and your component will be disabled. To work around this limitation, you can manage
the bindings yourself in code by directly reading from and writing to the recordset.

DataBinder Component

ADO defines the DataBinder component to perform simple data binding. This component
creates and manages the bindings between the fields in a recordset and the bindable
properties of WFC components. For more information about whether a property can be
bound, see the earlier section, "Bindable Properties."

Although a single DataBinder component can manage multiple bindings, it is associated
with only one recordset. To bind the fields of a second recordset, you must use another
DataBinder component. Additionally, the DataBinder component should be used only
to bind to components that exist on the same form.

If the component of a bound property supports a change notification for that property,
the DataBinder component marks the binding as dirty when the property value
changes. The recordset is updated when the user navigates to a new record or when
the DataBinder.commitChanges method is called in code. For more information, see
the previous section, "Property Change Notifications."

Example

The following example shows how to programmatically perform simple data binding
with the DataBinder component. Note that the DataBinder component uses an array of
DataBinding objects to manage the bindings.

```
import com.ms.wfc.data.*;
import com.ms.wfc.data.ui.*;
import com.ms.wfc.ui.*;

/* Use the Connection and Recordset components to
   connect to a database and retrieve a recordset. */
Connection c = new Connection();
c.setConnectionString("dsn=myDSN;uid=myUID;pwd=myPWD");
c.open();

Recordset rs = new Recordset();
rs.setActiveConnection(c);
rs.setSource("select * from authors");
rs.open();
```

```
/* Create a DataBinder component. To associate this
   component with rs, set the dataSource property. */
DataBinder db = new DataBinder();
db.setDataSource(rs);

/* Create the components whose properties will be bound. */
Edit edit1 = new Edit();
Edit edit2 = new Edit();

/* Set the DataBinder component's bindings property to
   an array of DataBinding objects. This array defines
   the bindings between the text property of each Edit
   component and the fields in the recordset. */
db.setBindings(new DataBinding[] {
     new DataBinding(edit1, "text", "firstName"),
     new DataBinding(edit2, "text", "lastName") } );
}
```

For more information about the DataBinder component's dataSource property, see the next section, "Complex Data Binding." For information about using the DataBinder component in the Forms Designer, see Chapter 4, "Accessing Data."

Complex Data Binding

Complex data binding refers to components that interact directly with a recordset. A complex data-bound component provides dataSource and dataMember properties that identify the recordset it is bound to. Note that the properties of complex bound components can still be simple bound via the DataBinder component.

dataSource and dataMember Properties

The dataSource property identifies an object that implements the IDataSource interface. This object exposes one or more recordsets. The dataMember property then specifies the name of the recordset that is currently bound to the component. For example:

```
/* Bind the component to the recordset named "Products",
   which is exposed by the data source, ds. */
dbComponent.setDataSource(ds);
dbComponent.setDataMember("Products");
```

If you do not set the dataMember property, then the data source's default recordset will be bound. (You can explicitly specify the default recordset by setting the dataMember property to null.)

```
/* Bind the component to the default recordset
   exposed by the data source, ds. */
dbComponent.setDataSource(ds);
dbComponent.setDataMember(null);  /* This line is optional. */
```

Note that the Recordset and DataSource components already implement the IDataSource interface. Therefore, you can set the dataSource property directly to one of these components. In this case, you do not have to set the dataMember property:

```
/* Set the dataSource property directly to the Recordset
   component,rs, without setting the dataMember property. */
dbComponent.setDataSource(rs);
```

Complex Bound Components in Visual J++

Visual J++ provides the following complex data-bound components:

Component	Description
DataBinder	Binds a field from a recordset to the property of a WFC component. (Although the DataBinder component is used to perform simple binding, the component itself exposes dataSource and dataMember properties.)
DataGrid	Binds multiple fields from a recordset and displays the data in a grid format.
DataNavigator	Allows the user to change the current record in a recordset. Any other component that is bound to the same recordset is then updated to reflect the new current row.

For information about using these components in the Forms Designer, see Chapter 4, "Accessing Data."

CHAPTER 19

Writing Windows-Based Applications with J/Direct

J/Direct is a new feature of Microsoft Visual J++ that provides easy access to Microsoft Windows dynamic-link libraries (DLLs). Using J/Direct, you can make direct calls to standard Win32 system DLLs (such as KERNEL32 and USER32) and third-party DLLs. J/Direct is far simpler to use than the older Raw Native Interface or the Java Native Interface (known as RNI and JNI, respectively), both of which require you to write a specialized wrapper DLL and perform all non-trivial data type translations yourself. With J/Direct, the vast majority of pre-existing DLL functions can be invoked by simply declaring the function and calling it. J/Direct uses the @dll.import directive, which is similar to Visual Basic's DECLARE facility.

To use J/Direct, you need to have installed Microsoft Visual J++ and Microsoft Internet Explorer, version 4.0 or higher. To quickly build applications that take advantage of the native power of J/Direct, use the J/Direct Call Builder, which is a part of the Visual J++ development environment.

This chapter explains how to use the @dll.import directive to invoke a DLL function from Java. It also offers details about how each data type is passed and received and describes how the @dll.struct directive is used to pass and receive structures from DLL methods.

Message Box Example

This section provides a message box application that uses the @dll.import directive.

Using J/Direct to call Win32 DLLs from Java code is straightforward. The following is a short Java application that displays a message box:

```
class ShowMsgBox {
    public static void main(String args[])
    {
        MessageBox(0, "It worked!",
                    "This messagebox brought to you using J/Direct", 0);
    }

    /** @dll.import("USER32") */
    private static native int MessageBox(int hwndOwner, String text,
                                         String title, int fuStyle);
}
```

The @dll.import directive tells the compiler that the MessageBox method will link to the Win32 USER32.DLL using the J/Direct protocol rather than the Raw Native Interface (RNI) protocol supported in previous versions. In addition, the Microsoft Virtual Machine (VM) for Java provides automatic type marshaling from String objects to the null-terminated strings expected by C.

It is not necessary to indicate whether the ANSI MessageBox (MessageBoxA) function or the Unicode MessageBox function (MessageBoxW) should be called. In the above example, the ANSI version is always called. "How the VM Chooses Between ANSI and Unicode," later in this chapter, explains how to use the auto modifier to call the optimal version of the function, depending on the version of Microsoft Windows that is hosting the application.

J/Direct Call Builder

Using the J/Direct Call Builder, you can quickly create J/Direct calls to the Win32 API. The J/Direct Call Builder automatically inserts Java definitions for the Win32 API elements into your code, along with the appropriate @dll.import tags.

To access the Win32 API with the J/Direct Call Builder

1. To open the J/Direct Call Builder, point to **Other Windows** on the **View** menu and click **J/Direct Call Builder**.

2. By default, the J/Direct Call Builder displays elements defined in the following Win32 DLLs: advapi32.dll, gdi32.dll, kernel32.dll, shell32.dll, spoolss.dll, user32.dll, and winmm.dll. (These DLLs are specified by the WIN32.TXT file, which is selected under **Source**.)

3. The **Target** box identifies the class to contain the J/Direct calls. By default, a class named Win32 will be added to your project and will contain these calls. (If your solution contains multiple Java projects, the Win32 class is added to the first project.)

   To specify a different target class, click the ellipsis button (**...**).

   - In the **Select Class** dialog box, select whether you want to view your classes in **Project View** or **Class View**. Project view displays a hierarchical list of the .java files in your solution, where each file node lists the names of the classes contained in that file. Class view displays a hierarchical list of class names.

   - Once you have chosen a view, select the name of the class to contain the J/Direct calls. (To copy the calls to the Windows Clipboard instead of to a class, select **Clipboard**.)

   - Click **OK**.

4. To filter the display of Win32 methods, structs, and constants, select or clear the **Methods**, **Structs**, and **Constants** options.

5. Now select the method, struct, or constant that you want to insert. (You can select multiple items using the SHIFT and CTRL keys.) Note that a Win32 struct will be added as a nested class inside your class.

> **Note** To search for an item by its initial characters, type the characters into the **Find** box. The first item that matches these characters is automatically selected.

6. To insert the associated Java definition into your class, click **Copy To Target**. (You can also double-click the method, struct, or constant to insert it into your class.)

When a Win32 API element is selected in the J/Direct Call Builder, the lower preview pane displays the associated Java definition. You can copy and paste this text into any file. To quickly find the online reference information for a Win32 API element, right-click the item and click **Display API Help** on the shortcut menu.

For information about the default settings for this builder, see the next section "Setting J/Direct Call Builder Options."

Setting J/Direct Call Builder Options

Visual J++ allows you to set two options to customize the functionality of the J/Direct Call Builder.

To set J/Direct Call Builder options

1. On the **Tools** menu, click **J/Direct Call Builder Options**.

2. In the **J/Direct Call Builder Options** dialog box, select or clear the following options:

Option	Description
Show Target window when copy to target	Selected by default. When you insert a J/Direct call into your class, the builder automatically opens the .java file in the Text editor, if it is not already opened.
Disable stack crawl security check	Cleared by default. The VM will initiate a stack-based security check for each J/Direct call. If any of the callers on the stack are not fully trusted, then a security exception is thrown and the J/Direct call will not be invoked. This mainly affects Java code deployed on Web pages.
	When you select this option to disable the security checks, the @security(checkDllCalls=off) tag is automatically added to your class the *next* time you insert a J/Direct call. (If you later clear this option, any existing occurrences of the @security tag remain in your files, but no new instances will be added.)

3. Click **OK** to save your settings.

Quick Syntax Reference

The following section gives a quick reference to the @dll.import, @dll.struct, and @dll.structmap directives. For each directive, the required syntax is shown and explained.

Syntax for @dll.import

The @dll.import directive should be placed just above the method declaration. The syntax of the directive is:

```
/**@dll.import("LibName",<Modifier>)*/
...method declaration...;
```

LibName is the name of the DLL that contains the function you want to invoke. *Modifier* is optional, and the value that you should supply for it varies depending on your needs. In the method declaration, you can use the function name that the DLL uses, or you can give the method a different name by using aliasing. For information on aliasing, see "Aliasing (Method Renaming)," later in this chapter. The Java data types that you choose for the parameters and for the return value of the method should be types that map to the types of the DLL function parameters and return value. See "How Data Types are Marshaled," later in this chapter, for more information about how Java data types map to native types.

The following table presents the @dll.import syntax for several situations that are described in this section.

Situation	Required Syntax	Explanation
Calling Win32 DLLs	`/**@dll.import("Libname")*/`	
Calling OLE APIs	`/**@dll.import("Libname", ole)*/`	
Aliasing	`/**@dll.import("Libname", entrypoint="DLLFunctionName")*/`	In the method declaration, use the Java name that you selected.
Linking by Ordinal	`/**@dll.import("Libname", entrypoint="#ordinal")*/`	"ordinal" is a 16-bit integer, specified in decimal, that indicates the DLL function that you are importing.

Syntax for @dll.struct

The @dll.struct directive is placed just above the class declaration. The syntax of @dll.struct is:

```
/**@dll.struct(<LinkTypeModifier>,<pack=n>)*/
...class declaration...;
```

LinkTypeModifier tells the compiler whether fields of type String and char represent ANSI or Unicode characters in native format. *LinkTypeModifier* can be *ansi*, *unicode*, or *auto*. If you do not specify *LinkTypeModifier*, *ansi* is used by default. See "How the VM Chooses Between ANSI and Unicode," later in this chapter, to help you learn more about the values to use for *LinkTypeModifier*.

You can also specify *pack=n* to tell the compiler to set the packing size of the structure to either 1, 2, 4, or 8, depending on the value you specify for *n*. If you omit the *pack=n* modifier, the packing size is set to 8 by default. See "Structure Packing," later in this chapter, for more information on setting the packing size.

Within the class declaration, you need to supply fields whose Java types map to the types of the fields in the native structure, in the order they occur in the native structure. See "Correspondence Between Types Inside Structures," later in this chapter, for information about choosing the data types of the fields.

The following table describes the syntax for several situations in which you might use the @dll.struct directive.

Situation	Required Syntax	Explanation
Declare a structure	`/**@dll.struct()*/`	When you do not specify *LinkTypeModifier*, char or String fields are assumed to represent ANSI characters.
Set a structure's packing size	`/**@dll.struct(pack=n)*/`	*n* can be 1,2,4, or 8.
Declare a structure that has a field of type char	`/**@dll.struct(ansi)*/`	The character field represents an ANSI character.
Declare a structure with a field of type string and set the packing size	`/**@dll.struct(unicode,pack=n)*/`	The String fields will be in Unicode format, and the packing size is set to 1,2,4, or 8, depending on the value of *n*.

Syntax for @dll.structmap

The @dll.structmap directive is used to declare fixed-size strings and arrays embedded in structures. It should be placed within a structure that is declared with @dll.struct, and directly above the declaration of the fixed-size string or array field. For more information on how to use @dll.structmap, see "Fixed-size Strings Embedded within Structures" and "Fixed-size Scalar Arrays Embedded within Structures." Both sections are later in this chapter.

The following table presents the syntax of the @dll.structmap directive.

Situation	Required Syntax	Explanation
Structure that contains a fixed-size string.	`/**@dll.structmap([type=TCHAR [Size]])*/`	*Size* is a decimal integer that indicates the number of characters in the string, including space for the null terminator.
Structure that contains a fixed-size array.	`/**@dll.structmap([type= FIXEDARRAY,size=n])*/`	*n* is a decimal integer that represents the size of the array.

How Data Types are Marshaled

Simply put, the Microsoft VM evaluates Java arguments, then converts them to native C++ types. The Microsoft VM infers the native type of each parameter and the return value from the declared (compile-time) Java type of the parameter. For example, a parameter declared as a Java integer is passed as a 32-bit integer; a parameter declared as a Java String object is passed as a null-terminated string, and so forth. There are no invisible attributes that provide information about the native types. In Java, what you see is what you get.

Quick Reference

The following two tables list the native type that corresponds to each Java type. The first table describes the mappings for parameters and return values, and the second table shows the mappings that are used with the @dll.struct directive.

Parameter and Return Value Mappings

Java	Native	Notes/Restrictions
byte	BYTE or CHAR	
short	SHORT or WORD	
int	INT, UINT, LONG, ULONG, or DWORD	

Parameter and Return Value Mappings *(continued)*

Java	Native	Notes/Restrictions
char	TCHAR	
long	__int64	
float	float	
double	double	
Boolean	BOOL	
String	LPCTSTR	Not allowed as return value, except in *ole* mode. In *ole* mode, String maps to LPWSTR. The Microsoft VM frees the string by using CoTaskMemFree.
StringBuffer	LPTSTR	Not allowed as return value. Set the StringBuffer capacity large enough to hold the largest string that the DLL function can generate.
byte[]	BYTE*	
short[]	WORD*	
char[]	TCHAR*	
int[]	DWORD*	
float[]	float*	
double[]	double*	
long[]	__int64*	
Boolean[]	BOOL[]	
Object	pointer to struct	In *ole* mode, an IUnknown* is passed instead.
Interface	COM interface	Use jactivex or similar tool to generate interface file.
com.ms.com.SafeArray	SAFEARRAY*	Not allowed as return value.
com.ms.com._Guid	GUID,IID,CLSID	
com.ms.com.Variant	VARIANT*	
@dll.struct classes	pointer to struct	
@com.struct classes	pointer to struct	
void	VOID	As return value only.
com.ms.dll.Callback	function pointer	As parameter only.

Mappings used with @dll.struct

Java	Native
byte	BYTE or CHAR
char	TCHAR
short	SHORT or WORD
int	INT, UINT, LONG, ULONG or DWORD
float	__int64
long	float
double	double
Boolean	BOOL[]
Java	Native
String	Pointer to a string, or an embedded fixed-size string
Class marked with @dll.struct	Nested structure
char[]	Nested array of TCHAR
byte[]	Nested array of BYTE
short[]	Nested array of SHORT
int[]	Nested array of LONG
long[]	Nested array of __int64
float[]	Nested array of floats
double[]	Nested array of doubles

Basic Scalar Types

The basic scalar types are mapped as follows:

Java type	DLL
int	signed 32-bit integer
byte	signed 8-bit integer
short	signed 16-bit integer
long	signed 64-bit integer
float	32-bit float
double	64-bit double

Note that there is no direct representation of unsigned integer types in Java. Since Java has no unsigned types, use the Java type which is the same size as the integer type you want. For example, the Java **int** type can be used without loss of representation for the common DWORD (unsigned 32-bit) type.

Chars

The Java char type becomes a CHAR (an 8-bit ANSI character) unless the *unicode* or *ole* @dll.struct modifier is in effect, in which case it becomes a WCHAR (a 16-bit Unicode character).

Booleans

The Java Boolean type maps to the Win32 BOOL type, which is a 32-bit type. As a parameter, the Java true maps to 1, and false maps to 0. As a return value, all non-zero values map to true.

Note that BOOL and VARIANT_BOOL (the internal Boolean type in Microsoft Visual Basic) are not interchangeable. To pass a VARIANT_BOOL to a Visual Basic DLL, you must use the Java short type and use –1 for VARIANT_TRUE, and 0 for VARIANT_FALSE.

Strings

This section explains how you can pass a string in ANSI or Unicode format to a DLL function. It also discusses two ways to return a string from a DLL function.

Passing a String to a DLL Function

To pass a standard null-terminated string to a DLL function, just pass a Java String.

For example, to change the current directory, you can access the Kernel32 function CopyFile as follows:

```
class ShowCopyFile
{
    public static void main(String args[])
    {
        CopyFile("old.txt", "new.txt", true);
    }
    /** @dll.import("KERNEL32") */
    private native static boolean CopyFile(String existingFile,
                                String newFile, boolean f);
}
```

Strings are read-only in Java, so the Microsoft VM will convert only the String object as an input. To allow virtual machine implementations to marshal Strings without copying the characters, String object parameters should not be passed to DLL functions that can modify the string. If the DLL function might modify the string, pass a StringBuffer object.

Strings are converted to ANSI unless the *unicode* or *ole* modifier is used, in which case the string is passed in Unicode format.

Strings cannot be declared as return types of a DLL function except in *ole* mode, where the native return type is assumed to be a LPWSTR allocated using the CoTaskMemAlloc function.

Receiving a String from a DLL Function

There are two common ways of passing a string back from a function: either the caller allocates a buffer that is filled in by the function, or the function allocates the string and returns it to the caller. Most Win32 functions use the first method, but OLE functions use the second method. (See "Invoking OLE API Functions," later in this chapter, to learn about the special support that J/Direct provides for calling OLE functions.) One function that uses the first method is the Kernel32 function GetTempPath, which has the following prototype:

```
DWORD GetTempPath(DWORD sizeofbuffer, LPTSTR buffer);
```

This function simply returns the path of the system temporary file directory (such as "c:\tmp\"). The *buffer* argument points to a caller-allocated buffer that receives the path, and *sizeofbuffer* indicates the number of characters that can be written to the buffer. (This is different from the number of bytes in the Unicode version.) In Java, strings are read-only, so you cannot pass a String object as the buffer. Instead, you can use Java's StringBuffer class to create a writable StringBuffer object. The following is an example that invokes the GetTempPath function:

```
class ShowGetTempPath
{
    static final int MAX_PATH = 260;
    public static void main(String args[])
    {
        StringBuffer temppath = new StringBuffer(MAX_PATH);
        GetTempPath(temppath.capacity(), temppath);
        System.out.println("Temppath = " + temppath);
    }

    /** @dll.import("KERNEL32") */
    private static native int GetTempPath(int sizeofbuffer,
                                          StringBuffer buffer);
}
```

To understand this example, it is important to distinguish between a StringBuffer's length and its capacity. The length is the number of characters logically in the string currently stored in the StringBuffer. The capacity is the actual amount of storage currently allocated to that StringBuffer. After the following statement executes:

```
StringBuffer sb = new StringBuffer(259);
```

the value of *sb.length* is zero, and the value of *sb.capacity* is 259. When you invoke a DLL method passing a StringBuffer, the Microsoft VM examines the capacity of the StringBuffer, adds one for the null terminator, multiplies by 2 if Unicode is the default character size, and then allocates that many bytes of memory for the buffer that is passed to the DLL function. In other words, you use the capacity, not the length, to set the size of the buffer. Be careful not to make the following mistake:

```
StringBuffer sb = new StringBuffer();   //Wrong!
   GetTempPath(MAX_PATH, sb);
```

Invoking the StringBuffer constructor with no arguments creates a StringBuffer object with a capacity of 16, which is probably too small. MAX_PATH was passed to the GetTempPath method, indicating that there was enough room in the buffer to hold 260 characters. Thus, GetTempPath will probably overrun the buffer. If you were planning to use GetTempPath extensively, you should wrap it in a Java-friendly wrapper in the following manner:

```
public static String GetTempPath()
{
    StringBuffer temppath = new StringBuffer(MAX_PATH-1);
    int res = GetTempPath(MAX_PATH, temppath);
    if (res == 0 || res > MAX_PATH) {
        throw new RuntimeException("GetTempPath error!");
    }
    return temppath.toString(); // can't return a StringBuffer
}
```

This method offers both convenience and safety, and it maps the error return value of the function to a Java exception. Notice that you cannot return StringBuffer objects.

Arrays

J/Direct automatically handles arrays of scalars. The following Java array types translate directly into native pointer types:

Java	Native	# bytes per element
byte[]	BYTE*	1
short[]	SHORT*	2
int[]	DWORD*	4
float[]	FLOAT*	4
double[]	DOUBLE*	8
long[]	__int64*	8
Boolean[]	BOOL*	4

The char[] array type maps to CHAR* unless the *unicode* modifier is in effect, in which case it maps to WCHAR*.

All scalar array parameters can be modified by the caller (such as [in, out] parameters).

Array types cannot be used as return types. There is no support for arrays of objects or strings.

Typically, this facility is used by OLE functions to return values. (OLE functions reserve the "function" return value to return the HRESULT error code.) See "Invoking OLE API Functions," later in this chapter, to learn how to obtain the return value for OLE functions.

Structures

The Java language does not directly support the concept of a structure. Although Java classes containing fields can be used to emulate the concept of a structure within the Java language, ordinary Java objects cannot be used to simulate structures in native DLL calls. This is because the Java language does not guarantee the layout of the fields and because the garbage collector is free to move the object around in memory.

Therefore, to pass and receive structures from DLL methods, you need to use the @dll.struct compiler directive. When applied to a Java class definition, this directive causes all instances of the class to be allocated in a memory block that will not move during garbage collection. In addition, the layout of the fields in memory can be controlled using the pack modifier (see "Structure Packing," later in this chapter). For example, the Win32 SYSTEMTIME structure has the following definition in the C programming language:

```
typedef struct {
   WORD wYear;
   WORD wMonth;
   WORD wDayOfWeek;
   WORD wDay;
   WORD wHour;
   WORD wMinute;
   WORD wSecond;
   WORD wMilliseconds;
} SYSTEMTIME;
```

The correct declaration of this structure in Java is as follows:

```
/** @dll.struct() */
class SYSTEMTIME {
   public short wYear;
   public short wMonth;
   public short wDayOfWeek;
   public short wDay;
   public short wHour;
   public short wMinute;
   public short wSecond;
   public short wMilliseconds;
}
```

The following example uses the SYSTEMTIME structure in a DLL method call:

```
class ShowStruct {
   /** @dll.import("KERNEL32") */
   static native void GetSystemTime(SYSTEMTIME pst);
   public static void main(String args[])
   {
      SYSTEMTIME systemtime = new SYSTEMTIME();
      GetSystemTime(systemtime);
      System.out.println("Year is " + systemtime.wYear);
      System.out.println("Month is " + systemtime.wMonth);
      // etc.
   }
}
```

Note   Classes declared with @dll.struct are considered unsafe and therefore cannot be used by untrusted applets.

Correspondence Between Types Inside Structures

The following table describes how scalar types map inside structures.

Java	Native
byte	BYTE
char	TCHAR (CHAR or WCHAR depending on @dll.struct definition)
short	SHORT
int	LONG
long	__int64
float	float
double	double
Boolean	BOOL (32-bit Boolean)

Reference types (Java objects and classes) normally map to embedded structures and arrays. Each supported mapping is described in the following table.

Java	Native
String	Pointer to a string, or an embedded fixed-string string
Class marked with @dll.struct	Nested structure
char[]	Nested array of TCHAR (CHAR/WCHAR)
byte[]	Nested array of BYTE
short[]	Nested array of SHORT
int[]	Nested array of LONG
long[]	Nested array of __int64
float[]	Nested array of floats
double[]	Nested array of doubles

There is no direct support for pointers inside structures due to the large number of possible ways referenced objects could be allocated and disposed of. To represent a structure with an embedded pointer, declare the pointer field as type int. You will need to make explicit DLL calls to the appropriate allocation functions and initialize the memory blocks yourself. (You could use DllLib.ptrToStruct to map the blocks onto @dll.struct classes.)

Nested Structures

A structure can embed another structure simply by naming the other structure as the field type. For example, the Windows MSG structure embeds a POINT structure as follows:

```
typedef struct {
    LONG x;
    LONG y;
} POINT;

typedef struct {
    int hwnd;
    int message;
    int wParam;
    int lParam;
    int time;
    POINT pt;
} MSG;
```

This translates directly into Java as follows:

```
/** @dll.struct() */
class POINT {
    int x;
    int y;
}
/** @dll.struct() */
class MSG {
    public int hwnd;
    public int message;
    public int wParam;
    public int lParam;
    public int time;
    public POINT pt;
}
```

Tip   Although embedding structures is handy, the fact remains that Java does not truly support embedded objects – only embedded references to objects. The Microsoft VM must translate between these two formats each time a nested structure is passed. Therefore, in a critical code path, you can improve performance by nesting structures manually (by copying the fields of the nested structure into the containing structure). For example, the *pt* field in the MSG structure could easily be declared as two integer fields, *pt_x* and *pt_y*.

Fixed-Size Strings Embedded Within Structures

Some structures have fixed size strings embedded in them. The LOGFONT structure is defined as follows:

```
typedef struct {
    LONG lfHeight;
    LONG lfWidth;
    /* <many other fields deleted for brevity> */
    TCHAR lfFaceName[32];
} LOGFONT;
```

This structure can be expressed in Java using an extension syntax to specify the size:

```
/** @dll.struct() */
    class LOGFONT {
        int lfHeight;
        int lfWidth;
        /* <many other fields deleted for brevity> */
        /** @dll.structmap([type=TCHAR[32]]) */
        String lfFaceName;
    }
```

The @dll.structmap directive indicates the size of the fixed string as measured in characters (including space for the null terminator).

For more information, see "Fixed-Size Scalar Arrays Embedded Within Structures."

Fixed-Size Scalar Arrays Embedded Within Structures

Fixed-size arrays of scalars embedded in structures can be specified using the @dll.structmap directive. The following is a C language structure that contains fixed-size scalar arrays:

```
struct EmbeddedArrays
{
    BYTE      b[4];
    CHAR      c[4];
    SHORT     s[4];
    INT       i[4];
    __int64   l[4];
    float     f[4];
    doubl     d[4];
};
```

You can specify the EmbeddedArrays structure by using @dll.structmap in the following way:

```
/** @dll.struct() */
class EmbeddedArrays
{
    /** @dll.structmap([type=FIXEDARRAY, size=4]) */
    byte b[];

    /** @dll.structmap([type=FIXEDARRAY, size=4]) */
    char c[];

    /** @dll.structmap([type=FIXEDARRAY, size=4]) */
    short s[];

    /** @dll.structmap([type=FIXEDARRAY, size=4]) */
    int i[];

    /** @dll.structmap([type=FIXEDARRAY, size=4]) */
    long l[];

    /** @dll.structmap([type=FIXEDARRAY, size=4]) */
    float f[];

    /** @dll.structmap([type=FIXEDARRAY, size=4]) */
    double d[];

}
```

Structure Packing

Structure fields are padded and aligned according to ANSI C draft 3.5.2.1. The packing size can be set using the *pack* modifier:

```
/** @dll.struct(pack=n) */
```

where *n* can be 1, 2, 4 or 8. The default is 8. For users of the Microsoft Visual C++ compilers, "pack=*n*" is equivalent to "#pragma pack(*n*)".

Understanding the Relationship Between @dll.struct and @com.struct

The @dll.struct directive is very similar to the @com.struct directive emitted by the jactivex tool and implicitly by the javatlb tool. (The javatlb tool, documented in previous versions of Microsoft Visual J++, has been replaced by jactivex.) The main difference is that the default type mappings are suited for Microsoft Windows function calling instead of COM object calling. Given this information, it follows that you can also generate @dll.struct classes by describing the structure in a type library and using the jactivex tool to generate the Java class. However, it's usually faster to generate the classes manually.

Pointers

Java does not support a pointer data type. However, instead of passing a pointer, you can pass a one-element array. You can store pointers in Java integers, and you can read and write data from raw pointers.

Return Value Pointers

Win32 functions that have multiple return values typically handle them by having the caller pass a pointer to a variable to be updated. For example, the GetDiskFreeSpace function has the following prototype:

```
BOOL GetDiskFreeSpace(LPCTSTR szRootPathName,
                      DWORD  *lpSectorsPerCluster,
                      DWORD  *lpBytesPerCluster,
                      DWORD  *lpFreeClusters,
                      DWORD  *lpClusters);
```

GetDiskFreeSpace is typically called as follows:

```
DWORD sectorsPerCluster, bytesPerCluster, freeClusters, clusters;
GetDiskFreeSpace(rootname, &sectorsPerCluster,
                &bytesPerCluster, &freeClusters, &clusters);
```

In Java, this is just a special case of passing scalar arrays where the array size is one element. The following example shows how to call the GetDiskFreeSpace function:

```
class ShowGetDiskFreeSpace
{
    public static void main(String args[])
    {
        int sectorsPerCluster[] = {0};
        int bytesPerCluster[] = {0};
        int freeClusters[] = {0};
        int clusters[] = {0};
        GetDiskFreeSpace("c:\\", sectorsPerCluster, bytesPerCluster,
                    freeClusters, clusters);
        System.out.println("sectors/cluster  = " + sectorsPerCluster[0]);
        System.out.println("bytes/cluster = " + bytesPerCluster[0]);
        System.out.println("free clusters = " + freeClusters[0]);
        System.out.println("clusters = " + clusters[0]);
    }

    /** @dll.import("KERNEL32") */
    private native static boolean GetDiskFreeSpace(String rootname,
                    int pSectorsPerCluster[], int pBytesPerCluster[],
                    int pFreeClusters[], int pClusters[]);
}
```

Raw Pointers

A pointer to an unknown or particularly difficult structure can be stored in a plain Java integer. If your application only needs to store the pointer and not dereference it, this is the simplest and most efficient approach. You might want to use this technique to store a pointer that has been returned by a DLL function that allocates a memory block. In fact, you can use this technique to store a pointer returned by any DLL function. Needless to say, using raw pointers eliminates many of the safety advantages of Java. An alternative approach should be used whenever possible. However, there are situations when you might choose to use raw pointers. With that in mind, there are two ways to read and write data from raw pointers.

Casting to a Reference to an @dll.struct Class

One way to read and write data through a raw pointer is to cast the raw pointer to a reference to an @dll.struct class. Once this is done, you can read and write the data using normal field access syntax. For instance, suppose you have a raw pointer that you wish to access as a RECT. You can use the system method DllLib.ptrToStruct as follows:

```
/** @dll.struct() */
   class RECT {
      int left;
      int top;
      int right;
      int bottom;
   }

   import com.ms.dll.*;

   int  rawptr = ...;
   RECT rect = (RECT)DllLib.ptrToStruct(RECT.class, rawptr);
   rect.left = 0;
   rect.top = 0;
   rect.right = 10;
   rect.bottom = 10;
```

The ptrToStruct method wraps the raw pointer in a RECT instance. Unlike instances created by the **new** operator, this RECT instance will not attempt to free the raw pointer upon reclamation by the garbage collector because the RECT object has no way of knowing how the pointer was allocated. In addition, because the native memory was already constructed at the time ptrToStruct was called, the RECT class constructor is *not* called.

Using the DllLib Copy Methods

Another method for reading and writing data through a raw pointer is to use the overloaded copy methods in DllLib. These methods copy data between Java arrays of various types and raw pointers. If you need to treat a raw pointer as a pointer to a string (LPTSTR), you can use one of the DllLib methods ptrToStringAnsi, ptrToStringUni, or ptrToString to parse the string and convert it into a java.lang.String object.

```
import com.ms.dll.*;

    int rawptr = ...;
    String s = DllLib.ptrToStringAnsi(rawptr);
```

Warning All Java objects are subject to movement in memory or reclamation by the garbage collector. Therefore, you should not attempt to obtain a pointer to a Java array by calling a DLL function that does generic casting. The following example shows you an incorrect way to obtain the pointer:

```
// Do not do this!
    /** @dll.import("MYDLL") */
    private native static int Cast(int javaarray[]);

    // Inside MYDLL.DLL
    LPVOID Cast(LPVOID ptr)
    {
        // Do not do this!
        return ptr; // comes in as a Java array; goes out as a Java int
    }
```

The value of *ptr* is guaranteed to be valid only for the duration of the call to the Cast function. This is because VM implementations are allowed to implement passing of arrays by copying and because garbage collection may cause the physical location of the array to be different after the call to the Cast function returns.

Polymorphic Parameters

Some Win32 functions declare a parameter whose type depends on the value of another parameter. For example, the WinHelp function is declared as follows:

```
BOOL WinHelp(int hwnd, LPCTSTR szHelpFile, UINT cmd, DWORD dwData);
```

The innocent-looking *dwData* parameter can actually be any one of the following: a pointer to a string, a pointer to a MULTIKEYHELP structure, a pointer to a HELPWININFO, or a plain integer, depending on the value of the *cmd* parameter.

J/Direct offers two ways to declare such a parameter:

- Declare the parameter as type Object.

- Use overloading to declare a separate method for each possible type.

For a comparison, see "Comparison Between the Two Methods," later in this chapter.

Declaring the Parameter as Type Object

The following shows how to declare WinHelp by declaring *dwData* as type Object:

```
/** @dll.import("USER32") */
static native boolean WinHelp(int hwnd, String szHelpFile,
                             int cmd, Object dwData);
```

When WinHelp is invoked, J/Direct will use the run-time type to determine how to translate *dwData*. The following table describes how the types are translated.

Type	Translated as
java.lang.Integer	4-byte integer
java.lang.Boolean	4-byte BOOL
java.lang.Char	CHAR (or WCHAR if the *unicode* or *ole* modifiers are in effect)
java.lang.Short	2-byte SHORT
java.lang.Float	4-byte FLOAT
java.lang.String	LPCSTR (or LPCWSTR if the *unicode* or *ole* modifier is in effect)
java.lang.StringBuffer	LPSTR (or LPWSTR if the *unicode* or *ole* modifier is in effect)
byte[]	BYTE*
char[]	CHAR* (or WCHAR* if the *unicode* or *ole* modifier is in effect)
short[]	SHORT*
int[]	INT*
long[]	__int64
float[]	float*
double[]	double*
@dll.struct	pointer to structure

Overloading the Function

Another way to declare the WinHelp function is to overload the function for each possible type:

```
/** @dll.import("USER32") */
static native boolean WinHelp(int hwnd, String szHelpFile,
                             int cmd, int dwData);

/** @dll.import("USER32") */
static native boolean WinHelp(int hwnd, String szHelpFile,
                             int cmd, String dwData);
```

```
/** @dll.import("USER32") */
static native boolean WinHelp(int hwnd, String szHelpFile,
                             int cmd, MULTIKEYHELP dwData);

/** @dll.import("USER32") */
static native boolean WinHelp(int hwnd, String szHelpFile,
                             int cmd, HELPWININFO dwData);
```

You cannot handle a polymorphic return value using overloading because Java methods cannot be overloaded on return value only. Therefore, you need to give each variant of the function a different Java name and use the *entrypoint* modifier to link them all to the same DLL method. See "Aliasing (Method Renaming)," later in this chapter, to learn more about renaming DLL methods.

Comparison Between the Two Methods

In most cases, overloading is the preferred approach because it offers superior run-time performance as well as better type checking. In addition, overloading avoids the need to wrap integer arguments inside an Integer object.

However, declaring the parameter as type Object can be useful in cases where there is more than one polymorphic parameter. You might also choose this method when you want to access a service that acts generically on a wide variety of types, such as a function that can accept any object declared with the @dll.struct directive.

Callbacks

Several Win32 APIs require your programs to provide Windows with the address of a callback function. You can write callbacks in Java by extending the system class com.ms.dll.Callback.

Declaring a Method that Takes a Callback

To represent a callback parameter in Java, declare the Java type to be either type com.ms.dll.Callback or a class that derives from it. For example, the Microsoft Win32 EnumWindows function is prototyped as follows:

```
BOOL EnumWindows(WNDENUMPROC wndenumproc, LPARAM lparam);
```

The corresponding Java prototype is:

```
import com.ms.dll.Callback;
   /** @dll.import("USER32") */
   static native boolean EnumWindows(Callback wndenumproc,
                                     int lparam);
```

Invoking a Function that Takes a Callback

To invoke a function that takes a callback, you need to define a class that extends
Callback. The derived class must expose one non-static method whose name is callback
(all lowercase). The C language definition of WNDENUMPROC is:

```
BOOL CALLBACK EnumWindowsProc(HWND hwnd, LPARAM lparam);
```

To author an EnumWindowsProc in Java, you declare a class that extends Callback
as follows:

```
class EnumWindowsProc extends Callback
    {
        public boolean callback(int hwnd, int lparam)
        {
            StringBuffer text = new StringBuffer(50);
            GetWindowText(hwnd, text, text.capacity()+1);

            if (text.length() != 0) {
                System.out.println("hwnd = " + Integer.toHexString(hwnd) +
                                   "h: Text = " + text);
            }
            return true;  // return TRUE to continue enumeration.
        }

    /** @dll.import("USER32") */
    private static native int GetWindowText(int hwnd, StringBuffer text,
                                            int cch);
    }
```

You can invoke EnumWindows with this Callback in the following way:

```
boolean result = EnumWindows(new EnumWindowsProc(), 0);
```

Restrictions on Types Accepted by the Callback Method

The return type of the callback method must be void, int, boolean, char, or short. The only
parameter type currently allowed is the int type. Fortunately, this is not as restrictive as it
sounds. You can use the DllLib methods ptrToStringAnsi, ptrToStringUni, and ptrToString
to treat a parameter as an LPTSTR. You can use the ptrToStruct method to treat a
parameter as a pointer to an @dll.struct class.

Associating Data with a Callback

Frequently, it is necessary to pass some data from the caller of the function to the callback. This explains why EnumWindows takes an extra *lparam* argument. Most Win32 functions that take callbacks accept one extra 32-bit parameter that is passed to the callback without interpretation. With the Callback mechanism, it is not necessary to pass data using the *lparam* argument. Because the callback method is non-static, you can store your data as fields in the EnumWindowsProc object.

The Lifetime of a Callback

Some care is required to ensure that the callback is not reclaimed by garbage collection before the native function is finished with it. If the callback is short-term (only callable for the duration of one function call), no special action is required because a callback passed to a DLL function is guaranteed not to be reclaimed by garbage collection while the call is in progress.

If a callback is long-term (used across function calls), you will need to protect the callback from being reclaimed, typically by storing a reference to it in a Java data structure. You can also store references to callbacks within native data structures by using the com.ms.dll.Root class to wrap the callback inside a root handle. The root handle is a 32-bit handle that prevents the callback from being reclaimed until the handle is explicitly freed. For example, a root handle to a WndProc can be stored in the application data area of an HWND structure, and then explicitly freed on the WM_NCDESTROY message.

Embedding a Callback Inside a Structure

To embed a callback inside a structure, you can first call the com.ms.dll.Root.alloc method to wrap the callback in a root handle. Then pass the root handle to the DllLib.addrOf method to obtain the actual (native) address of the callback. Then, store this address as an integer.

For example, the WNDCLASS structure can be declared in Java as:

```
/** @dll.struct() */
   class WNDCLASS {
      int style;
      int lpfnWndProc; // CALLBACK
      ... /* <other fields deleted for brevity> */
   }
```

Let's assume you have extended callback as follows:

```
class WNDPROC extends Callback
    {
        public int callback(int hwnd, int msg, int wparam, int lparam)
        {
        ...
        }
    }
```

To store a pointer to the callback inside the WNDCLASS object, use the following sequence:

```
import com.ms.dll.*;
    WNDCLASS wc = new WNDCLASS();
    int callbackroot = Root.alloc(new WNDPROC());
    wc.lpfnWndProc = DllLib.addrOf(callbackroot);
```

Invoking OLE API Functions

The following sections provide information on OLE API functions.

OLE Mode Syntax

The @dll.import directive includes a special mode tailored for importing OLE API functions. To use this mode, simply include the *ole* modifier as in the following example:

```
/** @dll.import("OLE32", ole) */
    public class OLE32 {
        ...
    }
```

Comparison of Win32 Functions with OLE Functions

In theory, the functions exported out of OLE32.DLL and OLEAUT32.DLL are no different from any other DLL function. In practice, the OLE functions follow a consistent calling style of their own. OLE functions differ from Win32 functions in the following ways:

- OLE functions only come in Unicode. There are no ANSI OLE functions.

- Virtually all OLE functions return a 32-bit status code known as an HRESULT through the normal function return value. The high-bit indicates whether the function succeeded (hi-bit off) or failed (hi-bit on). A few functions return multiple success values (typically S_OK and S_FALSE) but most return only one success value (S_OK).

- If an OLE function returns some value other than the status code, it does so by having the caller supply a pointer to a variable that will receive the value on exit. This return value pointer is, by convention, the last parameter.

- The Win32 style of returning strings is to fill in a caller-allocated buffer. OLE functions typically return strings by allocating them using CoTaskMemAlloc and expecting the caller to free them using CoTaskMemFree.

Comparing Win32 Code to OLE Code

The code for a simple Add function would look like this in the Win32 style of coding:

```
int sum;
sum = Add(10, 20);
```

In OLE style, the Add function would be written the following way:

```
HRESULT hr;
    int sum;
    hr = Add(10, 20, &sum);
    if (FAILED(hr)) {
        ...handle error..
    }
```

Invoking OLE Functions

The *ole* mode takes advantage of a consistent coding style to provide a Java-friendly way to call OLE functions. Invoking an OLE-style Add function from Java looks much like invoking a more traditional Win32-style function:

```
/** dll.import("OLELIKEMATHDLL", ole) */
    private native static int Add(int x, int y);
    int sum = Add(10, 20);
    // if we got here, Add succeeded.
```

How OLE Mode Works

Because of the *ole* modifier, the Microsoft VM automatically assumes that the native Add function returns an **HRESULT**. The VM notices that the Add function returns an integer. When invoking Add, the VM automatically allocates a temporary variable of type int and inserts a pointer to it as a third parameter. After the native Add function returns, the VM automatically checks the HRESULT and if it indicates a failure (high-bit on), a Java exception of type com.ms.com.ComFailException is thrown. If the HRESULT does not indicate a failure, the VM retrieves the Add function's true return value from the temporary variable it created, and it returns that value.

Unlike Java/COM integration, a return value of S_FALSE does not cause a ComSuccessException to be thrown. If you need to distinguish between success results, you need to use normal DLL calling mode and treat the HRESULT as an integer return value.

To summarize, *ole* mode alters the semantics of DLL calling as follows:

1. All strings and characters are assumed to be Unicode.

2. The function return value of the native function is presumed to be an HRESULT. The Microsoft VM throws a ComFailException if the returned HRESULT indicates failure.

3. If the Java method return type is not void, the Microsoft VM will assume that the native function returns an additional result through a pointer, which is the final argument to the function. The VM will supply this pointer argument and dereference it after the call to obtain the additional return value. This value will be returned as the value of the Java method.

Passing and Receiving Strings from OLE Functions

Declaring a parameter as type String on an *ole* mode function passes a LPCOLESTR. The Microsoft VM also includes a preceding length prefix so the string can also be treated as a BSTR.

Declaring a return value as type String in *ole* mode causes the Microsoft VM to pass a pointer to an uninitialized LPCOLESTR*. When the native function returns, the Microsoft VM will convert the returned LPCOLESTR to a Java String, and then call CoTaskMemFree to free the string.

Passing GUIDs (and IIDs and CLSIDs)

The system class com.ms.com._Guid is used to represent GUIDs. Passing a _Guid object as a parameter passes a pointer to a GUID to the native function. Declaring a return type of _Guid causes the Microsoft VM to pass a pointer to an uninitialized GUID that the function fills in (in *ole* mode only).

For example, OLE32 exports the functions CLSIDFromProgID and ProgIDFromCLSID to map between CLSIDs and the human-readable names used by the Visual Basic function CreateObject.

These methods have the following prototypes:

```
HRESULT CLSIDFromProgID(LPCOLESTR szProgID, LPCLSID pclsid);
HRESULT ProgIDFromCLSID(REFCLSID clsid, LPOLESTR *lpszProgId);
```

In Java, these methods are declared in the following way:

```
import com.ms.com._Guid;
    class OLE {
        /** @dll.import("OLE32", ole) */
        public static native _Guid CLSIDFromProgID(String szProgID);

        /** @dll.import("OLE32", ole) */
        public static native String ProgIDFromCLSID(_Guid clsid);
    }
```

> **Note**   Note that com.ms.com._Guid supersedes com.ms.com.Guid (with no underscore).

Passing VARIANTs

Declaring a parameter to be type com.ms.com.Variant passes a pointer to a VARIANT to the native function. Declaring a return value to be type com.ms.com.Variant (*ole*-mode only) passes a pointer to an uninitialized Variant for the native function to fill in.

Passing COM Interface Pointers

To pass a COM interface pointer, you must generate a Java/COM interface class using a tool such as jactivex.exe. You can then pass or receive COM interfaces by declaring a parameter to be of that interface type.

For example, the system class com.ms.com.IStream is a Java/COM interface that represents the Structured Storage IStream* interface. The OLE32 function CreateStreamOnHGlobal could be declared as follows:

```
import com.ms.com.*;
/** @dll.import("OLE32", ole) */
public static native IStream CreateStreamOnHGlobal(int hGlobal,
                                          boolean fDeleteOnRelease);
```

Aliasing (Method Renaming)

Sometimes you want to use a name for the Java method that is different from the name that the DLL uses when it exports the function. For example, you might want to have the Java name start with a lowercase letter so that it conforms to Java naming conventions. To do so, just use the @dll.import directive with the *entrypoint* modifier as in the following example:

```
/** @dll.import("USER32", entrypoint="GetSysColor") */
    static native int getSysColor(int nIndex);
```

You do not need to use aliasing to perform the ANSI/Unicode suffixing done by the Win32 APIs. The Microsoft VM automatically takes care of this (see "How the VM Chooses Between ANSI and Unicode," later in this chapter). Aliasing is also unnecessary when accessing functions that have been exported by a .def file. Such names are typically exported using "stdcall mangling." That is, a method such as the following sample method would be renamed to _sample@8 (where 8 denotes the number of parameter bytes accepted by the function):

```
extern "C"
   __declspec(dllexport)
   VOID sample(int x, int y){
      ...
   }
```

J/Direct automatically binds to stdcall-mangled names without an explicit entrypoint.

The Microsoft VM automatically provides aliases for the following KERNEL32 API functions.

Kernel32 Function	Alias
CopyMemory	RtlMoveMemory
MoveMemory	RtlMoveMemory
FillMemory	RtlFillMemory
ZeroMemory	RtlZeroMemory

Linking by Ordinal

Some DLLs export functions by ordinal (16-bit integer) rather than by name. To call such DLLs, you will need to use a method-level @dll.import directive to specify the ordinal. The syntax for ordinal linking is:

```
/** @dll.import("Libname", entrypoint="#ordinal") */
```

Note that *ordinal* is specified in decimal.

For example, to link a function exported as ordinal 82 in DLL "MyDll.DLL", you would write the following code:

```
/** @dll.import("MyDll", entrypoint="#82") */
   public static native void MySample();
```

Specifying @dll.import for an Entire Class

The @dll.import directive can also be used prior to the class definition to set a library name for all native methods declared in that class. The following declaration uses @dll.import for an entire class:

```
/** @dll.import("KERNEL32") */
class EnvironmentStrings
{
    public static native int GetEnvironmentStrings();
    public static native int GetEnvironmentVariable(String name,
                            StringBuffer value, int ccbValue);
    public static native boolean SetEnvironmentVariable(String name,
                                                String value);
}
```

It is equivalent to specifying @dll.import for each method, as in the following example:

```
class EnvironmentStrings
{
    /** @dll.import("KERNEL32") */
    public static native int GetEnvironmentStrings();

    /** @dll.import("KERNEL32") */
    public static native int GetEnvironmentVariable(String name,
                            StringBuffer value, int ccbValue);

    /** @dll.import("KERNEL32") */
    public static native boolean SetEnvironmentVariable(String name,
                                                String value);
}
```

Using the @dll.import directive at the class level saves space in the .class file and eliminates redundant information. However, class-level @dll.import directives are not inherited by subclasses.

How the VM Chooses Between ANSI and Unicode

Regarding the MessageBox example shown in the J/Direct topic "Getting Started," a subtle but important fact is that USER32 does not export a function named MessageBox. Because the MessageBox function takes a string, it (like all Win32 functions that deal with strings) must exist in two versions: an ANSI version and a Unicode version (named MessageBoxA and MessageBoxW, respectively). When you code a call to MessageBox in C or C++, the MessageBox "function" you call is actually a macro that expands to either MessageBoxA or MessageBoxW, depending on whether the UNICODE macro is defined.

Calling the ANSI Version of a DLL Function

By default, the Microsoft VM assumes that the ANSI version of the MessageBox function is the one that is needed. If you import the MessageBox function using @dll.import (without a modifier) as follows:

```
/** @dll.import("USER32") */
   static native int MessageBox(int hwnd, String text,
                                 String title, int style);
```

The Microsoft VM will go through the following steps:

1. The strings "text" and "title" are converted to ANSI null-terminated strings.

2. The VM attempts to find an export named MessageBox in USER32.DLL.

3. This attempt fails. The VM then appends an "A" onto the name and looks for an export named MessageBoxA.

4. This attempt succeeds, and the VM invokes the MessageBoxA function.

Calling the Unicode Version of a DLL Function

Suppose that instead of calling the ANSI version of the MessageBox function, you want to call the Unicode version. You can do this by using the *unicode* modifier with the @dll.import directive:

```
/** @dll.import("USER32",unicode) */
   static native int MessageBox(int hwnd, String text, String title,
                                int style);
```

Since the *unicode* modifier is present, the Microsoft VM will go through the following steps:

1. The strings "text" and "title" are converted to Unicode null-terminated strings.

2. The VM attempts to find an export named MessageBox in USER32.DLL.

3. This attempt fails. The VM appends a "W" onto the name and looks for an export named MessageBoxW.

4. This attempt succeeds, and the VM invokes the MessageBoxW function.

Calling the Optimal Version of a DLL Function

Unfortunately, neither calling the ANSI version or the Unicode version of a DLL function is an ideal way to invoke the Win32 functions. Using the default ANSI mode allows your code to run on any Win32 platform, but causes unnecessary performance penalties on fully Unicode systems such as Microsoft Windows NT. Using the *unicode* modifier removes the performance penalty but restricts you to running on systems that implement the Unicode API. Fortunately, you can use the *auto* modifier with the @dll.import directive to call the optimal version of a DLL function based on the host operating system.

Using the *auto* modifier gives you the best of both worlds. The following example shows how to call the optimal version of the MessageBox function:

```
/** @dll.import("USER32",auto) */
   static native int MessageBox(int hwnd, String text, String title,
                                int style);
```

When the *auto* modifier is present, the Microsoft VM determines at run time whether the underlying platform supports the Unicode APIs. If Unicode is supported, the VM acts as if the *unicode* modifier had been specified. Otherwise, the VM behaves as if the *ansi* modifier had been specified. Thus, the *auto* modifier allows you to generate a single binary which runs well on both ANSI and Unicode Windows systems using the optimal API set available on the given platform.

In general, the *auto* modifier should be used whenever you call Windows API functions. If you are calling your own DLLs, select either *ansi* (the default) or *unicode* depending on your needs.

The following list provides details of how the VM decides whether to use ANSI or Unicode when you use the *auto* modifier:

1. The VM opens the registry key HKEY_LOCAL_MACHINE\Software\Microsoft\Java VM and looks for the DWORD-named value DllImportDefaultType. This value can be one of the following:

    2 – ANSI: Uses the ANSI version always.

    3 – Unicode: Uses the UNICODE version always.

    4 – Platform: Uses ANSI or Unicode depending on the platform.

2. If the key does not exist, or if it is set to 4 (indicating platform), the VM calls the Win32 GetVersion function and examines the high bit to determine whether the underlying platform is Microsoft Windows 95 or Microsoft Windows NT. If the platform is Windows 95, ANSI mode is used. Otherwise, Unicode mode is used.

It is not necessary to set the DllImportDefaultType registry key yourself. It exists primarily so that the installation program can set the appropriate choice on future Windows platforms. You can programmatically query the preferred mode on your platform by reading the com.ms.dll.DllLib.systemDefaultCharSize field. This field will be set to 1 on ANSI systems, 2 on Unicode systems.

The *ansi*, *unicode*, and *auto* modifiers can also be used with the @dll.struct directive.

Obtaining the Error Code Set by a DLL Function

Do not invoke the Win32 function GetLastError to obtain an error code set by another DLL call. Because the Microsoft VM may execute function calls of its own in the process of executing Java code, the error code may have been overwritten by the time you get to it.

To reliably access the error code set by a DLL function, you must use the *setLastError* modifier to instruct the VM to capture the error code immediately after invoking that method. For performance reasons, this is not done by default. You can then invoke the com.ms.dll.DllLib.getLastWin32Error method to retrieve the error code. Each Java thread maintains separate storage for this value.

For example, the FindNextFile function returns status information through the error code. FindNextFile would be declared as follows:

```
/** @dll.import("KERNEL32",setLastError) */
   static native boolean FindNextFile(int hFindFile,
                             WIN32_FIND_DATA wfd);
```

A typical call would appear as:

```
import com.ms.dll.DllLib;

boolean f = FindNextFile(hFindFile, wfd);
if (!f) {
    int errorcode = DllLib.getLastWin32Error();
}
```

Dynamically Loading and Invoking DLLs

There may be times when you need more control over the loading and linking process than the @dll.import directive normally provides. For instance, your requirements might include:

- Loading a library whose name or path must be computed at run time or generated from user input.

- Freeing a library prior to process termination.

- Executing a function whose name or ordinal must be computed at run time.

The Win32 APIs have always provided the ability to control loading and linking. The LoadLibrary, LoadLibraryEx, and FreeLibrary functions allow you to have explicit control over the loading and freeing of DLLs. The GetProcAddress function allows you to link to a specific export. The GetProcAddress function returns a function pointer, so any language that can call through a function pointer can implement dynamic invocation without a problem.

J/Direct allows Java programmers to declare the requisite functions in the following way:

Note   If you are using the com.ms.win32 package, these declarations also appear in the Kernel32 class.

```
/** @dll.import("KERNEL32",auto) */
public native static int LoadLibrary(String lpLibFileName);

/** @dll.import("KERNEL32",auto) */
public native static int LoadLibraryEx(String lpLibFileName,
                                   int hFile, int dwFlags);
```

```
/** @dll.import("KERNEL32",auto) */
public native static boolean FreeLibrary(int hLibModule);

/** @dll.import("KERNEL32",ansi) */
public native static int GetProcAddress(int hModule, String lpProcName);
```

Notice that GetProcAddress is declared with the *ansi* modifier, not *auto*. This is because GetProcAddress is one of the few Windows functions without a Unicode equivalent. If we were to use the *auto* modifier, this function would fail on Microsoft Windows NT systems.

That only leaves the problem of invoking a function obtained by GetProcAddress. For your convenience, msjava.dll, (the DLL that implements the Microsoft VM) exports a special function named call. The call function's first argument is a pointer to a second function. All call does is invoke the second function, passing it the remaining arguments.

The following is an example of how an application could load a DLL and call AFunction exported by the DLL:

```
BOOL AFunction(LPCSTR argument);

    /** @dll.import("msjava") */
    static native boolean call(int funcptr,String argument);

    int hmod = LoadLibrary("...");
    int funcaddr = GetProcAddress(hmod, "AFunction");
    boolean result = call(funcaddr, "Hello");
    FreeLibrary(hmod);
```

Comparing J/Direct to Raw Native Interface

J/Direct and Raw Native Interface (RNI) are complementary technologies. Using RNI requires that DLL functions adhere to a strict naming convention, and it requires that the DLL functions work harmoniously with the Java garbage collector. That is, RNI functions must be sure to call GCEnable and GCDisable around code that is time-consuming, code that could yield, code that could block on another thread, and code that blocks while waiting for user input. RNI functions must be specially designed to operate in the Java environment. In return, RNI functions benefit from fast access to Java object internals and the Java class loader.

J/Direct links Java with existing code such as the Win32 API functions, which were not designed to deal with the Java garbage collector and the other subtleties of the Java run-time environment. However, J/Direct automatically calls GCEnable on your behalf so that you can call functions that block or perform UI without having a detrimental effect on the garbage collector. In addition, J/Direct automatically translates common data types such as strings and structures to the forms that C functions normally expect, so you don't need to write lengthy glue code and wrapper DLLs. The tradeoff is that DLL functions cannot access fields and methods of arbitrary Java objects. In this release, they can only access fields and methods of objects that are declared using the @dll.struct directive. Another limitation of J/Direct is that RNI functions cannot be invoked from DLL functions that have been called using J/Direct. The reason for this restriction is that garbage collection can run concurrently with your DLL functions. Therefore, any object handles returned by RNI functions or manipulated by DLL functions are inherently unstable.

Fortunately, you can use either RNI or J/Direct (or both). The compiler and the Microsoft VM allow you to mix and match J/Direct and RNI within the same class as your needs dictate.

Security Issues

Although J/Direct is a very powerful feature for stand-alone Java applications and trusted intranet Web applications, it is clearly too powerful to be used by normal Java applets on the Web. This section describes how J/Direct works with the security system of the Microsoft VM to prevent untrusted code from abusing the power provided by J/Direct.

Trusted Versus Untrusted Classes

J/Direct divides all loaded Java classes into one of two categories:

1. Fully trusted (indicating maximum permissions).

2. Untrusted.

Only fully trusted classes are allowed to use J/Direct. A Java class is considered fully trusted if one of the following statements is true:

- The class is digitally signed indicating full trust. An example of such a class would be a signed applet.

- The class is installed on the target computer's CLASSPATH or installed by the package manager. A downloadable, digitally signed library designed to be shared among multiple applets could meet this criterion.

- The class is running as a non-browser application using the JVIEW or the WJVIEW application.

An unsigned applet on the Web, on the other hand, constitutes untrusted Java code.

Security Checkpoints for J/Direct Method Calls

The Microsoft VM applies security checks to J/Direct methods at three different times:

1. At link time.

2. Upon first invocation.

3. Upon every invocation.

An attempted J/Direct call takes place only if each of the three security checks passes or is explicitly disabled.

Security Checks at Link Time

Linking is what occurs when one Java class invokes or accesses (using the Reflection API) a member of another class. At link time, the Microsoft VM checks to see whether the class being referenced is accessible and whether the arguments being passed are of the correct type and number. The class is considered accessible if it is in the same package or if it is declared public.

With the standard Java language, you are limited to a choice of two options for class accessibility: you can either declare a class public (so that anyone can link to it) or you can declare a class without the public modifier (so that only classes in the same package can link to it). However, with Microsoft Internet Explorer 4.0, there is now a third option. You can declare the class as "public for fully trusted callers only." You can declare any class with this type of accessibility, even if the class does not use J/Direct. To declare the class, place the following directive at the beginning of the class:

```
/** @security(checkClassLinking=on) */
```

It is important to notice that this security check only prevents untrusted callers from directly calling the "protected" class. It does not prevent indirect calls. A third (fully trusted) class can forward a call from an untrusted caller to the "protected" class. However, there is a safeguard. The intermediate class must either be installed on the target computer's CLASSPATH, or it must be digitally signed for maximum trust and installed using the browser.

Security Checks Upon First Invocation

The first invocation of a method is the first time the method is invoked from any caller. At this time, for each method marked with the native keyword, the Microsoft VM determines whether the method is a member of a fully trusted class. If it is not, a SecurityException is thrown that includes the message, "Only fully trusted classes can have native methods as members." Because this security check does not depend on the calling context, it only needs to be performed once. If it passes, the check does not take place on future invocations. There is no way to disable this security check.

Security Checks Upon Every Invocation

This is the most stringent check available. On every call, the entire call stack is examined. If even one caller that is not fully trusted is discovered on the call stack, a SecurityException is thrown. By default, all J/Direct methods perform this check. RNI methods do not perform this check due to backward compatibility requirements. RNI was designed to allow easy porting from the original JDK 1.0 native interface, which did not offer this security check.

Although this security check offers maximum safety, Microsoft offers a way to disable it. The mechanism for disabling is provided because this stringent security check has two important side effects:

Possible Performance Degradation	This security check requires a scan of the entire call stack each time a J/Direct method is called. The performance degradation is most noticeable on trusted applets, which generally run with a security manager present. Applications, on the other hand, usually do not see a significant performance drop. This is due to the fact that J/Direct omits the call stack scan for applications that run without a security manager.
Inflexibility	This security mechanism forces the use of maximum permissions, even in cases where only one specific permission is required. For example, consider a trusted library that uses J/Direct to expose a single permission to untrusted applets in a safe way. It would be appropriate for this library to turn off the call time security check and perform its own security check for the specific permission.

The @security directive disables the per-invocation security check. The syntax for this directive is:

```
/** @security(checkDllCalls=off) */
```

The @security directive applies to the entire class. Individual methods within a class cannot be tagged. The following example shows the placement of the @security directive:

```
/** @security(checkDllCalls=off) */
   class FastJDirectMethods{
      /** @dll.import(...) */
      static native void func();
   }
```

Be aware of the fact that disabling this security check transfers responsibility for security from the Microsoft VM to you. Remember that even with this security check disabled, you will still have to digitally sign the class for maximum trust. If you decide to use this directive, be sure to take the following precautions:

- All J/Direct methods should be declared private.

- Any publicly accessible methods should never blindly pass caller arguments to J/Direct. You must take responsibility for ensuring that only valid arguments are passed to native code.

- Your class should expose no more capability than is required, and it should guard all access to these capabilities with the appropriate security checks.

  Important Calls from within an applet's init, start, stop, or destroy methods may trigger a SecurityExceptionEx even if the applet is trusted. To avoid this situation, you should assert permissions by executing the following code:

  ```
  import com.ms.security.*;
      ...
  PolicyEngine.assertPermission(PermissionID.SYSTEM);
  ```

Security Checkpoints for J/Direct Structures

J/Direct also imposes security restrictions on classes that are marked using the @dll.struct directive. Because structures only become unsafe when they are instantiated, these security checks are more efficient than the checks used for J/Direct methods. The following two security checks are performed on @dll.struct classes:

Load time	Classes marked with the @dll.struct directive will load only if the context indicates full trust.
Link time	Code that is not fully trusted cannot link to classes declared using the @dll.struct directive. The Microsoft VM will throw a NoClassDefFoundError if such an attempt is made.

Security and the com.ms.win32 Classes

For maximum security, the J/Direct methods defined in the com.ms.win32 package do perform the call stack check on each invocation. If you are using these classes for a Java application (running under JVIEW or WJVIEW), the performance overhead will be negligible. If you are using com.ms.win32 classes from a trusted class and require maximum performance, you should copy the required J/Direct declarations into your own classes and disable the per-invocation security check. See "Security Checks upon Every Invocation," earlier in this chapter, for more information on disabling the per-invocation security check.

Error Messages

There are several types of exceptions that might be thrown by the Microsoft VM when you are using J/Direct. For each of the following run-time errors, possible causes and solutions are explained:

- java.lang.SecurityException [class.method]
- java.lang.IllegalAccessError
- java.lang.SecurityException
- java.lang.NoClassDefFoundError
- com.ms.security.SecurityExceptionEx

java.lang.SecurityException [class.method]

Exception Class	java.lang.SecurityException
Message	class.method: Only fully trusted classes can have native methods as members.
Possible Causes	The *native* keyword has been used on a method that is a member of a class that is not loaded with full permissions (for example, an unsigned applet). This exception is thrown only if an attempt is made to invoke the native method.
Possible Solutions	Digitally sign your applet requesting full permissions.

java.lang.IllegalAccessError

Exception Class	java.lang.IllegalAccessError
Message	Class has been marked as nonpublic to untrusted code.
Possible Causes	An untrusted class has attempted to refer to a field or method of another class that has been marked for trusted use only. Many of the system classes in the com.ms.com and com.ms.dll packages have been marked this way. A class can be marked as nonpublic to untrusted code using the @security directive in the following way:
| | ```
/** @security(checkClassLinking=on) */
public class ForTrustedUseOnly{
    ...
}
``` |
| Possible Solutions | Digitally sign your applet requesting full permissions. |
```

java.lang.SecurityException

Exception Class	java.lang.SecurityException
Message	J/Direct method has not been authorized for use on behalf of an untrusted caller.
Possible Causes	An untrusted class has invoked a trusted method that attempts to make a J/Direct call. Even if the class making the actual J/Direct call is trusted, the security manager will throw a SecurityException if any of the methods in the call stack belong to an untrusted class.
Possible Solutions	Digitally sign your applet requesting full permissions. Or, you can disable the security check by marking the class that attempts the J/Direct call with the @security directive, as shown in the following example:

```
/** @security(checkDllCalls=off) */
   public class SafeDllCalls{
      ...
   }
```

Note   Disabling this security check transfers responsibility for security from the Microsoft VM for Java to you. Remember that even with this security check disabled, you will still have to digitally sign the class for maximum trust. If you use the @security directive, you should ensure that the following statements are true:

- All J/Direct methods are declared private.

- Your class exposes only the functionality needed by the client.

- Your class guards all access to these capabilities with appropriate security checks.

java.lang.NoClassDefFoundError

Exception Class	java.lang.NoClassDefFoundError
Message	None.
Possible Causes	An untrusted class has attempted to load either a class marked with the @dll.struct directive or a class generated using the jactivex tool. Although this is really a security violation (not a class loader error), a NoClassDefFoundError is thrown for backward compatibility purposes.
Possible Solutions	Digitally sign your applet requesting full permissions.

com.ms.security.SecurityExceptionEx

Exception Class	com.ms.security.SecurityExceptionEx
Message	[host] J/Direct method has not been authorized for use on behalf of an untrusted caller.
Possible Causes	A J/Direct call was attempted from the init, start, stop, or destroy method of an applet. To make J/Direct calls during these methods, the applet must assert permissions even if the applet has been signed.
Possible Solutions	Execute the following code to assert permissions:

```
import com.ms.security.*;
    ...
    PolicyEngine.assertPermission(PermissionID.SYSTEM);
```

Troubleshooting Tips

The following sections describe problems that you may encounter when using J/Direct. For each situation, possible solutions are provided.

UnsatisifiedLinkError When Calling a Method

- Check your version of the compiler to see that it's current with this release of Microsoft Visual J++. If your compiler does not support J/Direct, the Microsoft VM will attempt to link native methods using the Raw Native Interface (and will not succeed).

- Make sure your DLL is visible on the system path. DLLs are searched for in the following locations (in order):

  1. The directory from which the application (typically JVIEW) loaded.

  2. The current directory.

  3. The Windows system directory.

  4. The Windows directory.

  5. The directories listed in the PATH environment variable.

  The Microsoft VM will not attempt to load the DLL until a method requiring it is actually called. Therefore, do not assume that the DLL load was successful simply because the Java class loaded successfully.

- Check the method qualifiers. Methods declared with the @dll.import directive must be native and static. They can have any level of access (public, private, and so on) supported by the Java language.

- Make sure that your method name matches the DLL export name exactly, including capitalization. The DLL linking mechanism in Win32 is case-sensitive.

- If you still have trouble linking to a method, use a utility such as dumpbin/exports (Visual C++) to verify that the DLL exports the method by the name you are using. Some DLLs may require you to link to exports by *ordinal* (an integer) rather than a name. In such a case, use the entrypoint override on the method using the "*#ordinal*" syntax as shown in the following example:

```
// This method is exported as ordinal #34.
/** @dll.import("MyDll",entrypoint="#34") */
public static native void MySample();
```

- Be aware that some so-called functions are actually C macros and the actual DLL export name may be quite different from the name of the macro.

Getting SecurityException When Calling a DLL Method or Using an @dll.struct Class

DLL calling and the use of @dll.struct classes is restricted to Java applications and signed Java applets.

StringBuffers Truncated on Return From DLL Function

You must ensure that the StringBuffer's capacity is sufficient to contain the string you need before you invoke the DLL function. You can specify the capacity in the StringBuffer's constructor, and you can use the StringBuffer.ensureCapacity method to guarantee a minimum capacity prior to the DLL call.

Syntax Errors Within @dll Directives

Extra white space within @dll.import and @dll.struct directives can cause syntax errors. Avoid using white space inside @dll constructs.

Compiler Cannot Find the com.ms.dll Package

An older version of Classes.zip is being used. Try renaming all older versions of Classes.zip on your disk drive reinstalling Visual J++.

@dll Directives Do Not Work on Applets (or Only Works Within the Microsoft Visual J++ Environment)

Because the use of J/Direct can compromise security, its use is restricted to Java applications and signed Java applets.

Using J/Direct Makes Class Untrusted

Any use of J/Direct within a class marks that class as unsafe and unusable by untrusted code, even if the J/Direct methods are not actually invoked.

J/Direct Throws a ParameterCountMismatchError After Calling a Native Function

The ParameterCountMismatchError exception alerts you to the fact that the called function consumed (popped off the stack) more or fewer parameters than was passed by J/Direct. This error normally indicates that the parameters in the Java method declaration do not match up with the parameters expected by the DLL function.

If the function pops off no arguments, it is assumed to be using the cdecl calling convention and an exception is not thrown, even if the Java method declares a non-zero number of arguments.

> **Caution**   You should not attempt to catch and deal with the ParameterCountMismatchError exception. This exception was designed to assist developers in catching errors during the development stage. For performance reasons, parameter count checking is performed only when the application is running under a Java debugger. It is also important to note that J/Direct performs this check after the function call has been completed. Because this exception indicates that one or more invalid parameters might have been passed to the function call, it cannot be guaranteed that the process can recover.

J/Direct Does Not Unload a DLL

J/Direct unloads a DLL when the Microsoft VM discards the Java class that imported the DLL. For a Java application running under JVIEW, this does not occur until the process exits. For a trusted Java applet, this happens at some undetermined time after the browser has left the page containing the applet. The Microsoft VM attempts to keep Java classes loaded for several pages afterward in order to optimize applet refresh time in case the page is revisited.

If you need explicit control over the loading and unloading of DLLs, you need to call the Windows loader explicitly and use the call entrypoint to invoke functions dynamically. For more information on how to do this, see "Dynamically Loading and Invoking DLLs," earlier in this chapter.

Errors and Warnings

Compiler Error J0001

INTERNAL COMPILER ERROR:

The compiler was unable to recover after detecting an error. Please consult your technical support help file, available from the **Help** menu, for instructions on how to search the Microsoft Knowledge Base for the latest information on this problem. Also, try to simplify the code where the compiler reported this error and compile again.

Compiler Error J0002

Out of memory

The compiler attempted to allocate some additional memory during processing, but was unable to do so. Check the location, size, and validity of your system swap file. Also, ensure that there is sufficient growth space available on the drive on which your swap file resides.

Compiler Error J0004

Cannot open class file 'filename' for reading

The compiler could not open the program source file for reading. This error usually occurs when another program has an exclusive lock on the source file. Close other processes that may be accessing the source file and compile again.

Compiler Error J0005

Cannot open class file 'filename' for writing

The compiler failed to generate the output .class file. This error usually occurs when the compiler cannot get write or create permission for the file. Ensure the file does not have its read-only attribute set, and that it is not currently in use by another process. This error can also occur when you are running or debugging the program that contains the specified .class file. Close all instances of the program and compile again.

Compiler Error J0006

Cannot read class file 'filename'

The compiler failed to read the specified .class file. This error usually occurs when the compiler encounters an error reading the storage device, or when the compiler cannot otherwise get read permission for the file. Ensure that the file is not in use by another process. Also, ensure the validity of the storage device you are attempting to use by using a disk scanning utility.

Compiler Error J0007

Cannot write class file 'filename'

The compiler failed while attempting to write the contents of a buffer to the specified .class file. This error usually occurs when space is exhausted on the targeted storage device. Free up any available space on the storage device and compile again.

Compiler Error J0010

Syntax error

The compiler could not determine the meaning of an expression or statement within the source program. This error usually occurs when the line, indicated in the error message, is syntactically invalid. This error typically accompanies a more descriptive error. Correct any accompanying errors and compile again.

The following example illustrates this error:

```
public class Simple {

    public void method1() {
        int i =; // error: missing assignment value
    }
}
```

illegal start of expression

Compiler Error J0011

Expected ':'

The compiler expected to find a colon following a **case** label or in a conditional expression that makes use of the ternary operator. This error usually occurs when a colon is accidentally omitted. Many times this error is caused on the line previous to the line the compiler has reported the error on. Ensure that the lines that require a colon are correct and compile again.

The following example illustrates this error:

```
public class Simple {

    private int i;
    private static int x = 1;

    public void method1(int arg1) {

        switch (arg1) {
            case 1 // error: ':' omitted after 'case 1'
        }

        i = ( arg1 < x) ? arg1  x; // error: ':' omitted after 'arg1'
    }
}
```

Compiler Error J0012

Expected ';'

The compiler expected to find a semicolon in the position indicated by the error message. This error usually occurs when the semicolon is accidentally omitted from the end of a statement. It can also occur when a conditional expression is not syntactically correct. This error is often caused on the line previous to the line the compiler has reported the error on. Ensure that semicolons are used properly and compile again.

The following example illustrates this error:

```
public class Simple {

    private static int x = 10 // error: ';' omitted

    public void method1(int arg1) {

        for (int i = 1; i < x i++) {
            // error: ';' omitted
        }
    }
}
```

Compiler Error J0013

Expected '('

The compiler expected to find a left parenthesis in the position indicated by the error message. This error usually occurs when the left parenthesis is accidentally omitted in any of the following situations:

- Type initializations
- **catch** statements
- Parenthesized expressions
- **while** loops
- **for** loops
- **if/else** statements

The following example illustrates this error:

```
public class Simple {

    private int i;

    public void method1(int arg1, int arg2) {

        if arg1 < arg2) // error: '(' omitted
            i = arg1;
        else
            i = arg2;

    }
}
```

Compiler Error J0014

Expected ')'

The compiler expected to find a right parenthesis in the position indicated by the error message. This error usually occurs when the right parenthesis is accidentally omitted in any of the following situations:

- Type initializations
- Type casts
- **catch** statements
- Parenthesized expressions
- **while** loops
- **for** loops
- **if/else** statements

The following example illustrates this error:

```
public class Simple {

    private int i;

    public void method1(int arg1, int arg2) {

        i = (arg1 < arg2 ? arg1 : arg2;
        // error: ')' omitted
    }
}
```

Compiler Error J0015

Expected ']'

The compiler expected to find a right square bracket in the position indicated by the error message. This error usually occurs when the right square bracket is accidentally omitted from an array declaration. This error is often caused on the line previous to the line the compiler has reported the error on. Ensure that all brackets match and compile again.

The following example illustrates this error:

```
public class Simple {

    private int x[ = new int[500]; // error: ']' omitted

}
```

Compiler Error J0016

Expected '{'

The compiler expected to find a left brace in the position indicated by the error message. This error usually occurs when the left brace is accidentally omitted from the beginning of a class declaration or method code block. This error is often caused on the line previous to the line the compiler has reported the error on. Ensure that all braces match and compile again.

The following example illustrates this error:

```
public class Simple // error: '{' omitted

    public void method1() {
        // do something meaningful
    }
}
```

Compiler Error J0017

Expected '}'

The compiler expected to find a right brace in the position indicated by the error message. This error usually occurs when a class or method's closing brace is not found. This error is often caused on the line previous to the line the compiler has reported the error on. Ensure that all braces match and compile again.

The following example illustrates this error:

```
public class Simple {
{
    int x,y;
    // error: no matching brace found for class
```

Compiler Error J0018

Expected 'while'

The compiler expected to find the keyword **while** in the position indicated by the error message. This error usually occurs when a **do/while** loop is not syntactically correct.

The following error illustrates this error:

```
public class Simple{
    public void method1(){
        do{
            // do something useful here
        }; // error: missing 'while' statement
}
```

The following code illustrates the correct form of a **do/while** loop:

```
public class Simple{
    public static void method1(){
        int x = 10;
        do{
            System.out.println(x);
            x--;
        }while(x != 0); // this is correct form for do/while loop
    }
    public static void main(String args[]){Simple.method1();}
}
```

Compiler Error J0019

Expected identifier

The compiler expected to find an identifier before the name of a class, interface, variable, or method declaration. This error usually occurs when the type is accidentally omitted in a declaration.

The following example illustrates this error:

```
public class Simple {

    private i;  // error: type omitted

}
```

Compiler Error J0020

Expected 'class' or 'interface'

The compiler expected to find either **class** or **interface** used within the corresponding declaration. This error usually occurs when the keywords are accidentally omitted from a **class** or **interface** declaration. Another possible cause of this error is unbalanced scoping braces.

The following example illustrates this error:

```
public Simple{ // error: missing the 'class' keyword
    // Do something here
}
```

This example illustrates this error caused by unbalanced scoping braces:

```
public class Simple {

    // do something meaningful

}}   // error: additional '}' not needed
```

Compiler Error J0021

Expected type specifier

The compiler expected to find a type specifier in the position indicated by the error message. This error usually occurs when a typographical error exists in an object instantiation or variable declaration.

The following example illustrates this error:

```
public class Simple {

    public Object o =new; // error: missing 'Object' type specifier
}
```

Compiler Error J0022

Expected end of file

The compiler expected to encounter an end-of-file character, but did not. This error usually occurs when the source file has been damaged in some way. Visually check the source file for obvious corruption, save any changes, and compile again.

Compiler Error J0023

Expected 'catch' or 'finally'

The compiler expected to find a **catch** or **finally** block immediately following a corresponding **try** block.

The following example illustrates this error:

```
public class Simple {
   public void method1(){
      try {
         // do something meaningful
      }
   } // error: 'catch' or 'finally' not found
}
```

The following example illustrates the correct syntax for using a **try/catch** block:

```
public class Simple{
   public void method1(){
      try{
         // Do something here. Possibly throw an exception type
      }
      catch(Exception e){
         /*Handle any errors here and use the 'Exception' object to
         determine the type of error that occurred */
      }
   }
}
```

Compiler Error J0024

Expected method body

The compiler expected to find a method body immediately following a method declaration. This error usually occurs when the braces surrounding the method body are missing. This error can also occur when the method was intended to be **abstract** or **native**, but the **abstract** or **native** keyword was mistakenly omitted from the method declaration.

The following example illustrates this error:

```
public abstract class Simple {

    public void method1();
    // error: 'abstract' omitted
    // This error would also exist if the class is not declared 'abstract'

}
```

Compiler Error J0025

Expected statement

The compiler expected to find a statement before the end of the current scope. This error usually occurs when the left brace, designating the beginning of the current scope, or both left and right braces are missing. Ensure that the braces for the current scope are balanced.

The following example illustrates this error:

```
public class Simple {

    void method1(int arg1) {

        if (arg1==1)
        // error: missing the left brace for the if statement
    }
}
```

Compiler Error J0026

Expected Unicode escape sequence

The compiler expected to find a valid Unicode escape sequence. This error usually occurs when a backslash is not followed by the letter "u" to signify a Unicode escape sequence. Check the syntax of your Unicode escape sequence and compile again.

The following example illustrates this error:

```
public class Simple {

    int i = \\u0032;
    // error: '\\' not valid

}
```

Compiler Error J0027

Identifier too long

The compiler detected an identifier name with a length greater than 1024 characters. Shorten the identifier name and compile again.

Compiler Error J0028

Invalid number

The compiler detected a numeric value that the Java language is not capable of supporting. This error usually occurs when the number specified is an amount that is outside of the range of any of Java's primitive data types. This error usually occurs when a numerical value is too large to be stored in the specified data type.

The following example illustrates this error:

```
public class Simple {

    long i = 12345678901234567890;
    // error: value out of range for 'long'

}
```

Compiler Error J0029

Invalid character

The compiler detected an ASCII character that could not be used in an identifier. This error usually occurs when a class, interface, method, or variable identifier includes an invalid character.

The following example illustrates this error:

```
public class Simple {

    private int c#;
    // error: '#' not supported

}
```

illegal character : \35

Compiler Error J0030

Invalid character constant

The compiler detected an attempt to assign an invalid character or character escape sequence to a variable of type **char**.

The following example illustrates this error:

```
public class Simple {

    char c = '\';
    // error: invalid escape character
    char x = '\\'; \* correct assignment of the backslash to the char
                      variable */

}
```

Compiler Error J0031

Invalid escape character

The compiler detected the use of an invalid escape character. This error usually occurs when a syntactical error is found in a Unicode escape sequence. The error can also occur if you use a "\" character in a string assignment.

The following example illustrates this error:

```
public class Simple {

    int i = \u032;
    // error: Unicode uses 4 hex digits
    int x = \u0032;
    // correct assignment of a Unicode escape sequence

}
```

The following example illustrates the error being caused by assigning the "\" character improperly to a string:

```
public class Simple{

    public String str = "C:\Windows\Desktop";
    // error: invalid assignment of the '\' character to a string
    // To assign it correctly use the '\\' character assignment
}
```

Compiler Error J0032

Unterminated string constant

The compiler did not detect a terminating double-quote character at the end of a string constant. This error usually occurs when the string terminator is accidentally omitted, or when the string constant is mistakenly divided onto multiple lines.

The following example illustrates this error:

```
public class Simple {

    String str = "Hello;
    // error: closing quote omitted

}
```

Compiler Error J0033

Unterminated comment

The compiler detected the beginning of a block comment, but did not detect a valid ending. This error usually occurs when the comment terminator is accidentally omitted.

The following example illustrates this error:

```
public class Simple {

    /* This comment block
     * does not have a valid
     * terminator

}
```

Compiler Error J0035

Initializer block cannot have modifiers except 'static'

The compiler detected a modifier other than **static** associated with an initializer. Use only the **static** keyword to specify the initializer as a **static** initializer or no modifier to signify that the initializer is an instance initializer. Remove the modifier from the initializer specified in the error message or add the **static** modifier to the initializer and compile again.

The following example illustrates this error:

```
public class Simple {
   protected{   // error: 'protected' is invalid here
      // do something here
   }
}
```

Compiler Error J0036

A data member cannot be 'native', 'abstract', or 'synchronized'

The compiler detected one of the modifiers shown above used in the declaration of a variable. The modifiers **synchronized** and **native** can only be applied to method declarations. The **abstract** modifier can be applied to methods, classes, and interfaces.

The following example illustrates this error:

```
public class Simple{

   native int myvar1;
   abstract int myvar2;
   synchronized int myvar3;
   // error: the vars above have invalid modifiers

}
```

Compiler Error J0037

A method cannot be 'transient' or 'volatile'

The compiler detected one of the modifiers shown above used in the declaration of a method. The modifiers **transient** and **volatile** can only be applied to field declarations.

The following example illustrates this error:

```
public class Simple{

   transient void Method1(){};
   volatile void Method2(){};
   // error: the methods above have invalid modifiers

}
```

Compiler Error J0038

'final' member 'identifier' must be initialized when declared in an interface

The compiler detected an uninitialized **final** variable in an interface definition. Variables declared as **final** in an interface definition must have their value set at declaration. Once set, the value cannot be programmatically changed.

The following example illustrates this error:

```
interface ISimple {

    final int COOL_RAD;
    // error: must have value set

}
```

Compiler Error J0040

Cannot define a method body for abstract/native methods

The compiler detected a method body defined immediately following the corresponding declaration of an **abstract** or **native** method. An **abstract** method must have its implementation code defined in a subclass. **Native** methods are implemented using code from a native language such as C++.

The following example illustrates this error:

```
public abstract class Simple{
    abstract void method1(){
        // Do something here
    }// error: abstract methods are implemented in subclasses
}
```

Methods declared within an interface are implicitly **abstract**. As such, this error can also occur when you attempt to define a method body in an interface. The following code illustrates this scenario:

```
public interface Simple {

    public void method1() {
        // error: must define this method body
        // in a class that implements the
        // 'Simple' interface
    }
}
```

Compiler Error J0041

Duplicate modifier

The compiler detected a modifier used twice in a declaration. This error usually occurs when the same modifier is mistakenly used more than once within a declaration.

The following example illustrates this error:

```
public class Simple {

    public public void method1() { // error: 'public' used twice
        // do something meaningful
    }
}
```

Compiler Error J0042

Only classes can implement interfaces

The compiler detected an interface declaration using the **implements** keyword. Interfaces cannot implement other interfaces. Interfaces can only be implemented by classes. This error usually occurs when an interface is mistakenly implemented instead of extending another interface using the **extends** keyword.

The following example illustrates this error:

```
public interface Simple implements color{
    // error: 'Simple' cannot implement the
    // 'color' interface

}
interface color {
    // do something meaningful
}

interface pattern extends color{
    // extending an interface is OK here
}
```

Compiler Error J0043

Redeclaration of member 'identifier'

The compiler detected the same identifier name being declared more than once within the same scope. This error usually occurs when a variable or method is mistakenly declared more than once. Ensure that you have not declared a method or variable more than once in the same class. Methods can have the same name but must differ in method parameters in order to be different.

The following example illustrates this error:

```
public class Simple {
   private int i;
   public void method1(){
      // do something here
   }

   // Other declarations for the class go here

   private int i; // error: 'i' declared twice
   public void method1(){
      // error: method declared twice
   }
}
```

Compiler Error J0044

Cannot find definition for class 'identifier'

The compiler could not locate the definition for the specified class. This error is usually caused by a typographical error. It can also occur when the package containing the specified class cannot be found.

The following example illustrates this error:

```
class NotSimple{
   // do something here
}

public class Simple {

   NotSimple smp = new NotSmple();
   // error: 'NotSmple' not a valid class name

}
```

Compiler Error J0045

'identifier' is not a class name

The compiler detected one of the following conditions:

- A class name provided as part of an **import** statement could not be found.

- The import statement was not syntactically valid.

- The class attempted to extend an interface. Only classes can be used with the **extends** statement.

- Ensure that that the package exists and that any classes you import exist in the package specified in the **import** statement and compile again.

The following example illustrates this error:

```
package non.existent;
import non.existent; /* error: the package is not existant and cannot be
                        imported */

public class Simple {

    // do something meaningful

}
```

Compiler Error J0046

'identifier' is not an interface name

The compiler detected that the identifier referred to by the keyword **implements** is not an interface. This error usually occurs when a class is used instead of an interface in an **implements** statement.

The following example illustrates this error:

```
class Simple2 {

    // do something meaningful

}

public class Simple implements Simple2 {

    // error: cannot implement class 'Simple2'

}
```

Compiler Error J0048

Cannot extend final class 'identifier'

The compiler detected an attempt to subclass a class declared with the keyword **final.** Classes declared as **final** cannot be subclassed.

The following example illustrates this error:

```
final class Simple2 {

    // do something meaningful

}

public class Simple extends Simple2 {

    // error: cannot extend 'Simple2'

}
```

Compiler Error J0049

Undefined name 'identifer'

The compiler detected a reference to a class, method, or variable that does not exist. Examples of when this error can occur include:

- A variable is referenced that does not exist or is mistyped.

- The object used with a method call does not exist or is mistyped.

- A class is imported that does not exist in the package specified or is mistyped.

Ensure that the reference to the class, method, or variable displayed in the error message is correct and compile again.

The following example illustrates this error:

```
import java.io.bogus; // error: unknown class name

public class Simple {

    public int method1(){
        return novar1;
        // error: 'novar1' does not exist
    }
    public void method2(){
        NotSimple nt = new NotSimple();
        np.methodx();
        // error: the object reference 'np' should be 'nt'
    }
}
```

```
class NotSimple{
    public void methodx(){
        // do something meaningful here
    }
}
```

Compiler Error J0051

Undefined package 'identifier'

The compiler detected a package name declaration, but was unable to locate the package definition. This error usually occurs when a syntactical error exists in an **import** statement. This error may also occur when the package cannot be found or does not exist.

The following example illustrates this error:

```
import java.lang.bogus.*;
// error: 'bogus' not a valid package name

public class Simple {

    // do something meaningful

}
```

Compiler Error J0053

Ambiguous name: 'identifier' and 'identifier'

The compiler could not resolve an ambiguity between the two identifiers shown. This error usually occurs when the same class name appears in two packages that are both imported into a source file using the "*" class import specifier. Ensure that you do not have two classes with the same name in the packages you are importing into your source file and compile again.

Compiler Error J0056

Missing return type specification

The compiler detected a method declaration without a return type specified. All method declarations must specify a return type. If the method is not meant to return a value, use the **void** keyword.

The following example illustrates this error:

```
public class Simple {

    public method1() { // error: no return type

        // do something meaningful

    }
}
```

Compiler Error J0057

Class file 'identifier' should not contain class 'identifier'

This compiler did not detect the class specified in the error in the specified class file. This error usually occurs when a class is compiled into a class file that later is renamed. Because the class file has a different name than the class contained inside of it, attempting to use the name of the class file as a class will fail. To avoid this situation you will need to change the class definition to have the correct name or rename the file back to the original class name.

Compiler Error J0058

Cannot have a variable of type 'void'

The compiler detected a variable declared as type **void**. The keyword **void** is not allowed in variable declarations. Rather, **void** can only be used as a method return type, noting that the method does not actually return a value.

The following example illustrates this error:

```
public interface Simple {

    public final static void i = 1;
    // error: 'void' not valid
}
```

Compiler Error J0059

Cannot reference member 'identifier' without an object

The compiler detected an attempt to reference a variable without a known object association. This error usually occurs when an instance field or method (a field or method declared without the keyword **static**) is referenced from within a **static** method without a valid instance. **Static** methods cannot use instance fields and methods without a valid instance of the class.

The following example illustrates this error:

```
public class Simple {

    private int x;
    public void method1(){
        // Do something here
    }
    public static void main(String args[]) {
```

```
    x = 0; /* error: 'x' must be static or referenced using class
              instance */
    method1(); /* error: 'method1' must be static or referenced with
                       a class instance */
  }
}
```

The following example illustrates the correct method to refer to a non-static member field or method:

```
public class Simple{

    private int x; // access level of member does not matter
    public void method1(){
        // Do something here
    }
    public static void main(String args[]){
        // Create an instance of the 'Simple' class
        Simple smp = new Simple();
        smp.x = 0; // valid reference to field
        smp.method1(); // valid call to method
    }
}
```

Compiler Error J0060

Invalid forward reference to member 'identifier'

The compiler detected an attempt to initialize a variable with another variable that had not yet been defined. To avoid this situation, reverse the field declarations order so that a variable that is referenced by another is defined first.

The following example illustrates this error:

```
public class Simple {
    private static int i = j;
    // error: 'j' not yet defined
    private static int j = 0;
}
```

The following example shows the correct way to initialize a field using another field in the same class:

```
public class Simple{
    private static int j = 0; // field is instantiated and populated
    private static int i = j; // with 'j' properly set, 'i' can be set
}
```

Compiler Error J0061

The members 'identifier' and 'identifier' differ in return type only

The compiler detected a subclass method attempting to overload a base class method, but the methods differed only in return type. In Java, overloaded methods must be distinguished by unique signatures. A unique signature consists of the method name, the number, type and positions of its parameters, and the return type.

The following example illustrates this error:

```
public class Simple extends Simple2 {

    public void method1() {
        // error: only return type differs
    }
}

class Simple2 {

    public int method1() {

        return 1;
    }
}
```

Compiler Error J0062

Attempt to reduce access level of member 'identifier'

The compiler detected an overridden method in the class being compiled that reduces the access level of its base class method. The base class access modifier for a method must be maintained by all derived classes that wish to overload the method.

The following example illustrates this error:

```
public class Simple{
    public void method1(){
        // Do something here
    }
}

class Simple2 extends Simple{
    private void method1(){
        /*error: cannot change access level of a method
        when overriding a base class's method. */
    }
}
```

Compiler Error J0063

Declare the class abstract, or implement abstract member 'identifier'

The compiler detected an **abstract** method defined in a class, a superclass, or an implemented interface but the method was never implemented. This error usually occurs when a class implements an interface or extends a class that contains an **abstract** method definition, but the class never implements the **abstract** method. This error can also occur if a class defines an **abstract** method but the class does not have the **abstract** modifier defined. Ensure that your class has implemented any **abstract** methods and compile again.

The following example illustrates this error:

```
interface ITest{
    public abstract void method1();
}

public class Simple implements ITest{
    // Do something meaningful here
    // error: the abstract method defined in 'ITest' is never implemented
}
```

Compiler Error J0065

Cannot assign to this expression

The compiler detected an expression in the position normally held by an **lvalue** for assignment. This error usually occurs when an expression is being assigned a value but the expression is not capable of accepting the assignment.

The following example illustrates this error:

```
public class Simple {

    public void method1() {

        int x = 0;
        int y = 1;

        x++ = y; // error: '++' not valid
    }
}
```

Compiler Error J0066

'this' can only be used in non-static methods

The compiler detected use of the keyword **this** within a class (or static) method. Class methods are not passed implicit **this** references. As such, they cannot reference instance (non-static) variables or methods.

The following example illustrates this error:

```
public class Simple {

    int x;

    public static void method1() {

        this.x = 12; // error: 'this' instance specific
    }
}
```

Compiler Error J0067

Cannot convert 'type' to 'type'

The compiler detected a variable type used out of its correct context. As such, the compiler could not implicitly convert the result to anything meaningful. Convert the value you are attempting to use to something the method or field definition requires and compile again.

The following example illustrates this error:

```
public class Simple {

    public void method1() {

        int i = 10;

        if (i--) {
            // error: conditional needs expression
            // or boolean field
        }
    }
}
```

Compiler Error J0068

Cannot implicitly convert 'type' to 'type'

The compiler could not convert the specified variable without an explicit typecast. This error usually occurs when a numerical field is assigned to a data type that is not numerical. Use a typecast to convert the data type to the appropriate data type and compile again.

The following example illustrates this error:

```
public class Simple {

    int i = 10;

    public void method1() {
        char c = i; // error: expected type char
        char c = (char)i; // this is the correct assignment statement
    }
}
```

Compiler Error J0069

Cannot apply '.' operator to an operand of type 'identifier'

The compiler detected the '.' operator applied to an invalid type. This error usually occurs when an invalid method call is made on an intrinsic data type. Ensure that your method call is using the correct object and compile again.

The following example illustrates this error:

```
public class Simple {

    int i = 123;
    int j = i.length; // error: 'i' not an array

}
```

Compiler Error J0072

'identifier' is not a member of class 'identifier'

The compiler detected a method call, but the method is undefined. This error usually occurs when the method name is either misspelled or cannot be found within the proper scope. This error can also occur when the method does not exist. Ensure that the member you are trying to reference exists in the specified class and compile again.

The following example illustrates this error:

```
public class Simple {

    public static void main(String args[]) {

        System.out.println("Hello");
        // error: 'printline' should be 'println'
    }
}
```

Compiler Error J0074

Operator cannot be applied to 'identifier' and 'identifier' values

The compiler detected an operator that cannot be correctly applied to the identifiers shown in the error message. This error usually occurs when two fields are non-numerical and operators used for numbers are applied to the fields.

The following example illustrates this error:

```
public class Simple {

    public void method1() {

        String s1 = "one";
        String s2 = "two";
        String result;

        result = s1 * s2; // error: invalid operands
    }
}
```

Compiler Error J0075

Invalid call

The compiler detected syntax for a method call, but the identifier does not represent a valid method name. This error usually occurs when a method name is misspelled or contains characters that are not recognized as valid in the Java language naming conventions.

The following example illustrates this error:

```
class Simple {
    int x = 1();
    // error: '1()' is not a valid method name
}
```

Compiler Error J0076

Too many arguments for method 'identifier'

The compiler detected a known method call, but the call contained more arguments than needed. Check the number of arguments for the method you are attempting to call and remove any additional arguments from the call.

The following example illustrates this error:

```
public class Simple {

    public void method1(int arg1) {

        // do something meaningful
    }

    public void method2() {

        method1(1, 2); // error: Too many arguments
    }

}
```

Compiler Error J0077

Not enough arguments for method 'identifier'

The compiler detected a known method call, but the call contained fewer arguments than needed. This error usually occurs when one or more arguments are accidentally omitted from the call.

The following example illustrates this error:

```
public class Simple {

    public void method1(int arg1) {
        // do something meaningful
    }

    public void method2() {

        method1(); // error: Too few arguments
    }
}
```

Compiler Error J0078

Class 'identifier' doesn't have a method that matches 'identifier'

The compiler identified a call to a known overloaded method within another class, but was unable to detect a matching method with the correct number of arguments. Ensure that the overloaded method call has the correct number and type of arguments and compile again.

The following example illustrates this error:

```
public class Simple {

    public void method1() {
        // do something meaningful
    }

    public void method1(int arg1) {
        // do something meaningful
    }
}

class Simple2 {

    public void method1() {

        Simple s = new Simple();
        s.method1(1, 2, 3); // error: too many arguments
    }
}
```

Compiler Error J0079

Ambiguity between 'identifier' and 'identifier'

The compiler could not distinguish the correct method to execute. This error usually occurs when two overloaded methods have related argument lists and the method call cannot be differentiated between the two methods. Ensure your method call is not using a parameter that conflicts with another overloaded method. Another way to avoid this error is to change the argument lists of the two overloaded methods so that they have a different number of arguments or more uniquely defined parameter data types.

The following example illustrates this error:

```
public class Simple {

    static void method1(Simple2 s2, Simple3 s3) {
        // do something meaningful
    }
```

```
   static void method1(Simple3 s3, Simple2 s2) {
      // do something meaningful
   }

   public static void main(String args[]) {

      Simple2 s2 = new Simple2();
      method1(s2, s2);
      // error: Ambiguity between Simple2 and Simple3
   }
}

class Simple2 extends Simple3 {
   // do something meaningful
}

class Simple3 {
   // do something meaningful
}
```

Compiler Error J0080

Value for argument 'identifier' cannot be converted from 'identifier' in call to 'identifier'

The compiler detected a method argument that does not match the parameters specified in the method declaration. This error usually occurs when a numerical field is passed as an argument to a method but the method requires a different numerical type. To pass different numerical types to arguments of a method, typecast the field being passed to the method.

The following example illustrates this error:

```
public class Simple {

   public void method1(int arg1) {
      // do something meaningful
   }

   public void method2() {

      float f = 1.0f;
      method1(f); // error: mismatched call types
   }
}
```

The following example illustrates how to avoid this error:

```
public class Simple{
    public void method1(int arg1){
        // do something meaningful
    }

    public void method2(){
        float f = 1.0f;
        method1((int)f); // typecast the 'float' to be treated as an 'int'
    }
}
```

Compiler Error J0081

Value for argument 'identifier' cannot be converted from 'identifier' in call to 'identifier'

The compiler detected a call to a method in a class located in a different class file, but was unable to convert one of the arguments from the supplied type to the type shown in the method declaration. This error usually occurs when a method is called with the arguments in the wrong order or the wrong method was called. Check the argument number that caused the error in the error message and ensure you passed the correct type of argument.

Compiler Error J0082

Class 'identifier' doesn't have a constructor that matches 'identifier'

The compiler did not detect a constructor matching the call identified in the error. This error usually occurs when a constructor is called with the wrong number of arguments. Ensure that the class has a constructor that matches the one you are attempting to call and compile again.

The following example illustrates this error:

```
public class Simple {

    Simple(int arg1) {
        // do something meaningful
    }

    public static void main (String args[]) {

        Simple s = new Simple(12, 13);
        // error: too many arguments
    }
}
```

Compiler Error J0083

'super()' or 'this()' may only be called within a constructor

The compiler detected use of either the **super()** or **this()** keyword outside of a constructor. The **super()** keyword is used to call a superclass constructor, while the **this()** keyword is used to call one constructor from another. To reference methods in a base class you must use the **super.** keyword.

The following example illustrates this error:

```
public class Simple {

    public void method1 () {

        super(); // error: 'super' cannot be called
    }
}
```

The following example illustrates using the **super.** keyword to reference a method in a base class:

```
class NotSimple{
    public class method1(){
        // do something here
    }
}

public class Simple{
    public method2(){
        super.method1(); // correct way to call a method of a superclass
    }
}
```

Compiler Error J0084

Cannot return a value from a 'void' method

The compiler detected an attempt to return a value from a method declared with a return type of **void**.

The following example illustrates this error:

```
public class Simple {

    public void method1() {
        return 1; // error: cannot return a value
    }
}
```

Compiler Error J0085

Expected return value of type 'identifier'

The compiler detected the keyword **return** within the body of a method which was declared to return a specific type, but the **return** had no associated value. The **return** statement with no associated value will not return a default value and thus must be assigned a valid return value.

The following example illustrates this error:

```
public class Simple {

    public int method1() {
        return; // error: must return int value
    }
}
```

Compiler Error J0086

'[]' cannot be applied to a value of type 'identifier'

The compiler detected array brackets used with a non-array type. Change the field to be a valid array declaration if you want to use the field as an array and compile again.

The following example illustrates this error:

```
public class Simple {

    public void method1() {
        int i = 0;
        int j, x;

        x = j[i]; // error: 'j' not declared as array
    }
}
```

Compiler Error J0087

'goto' statement is not currently supported by Java

The keyword **goto**, while defined as a keyword, has not yet been implemented in the Java language.

Compiler Error J0089

The case 'identifier' has already been defined in switch statement

The compiler identified two or more **case** statements with the same identifier or value occurring within the same **switch** statement.

The following example illustrates this error:

```
public class Simple {

   public int method1(int arg1) {

      switch (arg1) {
         case 1:
            return (int) 1;
         case 2:
            return (int) 2;
         case 2: // error: duplicate of above
            return (int) 3;
         default:
            return (int) 0;
      }
   }
}
```

Compiler Error J0090

'default' has already been defined in switch statement

The com/piler identified two or more instances of the keyword **default** occurring within the same **switch** statement.

The following example illustrates this error:

```
public class Simple {

   public int method1(int arg1) {

      switch (arg1) {
         case 1:
            return (int) 1;
         case 2:
            return (int) 2;
         default:
            return (int) 3;
         default: // error: duplicate of above
            return (int) 0;
      }
   }
}
```

Compiler Error J0091

'case' outside of switch statement

The compiler identified the keyword **case** used outside the scope of a **switch** statement.

The following example illustrates this error:

```
public class Simple {

    public int method1() {
        case 1: // error: no switch statement
            return 1;
    }
}
```

Compiler Error J0092

Constant expression expected

The compiler detected an expression that used a non-constant value when a constant value was required. This error usually occurs when a variable is used in a **case** statement. Check the expression to be sure that a constant value is being used and compile again.

The following example illustrates this error:

```
public class Simple{
    int var1 = 10;
    int var2 = 20;
    public void method1(){
        switch(var1){
        case var2:
            // error: cannot use variable with case
        }
    }
}
```

Compiler Error J0093

'break' only allowed in loops and switch statements

The compiler detected the keyword **break** occurring outside the scope of a loop or **switch** statement.

The following example illustrates this error:

```
public class Simple{
    public void method1(){
        if (true)
            break;
            // error: break allowed in loops only
    }
}
```

Compiler Error J0094

Label 'identifier' not found

The compiler detected a label name associated with one of the keywords **continue** or **break**, but could not find the label. This error usually occurs when a label does not exist, yet it is being referenced by a **break** or **continue** statement. This error can also occur if the label is placed outside the **break** or **continue** statement's scope. A **break** or **continue** statement must reference a label that precedes an enclosing loop or block. Ensure that the **break** or **continue** statement can access a valid label and compile again.

The following example illustrates this error:

```
public class Simple{
    public int method1(){
        int y;
        for (int x = 0; x < 10; x++){
            y = x *2;
            if (x == 5)
                break test; // error 'test' is not defined as a label
        }
        return y;
    }
}
```

The following example illustrates the correct usage of a label when used with the **break** or **continue** statements:

```
public class Simple{
    public int method1(int arg1){
        int x,y = 0;
        test: // label precedes the loop.
        if (arg1 = 0)
            return y;
        for (x=1; x < 10; x++){
            y = x * arg1;
            if (y <= arg1){
                y = -1;
                break test;
            }
        }
        return y;
    }
}
```

Compiler Error J0095

'continue' only allowed in loop

The compiler detected attempted use of the keyword **continue** outside the scope of a loop. This error usually occurs when a loop is removed and **continue** statements are left in the code. Remove any **continue** statements that are outside of a loop and compile again.

The following error illustrates this error:

```
public class Simple{
    public void method1(int arg1){
        if (arg1 ==1)
            continue;
            // error: continue only allowed in loops. Remove 'continue;'.
    }
}
```

Compiler Error J0096

Class value expected

The compiler detected a synchronization block, but the **synchronized** statement was applied to an invalid type. This error usually occurs when an identifier other than a class object instance is used with the **synchronized** statement.

The following example illustrates this error:

```
public class Simple {

    public void method1() {
        int i;
        synchronized (i){ // error 'i' must resolve to an object reference
            // Do something here
        }
    }
}
```

Compiler Error J0097

'instanceof' operator expected class or array

The compiler detected the **instanceof** operator applied to a type that did not resolve to a class or array. The **instanceof** operator is used to determine if identifier is an instance of a specific class or array. Ensure the **lvalue** used with the **instanceof** operator references a class instance or array and the **rvalue** references a valid class name or array and compile again.

The following example illustrates this error:

```
public class Simple {

    public void method1() {

        Simple2 obj = new Simple2();

        if (obj instanceof int) // error: 'int' is not a class name
            // do something meaningful
    }
}

class Simple2 {
    // do something meaningful
}
```

Compiler Error J0098

Attempt to access non-existent member of 'identifier'

The compiler detected an array member specified, but could not identify it. This error usually occurs when an attempt to reference the **length** method of an array is mistyped. This error can also occur when an attempt is made to call a method in an array of objects but the call does not reference an element of the array.

The following example illustrates this error:

```
public class Simple {

    public void method1() {
        String j[] = new String[10];
        // intialize the array elements here
        String str = j.toUpperCase();
        // error: missing array brackets '[]'
    }
}
```

Compiler Error J0100

Cannot throw 'identifier' — the type does not inherit from 'Throwable'

The compiler detected an object in a **throw** statement that was not derived from the class **Throwable**. This error usually occurs when a **throw** statement uses a class that does not inherit from the **Throwable** class. Ensure that the exception class you are throwing is a valid exception class.

The following example illustrates this error:

```
class BogusException{
    // Do something useful here
}

public class Simple{

    public void method1(int arg1){
        // Do something meaningful
        if (arg1 == 0){
            throw new BogusException();
            // error: BogusException is not a valid exception class
        }
    }
}
```

Compiler Error J0101

The type 'identifier' does not inherit from 'Throwable'

The compiler detected an invalid class argument used as an argument in a **catch** statement. When using a **catch** statement to handle exceptions, you must define it with a class derived from **Throwable** as a parameter. Ensure that the class you defined for the **catch** statement is derived from **Throwable** and compile again.

The following example illustrates this error:

```
public class Simple {

    public void method1() {

        try {
            // do something meaningful
        } catch (String s) {
            // error: 'String' not a subclass
            // of 'Throwable'
        }
    }
}
```

The following example illustrates the correct way to use the **catch** statement to trap exceptions:

```
public class Simple{
    public void method1(int arg1){
        try{
            // do something here
            if (arg1 == 0)
                throw new myException(); // throw a valid exception object
        }
```

```
        catch(myException c){ // this is a valid exception object to catch
            // handle exception here
        }
    }
}
class myException extends Throwable{
    // class definition goes here
}
```

Compiler Error J0102

Handler for 'identifier' hidden by earlier handler for 'identifier'

The compiler detected an exception handler that will never be executed because an earlier handler would have already caught the exception. This error usually occurs when **catch** statements are written in the wrong order.

The following example illustrates this error:

```
class Simple {

    static
    {
        try
        {
        }
        catch (Exception e)
        {
        }
        catch (ArithmeticException e)
        {
        }
        // error: any exceptions this block
        // could have caught are already caught
        // by the first catch statement
    }
}
```

Compiler Error J0103

Cannot override final method 'identifier'

The compiler detected a class method attempting to override one of its base class methods, but the base class method was declared with the keyword **final**. Methods defined with the **final** modifier cannot be overridden by a derived class.

The following example illustrates this error:

```
public class Simple extends Simple2 {

    public void method1() {
        // error: 'method1' final in superclass
    }
}

class Simple2 {

    public final void method1() {
        // do something meaningful
    }
}
```

Compiler Error J0104

Unreachable statement or declaration

The compiler detected a statement or declaration that cannot be reached under any circumstances. This error usually occurs when a **return** statement is called from a method, and code is placed below the **return** statement. This error can also occur if a **break** statement is used in a loop without any flow control to allow code below it to be run.

The following example illustrates this error:

```
class Simple {
    public int method1(int arg1){
        for (int y = 10; y < 10;y++){
            break;
            int z = y +10; // error: break causes this line to never be run
        }
        // do something here
        return arg1;
        int x = arg1 /2;
        /*error: this line of code cannot be reached because of return
                statement */
    }
}
```

Compiler Error J0105

Method 'identifier' must return a value

The compiler detected a method declaration that included a return type other than **void**, but the keyword **return** was not found in the method body. This error usually occurs when a method that returns a value is missing a valid **return** statement. This error can also occur if a **return** statement is called within a flow control block and cannot always be accessed due to the logic of the method.

The following example illustrates this error:

```
public class Simple {

    public int method1(int arg1) {
        if (arg1==0)
            return arg1 + 2;
    } // error: flow control prohibits a value from always being returned
}
```

Compiler Error J0106

Class 'identifier' has a circular dependency

The compiler detected two or more classes directly or indirectly attempting to subclass each other. This error usually occurs when two classes extend each other. One class should act as the base class of the other.

The following example illustrates this error:

```
public class Simple extends Simple2 {

    // error: extending 'Simple2'
}

class Simple2 extends Simple {

    // error: also extending 'Simple'
}
```

Compiler Error J0107

Missing array dimension

The compiler detected the initialization of an array, but failed to detect a valid array dimension. This error usually occurs when an array is defined but one of the dimensions of the array is not defined. In order to use an array, all dimensions must be defined.

The following example illustrates this error:

```
public class Simple {

    public void method1() {

        int [][] i = new int[][12];
        // error: missing first array dimension
    }
}
```

Compiler Error J0108

Cannot 'new' an instance of type 'identifier'

The compiler detected an attempt to instantiate a data type that does not require the use of the keyword **new**. This error usually occurs when an attempt is made to use the **new** keyword with an intrinsic data type and the declaration is not an array. Ensure your member declaration does not use the **new** keyword unless it is a class object or array declaration.

The following example illustrates this error:

```
public class Simple {

    public void method1() {
        String myString = new String(); /*usage OK since it is a class
                                           object*/
        int x[] = new int[10]; // usage of new here is OK
        int i = new int(5);
        // error: cannot use 'new' on 'int' types
    }
}
```

Compiler Error J0109

Cannot 'new' an instance of abstract class 'identifier'

The compiler detected an attempt to instantiate a class object declared as **abstract**. A class declared as **abstract** cannot be instantiated and exists only as a base class for other classes to derive from.

The following example illustrates this error:

```
abstract class Simple2 {
    // do something meaningful
}

public class Simple {

    public void method1() {

        Simple2 s2Object = new Simple2();
        // error: class 'Simple2' declared as abstract
    }
}
```

Compiler Error J0110

Cannot 'new' an interface 'identifier'

The compiler detected an attempt to instantiate an interface object declared as **abstract**. Interfaces can only be implemented by a class, and thus cannot be instantiated in the way a class can.

Note Interfaces are abstract by default, regardless of whether or not the keyword **abstract** is used in their declaration.

The following example illustrates this error:

```
interface Simple2 {
   // do something meaningful
}

public class Simple {

   public void method1() {

      Simple2 s2Object = new Simple2();
      // error: interface Simple2 is abstract

   }
}
```

Compiler Error J0111

Invalid use of array initializer

The compiler detected an attempt to initialize an array, but the initialization statement was not syntactically correct. Arrays can be initialized at declaration with an initial set of values. This error usually occurs when trying to initialize an array of arrays with the incorrect number or positioning of braces and commas. Ensure that the syntax of your array initialization is correct and compile again.

The following example illustrates this error:

```
public class Simple{
   public void method1(){
      int[]i = {{1,2,3}, {4,5,6}};
      // error: 'i' delcared for only one dimension
   }
}
```

The following example illustrates the proper syntax for array initialization:

```
public class Simple{
   public void method1(){
      int[]i = (1,2,3,4,5,6}; // single dimension initialization
      int [][]x = {{1,2,3},{4,5,6}}; // multi-dimension initialization
   }
}
```

Compiler Error J0112

Cannot assign final variable 'identifier'

The compiler detected an attempt to change the value of a field declared as **final**. A field declared as **final** cannot be assigned a value once it has been initialized with a value either at declaration, in an instance initializer, or constructor.

The following example illustrates this error:

```
public class Simple {
   private final int i = 3;

   public void method1(int arg1) {
      i = arg1;
      // error: variable 'i' declared final
   }
}
```

Compiler Error J0113

Call to constructor must be first statement in constructor

The compiler detected a constructor called from within the body of a second constructor, but the constructor call was not placed at the beginning of the second constructor body. In a constructor, calls to another constructor must be the first line of code in the constructor's body. Ensure that the constructor call is the first line of code in the constructor body and compile again.

The following example illustrates this error:

```
public class Simple {

   int i, j;
   Simple () {

      i = 0;
   }

   Simple(int arg1) {

      j = arg1;
      this(); // error: call to Simple() must be first
   }
}
```

Compiler Error J0114   √

Cannot reference 'this' in constructor call

The compiler detected an improper reference to **this** in a constructor. The **this** statement is usually used in a constructor to access methods and fields of the constructor's class. Usage of **this(this)** or **super(this)** in a constructor will cause this error to occur because the instance of the class has not yet been created and thus cannot be passed to another constructor.

The following example illustrates this error:

```
class SuperSimple {
   SuperSimple(){}
   SuperSimple(Object o) { }
}

public class Simple extends SuperSimple {
   int x;
   public Simple()
   {
      this(10); // this is OK; calls another constructor
      super(this);
      // error: cannot pass this to a super constructor
      this.x = 1; // this is OK
      this.method1(); // this is OK too
   }
   public Simple(int arg1){
      this.x = arg1; // this is OK
   }
   public void method1(){}
}
```

Compiler Error J0115

Cannot call constructor recursively (directly or indirectly)

The compiler detected a recursive constructor call. This error usually occurs when a constructor has a call to the same constructor. This error can also occur if one constructor calls a second constructor and the second constructor has a call back to the first constructor.

The following example illustrates this error:

```
public class Simple {

   Simple (int arg1) {

      this(1);
      // error: constructor calling itself
   }
}
```

Compiler Error J0116

Variable 'identifier' may be used before initialization

The compiler detected an attempt to use a variable before it was properly initialized.
In order to use a variable in an assignment or expression, you need to assign it a value.
Initialize the variable in a constructor or field initializer and compile again.

The following example illustrates this error:

```
public class Simple {

    static
    {
        int i;
        int j = i;
        // error: 'i' not yet initialized

    }
}
```

Compiler Error J0117

Cannot declare an interface or outer class to be 'private'

The compiler detected use of the modifier **private** in an outer class or interface declaration.
This modifier may only be used with fields, methods, and inner class declarations.

The following example illustrates this error:

```
private class Simple {

    // error: a class cannot be 'private'

}
```

Compiler Error J0120

Divide or mod by zero

The compiler detected a division by zero error.

The following example illustrates this error:

```
public class Simple {

    final int x = 0;
    int y = 1 % x;
    // error: x cannot be 0

}
```

Compiler Error J0121

Unable to recover from previous error(s)

The compiler encountered a serious error and could not continue processing the file reliably. Fix whatever errors are already flagged and compile again.

Compiler Error J0122

Exception 'identifier' not caught or declared by 'identifier'

The compiler detected an exception that was thrown but never caught within the exception class. This error usually occurs when a method calls another method that is declared to throw an exception. In order for a method to call another method that throws an exception, the method must either be declared to throw the exception or handle the error using a **try/catch** combination.

The following example illustrates this error:

```
class SimpleException extends Exception {
   // do something meaningful
}

class Simple {

   void method1() throws SimpleException { }
   void method2() { method1(); }
   // error: exception not declared for method2
}
```

The following examples illustrates how to call a method that is declared to throw an exception:

```
/*This example illustrates handling by declaring the other method as
throwing an exception duplicate to the method it is calling.*/
class SimpleException extends Exception{
   // do something here
}

public class Simple{
   void method1() throws SimpleException{
      // do something here
   }
   void method2() throws SimpleException{
      method1(); // caller of method2 now is forced to handle exception
   }
}
```

```
/*This example illustrates handling the exception using a try/catch
  combination.*/
class SimpleException extends Exception{
    // do something here
}

public class Simple{
    void method1() throws SimpleException{
        // do something here
    }
    void method2(){
        try{
            method1();
        }
        catch(SimpleException e){
            // handle exception here
        }
    }
}
```

Compiler Error J0123

Multiple inheritance of classes is not supported

The compiler detected a class attempting to apply the keyword **extends** to more than one base class. This is defined as multiple inheritance in other languages and is not supported in Java.

The following example illustrates this error:

```
public class Simple extends BaseClass1, BaseClass2 {
    // error: multiple inheritance not supported in Java
}

class BaseClass1 {

    // do something meaningful
}

class BaseClass2 {

    // do something meaningful
}
```

Compiler Error J0124

Operator cannot be applied to 'identifier' values

The compiler detected an operator being applied to a type it cannot be used with. Ensure that the operator you are attempting to use is valid for that type of variable or object and compile again.

The following example illustrates this error:

```
public class Simple {

    void method1(boolean b) {

        b++;
        /* error: post increment operator cannot
           be applied to boolean variables */
    }
}
```

Compiler Error J0125

'finally' block used without 'try' statement

The compiler detected a **finally** block but did not find a corresponding **try** statement. A **finally** block is used to execute code after a **try** statement, regardless of the results of the **try** statement.

The following example illustrates this error:

```
public class Simple {

    public void method1() {

        finally {
            // error: missing corresponding try statement
        }
    }
}
```

The following example illustrates the correct usage of the **finally** block:

```
public class Simple{

    public int method1(int arg1){
        try{
            arg1/10;
        }
        catch(Exception e){
            // handle exception here; must come before 'finally'
        }
        finally{
            // do something here; this section is run regardless of 'try'
        }
    }
}
```

Compiler Error J0126

'catch' block used without 'try' statement

The compiler detected a **catch** statement but did not find a corresponding **try** statement. In order to use a **catch** statement you must have a **try** statement preceding it. Ensure that you have a valid **try** statement preceding your catch statement and compile again.

The following example illustrates this error:

```
public class Simple {

    public void method1() {

        catch {
            // error: missing corresponding try statement
        }
    }
}
```

The following example illustrates the proper usage of the **catch** block:

```
public class Simple {

    public void method1() {
        try{
            // do something here
        }
        catch (Exception e){
            // handle exceptions from try statement here
        }
    }
}
```

Compiler Error J0127

'else' keyword used without 'if' statement

The compiler detected the keyword **else** but did not find a corresponding **if** statement. This error usually occurs when there are scoping issues regarding the placement of an **else** statement. It can also occur if an **else** statement's corresponding **if** statement is missing.

The following example illustrates this error:

```
public class Simple {

    public void method1(int arg1) {
        if (arg1 == 0){
            // Do something here
            else{}
                // error 'else' is inside of the 'if' block instead of outside
        }
    }
}
```

Compiler Error J0128

Cannot declare an interface to be 'final'

The compiler detected an interface declared with the keyword **final**. Interfaces cannot be defined as final and thus cannot use the **final** modifier. Remove the **final** keyword from the interface declaration and compile again.

The following example illustrates this error:

```
final interface Simple {

    /*error: 'final' only applies to
        classes, methods,or variables*/

}
```

Compiler Error J0129

Cannot declare a class to be 'identifier' and 'identifier'

The compiler detected a class declared with modifiers that cannot be combined. Ensure that the modifiers you have applied to the class do not conflict with each other and compile again.

The following example illustrates this error:

```
public abstract final class Simple {

    /*error: 'abstract' and 'final' cannot
        be used together in a class declaration*/

}
```

Compiler Error J0130

Cannot declare an interface method to be 'native', 'static', 'synchronized' or 'final'

The compiler detected one of the keywords shown in the error message used in the declaration of an interface method. Because an interface method does not have implementation code, it cannot be declared as **native**, **static**, **synchronized**, or **final**.

The following example illustrates this error:

```
interface Simple {

    public final void method1();
    /*error: 'method1' cannot be declared
        as final in an interface*/
}
```

Compiler Error J0131

Cannot declare a method to be 'identifier' and 'identifier'

The compiler detected the use of two or more incompatible modifiers in the declaration of a method. This error usually occurs when a method has been defined with two access modifiers such as **public** and **private**. Ensure that the modifiers for the method do not conflict with each other and compile again.

The following example illustrates this error:

```
public class Simple {

    public private void method1() {

        // error: modifiers 'public' and 'private'
        // cannot be combined in a declaration
    }
}
```

Compiler Error J0132

Cannot declare a field to be 'identifier' and 'identifier'

The compiler detected the use of two or more incompatible modifiers in the declaration of a variable. This error usually occurs when a field has been defined with two access modifiers such as **public** and **private**. Ensure that the modifiers for the field do not conflict with each other and compile again.

The following example illustrates this error:

```
public class Simple {

    public private int i;
    // error: modifiers 'public' and 'private'
    // cannot be combined in a declaration
}
```

Compiler Error J0133

Constructors cannot be declared 'native', 'abstract', 'static', 'synchronized', or 'final'

The compiler detected the use of one of the modifiers shown above in the declaration of a constructor. Ensure that the constructor is not defined with any of the modifiers mentioned in the error message and compile again.

The following example illustrates this error:

```
public class Simple {

    final Simple() {}
    // error: constructors cannot be 'final'

}
```

Compiler Error J0134

Interfaces cannot have constructors

The compiler detected an interface containing a constructor declaration. Because an interface cannot be instantiated, constructors cannot be defined for an interface. If you are defining a method with the same name as the interface, ensure that it has the appropriate modifiers to differentiate it from a constructor declaration.

The following example illustrates this error:

```
interface Simple {

    Simple();
    // error: interfaces cannot
    // declare constructors

}
```

Compiler Error J0135

Interface data members cannot be declared 'transient', 'volatile', 'private', or 'protected'

The compiler detected one of the modifiers shown above used in the declaration of an interface member variable. Because interfaces are public and cannot be instantiated, these modifiers are not applicable and should be used with classes only.

The following example illustrates this error:

```
interface Simple {

    volatile int i = 1;
    // error: 'volatile'cannot be used

}
```

Compiler Error J0136

Public class 'identifier' should not be defined in 'identifier'

The compiler detected more than one class declared with the modifier **public** in a source file. Remove the **public** access modifier from other classes and ensure that the class that will be exposed through the class file is declared as **public**. You can also move classes that need to remain declared as **public** to their own source file. This error can also occur if a source file has a different name than the **public** class defined within it, or the **public** class and the source file do not match in case. Rename the source file or the name of the **public** class defined within it so that they are the same and compile again.

The following example illustrates this error:

```
public class Simple {

    // do something meaningful

}

public class Errorclass {

    // error: only one class may be defined as
    // 'public' within the same source file

}
```

Compiler Error J0138 ✓

Interface cannot have static or instance initializer

The compiler detected a **static** initializer or instance initializer within an interface. Because an interface does not get instantiated, initializers cannot be defined in an interface. To set the values of interface fields, initialize them at the time of declaration.

The following example illustrates this error:

```
interface Simple {
   int x = 10; // This is OK
   {
      // error: initializers cannot
      // be used in interfaces
   }
}
```

Compiler Error J0139

Invalid label

The compiler detected an invalid label. Labels must start with a non-numeric character. Change the label and compile again.

The following example illustrates this error:

```
public class Simple {

   public int method1(int arg1) {
      123:
         // error: label cannot begin with a number.
         return arg1 * 2;
   }
}
```

Compiler Error J0140

Cannot override static method 'identifier' with non-static method 'identifier'

The compiler detected an attempt to override a **static** method from within a subclass. A method that has been declared as **static** cannot be overridden.

The following example illustrates this error:

```
public class Simple {

    static void method1() {}
}

class SimpleSubclass extends Simple {

    void method1() {}
    // error: cannot override
    // static method
}
```

Compiler Error J0141

Argument cannot have type 'void'

The compiler detected a method argument defined as type **void**. The **void** type can only be used for method return values to declare a method has no return value. Change the data type of the argument and compile again.

The following example illustrates this error:

```
public class Simple {

    public void method1(void i) {
        // error: type void can only
        // be used as a return value
    }
}
```

Compiler Error J0142

Cannot make static call to abstract method 'identifier'

The compiler detected an attempt to directly call an abstract method. Abstract methods are defined to provide a definition of a method to be implemented by subclasses; therefore, **abstract** methods do not have implementation code. Because of this lack of implementation in an **abstract** method, calling an abstract method using the **super** keyword is invalid.

The following example illustrates this error:

```
public abstract class Simple {

    abstract int method1();
}

class SimpleSubclass extends Simple {

    int method1() {

        return super.method1();
        // error: cannot call abstract method
    }
}
```

Compiler Error J0143

Cannot throw exception 'identifier' from static initializer

The compiler detected an attempt to throw an exception from within a static initializer. This error usually occurs when a **throw** statement is called or when an initialization of a static class instance occurs within a static initializer. To capture exceptions from static class instance initializations in a static initializer, use a **try/catch** block combination.

The following example illustrates this error:

```
public class Simple {

    static {
        ThrowClass TClass = new ThrowClass();
        // error: cannot throw exceptions
        // within static initializers
    }
}

class ThrowClass {

    ThrowClass() throws Exception{}

}
```

The following example illustrates how to use the **try/catch** block combination to capture potential errors when initializing static class instances in a static initializer:

```
public class Simple{
    static ThrowClass thr;
    static{
        try{
            ThrowClass thr = new ThrowClass();
        }
        catch (Exception e){
            // Handle errors here from initialization of 'ThrowClass'
        }
    }
}

class ThrowClass {
    ThrowClass() throws Exception(){
        // Do something here
    }
}
```

Compiler Error J0144

Cannot find definition for interface 'identifier'

The compiler could not locate a definition for the named interface. This error usually occurs when an implemented interface is either missing or misspelled. Verify the location and name of the interface you are implementing and compile again.

The following example illustrates this error:

```
public class Simple implements Bogus {
    // error: the interface 'Bogus' does not exist

}
```

Compiler Error J0145

Output directory or file too long: 'identifier'

The output directory or source file being saved exceeds 228 characters in length. Shorten the length of the output directory path or source file and compile again.

Compiler Error J0146

Cannot create output directory 'identifier'

The output directory could not be created. This error usually occurs when you do not
have write permission on the specified drive.

Compiler Error J0147

Cannot access private member 'identifier' in class 'identifier' from class 'identifier'

The compiler detected an invalid attempt to access a private member contained within
another class. Private class members are only accessible from within the member's class.
A class's private members are also available from its inner classes.

The following example illustrates this error:

```
class AccessClass {

    private int i = 0;

}

public class Simple {

    public void method1() {

        AccessClass ac = new AccessClass();

        ac.i = 1;
        // error: cannot access 'i'
    }
}
```

Compiler Error J0148

**Cannot reference instance method 'identifier' before superclass constructor has
been called**

The compiler detected an attempt to reference an instance method before the superclass
constructor was called. This error usually occurs when a base class method is called from
within a subclass's constructor using the **super()** statement. This error can also occur if the
subclass calls its own methods from the constructor using the **this()** statement. This error
occurs because instances of the subclass and base class have not been instantiated at the
time the constructor is called. To avoid this situation, use the **super.** statement to call a
base class method, and use the **this.** statement to call a subclass method.

The following example illustrates this error:

```
abstract class Simple {

    Simple(int i) {}

    int method1() {

        return 0;
    }
}

class SimpleSubclass extends Simple {

    SimpleSubclass() {

        super(method1());
        // error: constructor must be called first
    }
}
```

Using the abstract class from the example above, the following example illustrates how to call the base class method from the constructor:

```
class SimpleSubclass extends Simple{

    SimpleSubclass(){
        super.method1();
    }
}
```

Compiler Error J0150

Cannot have repeated interface 'identifier'

The compiler detected an interface name being repeated within a class declaration. This error is usually caused when a class implements a large number of interfaces and one of the interfaces has a duplicate entry in the **implements** list. Ensure that you do not have a duplicate interface entry and compile again.

The following example illustrates this error:

```
interface SimpleI {
    // do something meaningful
}

class Simple implements SimpleI,IColor,IFont, SimpleI {
// error: 'SimpleI' repeated
}
```

Compiler Error J0151

Variable 'identifier' is already defined in this method

The compiler detected two variables with the same name that are defined twice within the same scope of a method. Ensure that a variable has not been defined twice in the same scope or that a variable has not been defined the same name as an argument passed to the method and compile again.

The following example illustrates this error:

```
public class Simple {

    public void method1() {

        int i = 1;
        int j = i;
        // more code here
        int i = 0;
        // error: 'i' defined twice within
        // the same scope

    }
}
```

Compiler Error J0152

Ambiguous reference to 'identifier' in interfaces 'identifier' and 'identifier'

The compiler detected an ambiguous reference to an identifier. The identifier may have been declared in two or more interfaces, and the compiler could not determine which reference to use. Ensure that you do not have two interfaces with the same field defined.

The following example illustrates this error:

```
interface Interface1 {
    final int i = 0;
}

interface Interface2 {
    final int i = 1;
}

public class Simple implements Interface1, Interface2 {

    int method1() {
        return i; // error: cannot determine which instance of 'i' to use
    }
}
```

Compiler Error J0158

Class 'identifier' already defined

The compiler detected two or more classes defined with the same name. Ensure that you do not have the class defined more than once (as an outer class) in the same source file or package. This error can also occur if a class is duplicated by an imported class. Rename one of the classes or remove the duplicate instance and compile again.

The following example illustrates this error:

```
public class Simple {
    // do something meaningful
}

class Simple {
    // error: class 'Simple' already defined
}
```

Compiler Error J0159

'@' must be followed by the response filename

The compiler detected the @ character on the JVC command line, but did not detect a valid response filename immediately following it. Supply the response filename and compile again.

Compiler Error J0160

Response file 'identifier' could not be opened

The compiler could not open the specified response file. This error usually occurs when the response file name is misspelled or the file does not exist. Check the location of the response file and compile again.

Compiler Error J0161

Cannot open source file: 'identifier'

The source file specified in the error message could not be opened. This error usually occurs when either the filename specified is misspelled or the file does not exist. Check the location of the specified source file and compile again.

Compiler Error J0162

Failed to initialize compiler

The compiler failed to properly initialize. This error most often occurs because the compiler and/or the Microsoft Virtual Machine for Java (VM) are not properly installed or are the incorrect version. Confirm the correct version and installation of the VM and compiler.

Compiler Error J0163

Array 'identifier' missing array index

The compiler detected access to an array type, but the index value was missing. To access an element of an array, you must provide a valid integer index for the array. Ensure that a valid integer is used to reference an index of the array and compile again.

The following example illustrates this error:

```
public class Simple {

    int j[] = {1, 2, 3};

    void method1() {
        j[] = 0;
        // error: 'j' missing index value
    }
}
```

Compiler Error J0164

Ambiguous import of class 'identifier' from more than one package

The compiler detected two or more **import** statements attempting to import identical class names from different packages. This error usually occurs when two packages contain duplicate classes and both packages are imported into the same source file. Check the packages imported into the source file for duplicate classes. Remove the duplicate class from one of the packages or remove one of the **import** statements from the source file.

The following example illustrates this error:

```
import Box.Test; // This package contains a class named 'Test'
import Carton.Test; // This package contains a class named 'Test' also
// error: which 'Test' class should be used by the compiler?

public class Simple{
    // Do something here
}
```

Compiler Error J0165

Cannot throw exception 'identifier' from method 'identifier' — it is not a subclass of any exceptions thrown from overridden method 'identifier'

The compiler detected an overridden method attempting to throw more exceptions than the method it overrides. In Java, an override method cannot be declared to throw more exceptions than the overridden method. Either change the exception thrown to one that the base class **throws,** or change the base class declaration to throw the exception type that the subclass needs to throw.

The following example illustrates this error:

```
class ExceptionA extends Exception {
    // do something meaningful
}

class ExceptionB extends Exception {
    // do something meaningful
}

class AnotherClass {

    public void method1() throws ExceptionA {
        // do something meaningful
    }
}

public class Simple extends AnotherClass {

    public void method1() throws ExceptionA, ExceptionB {
        // error: cannot throw greater than
        // one exception here
    }
}
```

Compiler Error J0166

Cannot access member 'identifier' in class 'identifier' from 'identifier' — it is in a different package

The compiler detected an invalid attempt to reference a member variable or method defined within a different package. This error usually occurs when an attempt is made to access a **protected** or default access member defined within another package. **Protected** or default access members of a class located in a different package are not accessible. Ensure that the member you are attempting to access in another package is not a **protected** or default access member.

Compiler Error J0167

Cannot override non-static method 'identifier' with static method 'identifier'

The compiler detected an attempt to override a superclass method with a subclass method declared with the modifier **static**. When a method is overridden in a subclass, the method cannot raise or lower the access level of the method or apply the **static** modifier. Remove the **static** modifier from the overridden method declaration and compile again.

The following example illustrates this error:

```
public class Simple {

    public void method1() {
        // do something meaningful
    }
}

class Simple2 extends Simple {

    static public void method1() {
        // error: overriding superclass 'method1'
        // with a static method is not valid
    }
}
```

Compiler Error J0168

The declaration of an abstract method must appear within an abstract class

The compiler detected a method declared with the modifier **abstract** within a class which was not defined as **abstract**. This error usually occurs when a class is intended to be **abstract** but is missing the **abstract** modifier in the class declaration. Either change the class so it is declared as **abstract** or remove the modifier from the methods defined in the class.

The following example illustrates this error:

```
public class Simple {

    abstract void method1();
        // error: class must also be abstract
}
```

Compiler Error J0169

Cannot access 'identifier' — only public classes and interfaces in other packages can be accessed

The compiler detected an attempt to access a non-public class or interface contained within another package. Only classes or interfaces defined with the modifier **public** can be accessed in other packages. Check the access level of the class or interface you are accessing in the other package to ensure that it is **public** and compile again.

The following example illustrates this error:

```
// Source located in 'Boxes.Java' in the 'Box' package
package Box;
public class Box{
    TapeRoll tr = new TapeRoll();
    // Do meaningful stuff here
}
class TapeRoll{
    // Define the class here
}

// Source located in 'Simple.java'
import Box.TapeRoll;
public class Simple{
    public static void main(String args[]){
        Box.TapeRoll tr = new Box.TapeRoll();
        // error: cannot access a 'non-public' class in a different package
    }
}
```

Compiler Error J0170 ∨

Cannot load predefined class 'identifier'

The compiler attempted to load a predefined class, but was unable to find the appropriate file. This error usually occurs when the Java API class files cannot be found on the system or the correct version of the Microsoft Virtual Machine for Java (VM) is not properly installed. Ensure that your Java API class files and the VM have been installed properly on the system and compile again.

Compiler Error J0173

Found class 'identifier' in package 'identifier' rather than package 'identifier'

The compiler found the specified class, but the class was not defined as a member of the correct package. This error usually occurs when the class file is being imported from the wrong directory. Ensure that the class you are importing is located in the correct package directory and compile again.

Compiler Error J0175

Cannot invoke method on 'null' literal

The compiler detected an attempt to call a method from the **null** keyword. **Null** is not a class object and provides no methods. Remove the statement that attempted a method call from the **null** keyword and compile again.

The following example demonstrates this error:

```
public class Simple{
   public String methdo1(){
      // Do something meaningful here
      return null.toString();
      // error : cannot invoke a method from 'null'
   }
}
```

Compiler Error J0176

Duplicate label 'identifier' nested inside another label with same name

The compiler detected a nested label that was the same as another label. Rename the label to something different. Change all **break** and **continue** statements that reference the label and compile again.

The following example illustrates this error:

```
public class Simple{
   void method1(){
      outsideLoop:
      for (int i=0;i<10;i++)
      {
         outsideLoop:  // error: duplicate label
         for (int x=0;x<10;x++)
         {
            break outsideLoop;
         }
         break outsideLoop;
      }
   }
}
```

Compiler Error J0189

'return' not allowed in a static initializer or instance initializer

A **return** statement was found in a static or instance initializer. Initializers, like constructors, can not return a value. Remove the **return** statement and compile again.

The following example illustrates this error:

```
public class Simple{

    static int var1;

    static{
        var1 = 0;
        return;
        // error: return statement not allowed in static initializer
    }
}
```

Compiler Error J0191

Expected '.class'

The compiler detected usage of an intrinsic type name in an expression or assignment statement but did not find **.class** after the name. This error usually occurs when the **.class** keyword is omitted. Add the **.class** extension to the end of the intrinsic type and compile again.

The following example illustrates this error:

```
public class Simple{
    public static void main (String args[]){
        Class x = int; // error: missing '.class'
    }
}
```

Compiler Error J0192

'.class' on intrinsic type requires Java 1.1 compatible class libraries

The compiler detected usage of the **.class** keyword with an intrinsic data type, but either the Microsoft Virtual Machine (VM) for Java or the Java class libraries are based on Java 1.0. Ensure that your class libraries and Java VM are the Java 1.1 versions and compile again.

Compiler Error J0193

Cannot have an array of type 'void'

An attempt to define an array of type **void** was found by the compiler. The **void** data type is for use with methods to declare that the method has no return value and can not be used as an array.

```
public class Simple{

    void MyArray[]; // error: void arrays not supported

}
```

Compiler Error J0194

Class or interface cannot be declared 'volatile', 'native', 'transient', or 'synchronized'

The compiler detected that an inner class or interface was declared with one of the above mentioned modifiers. This error usually occurs when a method or field modifier is applied to an inner class or interface definition. Inner classes and interfaces can use the **private**, **public**, and **protected** access modifiers. Inner classes can also use modifiers such as **abstract**, **static**, and **final**.

The following example illustrates this error:

```
public class Simple{
    // Do something here
    volatile class InnerClass{
        /*error: like outer class, inner classes cannot be defined as
                 volatile */
    }
}
```

Compiler Error J0195

Cannot declare 'identifier' as 'static' in inner class 'identifier'

The compiler detected an attempt to declare a variable or method as **static** from within an inner class. Unlike regular class declarations, inner classes do not support static members. Classes defined within another class, that are declared as **static**, can have static members but the class is considered an outer class. This error can also occur if an interface was defined within an inner class.

The following example illustrates this error:

```
public class Simple{

    // Do something meaningful here

    class InnerClass{

    static int var1; /* error: cannot declare static
                               members in inner class*/
    }
}
```

The following example illustrates how to define a class within a class that can contain **static** members:

```
public class Simple{

    // Do something meaningful here

    /*Because 'InnerClass' class is declared as static it is now treated
        as an outer class enclosed within the 'Simple' class*/
    static class InnerClass{
        static int var1 = 100; // This is OK as long as the class is static
    }
}
```

Compiler Error J0196

Nested class 'identifier' cannot have the same name as any of its enclosing classes

The specified inner class has the same name as one of the classes that it is nested under. Ensure that you have not duplicated the name of a class in which your inner class is nested within and compile again.

The following example illustrates this error:

```
public class Simple{

    // Do something meaningful here
    class InnerClass{
        // Do something meaningful here
        class Simple{
            // error: inner class has same name as a parent class
        }
    }
}
```

Compiler Error J0197

Cannot declare interface in inner class 'identifier'

The compiler detected an attempt to declare an interface inside an inner class. Inner class definitions do not support interfaces declared within them. Remove the interface declaration from within the inner class declaration and compile again.

The following example illustrates this error:

```
public class Simple{
   // Do something meaningful here
   class InnerClass{
   // Do something meaninful here
      interface MyInterface{
         /*error: interfaces cannot be declared
                  inside inner classes */
      }
   }
}
```

Compiler Error J0198

An enclosing instance of type 'identifier' is required

The compiler detected that an inner class definition tried to reference something outside of its scope. Examples of when this can occur are:

A class declared within another class as **static** referenced one of the parent class's non-static variables or methods. Since the inner class is declared **static** it cannot reference any members of the parent class without an instance of the parent class defined.

An inner class tried to reference a class that was not its outer class using the **this** keyword with the classes name preceding it. Since the referenced class is not the inner class's parent class, an instance cannot be implied.

The following examples illustrate this error:

```
// This example illustrates the first error situation
public class Simple{
   int x = 10;
   static class InnerClass{
      public void method1(){
         int y = x; /*error: instance variable needed
                        to reference parent
                        variables. */
      }
   }
}
```

```
// This example illustrates the second error situation
class A{
    int x;
}
class B{
    // Do something meaningful here
    class InnerClass{
        void method1(){
            int y = A.this.x;
            /*error: no instance of A defined. Cannot use
              the <classname.this.variable> syntax here.*/
        }
    }
}
```

Compiler Error J0199

Call of 'this()' cannot be qualified

The compiler detected that an inner class's constructor attempted to call it's outer class constructor using the class name with the **this()** method. Inner classes cannot call their outer class's constructors. Remove the call to the outer class constructor from the inner class constructor and compile again.

The following example illustrates this error:

```
public class Simple{
    int x;
    Simple(int x){
        this.x = x;
    }
    class InnerClass{
        InnerClass(){
            Simple.this(10);
            // error: cannot call outer class constructor
        }
    }
}
```

Compiler Error J0200

'this' must be qualified with a class name

The compiler detected that an attempt was made in an inner class to reference an outer class member using the **this** keyword with a name other than an outer class's name. Only the name of the outer class can be used from an inner class to reference members of the outer class.

The following example illustrates this error:

```
public class Simple{
    int x;
    class InnerClass{
        void method1(){
            int j = x.this;
            /*error: only a class name can be used with
            this to reference outer class */
        }
    }
}
```

The following example illustrates the proper way to reference an outer class's members:

```
public class Simple{
    int x;
    int method2(int arg1){
        return arg1 * ;
    }
    class InnerClass{
        void method1(){
            int j = Simple.this.x; // This is OK!
            int z = Simple.this.method2(10);
        }
    }
}
```

Compiler Error J0201

'super' cannot be qualified except as a superclass constructor call

The compiler detected the usage of the **super** keyword with an instance of the superclass preceding it to access a field or method of the superclass. Using an instance of a superclass, along with the keyword **super,** is limited to referencing a superclass constructor when the superclass has inner classes defined within it.

The following example illustrates this error:

```
class Simple{
    int x;
}

class NotSimple extends Simple{
    NotSimple(Simple smp){
        smp.super.x = 100;
        /*error Cannot reference field with superclass
                name */
        super.x = 100; // This is OK!
    }
}
```

Compiler Error J0202

'super()' cannot be qualified; superclass 'identifier' is not an inner class

The compiler detected a call to a superclass constructor using an instance of the superclass but the superclass is not an inner class. The usage of an instance of a superclass combined with the **super** keyword is only used when a superclass is an inner class.

The following example illustrates this error:

```
class Simple{
    // Do something meaningful here
}

class NotSimple extends Simple
{
    NotSimple(Simple smp){
        smp.super();
        /*error: cannot call 'super' with instance when
          superclass does not contain inner classes*/
    }
}
```

The following example shows the usage of a superclass instance with the **super** keyword:

```
class Simple{
    // Do something here
    class InnerClass{
        int var1, var2;
    }
}

public class NotSimple extends Simple.InnerClass{
    NotSimple(Simple smp){
        smp .super();
        // This is OK!
    }
}
```

Compiler Error J0203 √

Cannot access protected member 'identifier' in class 'identifier' from class 'identifier'

The compiler detected an attempt to access a protected member from a class in a different package. A protected member of a class may be accessed from outside the package in which it is declared only by code that is responsible for the implementation of that class. Remove the call to the other package's protected member or make your class a subclass of the other package's class and compile again.

The following example illustrates this error:

```
/*(source located in a file called PublicClass.java in
   the the Boxes Package directory) */
package Boxes;

public class PublicClass{
   protected void method1(){
      // Do something here
   }
}

// (source located in a file called Simple.java)
import Boxes.PublicClass;

public class Simple extends PublicClass{
   public void method1(){
      PublicClass pub = new PublicClass();
      pub.method1();
      /*error: Cannot access protected method 'method1' because it
               is located in a different package.*/
   }
}
```

Compiler Error J0204

Cannot access protected member 'identifier' in class 'identifier' via a qualifier of type 'identifier'

The compiler detected that a class in one package, that is extending a class in another package, attempted to access a protected member of the base class using an instance of the base class. This error usually occurs when a class attempts to access members of its base class through an instance other than **this**, **super**, or an instance of the derived class. Ensure that the base class's protected member is accessed using the **this** or **super** keyword, or an instance of the derived class and compile again.

The following example illustrates this error:

```
/*(source located in a file called Point.java located in the Boxes package directory) */
package Boxes;

public class Point{
   protected int x, y;
   // Do other meaningful code here
}
```

```
// (source located in a file called simple.java)
import Boxes.Point;

public class Simple extends Point{
    public void method1(Point p){
        super.x = 0; // this is OK!
        p.x = 0; /*error: cannot use a protected member
                    for usage other than extending it. */
    }
}
```

Compiler Error J0205

Cannot use non-final local variable 'identifier' from a different method

The compiler detected that a local variable, which was not declared as final, was referenced in a method. This error can occur if an inner class is defined in a local block or method declaration and the inner class attempts to reference a parameter or local variable defined outside of its scope.

The following example illustrates this error:

```
public class Simple{
    void method1(int var1){
        class InnerClass{
            boolean getVar1(){
                return(var1 == 1);
                /*error cannot reference local variable of
                  method from within inner class. */
            }
        }
    }
}
```

Compiler Error J0206

Cannot assign a second value to blank final variable 'identifier'

The compiler detected an attempt to assign a value to a **final** variable more than once. This error usually occurs when a blank **final** variable is initialized more than once in a constructor or initializer. Check for duplicate initializations of the **final** variable mentioned in the error message and compile again.

The following example illustrates this error:

```
public class Simple{
    final int var1;

    {
        var1 = 10;
        // Do other initializations here
        var1 = 20; // error: duplicate assignment
    }
}
```

Compiler Error J0207

Cannot assign blank final variable 'identifier' in a loop

The compiler detected that a **final** variable was assigned a value from within the scope of a program control loop. A **final** variable can only be assigned a value once and thus cannot be initialized within a loop. Move the initialization of the **final** variable specified in the error message outside of the loop and ensure that it is initialized only once.

The following example illustrates this error:

```
public class Simple{
    final int x;

    public Simple(){
        for (int z=0;z<10;z++){
            x = z; /*error: cannot assign final variable
                     in loop */
        }
    }
}
```

Compiler Error J0208

Constructor or instance initializer must assign a value to blank final variable 'identifier'

The compiler detected that a **final** variable was declared but never assigned a value in either an initializer or constructor. In order for a variable to be properly declared **final** it must be assigned a value.

The following example illustrates this error:

```
public class Simple{
    final int x; // error: final variables must be assigned a value
    final int z = 10; // This is OK
}
```

Compiler Error J0209

Expected '='

The compiler detected that an equal sign was missing from a comment tag (for example **@com, @security, @dll**) attribute. This error usually occurs when an equal sign is missing from an attribute in a comment tag declaration. This error can also occur if another symbol or character obscures the equal sign from being evaluated by the compiler. Ensure that all comment tag attributes have proper equal signs applied and compile again.

The following example illustrates this error:

```
/**@com.interface(iid 31415926-5358-9793-2384-612345678901)*/
// error: missing equal sign in 'iid' parameter
interface Itest{
    // Do something meaningful here
}
```

Compiler Error J0210

Expected '.'

The compiler detected that the specified comment tag's declaration (for example **@com, @dll**) is missing a period after the comment tag (for example **@com.method**). This error can also occur if another symbol or character obscures the period symbol from being evaluated by the compiler. Ensure that your comment tag declaration contains a period after the comment tag and compile again.

The following example illustrates this error:

```
/**@com class*/
// error: missing '.' from @com statement

public class Simple{
    // Do something meaningful here
}
```

Compiler Error J0214

Invalid GUID specified

The compiler detected that an **@com** attribute that requires a GUID has an invalid GUID entry. This can be caused by a syntax error in entering the GUID. Check the syntax for the GUID and compile again.

Compiler Error J0215

Syntax error in @com declaration

A syntax error was found in the specified **@com** declaration. This is most often caused by incorrectly typing the declaration. Check the syntax of the **@com** declaration and compile again.

The following example illustrates this error:

```
/** @com.inteface (iid=31415926-5358-9793-2384-612345678910)
// error:  The word 'interface' is misspelled.
interface ITest{
   // Do something here
}
```

Compiler Error J0216

@com attribute 'identifier' on 'identifier' is illegal in this context

The compiler has detected that a value assigned to an attribute within an **@com** declaration is illegal. This error most often occurs when an attribute is specified but usage of the attribute requires that other specific attributes be specified. This error can also occur if an attribute is specified in the wrong location within an **@com** declaration.

Compiler Error J0217

@com attribute 'identifier' was not specified for 'identifier' but is required in this context

The compiler detected an attribute (for the **@com** declaration shown in the error) that is missing and that is required for this type of declaration. Each type of **@com** declaration has attributes that are required. See the documentation on **@com** for more details on what attributes are required for the **@com** declaration that is listed in the error message.

The following example illustrates this error:

```
/**@com.class() */
// error: must specify classid for @com.class
public class Simple{
   // Do something here
}
```

Compiler Error J0218

@com attribute 'identifier' on 'identifier' has an invalid value

The compiler detected that the value specified in the error message is either not the correct type for the attribute specified in the error or is outside the valid range for the attribute. Check the value assigned to the specified attribute and compile again.

The following example illustrates this error:

```
/** @com.class(classid=911CAED0-2957-11d1-A55E-00A0C90F26EE) */
class Simple{
    /** @com.parameters([type=CUSTOM, customMarshal="foo.bar",
        customMarshalFlags = 5] i) */
        // error: customMarshalFlags cannot be set higher than 3
    native void method1(Object i);
}
```

Compiler Error J0219

An @com attribute cannot be placed on member 'identifier' unless the containing class or interface also has an @com attribute

The compiler detected that an **@com** declaration was placed on a member of a class or interface, but the class or interface was not declared with an **@com** declaration. Ensure that the class or interface which contains the method specified in the error has a valid **@com** declaration defined and compile again.

The following example illustrates this error:

```
interface Simple{
    /**@com.method(dispid=777); */
    public void method1();
    /*error: interface does not have an @com comment tag
            assigned*/
}
```

Compiler Error J0220

An @com attribute cannot be placed on static member 'identifier'

The compiler detected that an **@com** declaration was placed on a static member of a class. Static members cannot be exposed through COM. Remove the **static** keyword from the method or field and compile again.

The following example illustrates this error:

```
/*@com.class(classid=31415926-5358-9793-2384-612345678910)
public class Simple{
    /**@com.method(dispid=777);*/
    static void method1(){}
    // error: cannot expose static method via COM
}
```

Compiler Error J0221

The @com attribute on member 'identifier' cannot be used in this type of class or interface

The compiler detected that an **@com** declaration was placed on a member of a class or method but because of the type of **@com** attribute used with the class or interface, it is not allowed. This error can occur in the following situations:

Using an **@com.structmap** declaration on a member of a class or interface that has the **@com.class** or **@com.interface** declaration applied.

Using an **@com.method** declaration on a member of a class that has the **@com.struct** declaration applied.

The following example illustrates this error:

```
/**@com.struct()*/
class Simple{
    /**@com.method(dispid=777)*/
    public native void method1();
    /*error: cannot use @com.method inside of
              @com.struct*/
}
```

Compiler Error J0222

@com attribute cannot be placed on method 'identifier'— it must be declared 'native' or be in an interface

The compiler detected that a method was specified with an **@com.method** or **@com.parameters** attribute, but the method was not declared with the **native** modifier or declared in an interface definition. For methods to be exposed through a COM interface they must either be declared in an interface declaration or declared **native** from within a class declaration.

The following example illustrates this error:

```
public class Simple{

    /** @com.method(dispid=306); */
    public void method1(){}
    /*error: method must be declared 'native' or
            declared in an interface */
}
```

Compiler Error J0223

The @com.parameters declaration on member 'identifier' has the wrong number of parameters

The compiler detected that the @**com.parameters** attribute (specified in the error message) has a different number of parameters than the method it is exposing through COM. Ensure that both the method's declaration and the @**com.parameters** attribute have the correct number of parameters and compile again.

The following example illustrates this error:

```
/**@com.interface(iid=31415926-5358-9793-2384-612345678910)*/
interface Itest{
    /** @com.method(dispid=306);
        @com.parameters([type=BOOLEAN] var1, var2, var3)
    */
    public void method1(boolean var1, int var2);
      /*error: extra parameter added to com.parameters
              declaration */
}
```

Compiler Error J0224

'return' must be the last item in an @com.parameters declaration

When declaring @**com.parameters** for a method, the **return** parameter must be the last parameter in the list. The compiler detected the **return** parameter in a different position within the parameter list. Check the location of the return parameter in the @**com.parameters** attribute specified in the error message, make the appropriate changes, and compile again.

The following example illustrates this error:

```
/** @com.class(classid=911CAED0-2957-11d1-A55E-00A0C90F26EE) */
class Simple{
    /** @com.parameters([type=I4] return, [type=CUSTOM,
        customMarshal="foo.bar", customMarshalFlags = 3] i) */
        // error: 'return' cannot be defined as the first parameter
    native int method1(Object i);
}
```

Compiler Error J0225

An @com. 'identifier' declaration is illegal for this type of item

The compiler detected that an **@com** declaration was defined for the wrong type of item. This error usually occurs as a result of a change to your code, but it is not due to the syntax or placement of an **@com** declaration. Ensure that the proper **@com** declaration is used on the specified item in your code.

The following example illustrates this error:

```
/**@com.interface(iid=31415926-5358-9793-2384-612345678901,dual)*/
interface Itest{
   /**@com.struct()*/
   public int method1();
   // error: wrong type of @com declaration applied
}
```

Compiler Error J0226

The @com declared type of 'identifier' is illegal for a dispatch or dual interface

The compiler detected that an **@com** interface declaration, declared as either a **dual** or **dispatch** interface, has a member that contains an **@com.parameters** declaration with an incorrect **type**. Certain **@com.parameters** types are not allowed when the interface they are defined in is declared as either a **dual** or a **dispatch** interface. The following list shows which values are invalid for **type**:

- FIXEDARRAY
- SYSFIXEDSTRING
- I8
- U8
- STRUCT
- CUSTOM, CUSTOMBYREF/CUSTOMBYVAL
- PTR (except PTR to VARIANT)
- Arrays of any of the above listed values

The following example illustrates this error:

```
/**@com.interface(iid=31415926-5358-9793-2384-612345678901,dual) */
interface Itest{
   /**@com.parameters([in,out] n , [type = I8] j); */
   /*error: cannot use 'I8' as a type in a dual
          interface */
   public void method1(int n, int j);
}
```

Compiler Error J0227

It is impossible for an expression of type 'identifier' to be an instance of 'identifier'

The compiler detected that a comparison of two classes using the **instanceof** operator could never be instances of each other. In order to use the **instanceof** operator correctly you must compare classes that have some common class lineage. Either change the expression containing the **instanceof** operator so that it uses a related class and instance for its comparison or remove the expression and compile again.

The following example illustrates this error:

```
class Simple1{
    // do something meaningful here
}

class Simple2{
    // do something meaningful here
}

class CompClasses{
    Simple1 x = new Simple1();
    public static void main(String args[]){

    if(smp.x instanceof Simple2){
        /*error: non related classes cannot be instances of each other*/
    }
}
```

The following example illustrates the correct usage of the **instanceof** operator to determine if a class instance is an instance of a specific class:

```
class Simple1 extends Simple2{
    // do something meaningful here
}

class Simple2{
    // do something meaningful here
}

class CompClasses{
    Simple1 x = new Simple1();
    public static void main(String args[]){

    if(smp.x instanceof Simple2){
        // This is OK since 'Simple1' is a subclass of 'Simple2'
    }
}
```

Compiler Error J0228

Syntax error in @dll declaration

The compiler detected a syntax error in an **@dll** comment tag. This error usually occurs when an **@dll** comment tag has been mistyped. Check the statement for syntactical errors and compile again.

The following example illustrates this error:

```
public class Simple{
    /**@dll.import(kernel32, ansi)*/
    /* error: missing quotes around 'kernel32' */

    public static native boolean GetComputerName(StringBuffer s, int[]cb);
}
```

Compiler Error J0229

Expected string constant

The compiler detected that a string constant parameter of a comment tag's declaration (for example **@com**, **@dll**, or **@security**) was either missing the string constant or the string constant was incorrectly entered. This error most often occurs when matching quotes are missing around a value passed to an attribute. Check your comment tag declaration's attributes and compile again.

The following example illustrates this error:

```
/**@com.interface(iid=31415926-5358-9793-2384-612345678901,dual)*/
interface ITest{
    /**@com.method(name=method1);*/
    // error: Missing quotes around 'method1'
    public void method1();
}
```

Compiler Error J0230

Class or interface name 'identifier' conflicts with import 'identifier'

The specified class or interface conflicts with a class that has been imported. This can be caused by declaring a class or interface that is already declared in the Java API, and you are trying to import that API class or interface into your source file.

The following example illustrates this error:

```
import java.lang.Cloneable;

class Cloneable{ /*error Cloneable has already been
                           imported */
   // class implementation
}
```

Compiler Error J0231

Expression statement must be assignment, method call, increment, decrement, or "new"

The compiler detected an invalid expression statement. An expression statement is a statement that can reside on its own line of source code. The following are some examples of valid expression statements:

```
m_cars.changeColor(); // Method calls
int x = y + z; // Assignment statements
j++; // Increment statement
m_tempVar1 += 3;
new Simple();
```

The following are examples of invalid expression statements:

```
1+2;  // error: No assignment statement
j+k-method1();  // A method call but not a valid assigment statement
var1 == var2;  /*Comparison statements should be contained in flow
                 control statements*/
```

Compiler Error J0232 ✓

Expected '{' or ';'

The compiler detected an error with a method declaration in a class or interface. This error usually occurs if an interface's method declaration is missing a semicolon at the end of the declaration or a class's declaration is missing its opening brace '{'. Check the specified class or interface method declaration and for a missing semicolon or opening brace and compile again.

The following example illustrates this error:

```
interface ISimple{
   public void method1()
   // error: missing semicolon to end declaration
}

public class Simple{
   public void method1()
   // error: missing opening brace
}
```

Compiler Error J0233

Catch clause is unreachable; exception 'identifier' is never thrown in the corresponding try block

The compiler detected that the specified **catch** clause will never be executed because the corresponding **try** statement block never throws the **catch** statement's exception type. **Catch** statements are required to catch exceptions or derivations of exceptions that the **try** statement block can throw. This error can be avoided by changing the **catch** statement so it does not catch a specific exception type, but instead, catches the base **Exception** class. Change the exception class your **catch** statement will trap and compile again.

The following example illustrates this error:

```
class Simple{
    void method1(){
        int I = 0;
        try{
            I = I + 1; // This try block has nothing to do with clones
        }
        catch (CloneNotSupportedException c){
            // error: The exception type can never be caused by try block
        }
    }
}
```

The following example illustrates how to avoid this error by using the base **Exception** class:

```
class Simple{
    void method1(){
        int I = 0;
        try{
            I = I + 1; // This try block has nothing to do with clones
        }
        catch (Exception e){
            // This is OK since all exceptions must derive from this class
        }
    }
}
```

Compiler Error J0234

'identifier' is not a field in class 'identifier'

The compiler detected a field reference but the field does not exist in the specified class. This error usually occurs when the field reference is mistyped or the field reference was meant to reference a field in a different class. Ensure that the field exists in the specified class, that your reference to the field is syntactically correct, and compile again.

The following example illustrates this error:

```
public class Simple{
    int var1;
    public Simple(){
        this.var = 10;
        // error: 'var' is not a field in this class
    }
}
```

Compiler Error J0235

'identifier' is not a method in class 'identifier'

The compiler detected a method call but the method does not exist in the specified class. This error usually occurs when the method call is called incorrectly or the method call was meant to reference a method in a different class. Ensure that the method exists in the specified class, that your method call is syntactically correct, and compile again.

The following example illustrates this error:

```
class Simple{
    public void method1(){
        // do something here
    }
}

class Simple2{
    public void method1(){
        Simple smp = new Simple();
        smp.method2();
        // error: 'method2' does not exist in the class 'Simple'
    }
}
```

Compiler Error J0236

'identifier' is not a nested class or interface in class 'identifier'

The compiler detected a reference to a nested class or interface but the nested class or interface does not exist in the specified class. This error usually occurs due to a syntactical error in referencing a nested class or interface. Check the reference to the inner class for syntax errors and ensure that the class or interface exists inside the specified class, and compile again.

The following example illustrates this error:

```
class NotSimple{
}

public class Simple{
    void method1(){
        NotSimple nt = new NotSimple();
        Object o = nt.new InnerClass();
        // error: 'InnerClass' is not an inner class of 'NotSimple'
    }
}
```

Compiler Error J0237

'identifier' is not a field or nested class in class 'identifier'

The compiler detected a reference to a nested class or field but the nested class or field does not exist in the specified class. This error usually occurs due to a syntactical error in referencing a nested class or field. This error can also occur if a reference to a field in an inner class is made but the field does not exist within the inner class definition. Ensure that the inner class or field exists and compile again.

The following example illustrates this error:

```
class Simple1{
    int var1;
}

class Simple2{
    static class InnerClass{
        int var1;
    }
    static Simple1 smp;
}

public class Simple{
    void method1(){
        int x, y;

        x = Simple2.innerclass.var1; /*error: 'innerclass' is not name of
                                an inner class. 'InnerClass' is */
        y = Simple2.smt.var1; /*error: 'smt' is not the name of a field in
                            'Simple2'. Should be 'smp' */
    }
}
```

Compiler Error J0238

Cannot throw exception 'identifier' from field initializer

The compiler detected that an exception was thrown within a field initializer. This error usually occurs when an exception is throwable from a constructor of a class, and an instance of that class is declared and instantiated as a member of another class. To resolve this problem, have the class object that throws the exception instantiated inside a constructor so it can use a **try/catch** combination to trap any exceptions from the other class's constructor call.

The following example illustrates this error:

```
public class Simple{
    public int i;
    public Simple(boolean var1) throws Exception{
        if (var1 = true)
            i = 0;
        else
            throw new Exception();
    }
}
// This is the incorrect way to instantiate this class
class Simple2{
    Simple smp = new Simple(true);
    /* error: cannot call constructor that throws exception in field
                initializer*/
}
```

The following code replaces the 'Simple2' class code in the example above to show the correct way to instantiate the 'Simple' class instance:

```
// This is the correct way to instantiate Simple
class Simple2{
    Simple smp;
    public Simple2(){
        try{
            smp = new Simple(true);}
        catch(Exception e){}
    }
}
```

Compiler Error J0239

Static initializer must assign a value to blank final variable 'identifier'

The compiler detected that a **static final** variable was not initialized to a value using a static or field initializer. In order to declare a variable as **static** and **final** you must use a static or field initializer to set an initial value. This error can also occur if a field is declared as **static** and **final** and assigned a value in a constructor.

The following example illustrates this error:

```
public class Simple{
    static final int MAX_CONTROL;
} // error: static final variables must have value assigned
```

Compiler Error J0240

Syntax error in @security declaration

The compiler detected a syntax error in the specified **@security** comment tag. This error usually occurs when the comment tag is missing a closing parenthesis or the tag's attributes are incorrect. Ensure the syntax of the specified **@security** comment tag declaration is correct and compile again.

The following example illustrates this error:

```
/**@security()*/   // error: invalid @security syntax
public class Simple{
    // class members defined here
}
```

Compiler Error J0241

'@security' can only be specified on a class or interface

The compiler detected that the **@security** comment tag was applied to something other than a class or interface declaration. The **@security** comment tag is used to define the security settings for a class or interface definition and cannot be applied to methods or fields of a class or interface.

The following example illustrates this error:

```
public class Simple{
    /**@security(checkDllCalls=on)*/
    public void method1(){
    // error: cannot use @security tag on method
    }
}
```

Compiler Error J0242

Cannot make static call to non-static method 'identifier'

The compiler detected that a method was called by using the static method call syntax '*<classname>*.*<method>*', but the method is not a static method. Change the method call to use an instance of the class that contains the method instead of the class name itself and compile again.

The following example illustrates this error:

```
public class Simple{
    public void method1(){
        // do something here
    }
}

class NotSimple{
    public void methodx(){
        Simple.method1();
        // error: 'method1' is not a static method
    }
}
```

Compiler Error J0243

'identifier' is obsolete; use 'identifier' instead

The compiler detected a comment tag (for example **@com**, **@dll**, **@security**) that is using a format that is now considered obsolete. To avoid this error change the line of code that the error occurred on to the newer format specified in the error message and compile again.

The following example illustrates this error:

```
public class Simple{
    /**@dllimport("kernel32", ansi)*/
    /* error: 'dllimport' is no longer a supported format for
       @dll.import declarations */
    public static native boolean GetComputerName(StringBuffer s, int[]cb);
}
```

Compiler Error J0244

@conditional allowed only on void-returning methods

The compiler detected an **@conditional** comment tag for a method that has a non-void return value. The **@conditional** comment tag can only be used for methods without a return value. Change the method declaration to return **void** or remove the **@conditional** comment tag and compile again.

The following example illustrates this error:

```
public class Simple{
    /**@conditional(DEBUG)*/
    public int method1(int x){
        // error: conditional methods cannot return a value
    return x * 2;
    }
}
```

Compiler Error J0245

Warning treated as error

The compiler was run using the **/wx** switch, and a warning was found during compilation. The **/wx** compiler switch treats all warnings as errors. In order for the **/wx** compiler switch to display this error, the warning level switch (**/w{0-4}**) must be set high enough to display the warning. Determine the cause of the warning and compile again. You can also remove this switch from your compiler options and compile again.

Compiler Error J0246

Invalid token on a # directive

The compiler detected an invalid token for a conditional compilation expression. This error usually occurs when a token is mistyped or the token used is not a legal token. Ensure that the conditional compilation directive specified in the error is correct and compile again.

The following example illustrates this error:

```
public class Simple{
    public void method1(){
        #iff DEBUG // error: 'iff' is not a valid token
            System.out.println("Do something meaningful here");
        #endif
    }
}
```

Compiler Error J0247

#elif without matching #if

The compiler detected a **#elif** conditional compilation directive, but did not detect a matching **#if** directive. Ensure that you have a valid **#if** conditional compilation directive to match your **#elif** directive and compile again.

The following example illustrates this error:

```
public class Simple{
    public void method1(){
        // error: need to have '#if' before '#elif'
        #elif DEBUG
            System.out.println("Do something meaningful here");
        #endif
    }
}
```

Compiler Error J0248

#endif without matching #if

The compiler detected a **#endif** conditional compilation directive, but did not detect a matching **#if** directive. This error usually occurs because an extra **#endif** directive was supplied. This error can also occur when a **#if** conditional compilation directive was deleted or commented out but the matching **#endif** directive was not deleted. Ensure that you have matching directives and compile again.

The following example illustrates this error:

```
public class Simple{
    public void method1(){
        // #if SIMPLE
        // do something here
        #if DEBUG
            // do something here
            #if WIN95
                // do something here
            #endif
        #endif
        #endif // error: extra '#endif' directive not permitted
    }
}
```

Compiler Error J0249

#else without matching #if

The compiler detected a **#else** conditional compilation directive but, did not detect a matching **#if** directive. This error usually occurs because an extra **#else** directive was supplied. This error can also occur when a **#if** conditional compilation directive was deleted or commented out but a **#else** directive was not deleted. Ensure that you have matching directives and compile again.

The following example illustrates this error:

```
public class Simple{
    public void method1(){
        // do something here
        #else /*error: this '#else' directive has no matching '#if'
                directive */
    }
}
```

Compiler Error J0250

Already had an #else

The compiler detected a duplicate **#else** conditional compilation directive in a **#if** directive block. A **#if** directive can only have one **#else** directive. Ensure that you have only one **#else** conditional compilation directive for the **#if** directive in which the error occurred and compile again.

The following example illustrates this error:

```
public class Simple{
   #if A
      #if B
      void method1{
      // do something here
      }
   #else
      void method2{
      // do something here
   #else  // error: extra '#else' directive supplied
   #endif
}
```

Compiler Error J0251

Unexpected EOF while looking for #endif

The compiler detected a **#if** conditional compilation directive but did not find a matching **#endif** directive, and the symbol used by the **#if** directive was not defined. This error usually occurs when a **#if** conditional compilation directive is used but a matching **#endif** directive was not defined to close the conditional compilation block. Ensure that you have a matching **#endif** directive for the **#if** directive specified in the error and compile again.

The following example illustrates this error:

```
public class Simple{
   void method1(){
      #if DEBUG // debug has not been defined
         System.out.println("Do something here");
   // error: '#endif' not specified for the '#if' directive
   }
}
```

Compiler Error J0252

#if nested too deeply

The compiler detected nested **#if** conditional compilation blocks that were nested too deeply. Nesting of **#if** conditional compilation blocks is limited to 64 levels. Ensure that your nesting of **#if** blocks is within the limit and compile again.

Compiler Error J0253

Cannot have #define/#undef after source

The compiler detected a **#define** or **#undef** conditional compilation directive after other Java source code. The **#define** and **#undef** directives must be placed before other Java source code (except for other conditional compilation directives and source comments). Move the **#define** or **#undef** directive indicated by the error to the front of all Java source code in the file and compile again.

The following example illustrates this error:

```
package boxes;

#define DEBUG
// error: '#define' must occur before the 'package' statement

public class Simple{
}
```

Compiler Error J0254

Cannot change predefined symbol

The compiler detected an attempt to use the **#define** or **#undef** directive on a symbol already defined in Java. This error occurs when a symbol such as **true** or **false**, which are already defined for conditional compilation, is redefined using the **#define** or **#undef** conditional compilation directives. Remove or change the **#define** or **#undef** directives specified in the error and compile again.

The following example illustrates this error:

```
#undef false // error: cannot undefine the 'false' symbol
#define true // error: cannot define the predefined 'true' symbol

public class Simple{
    // do something here
}
```

Compiler Error J0255

Expected #endif

The compiler detected a **#if** conditional compilation directive but did not find a matching **#endif** directive; however, the symbol used by the **#if** directive was defined. This error usually occurs when a **#if** conditional compilation directive is used but a matching **#endif** directive in not defined to close the conditional compilation block, and the code is intended to be compiled. Ensure that you have a matching **#endif** directive for the **#if** directive specified in the error and compile again.

The following example illustrates this error:

```
#define DEBUG

public class Simple{
    void method1(){
        #if DEBUG
            System.out.println("Do something here");
    // error: '#endif' has not been specified for the '#if' directive
    }
}
```

Compiler Error J0256

Expected 'class', 'interface', or 'delegate'

The compiler expected to find the **class**, **interface**, or **delegate** keywords used within the corresponding declaration. This error usually occurs when the keywords are accidentally omitted from a **class**, **interface**, or **delegate** declaration. Another possible cause of this error is unbalanced scoping braces.

> **Note** This error will only occur if the Microsoft Extensions are enabled in your project. Otherwise, compiler error J0020 will be displayed.

The following example illustrates this error:

```
public Simple{ // error: missing the 'class' keyword
    // Do something here
}
```

This example illustrates this error caused by unbalanced scoping braces:

```
public class Simple {

    // do something meaningful

}}   // error: additional '}' is not permitted
```

Compiler Error J0257 ✓

Delegate cannot be initialized with static method 'identifier'

The compiler detected a **delegate** instantiation but the method reference, passed as a parameter, was a **static** method. When instantiating a **delegate**, you must pass a non-static method as a parameter. Ensure that the method you are defining the **delegate** to use is a non-static method and compile again.

The following example illustrates this error:

```
delegate int MyDelegate (int var1, String var2)throws Exception;

public class Simple{

    public static int method1(int var1, String var2) throws Exception{
        // do something here
        return var1;
    }

    public static void main (String args[]){
        Simple smp = new Simple();
        MyDelegate md = new MyDelegate(smp.method1);
        /*error: the method passed as a parameter to the delegate is a
                 static method */
    }
}
```

Compiler Error J0258 ✓

Cannot declare delegate in inner class 'identifier'

The compiler detected an attempt to declare a **delegate** inside an inner class. Inner class definitions do not support **delegates** declared within them. Remove the **delegate** declaration from within the inner class declaration and compile again.

The following example illustrates this error:

```
public class Simple{
    // Do something meaningful here
    class InnerClass{
    // Do something meaninful here
        delegate int MyDelegate (int var1, String var2);
            /*error: delegates cannot be declared
                     inside inner classes */
    }
}
```

Compiler Error J0259 ✓

Exception 'identifier' from method 'identifier' is not a subclass of any exceptions declared thrown by delegate 'identifier'

The compiler detected a **delegate** that was initialized with a method that throws an exception that is incompatible with the **delegate's** declared set of exceptions. Each exception thrown by the method must be the same class or a subclass of an exception that the delegate throws. Change the set of exceptions thrown by either the delegate or the method and compile again.

The following example illustrates this error:

```
delegate void SimpleDelegate(String var1) throws Exception;

public class Simple{
    public void method1(String var1) throws Throwable{
        // do something here
    }
    public static void main (String args[]){

        Simple smp = new Simple();
        SimpleDelegate del1 = new SimpleDelegate(smp.method1);
        /* error: the method reference argument throws an exception that is
                  not the same or a subclass of the exception declared by the
                  delegate */

    }
}
```

Compiler Error J0260

Cannot declare an interface method to be 'protected' or 'private'

The compiler detected an interface with a method declared as **protected** or **private**. Interface methods must be declared as either **public** or with no access modifier (default). Change the interface method declaration specified in the error so that it is not declared **protected** or **private** and compile again.

The following example illustrates this error:

```
interface ISimple{
    public void method1(); // this is OK!
    void method2(); // this is OK! Declared as "default" access
    protected void method3(); /*error: cannot declare interface method as
                                      protected */
    private void method4(); /*error: cannot declare interface method as
                                      private */
}
```

Compiler Error J0261

An explicit enclosing instance of class 'identifier' is needed to instantiate inner class 'identifier'

The compiler detected an attempt to create an instance of an inner class without specifying an instance of its enclosing class. This error usually occurs when an attempt is made, within a static method, to instantiate an inner class as you would an outer class. To create an instance of an inner class, you must use an existing instance of its outer class. Create an instance of the enclosing class and use it to instantiate the inner class and compile again.

The following example illustrates this error:

```
public class Simple{
    class InnerClass{
        // do something here
    }

    public static void main(String args[]){
        InnerClass inc = new InnerClass();
        /*error: an instance of the outer class is required to instantiate
                its inner class */
    }
}
```

The following example illustrates how to create an instance of an inner class using an instance of its outer class:

```
public class Simple{
    class InnerClass{
        // Do something here
    }
    public static void main(String args[]){
        Simple smp = new Simple();
        /*use the instance of 'Simple' to create an instance of its inner
          class*/
        InnerClass inc = smp.new InnerClass();
    }
}
```

Compiler Error J0262

An explicit enclosing instance of class 'identifier' is needed to call constructor of superclass 'identifier'

The compiler detected an attempt by a derived class to call its superclass constructor without an instance of the superclass. This error usually occurs because the superclass is also an inner class. When a derived class is instantiated, an instance of its superclass is also created (and the superclass constructor is invoked). In order to create an instance of an inner class you must instantiate the inner class using an instance of its outer class.

The following example illustrates this error:

```
class OuterClass{
    class InnerClass{
    // do something here
    }
}

public class Simple extends OuterClass.InnerClass{
    // do something here
}
/*error: superclass 'InnerClass' cannot be instantiated without its
    outer class 'OuterClass' being instantiated */
```

The following example illustrates how to instantiate a class that is derived from an inner class:

```
class OuterClass{
    class InnerClass{
    // do something here
    }
}

public class Simple extends OuterClass.InnerClass{
    Simple(){
        /*this line creates an instance of the outer class and calls
            the superclass (the inner class) constructor */
        new OuterClass().super();
    }
}
```

Compiler Error J0264

Array cannot have a dimension

The compiler detected an attempt to initialize an array dimension incorrectly. This error usually occurs when an array dimension size is specified before the instance is created. This error can also occur when an array is given a dimension in the proper place but an initialization list is also provided to set the values of the array (you cannot specify an array size for the dimension when using an initialization list). Correct the initialization of the array specified by the error and compile again.

The following example illustrates this error:

```
public class Simple{
    public void method1(){
        String[3] var1; /* error: cannot specify array size here since
                            array is not instantiated yet */
        String[] var2 = new String[3]; // this is OK!

        boolean var3 = new boolean[3]{true,false,true};
        /*error: cannot specify an array size for the dimension when using
                an initialization list */
        boolean var4 = new boolean[]{true, false,true}; // this is OK!
    }
}
```

Compiler Error J0265

@dll attribute cannot be placed on method 'identifier' — it must be declared 'native'

The compiler detected an **@dll** comment tag placed on a method that is not declared with the **native** modifier. This error usually occurs if an **@dll** comment tag is defined but the method it was applied to was removed or commented out, and other methods in the class can have the comment tag applied to them. Ensure that the method declared with the **@dll** comment tag is declared as **native** or remove the **@dll** comment tag and compile again.

The following example illustrates this error:

```
public class Simple{
    /** @dll.import("USER32") */
    // private native static int MessageBox(int hwndOwner, String text,
                                            String title, int fuStyle);

    /*error: the @dll comment tag cannot applied to 'method1' which is a
            non-native method instead of the intended native method*/
    public void method1(){
        // do something here
    }
}
```

Compiler Error J0266

Compilation canceled by user

The user canceled compilation. This error simply informs the user that the request to cancel compilation was successful.

Compiler Error J0267

A delegate cannot be 'identifier'

The compiler detected an attempt to declare a **delegate** with an invalid modifier. Only the **public** and **final** modifiers can be applied to a **delegate** declared outside of a class. A **delegate** declared within a class can have the **public**, **final**, **protected**, and **private** modifiers applied. Ensure that your **delegate** declaration is not using an invalid modifier and compile again.

> **Note** Although you can use the **final** modifier in a **delegate** declaration, it is not needed as delegates are implicitly **final**.

The following example illustrates this error:

```
private delegate void Simple(int var1, int var2);
// error: cannot declare a delegate as 'private'
```

Compiler Error J0268

A delegate cannot be 'identifier' and 'identifier'

The compiler detected a delegate declaration, within a class, attempted to use a combination of access modifiers that are not allowed. This error usually occurs when a delegate is declared with two access modifiers applied. Remove the additional access modifier applied to the specified delegate declaration and compile again.

The following example illustrates this error:

```
public class Simple{
    public private delegate void SimpleDelegate();
    // error: cannot declare a delegate to be 'public' and 'private'
}
```

Compiler Error J0269

Ambiguous name: inherited 'identifier' and outer scope 'identifier' — an explicit 'this' qualifier is required

The compiler detected reference to a variable or method from within an inner class that is defined in both its outer class and its superclass. The compiler cannot determine which variable or method is to be used. You can reference the outer class variable or method by using *class*.**this**.*name*, where *class* is the name of the outer class whose variable or method you wish to reference and *name* is the variable or method name. To reference the superclass variable or method you can use the **this super** keyword before the reference.

The following example illustrates this error:

```
class NotSimple{
    int var1 = 20;
}

public class Simple{
    int var1 = 10;
    class InnerClass extends NotSimple{
        int var2 = var1;
        // error: cannot determine which 'var1' to use
    }
}
```

The following example illustrates how to resolve name ambiguity between the outer class and superclass variables:

```
class NotSimple{
    int var1 = 20;
}

public class Simple{
    int var1 = 10;
    class InnerClass extends NotSimple{
        int var2 = Simple.this.var1;
        // this is OK and references the outer class variable
        int var3 = super.var1;
        // this is OK and references the superclass variable
    }
}
```

Compiler Error J0270

Ambiguous reference to 'identifier' in interface 'identifier' and class 'identifier'

The compiler detected an ambiguous reference to a field. This error usually occurs when a class's superclass and an interface the class implements have the same field declared. The compiler cannot determine which instance of the field to use. Ensure that you do not have a superclass and implemented interface that have the same field defined and compile again.

The following example illustrates this error:

```
public class Simple extends SuperClass implements SuperInterface{
    public static void main (String args[]){
        float x = var1; /*error: cannot determine which instance of 'var1'
                                    to use */
    }
}
```

```
class SuperClass{
    float var1;
}

interface SuperInterface{
    float var1=6.0f;
}
```

Compiler Error J0271

Expected 'delegate'

The compiler detected the **multicast** modifier but did not detect the **delegate** keyword. The **multicast** modifier can only be used in conjunction with the **delegate** keyword to create multicast delegates. Ensure that you have the **delegate** keyword in the declaration specified by the error message and compile again.

The following example illustrates this error:

```
public multicast void SimpleDelegate(String x, int y);
// error: the 'delegate' keyword is missing after the 'multicast' modifier
public class Simple{
    // Do something here
}
```

Compiler Error J0272

A multicast delegate cannot return a value

The compiler detected a return type other than **void** for a **multicast delegate** declaration. Although **delegates** can return a value other than **void**, **multicast delegates** cannot return a value other than **void**. Ensure that the **multicast delegate** declaration specified by the error returns **void** and compile again.

The following example illustrates this error:

```
multicast delegate int SimpleDelegate(int x, int y);
// error: cannot declare multicast delegate with non-void return type
public class Simple{
    public int method1(int x, int y){
        // Do something here
    }

    public static void main (String args[]){
        Simple smp = new Simple;
        SimpleDelegate sd = new SimpleDelegate(smp.method1);
    }
}
```

Compiler Error J0273

Cannot cast to 'void'

The compiler detected an attempt to cast the return value of a method call to **void**. Casting a method call to **void** is not allowed in the Java language. Remove the **void** cast for the method call specified by the error and compile again.

The following examples illustrates this error:

```
public class Simple{
    public void method1(){
        // Do something meaningful here
    }
    public static void main (String args[]){
        Simple smp = new Simple();
        (void) method1();
        // error: cannot cast method's return value to 'void'.
    }
}
```

Compiler Error J0274

Expected 'identifier' within single comment preceding class 'identifier'

The compiler detected that the class, specified in the error message, was declared with either the **@com.typeinfo** or **@com.transaction** comment tag and a corresponding **@com.register** comment tag was not found within the same comment. This error can occur when an **@com.register** comment tag is declared but is within a separate comment. Ensure that an **@com.register** comment tag is defined within the same comment as the **@com.typeinfo** or **@com.transaction** comment tags defined for the class specified in the error message and compile again.

The following example illustrates this error:

```
/** @com.register ( clsid=AE032C46-E6A0-11d0-8C83-00C04FC2AAE7) */
/** @com.typeinfo(attrid=31415926-5358-9793-2384-612345678901,
value="Help") */
public class Simple{
    /error: the '@com.register' tag is ignored since it is in a separate
            comment */
}

/** @com.register ( clsid=AE032C46-E6A0-11d0-8C83-00C04FC2AAE7)
    @com.typeinfo(attrid=31415926-5358-9793-2384-612345678901,
value="Help")*/
public class Simple2{
    // This comment is OK. It combines both tags in a single comment.
}
```

Compiler Error J0275

Class or interface name 'identifier' conflicts with package 'identifier'

The specified class or interface name conflicts with a package name. This error can
be caused by declaring a class or interface within a package with the same name as a
subpackage. Rename either the subpackage or the class or interface that is causing the
ambiguity and compile again.

The following example illustrates this error:

```
// located in a file called Plastic.java
package Boxes.Dishes;
public class Plastic{
    // do something here
}

// located in a file called Dishes.java
package Boxes;
public class Dishes{
    // error: the name 'Dishes' is also the name of the subpackage
}
```

Compiler Error J0500

#error 'text'

This error message is generated when there is a **#error** conditional compilation directive
in the program.

The following example illustrates this error:

```
#define DEBUG
public class Simple{
    public void method1(){
        #if DEBUG
            #error You should not be running in debug mode here!
            // error: displayed when 'DEBUG' is defined
        #endif
    }
}
```

Compiler Warning J5001

Local variable 'identifier' is initialized but never used

The compiler detected an initialized variable that was not referenced in any class code.
This message occurs at warning level 3 or greater. Use the variable or remove its
declaration.

The following example illustrates this warning:

```
public class Simple {

    public int method1() {

        int i = 1;
        return 1;
        // warning: 'i' is never used
    }
}
```

Compiler Warning J5002

Compiler option 'identifier' is not supported

The compiler detected that an unsupported command line option was specified. Check your compiler switch settings and compile again.

Compiler Warning J5003

Ignoring unknown compiler option 'identifier'

The compiler detected an unknown option specified on the JVC command line. This warning usually occurs when a typographical error exists. For example, specifying **/W4** on the command line will cause this warning because the warning level option must use a lowercase 'w.'

Compiler Warning J5004

Missing argument for compiler option 'identifier'

The compiler detected a valid command line option, but the required argument was not specified. Check your compiler switch settings and compile again.

Compiler Warning J5005

Package 'identifier' was already implicitly imported

The compiler detected an **import** statement for a package that was already implicitly imported, such as **java.lang**. This message occurs at warning level 1 or greater.

The following example illustrates this warning:

```
import java.lang.*;
// warning: process is already imported in the first import statement
import java.lang.Process;

public class Simple{
    // Do something meaningful here
}
```

Compiler Warning J5006

'private protected' not supported, using 'protected'

The compiler detected use of the modifier combination **private protected**. This combination is now obsolete and has been replaced by **protected**. This message occurs at warning level 1 or greater.

Compiler Warning J5014

'identifier' has been deprecated by the author of 'identifier'

The method or class referenced has been marked as deprecated. Deprecated methods or classes are marked by the creator of the source code as outdated and subject to removal. To keep code stable, avoid calling functions that have been flagged as deprecated.

Compiler Warning J5015

The parameter 'identifier' in an @com.parameters declaration does not match the corresponding argument 'identifier'

An **@com.parameters** declaration does not match the method that implements the interface. This error could indicate data type inconsistencies or mismatched parameter locations. Ensure that your **@com.parameters** declaration has the same number of parameters, the correct types, and correct order with the method being declared and compile again.

The following example illustrates this warning:

```
/** @com.interface(iid=31415926-5358-9793-2384-612345678901, dual) */
interface ExampleInterface
{
/**
@com.method(dispid=306)
@com.parameters([type=BOOLEAN] when, on)
*/
// error: @com.parameters declaration has parameters in wrong location

public String Method1(boolean on, int when);
}
```

Compiler Warning J5016

This 'instanceof' operator will always be true

The compiler determined that the specified **instanceof** expression will always evaluate to true. This can occur when **instanceof** is used to determine if a subclass instance is a member of a base class or an implemented interface. Although it is not an error to use the **instanceof** operator in this fashion, it's not particularly useful since the expression will always evaluate to true.

The following example illustrates this warning:

```
interface I {}
class X {}
class Y extends X implements I {}

public class Simple{
    void f()
    {
        Y y = new Y();
        X x = new X();
        Object o;

        // These statements give J5016 warnings...
        if (y instanceof X){
            // y is of type Y, which extends X, so this is always true
        }
        if (y instanceof I){
            // type Y implements I, so this is always true.
        }
        if (x instanceof Object){
            // everything is of type Object
        }
    }
}
```

Compiler Warning J5018

Class, interface, or package name contains characters not in the ASCII character set

The compiler detected a character that is not in the ASCII character set used for a **class**, **interface**, or **package** name. Some computer systems may not support this character. To ensure that your **class**, **interface**, or **package** name can be interpreted by Virtual Machines (VM) on other computer systems, change the invalid character to a valid character from the ASCII character set and compile again.

Compiler Warning J5019

Public member of COM-exposed class or interface contains characters not in the ASCII character set

The compiler detected a character that is not in the ASCII character set used for a method or field that is accessible to other languages via COM. Other languages may not support this character. To ensure that your member name can be accessed from other languages, change the character to a valid character from the ASCII character set and compile again.

Compiler Warning J5020

Directive 'identifier' ignored — extensions are turned off

The compiler detected a comment tag such as **@com** or **@dll** applied in your source code but Microsoft Language Extensions were disabled. In order to use comment tags and other Microsoft Language Extensions, the extensions option must be enabled.

> **Warning** With the Microsoft Language Extensions option disabled, any code that utilizes Microsoft Language Extensions may not work correctly.

The following example illustrates this warning:

```
// Microsoft Language Extensions are 'disabled'
public class Simple{
    /**@dll.import("User32")*/
    public static native int MessageBox(int hWnd, String text, String
                                        caption, int type);
    // warning: the 'MessageBox' method may not work correctly
```

Compiler Warning J5021

Package 'identifier' should not be defined in directory 'identifier'

The compiler detected a **package** statement in your source file but the directory name where the source file resides does not match the **package** statement. Although the source code will compile, other source files will not be able to reference classes, interfaces, and delegates defined in this source file using the **package** name.

The following example illustrates this warning:

```
// source file resides in c:\files\simple
package boxes; // warning: package 'boxes' does not match directory name
'simple'
public class NotSimple{
    // warning: this class is not accessible using the current package name
}
```

Compiler Warning J5022

Referenced class file 'filename' may be older than 'filename'

The compiler detected a class file, which is referenced by the source file being compiled, that is out of date or not found. This warning usually occurs when automatic re-compilation of referenced classes has been disabled (using the **ref-** compiler option). If you are compiling within Visual J++, the **ref-** option is passed to the compiler by default. If any of your source files reference a class file that is not in your project and the file is out of date with its source, you will need to update the referenced class files. You can either recompile the external class files to make them up to date, add the external files to your project, or add the **ref** compiler option. You can add the **ref** compiler option by entering it in the **Additional Compiler Options** text box in the Compile tab of the Project Settings dialog box.

Compiler Warning J5023

File 'filename' has more than 65535 lines — debug information may be incorrect

The compiler attempted to place debugging information in a source file that contains more than 65535 lines of code. Your code may compile, however; not all the debugging code needed for your application will be contained in this file. Reduce the size of your source file so that the debugging information can be added and compile again.

Compiler Warning J5024

Package 'identifier' was already imported

The compiler detected a **package** imported more than once in the specified source file. Although this will not cause the compiler to fail, you should remove the extra **import** statement for the **package** specified in the warning message.

Compiler Warning J5500

#warning 'text'

This warning message is generated when there is a **#warning** conditional compilation directive in the program.

The following example illustrates this error:

```
#define DEBUG
public class Simple{
    public void method1(){
        #if DEBUG
            #warning You are compiling for debug mode
            // warning: displayed when 'DEBUG' is defined
        #endif
    }
}
```

COM Registration Errors (Visual J++)

During registration of a COM class, you may be prompted with an error or warning message. The following is a list of the more common errors and warnings. Each error or warning includes information as to the possible reasons the error occurred and, where applicable, suggestions on how to resolve the error or warning.

No registration attribute in class file 'filename'

Registration of the class file referenced in the error message was attempted but the class file did not contain a @com.register comment tag. Ensure that the COM class in the class file you are attempting to register has a valid @com.register comment tag.

Cannot create instance of class 'identifier'

In order to create a type library and register your COM class, a class must be able to be instantiated and call the standard constructor (the constructor that does not contain any parameters). This error can occur if any dependent classes of your COM class cannot be located or if there is an error in the standard constructor for your class. Ensure that the dependent classes for your COM class can be accessed and that your class's standard constructor contains no errors.

Cannot open filename 'filename'

During the COM registration process, a temporary type library file is generated. This error occurs when the temporary filename cannot be copied and renamed to the final type library name. Ensure that the file is not read-only, in a read-only directory, or in use by another application.

Unable to create registry keys for class 'identifier'

While attempting to register your COM class, the COM registration process could not create a key in the system registry. This error can also occur if the COM registration process cannot open a specific key or write a value into the registry. Ensure that your system registry is not damaged.

Class file 'filename' does not have the extension '.class'

In order to register a COM class, the compiled class file must have the .class extension. This error can also occur if the file to be registered as a COM class is not a valid Java class file. Ensure that the class file you are attempting to register as a COM class contains the .class extension and that it is a valid Java class file.

The internal class name 'identifier' does not match the file or directory name of class file 'filename' — it cannot be loaded

The COM class that is being registered has a different class name than the class file it is located in, or the class file is located in a directory that conflicts with the class's defined package. Ensure that the COM class name and its defined package match the location and name of the class file.

Classes contain more than one type library id. Only one type library can be created at a time

Only one type library can be specified in your Visual J++ project at a time. This error usually occurs when a COM class's @com.register comment tag has a different typelib GUID than the other COM classes in your project. All COM classes in a project must have the same typelib GUID specified. You can resolve this conflict by clearing the check box next to the class in the COM Classes tab of the Project Properties dialog box, apply the changes, and then recheck the check box for the class. This will reassign the class as a COM class and specify the same typelib GUID.

Base name of class 'identifier' conflicts with another class in the same type library

A class was found that was defined already within the type library. This error usually occurs when a COM class is defined in one package, and a COM class, with the same name, in a different package are both being added to the same type library. Change the name of one of the classes being added to the type library so that the conflict is resolved.

Windows EXE/COM DLL Packaging Errors (Visual J++)

During the creation of a Windows EXE or COM DLL, you may be receive an error message. The following is a list of the error messages that might occur. Each error includes information as to the possible reasons the error occurred and, where applicable, suggestions on how to resolve the error.

Path too long: 'path'

The path and filename of a Windows EXE or COM DLL is larger than 256 characters. Reduce the size of the path and filename and rebuild your project.

No main class file specified

An attempt was made to create a Windows EXE but a main class (a class with a main method defined) was not specified. In order for a Windows EXE to be created, you must specify a main class in the Launch tab of the Project Properties dialog box.

No class files found

An attempt was made to create a Windows EXE or COM DLL but no class files were found or specified to create the EXE or DLL. Ensure that your project contains at least one class file and that a class file is specified in the Output Format tab of the Project Properties dialog box.

Unable to open output file: 'filename'

The file specified in the error message could not be opened. Ensure that the specified file is not read-only or in use by another program. This error can also occur if the specified file is located in a directory in which you do not have write permission.

Unable to update resources in file: 'filename'

An attempt was made to write resource information to the resource file specified in the error message, but was unable to update the resource file. Ensure that you have enough available free disk space on your computer.

Badly formatted class file: 'filename'

The class file specified in the error message is in an invalid format. This error usually occurs when a class file is damaged or is a file with the class extension, but is not a valid Java class file. Delete the class file specified in the error message and rebuild your project.

File not found: 'filename'

The file specified in the error message was not found. Ensure that the proper location of the file is specified in the Output Format tab of the Project Properties dialog box and rebuild your project.

Unable to load resources from file 'filename'

The resource file specified in the error message could not be opened. Ensure that the resource file is a valid Windows resource file and that the resource file is not in use by another program.

Unable to read typelib file 'filename'

The type library file specified in the error message could not be opened. Ensure that the type library file is a valid type library file and that the file is not in use by another program.

Corrupt registration attribute in class 'identifier'

A COM registration attribute for the class specified in the error message is corrupt. This error usually occurs when the class file for the specified class is damaged or in an invalid file format. Delete the class file for the specified class and rebuild your project.

Class 'identifier' does not have a method of the form 'static public void main (String[])'

A class was specified as the main class of a Windows EXE, but the class did not contain a main method. The main method provides a starting point for the Windows EXE and must be specified. Add a main method to the class specified in the error message or choose a different main class in the Launch tab of the Project Properties dialog box and rebuild your project.

Main class name 'identifier' is too long

The main class name specified in the error message is larger than 256 characters. Reduce the size of the class name and rebuild your project.

Specified main class 'identifier' not found

While creating a Windows EXE file, the class specified as the main class for the Windows EXE was not found. This error usually occurs when a main class was specified in the Launch tab of the Project Properties dialog box, but the main class has been removed or renamed from the class file. Specify a new main class in the Launch tab of the Project Properties dialog box and rebuild your project.

Unable to read from file 'filename'

The file specified in the error message could not be opened for reading. Ensure that the specified file is not in use by another program.

Cannot create a DLL with no COM classes

An attempt was made to create a COM DLL, but the project does not contain any COM classes. You can create a COM class by selecting a class from the list of classes in the COM Classes tab of the Project Properties dialog box. If you do not wish to expose any of your classes as COM classes, change the type of package you want to create in the Output Format tab of the Project Properties dialog box and rebuild your project.

Failure during auto-registration of 'filename'

A COM DLL failed to auto-register after being created. This error usually occurs when the system registry is damaged.

Out of memory

Insufficient memory was available when creating a Windows EXE or COM DLL. Close other programs that are currently running to provide more available memory and rebuild your project.

Conditional Compilation

Visual J++ provides two new mechanisms for conditionally compiling code in Java: conditional directives and conditional methods. The table below describes all the conditional directives available. For an overview, see "Conditional Directives." For an overview describing the syntax and use of conditional methods, see "Conditional Methods." Both section are later in this appendix.

> **Note** The conditional directive and conditional method mechanisms provided with Visual J++ are extensions to the Java language, provided by Microsoft. Thus, source code containing these mechanisms will not compile properly with other Java development tools.

Conditional Directive	Description
#if	Conditionally includes or excludes source code, depending on the resulting value of its expression or identifier.
#elif	Optional use with the #if directive. If the previous #if test fails, #elif includes or excludes source code, depending on the resulting value of its own expression or identifier.
#else	Optional use with the #if directive. If the previous #if test fails, source code following the #else directive will be included.
#endif	Required use with the #if directive. The #endif directive closes a conditional block of code.
#define	Defines an identifier used in preprocessing.
#undef	Undefines an identifier used in preprocessing.
#error	Generates a developer-defined error message at compile time.
#warning	Generates a developer-defined warning message at compile time.

The #if, #elif, #else, and #endif Conditional Directives

The #if, #elif, #else, and #endif directives are used together to allow lines of source code to be conditionally included or excluded from the compilation of a source file. The #if directive, which begins all conditional blocks, must be matched by a closing #endif directive.

Syntax

#if <*expression1*>
    code to be included
#elif <*expression2*>
    code to be included
#else
    code to be included
#endif

The expression following the #if and #elif directives must be a valid Boolean expression, comprised of Boolean operators and using identifiers declared with the #define or #undef compiler directives. If the expression following the #if directive evaluates to true, lines immediately following the directive are retained in the source file. If, however, the expression has the value false, the lines immediately following the directive are excluded from the source file until the #elif, #else, or #endif directive is encountered.

Only one #else directive can be included in a conditional block. Lines following the #else directive are retained in the source file only if the associated expression evaluated by the #if directive evaluates to false.

Zero or more #elif directives can be included within a conditional block of code. The #elif directive, an abbreviation of "else if," is used for subsequent evaluation of expressions, where the #if directive has already been evaluated and proven to be false.

Expressions used in conditional compilation have some of the same limitations and behaviors as those imposed by the Java language. For example, all the Java defined Boolean and bitwise operators are accepted, and operator precedence is identical. Furthermore, the Java language also defines the use of parenthesis to force the order of evaluation.

The following example illustrates using each of these conditional directives:

```
#define DEBUG
#undef RETAIL

public class test {

    #if DEBUG
        if (cmdStatus.equals(invokeError))
        {
            // The following line displays a diagnostic message:
            System.out.println("Error: command timed out.");
            // appropriate actions
            // taken here
        }
    #elif RETAIL
        if (cmdStatus.equals(invokeError))
        {
            // appropriate actions
            // taken here
        }
    #else
        #error Must define DEBUG or RETAIL;
    #endif
}
```

The #define Conditional Directive

The #define directive is used to include a conditional identifier into a source file. When defined, the identifier can be used in all the classes contained within the source file. The directive must be placed at the top of the source file, with only comments and other conditional compilation directives preceding it.

By convention, the value of the identifier declared by the #define directive will always be true.

Syntax

#define *<identifier>*

The identifier shown above can be up to 1,024 characters in length. By convention, identifiers are composed of uppercase characters to clarify their usage.

The following example illustrates use of the #define directive in a Java application:

```
#define DEBUG   // DEBUG evaluates as true.

#if DEBUG
    // code to be included
#endif
```

Note The Visual J++ build process does not allow per-file build settings. This means that in order to turn on and off conditional identifiers within a single source file, the #define and #undef directives must be explicitly declared within each file.

The #undef Conditional Directive

The #undef directive, as its name implies, is used to remove an identifier from a source file. The identifier need not be defined beforehand, and can be redefined again within the source file using the #define directive. The #undef directive must be placed at the top of the source file, with only comments and other conditional directives preceding it.

Syntax

#undef <*identifier*>

The identifier shown above can be up to 1,024 characters in length. By convention, identifiers are usually composed of uppercase characters to clarify their usage.

The following example illustrates use of the #undef directive in a Java application:

```
#undef DEBUG   // DEBUG evaluates to false

#if DEBUG      // now set to false.
    // lines extracted at compile time
#endif
```

Note The Visual J++ build process does not allow per-file build settings. This means that in order to turn on and off conditional identifiers within a single source file, the #define and #undef directives must be explicitly declared within each file.

The #error Conditional Directive

The #error directive takes a string as an argument and produces an error message at compile time. Errors produced by this directive are displayed as normal compiler errors.

Like the #warning directive, this directive is most useful for detecting predefined constraints and inconsistencies during preprocessing of the source file.

Syntax

#error *<message string>*

The message string identifier shown above indicates the error message to be displayed. The following example illustrates use of the #error directive:

```
#if DEBUG
   ...
#elif RETAIL
   ...
#else
   #error DEBUG or RETAIL must be defined!
#endif
```

When the error above is encountered, the following line will be output:

```
#error 'DEBUG or RETAIL must be defined' (J0500)
```

The #warning Conditional Directive

The #warning directive takes a string as an argument and produces a warning message at compile time. Warnings produced by this directive are displayed as normal compiler warnings.

Like the #error directive, this directive is most useful for detecting predefined constraints and inconsistencies during preprocessing of a source file.

Syntax

#warning *<message string>*

The message string identifier shown above indicates the warning message to be displayed. The following example illustrates use of the #warning directive:

```
#if !TRACING
   #warning This interface has not been completely tested yet!
#endif
```

When the warning above is encountered, the following line will be output:

```
#warning 'This interface has not been completely tested yet!' (J5500)
```

Conditional Methods

Conditional methods use the @conditional tag embedded within Java documentation comments to conditionally include or exclude entire methods from a source file. When a conditional method is excluded from a source file, the compiler automatically eliminates calls to the method from elsewhere within the program.

Syntax

```
/** @conditional (expression) */
void someMethod(args)
{
    ...
}
```

The expression shown above can be any valid Java expression, using identifiers declared with the #define or #undef compiler directives.

The greatest benefit conditional methods provide is a simple way to include or exclude large amounts of debug information from an application. For example, a number of conditional methods may be created to generate vital diagnostic information during the development process. Once development is complete and the application is ready for release, all conditional methods, the expressions used to include them, and any calls can be easily eliminated from the compiled application by merely changing the value of an identifier.

The following example illustrates use of a conditional method:

```
#define DEBUG    // DEBUG is true
...
    public class someClass {
     . . .
        /** @conditional (DEBUG) */
        trackDisplay(int dTrack)
        {
            System.out.println("Variable dTrack assigned: %d", dTrack);
        }
}
```

In the code above, defining the DEBUG identifier allows the trackDisplay conditional method to be compiled. Once the method is no longer useful to the developer, replacing the #define directive with the #undef directive will cause the compiler to extract the method from compilation of the source file, and nullify any calls made to the method from elsewhere within the program.

Conditional Directives

Conditional directives are used to include or exclude blocks of code from a source file, based on the result of an expression, or the value of a single identifier. Conditional directives are useful in many aspects of development, among them:

- They can be used to selectively include or exclude vital diagnostic, or debug code. Once an application containing conditional directive-based code is ready for release, the code can be easily eliminated from the project.

- They can be used to experiment with several possible code optimizations. For example, if various implementations of an algorithm need to be examined for efficiency, setting the appropriate conditional identifier can instantly switch the code execution path to a different algorithm.

The following example demonstrates the use of conditional directives:

```
# define PRINTHELLO    // PRINTHELLO has the value 'true'

public class sample {

    public static void main(String args[])
    {
      #if PRINTHELLO
          System.out.println("Hello!");
      #else
          System.out.println("Goodbye.");
      #endif
    }
}
```

In the example shown above, the string "Hello!" will be displayed. Removing the #define directive will display the string "Goodbye."

Like standard conditional constructs in Java, several of the conditional compilation directives also make use of expressions that govern their flow. For example, the #if compiler directive, like it's Java language equivalent — the if statement, makes use of Java identifiers and operators to form expressions. Thus, most of the rules that govern the syntax of creating syntactically correct statements in the Java language also apply to the creation of expressions for conditional directives. One notable exception where the language syntax rules do not apply is in the use of multi-line comment blocks.

Conditional directives must be alone on a line, except for single-line comments. Multi-line comments may not begin or end on the same line as a conditional directive.

Used wisely, conditional directives can save you considerable time and effort in debugging code.

Reserved Words (Keywords)

abstract

The **abstract** keyword can be used in the declaration of classes and methods. Use of the keyword in a class declaration typically means that one or more of the methods within the class body are declared as abstract. If the keyword is left off the class declaration, and a method within the body of the class is declared using the **abstract** keyword, then the class is implicitly defined to be abstract. In other words, the keyword **abstract** need not be provided as part of the class declaration in this circumstance, and the code will compile successfully. (For readability it is recommended that abstract class declarations include the keyword to make the class intention clear.)

Classes declared to be abstract cannot be instantiated. Instead, abstract classes force the programmer to provide a body for each abstract method within a new derived class. The following example shows a simple abstract class and a class derived from it:

```
public abstract class FruitClass
{

    public boolean isPeelable( );


        .
        .
        .

}


public class BananaClass extends FruitClass
{

    private boolean bPeel;

    public boolean isPeelable( ) {
        .
        .
        .
        return bPeel;
    }

}
```

The derived class (BananaClass) may be instantiated, and any non-abstract methods of the abstract class (FruitClass) will be inherited unless they are overridden.

Note that a class declaration cannot use abstract and final.

The **abstract** keyword can also be used to define methods. As already shown above, a class containing abstract methods is then also (either implicitly or explicitly) defined as abstract and must be subclassed in order to be instantiated. An abstract method cannot have the implementation defined within the abstract class. Rather, it is declared with arguments and a return type as usual, but the body that is enclosed in curly braces is replaced with a semicolon.

Consider the following example declaration of an abstract method:

```
abstract public int someMethod( int arg1, int arg2);
```

Note that a method declared with the keyword **abstract** cannot be declared with the keywords **static**, **private**, or **final**.

boolean

The **boolean** keyword is used to declare a primitive Java data type containing a truth value. The two possible values of a Boolean variable are **true** and **false**. Note that **true** and **false** are defined as keywords in the Java language, but they are actually literal values. Hence, the keywords **true** and **false** can be used as return values, in conditional tests, and in assignments and comparisons to other Boolean variables.

The contents of Boolean variables cannot be cast to or from other types; the current value of a Boolean variable can be converted to a string however.

The following code demonstrates declaration and assignment for a Boolean variable:

```
private boolean isRunning;

isRunning = true;
```

break

The **break** keyword is used to define a break statement which, without a label, transfers control out of the innermost enclosing while, do, for, or switch statement. If the break statement includes a label and the statement is executed, control will be transferred out of the enclosing statement to the line immediately following the label declaration. (In this case, the break target need not be a while, do, for or switch statement.)

The break statement also transfers control outside of try/catch blocks. Note that if the break statement with a label is executed within a try or catch block, and an associated finally block is defined for the try/catch block, then the contents of the finally block will first be executed. After the entire finally block has executed, control will once again transfer to the first statement immediately following the label declaration.

The following example demonstrates a break statement used with a label:

```
block1:

    recordsRemain = getUpdateStatus( );

while (recordsRemain)
{
    if (isRunning)
        System.out.println("Update another record");
    else
        break block1;
}
```

byte

The **byte** keyword is used to declare a primitive Java data type containing an integer value in the range of negative *128* to positive *127*. A byte is defined as 8 bits in length, regardless of the platform the Java bytecode executes on.

Note that byte variables can be cast to and from other numeric types.

The following example demonstrates declaration and assignment for a byte variable:

```
private byte stripThis;

stripThis = 64;
```

case

The **case** keyword can only be used within a switch statement block. It is used repeatedly to provide any number of unique constants (or numeric labels) for comparison within a switch statement block. If the case constant equals the value of the expression at the top of the switch statement, then control is passed to the statement immediately following the case statement. If, on the other hand, the expression at the top of the switch statement block and the case label do not match, control is passed to the next case for comparison.

In the event that no case constants match the value of the expression given at the top of the switch statement, often a default case is provided.

For an example of how the **case** keyword can be used, see the keyword switch.

catch

The **catch** keyword is used to introduce an exception-handling block of code. The keyword is followed by an exception type, an argument name in parentheses, and a block of code to execute should the specified exception actually occur. A **try** statement and its corresponding block of code always precede a catch statement. When an exception is thrown within the corresponding try statement block, the catch statement's exception type is evaluated to determine whether it is capable of handling the exceptional condition. If the exception type can be handled, the argument is assigned to the specified type and the code within the catch block is executed.

For an example of how the **catch** keyword can be used, see the keyword **try**.

char

The **char** keyword is used to declare a primitive Java data type containing a single 16-bit Unicode character in the range \u0000 to \uffff. Unicode characters are used to represent a majority of known written languages throughout the world. (ASCII characters make up a very small part of the Unicode character set.)

Note that values stored by char may be cast to and from other numeric types. However, because character data is implicitly unsigned, casts of char to byte or short can result in a negative number.

The following example demonstrates declaration and assignment for a char variable:

```
private char hitChar;

hitChar = 'a';
```

class

The **class** keyword is used in the declaration of a new class. A class declaration defines a new reference type (or object) and describes its implementation through the use of constructors, methods, and fields. These implementation details can be inherited from superclasses, or uniquely defined as part of the class declaration.

continue

The **continue** keyword is used in nested loops to define a continue statement, which, without a label, transfers control to the end of the innermost enclosing while, do, or for loop. Once control is passed, the current loop iteration ends and a new one begins. If the continue statement includes a label and is executed, control is transferred to the last statement of the outer loop. In this case, the continue target *label* must point to a while, do, or for loop. (Contrast this with the labeled break statement, where the target need not be a loop, or iteration, statement.)

Note that if the continue statement with a label is executed within a try or catch block, and an associated finally block is defined for the try/catch block, then the contents of the finally block will be executed first. After the entire finally block has executed, control will once again transfer to the last statement of the loop immediately following the label declaration.

The following code demonstrates the **continue** keyword used with and without a label:

```
block1:
for ( int i = 0; i < 10; i++ )
{
    while ( statusOkay )
    {
        if ( someNum < 0 )
        {
            someNum++;
            System.out.println("Do it again");
            continue;
        }

        if (string1[i] == null)
        {
            System.out.println("null string here");
            continue block1;
        }
        else
        {
            string2[i] = string1[i];
        }
    // continue statement without label points here
    }
// continue statement with label points here
}
```

default

The **default** keyword can only be used within a switch statement block. It can be used only once, and is typically located at the end of the switch statement block. The **default** keyword is used to label statements that are to be executed by default. That is, the default statement block is only executed when the result value of the switch expression does not match any of the case labels within a switch statement block.

For an example of how the default keyword is used, see the keyword **switch**.

delegate

The **delegate** keyword is used as part of a delegate declaration to define a class that extends com.ms.lang.Delegate, or com.ms.lang.MulticastDelegate. Delegates are commonly used within the Microsoft Windows Foundation Classes (WFC) library to build event-handling mechanisms.

Delegates roughly equate to function pointers, commonly used in C++ and other object-oriented languages. Unlike function pointers however, delegates are object-oriented, type-safe, and secure. In addition, where a function pointer contains only a reference to a particular function, a delegate consists of a reference to an object, and references to one or more methods within the object.

Either "regular" or multicast delegates may be declared, depending on the presence or absence of the multicast keyword. A "regular" delegate encapsulates a reference to a single method within an instance. When this type of delegate is invoked, the underlying method is called.

A multicast delegate differs from a regular delegate in that it may contain references to more than just one method. Methods in a multicast delegate are executed synchronously when the delegate is invoked, and in the order which they appear. If one of the called methods raises an exception, then the delegate ceases, and the exception is propagated to the delegate caller.

> **Note**   The **delegate** keyword is an extension to the Java language, provided by Microsoft.

do

The **do** keyword is used as part of a do/while loop. Unlike the other, more commonly used loop constructs, a do/while loop expression is evaluated only after the block of code within its body has been executed. Thus, you are ensured that the code within the loop body is executed at least once, even if the expression tested causes the loop to end.

Note   Don't forget that a semicolon is required after the condition in a do/while loop.

The following code shows a typical do/while loop construct:

```
int i = getValue( );

do
{
   System.out.println("Printing at least once");
   .
   .
   .
} while ( i <= 10 );
```

double

The **double** keyword is used to declare a primitive Java data type containing a 64-bit floating-point number in IEEE 754 format. Variables of type double store values in the range negative *1.7E308* to positive *1.7E308* within approximately 14 significant digits of accuracy. When you want a floating-point literal value to be treated as a double, append the letters 'd' or 'D' to the end of the value.

Note that double variables may be cast to and from other numeric types. However, doubles cannot be cast to or from values of type **boolean**.

The following example demonstrates declaration and assignment for a double variable:

```
private double dCalcSet;

dCalcSet = 1.23d;
dCalcSet = 3e2;
dCalcSet = .25;
```

else

The **else** keyword is used to provide an alternative clause to an if statement. If the expression defined by the if statement evaluates to *false*, then control transfers to the first statement following the **else** keyword. If the expression defined by the if statement evaluates to *true*, then control transfers to the first statement following the if keyword.

Note that if/else conditional testing is a frequent source of program bugs. Consider the following example of a poorly formatted if/else condition:

```
if ( numPrints < 1000 )
    if ( paperFeed == fullTray )
    {
        printPaperCopy( );
        showStatus( );
        paperFeed--;
    }
else
    suspendPrintJob( ) // Bad indenting!;
```

In the example shown above, the beginning of the else statement block is formatted to fall into the same column as the outermost if statement, even though it's proper association is with the closest if statement. Problems of this nature can be easily overlooked unfortunately, and it is up to the programmer to use good formatting to illustrate the logical intent of the code.

extends

The **extends** keyword is used in a class declaration to specify the direct *superclass* of the class being declared. The superclass can be thought of as the class from whose implementation the implementation of the current class is derived. The class being declared is said to be the direct *subclass* of the class it extends. If no class is explicitly defined as the superclass with the **extends** keyword, then that class has the class java.lang.Object as its implicitly declared superclass.

When a class is extended, the class declared has access to all the public and protected variables and methods of its superclass. Note that classes declared with the keyword **final** cannot be subclassed.

The following example shows typical use of the keyword **extends**:

```
public class TransactionApplet extends Applet
{
    .
    .
    .
}
```

false

The **false** keyword can be used as one of the two possible Boolean values. Strictly speaking, **false** is not a keyword of the Java language; rather, it is a literal value to be assigned to a variable of type **boolean**.

For an example of how the **false** keyword can be used, see the keyword **boolean**.

final

The **final** keyword is used as a modifier for classes, methods, and variables.

When the **final** keyword appears in a class declaration, it means that the class may never be subclassed or overridden. This prevents over-specialization of a particular class. In some sense, the person who created the class considered any further changes to be tangential to its primary purpose.

When the **final** keyword appears in a method declaration, it means that the method may never be overridden. (Note that methods declared with the keywords **static** or **private** are implicitly **final**.)

When the **final** keyword appears in a variable declaration, it means that the variable has an assigned value that can never be changed.

finally

The **finally** keyword is used to define a block of code following a try/catch exception block. The finally block is optional, and appears after the try block and after any catch blocks. The code in a finally block is always executed once, regardless of how the code in a try block executes. In normal execution, control reaches the end of the try block and then proceeds to the finally block, which typically performs any necessary cleanup.

Note that if control leaves the try block because of a return, continue, or break statement, the contents of the finally block are still executed before control transfers out of the try block.

If an exception occurs in the try block, and there is an associated catch block to handle the exception within the method, control transfers first to the catch block, and then to the finally block. If there is not a local catch block to handle the exception, control transfers first to the finally block, and then moves up the series of prior method calls until the exception can be handled.

float

The **float** keyword is used to declare a primitive Java data type containing a 32-bit floating-point number represented in IEEE 754 format. Variables of type double store values in the range positive *3.40282347E+38* to negative *1.40239846E-45*. When you want a floating-point literal value to be treated as a float, append the letters 'f' or 'F' to the end of the value.

The following example demonstrates declaration and assignment for a float variable:

```
float fCalcSet;

fCalcSet = 1.23f;
fCalcSet = 3e2f;
fCalcSet = .25f;
```

for

The **for** keyword is used to create a loop construct. An initialization section, an expression section, and an update section immediately follow the keyword. A semicolon separates each section, and all appear together within at least one set of parentheses.

The initialization section allows the programmer to declare one or more local loop variables. Once the loop ends, these variables are no longer valid.

The expression section contains an expression that is evaluated to determine whether the loop should continue. A *true* result allows the loop to continue; a *false* result allows control to transfer to the statement following the loop body.

The update section allows the programmer to increment loop counters or perform other updates. Typically, the update section is used to increment or decrement whatever loop counters the programmer defines.

The following example shows a typical **for** loop construct:

```
for ( int i = 0; i < 10; i++ )
```

if

The **if** keyword is used to execute a statement or block of statements when it's associated expression evaluates to *true*. An if statement may also have an alternative else clause. If the expression defined by the if statement evaluates to *false*, then control transfers to the statement (or block of statements) following the **else** keyword. If the expression defined by the if statement evaluates to *true*, then control transfers to the first statement following the **if** keyword.

Note that if/else conditional testing is a frequent source of program errors. Consider the following example of a poorly formatted if/else condition:

```
if ( numPrints < 1000 )
    if ( paperFeed == fullTray )
    {
        printPaperCopy( );
        showStatus( );
        paperFeed--;
    }
else
    suspendPrintJob( );   // Bad indenting!
```

In the example shown above, the beginning of the else statement block is formatted to fall into the same column as the outermost if statement, even though it's proper logical association is with the if statement closest to it. Problems of this nature can be easily overlooked, unfortunately, and it is up to the programmer to use good formatting techniques to illustrate the logical intent of the code.

implements

The **implements** keyword is used in a class declaration to indicate that the class provides an implementation for one or more interfaces. If more than one interface is implemented within the class, the interface names must be separated by commas in the declaration. The **implements** keyword must also follow the **extends** clause in the class declaration.

The following example demonstrates use of the keyword **implements** in a class declaration:

```
public class PotatoHead implements InterchangeableParts
{

}
```

import

The **import** keyword is used by Java to make classes available to the current file using an abbreviated name. Any number of import statements may appear in a Java program, but they must appear after the optional package statement at the top of the file, and before the first class or interface definition in the file.

The following examples demonstrate use of the keyword **import**:

```
import my.package.*;    // all classes in my.package are imported
import my.package.cool; // only the cool class is imported from my.package
```

instanceof

The **instanceof** keyword is used as an operator that returns *true* if an object on its left side is an instance of the class specified on its right side. The instanceof operator will also return *true* when comparison is done with an object implementing an interface. The instanceof operator returns *false* if the object is not an instance of the specified class or does not implement the specified interface. It also returns *false* if the specified object is null.

int

The **int** keyword is used to declare a primitive Java data type that contains an integer value in the range of negative *2147483648* to positive *2147483647*. An int is defined as 32 bits in length, regardless of what platform the Java bytecode executes on.

The contents of int variables can be cast to or from other numeric types.

The following example demonstrates declaration and assignment for an int variable:

```
private int iValueK;

iValueK = 1024;
```

interface

The **interface** keyword is used in the declaration of an interface. An interface can be thought of as a template for a class that you may need to implement, but you don't have to do all the design work yourself.

Interfaces differ from classes in the following ways:

- Interfaces cannot implement other interfaces. (They may extend other interfaces.)

- Interfaces cannot contain constructors, instance variables, class methods, or static class initializers.

- All methods declared within an interface are implicitly declared to be public and abstract. Methods within an interface cannot be declared as final, native, static, or synchronized.

- All variables declared within an interface are implicitly declared to be static and final, and thus, must be assigned a constant value. Variables are also implicitly public, and cannot be declared as either transient or volatile.

long

The **long** keyword is used to declare a primitive Java data type containing a value in the range negative *9223372036854775808* to positive *9223372036854775807*. A long is defined as 64 bits in length, regardless of what platform the Java bytecode executes on.

The contents of long variables can be cast to or from other numeric types.

The following example demonstrates declaration and assignment for a long variable:

```
private long iLedgerBalance;

iLedgerBalance = 1234567890;
```

multicast

The **multicast** keyword is used in a delegate declaration to define a class that extends com.ms.lang.MulticastDelegate. For more information on multicast delegates, see the **delegate** keyword.

> **Note**   The **multicast** keyword is an extension to the Java language, provided by Microsoft.

native

The **native** keyword is a modifier used in the declaration of a method to indicate that the method is implemented in another programming language. Because a native method is implemented outside of a Java program, the method declaration ends with a semicolon rather than a method body.

Note that native methods cannot be declared with the keyword **abstract**. For easy access to the Windows API, see Chapter 19, "Writing Windows-Based Applications with J/Direct."

new

The **new** keyword is used as an operator for creating a new object or array.

When **new** is used to create an object, it first creates an instance of the specified class, then initializes all of the instance variables to their default values, and last invokes the appropriate constructor for the class, depending on the arguments provided in the argument list.

Using the **new** keyword to create a class object typically looks like this:

```
Button b = new Button("OK");
```

The new operator can also be used to allocate dimensional arrays for any numeric or object type. Once an array has adequate space allocated, all the elements of the array are initialized to a default value, and it is then up to the programmer to supply values other than the defaults.

Using the **new** keyword to create an array typically looks like this:

```
int array[] = new int[ 10 ];
```

null

The **null** keyword represents a special value that indicates a variable does not refer to any object. The value null may be assigned to any class or interface variable to aid garbage collection. (Assigning the value null to any of the items above indicates to the garbage collection system that the object or variable is no longer in use.) It cannot be cast to any other type, and should not be considered to have a known numeric value.

package

The **package** keyword is used by Java to specify which package the code in the file is located in. Java code that is part of a particular package has access to all classes in the package, and all non-private methods and variables in those classes.

The package statement must come before anything else (except comments and conditional compilation directives) in a Java file. If the package statement is omitted from a Java file, the code in that file becomes part of an unnamed default package.

private

The **private** keyword is a modifier that can be used in the declaration of methods or variables. (Note that the **private** keyword cannot be used in the declaration of local variables.) Using the private modifier in the declaration for either of these types hides the methods and variables so they cannot be directly referenced outside of the class they're declared in. One exception to this rule is that private methods or variables declared within a class can also be used by inner classes.

protected

The **protected** keyword is a modifier that can be used in the declaration of methods or variables. (Note that the **protected** keyword cannot be used in the declaration of local variables.) A protected variable or method is only visible within its class, within its subclasses, or within the class package. Note that the subclasses may reside within different packages, however.

public

The **public** keyword is a modifier that can be used in the declaration of classes and interfaces. (Note that the **public** keyword cannot be used in the declaration of local variables.) The **public** keyword can also be used as a modifier in the declaration of methods and variables. Classes or interfaces declared as public are visible everywhere. Methods and variables declared as public are visible everywhere their corresponding classes are visible.

Note that public classes must have a class name that exactly matches the name of the .java file in which they appear.

return

The **return** keyword returns control to the invoker of a method or constructor. A return statement used in a method can either return a value, or simply return to the invoker without specifying a value. If a return value from a method is not needed, the **return** keyword is followed immediately by a semicolon (rather than a value) and the method's declaration must specify a return type of void. If a return value from a method is needed, the method's declaration must specify a return type that matches the type of value being returned.

Note that in constructors, return statements cannot return values.

short

The **short** keyword is used to declare a primitive Java data type containing a value in the range negative 32,768 to positive 32,767. A short is defined as 16 bits in length, regardless of what platform the Java bytecode resides on.

The contents of short variables can be cast to or from other numeric types.

The following example demonstrates declaration and assignment for a short variable:

```
private short squareFeet;

squareFeet = 4600;
```

static

The **static** keyword is used as a modifier for methods and variables. The keyword can also be used to define static initializing blocks.

When the **static** keyword appears in a method or variable declaration, it means that there will be only one copy of the method or variable that each class object may reference, regardless of the number of instances of the containing class that are created.

The **static** keyword can also be used to create a static initializing block of code that runs only once, when the class object is first loaded into memory.

super

The **super** keyword is typically used to access hidden variables or overridden methods in a superclass. This keyword can also be used, along with an optional list of arguments, as the first line in a constructor body to call a superclass constructor.

switch

The **switch** keyword is used along with the keyword **case**, and sometimes the keyword **default**, to create a conditional statement. In a switch statement, the **switch** keyword is followed by an expression within parentheses whose value must evaluate to a primitive Java data type. Once the expression has been evaluated, its value is compared against the label following each case statement within the switch statement body. When a label has the same value, the lines following that case statement are executed. An optional default label is included within the body of a switch statement when there is no guarantee that the labels provided by each case statement are the only values the switch expression may evaluate to.

The following example shows a typical switch statement construct:

```
switch ( someExpression )
{
    case 1:
        {
        doCase1( );
        break;
        }
    case 2:
        {
        doCase2( );
        break;
        }
    case 3:
        {
        doCase3A( );
        doCase3B( );
        }
    default:
        doDefault( );
}
```

The **break** keyword is also, at times, used within the body of a switch statement. Once the lines following a case statement have executed, the break statement is included to jump over the remaining body of the switch condition. Without a break statement, subsequent case statements would continue being evaluated, and eventually the default statement, if one were included, would execute.

synchronized

The **synchronized** keyword can be used as a modifier to specify thread-safe methods, and as a statement to specify critical sections of code. Used as a method modifier, **synchronized** indicates that the method should only be available to one thread at a time. Used as a statement, synchronized is followed by an expression in parentheses and a block of statements. If the expression within parentheses evaluates to an object type or array, the program obtains a lock on the item before executing the statement block.

this

The **this** keyword is used with instance methods and constructors to refer to the current object. Use of the keyword **this** in the very first statement in the body of a constructor means that another constructor in the same class is being called to assist in creation of the object. For example:

```
public class MyClass
{

    private long birthday;
    private String name;

    // first constructor
    MyClass( String bDay )
    {
        birthday = formatBirthday( bDay );

    }

    // second constructor
    MyClass(String nm, String bDay )
    {    this ( bDay );

        name = new String(nm);

    }
}
```

Note The keyword **this** must appear as the first statement in the body of a constructor, otherwise your code will not compile.

Use of the keyword **this** in an instance method is helpful when a variable using the same name appears within the method body. For example, when you refer to a class scope variable in a method containing the variable name *x*, the class scope variable would be known as *this.x*.

throw

The **throw** keyword is typically used within a try block to indicate that an exceptional condition has occurred. The **throw** keyword is followed by an exception object, derived from the class Throwable, indicating the type of exception being thrown. A throw statement causes a program to immediately stop and resume at the nearest catch statement that can handle the specified exception object. Hence, throw statements may also be outside a try block, if the exception will be caught elsewhere within the program.

The following example shows use of the **throw** keyword:

```
public void someMethod( int div ) throws Exception1
{
    try
    {
        if ( div == 0 )
            throw new Exception1( );
    }
    catch(Exception1 e1)
    {
        // Exception can be handled in this catch
        // block
        .
        .
        .
    }
}
```

throws

The **throws** keyword is used in a method declaration to list any exceptions *not* derived from Error or RuntimeException that a method can throw. (Exceptions derived from type RuntimeException are typically avoidable. Exceptions derived from type Error are usually related to serious system problems; thus, little can be done about them.)

The following example shows a typical method declaration using the **throws** keyword:

```
public int someMethod( int argument ) throws Exception1, Exception2
{
    // This method may contain a try/catch block
    // for detecting and possibly handling any caught
    // exceptions.

}
```

transient

The **transient** keyword is a modifier used in the declaration of variables. Use of this keyword specifies that the current value of the variable need not be serialized (or saved) along with other data stored in a class object.

The following example shows the declaration of a variable with the transient modifier:

```
private transient int currentTime;
```

true

The **true** keyword can be used as one of the two possible Boolean values. Strictly speaking, **true** is not a keyword of the Java language; rather, it is a literal value that is assigned to a variable of type **boolean**.

For an example of how the **true** keyword can be used, see the keyword **boolean**.

try

The **try** keyword is used to indicate a block of code in which an exception might occur. For each try statement, there must be at least one corresponding catch clause. If the exception occurs, the catch clause parameter is evaluated to determine whether it is capable of handling the exceptional condition. If the exceptional condition cannot be handled by any of the catch clauses corresponding to the try statement, then control is transferred up the chain of method calls and all the previous exception types are evaluated until one capable of handling the condition is found.

Note that if the try statement has a corresponding finally clause, then the body of the finally clause will be executed no matter whether the try block completes normally or abruptly, and no matter whether a catch clause is first given control.

The following example shows a typical try/catch/finally construct:

```
try
{
    // code within this block may cause an exception.
    .
    .
    .
}
catch( Exception1 e1 )
{
    // code within this block is executed only
    // when an exception of type Exception1 occurs,
    // otherwise it is skipped over.
    .
    .
    .
}
catch( Exception2 e2 )
{
    // code within this block is executed only
    // when an exception of type Exception2 occurs,
    // otherwise it too is skipped over.
    .
    .
    .
}
finally
{

    // code within this block is always executed,
    // regardless whether an exception within the
    // try block occurs or not. This block is
    // typically used for cleaning up.
    .
    .
    .
}
```

void

The **void** keyword is used in the declaration of a method to indicate that the method returns no value.

Note that Java provides only this very limited use of the **void** keyword. Unlike in the C language, the **void** keyword cannot be used to declare the absence of method parameters, void pointers, and so on.

volatile

The **volatile** keyword is a modifier used in the declaration of variables. Use of this keyword specifies that the value the variable contains may change asynchronously, and, therefore, the compiler should not attempt to perform optimizations with it.

while

The **while** keyword is used to create a loop construct. In a while loop, the expression in parentheses immediately following the keyword is evaluated, and if the Boolean result is *true*, the statements appearing within the loop body are executed. If multiple statements make up the body of the loop, they must be enclosed with curly braces. Once the loop body has executed, control transfers back to the top of the loop where the test is performed again, and the execution of the loop body is repeated until the value of the expression evaluates to *false*.

The following example shows a typical while loop construct:

```
while ( i < 10 )
{
    // statements here execute if above expression is true
    .
    .
    .
}
```

Index